LAWS *of* IMAGE

PRIVACY AND PUBLICITY IN AMERICA

Samantha Barbas

STANFORD LAW BOOKS

An Imprint of Stanford University Press

Stanford, California

Stanford University Press
Stanford, California
©2015 by the Board of Trustees of the Leland Stanford Junior University.

Library of Congress Cataloging-in-Publication Data
Barbas, Samantha, author.
  Laws of image : privacy and publicity in America / Samantha Barbas.
    pages cm
  Includes bibliographical references and index.
  ISBN 978-0-8047-9144-1 (cloth : alk. paper)
    1. Privacy, Right of—United States—History. 2. Personality (Law)—
  United States—History. 3. Libel and slander—United States—History.
  4. Publicity (Law)—United States—History. I. Title.
    KF1262.B37 2015
    342.7308'58—dc23
                                                        2015010587
  ISBN 978-0-8047-9671-2 (electronic)

Typeset at Stanford University Press in 10/15 Adobe Garamond

To the memory of my mother and my father

Acknowledgments

I am indebted to the friends, colleagues, librarians, and research assistants who made this book possible. Special thanks go to David Engel, Fred Konefsky, and Dianne Avery, who took time to read the manuscript closely and offer important and insightful suggestions. Research assistants Tara Ward, Rebecca Kujawa, Sarah Handley-Cousins, Megan Furrer, and Danielle Okst provided invaluable assistance with research and notes. The amazing librarians at the SUNY Buffalo Law School—Joe Gerken, Nina Cascio, John Mondo, Marcia Zubrow—are to be commended for their patience with my numerous requests. Research for this book was made possible by a generous grant from the Baldy Center for Law and Social Policy at the SUNY Buffalo Law School. My deepest gratitude goes to Mike Scanlon, who has listened to these ideas many times for many years. My father and mother, Louis and Mie Barbas, would have been thrilled to see this book. I dedicate it to their memory.

Contents

LAWS OF IMAGE

Introduction

Our Images, Our Selves

After receiving calls from her neighbors, a woman found that her daughter's picture had been used in an ad for a local ice cream store, without the daughter's or the mother's consent. Her daughter had simply "liked" the ice cream store on Facebook. The woman was outraged and embarrassed. People across the country whose photographs had been similarly exploited under Facebook's Sponsored Stories advertising program sued Facebook.[1]

In 1948, the *Saturday Evening Post* ran a critique of cabdrivers in Washington, D.C., that accused them of cheating their customers. A photograph appeared with the article that depicted a woman cabdriver, Muriel Peay, talking to the article's author on the street. The caption did not name her, and the article did not refer to her. Although the woman had consented to be photographed, she did not know that the picture would be used in an article on cheating cabbies. She was humiliated, and she sued the magazine.[2]

In the early 1940s, Zelma Cason, who was the inspiration for a character in a book by a famous writer, sued the author. The portrayal of Cason was highly complimentary, although in one part of the book the author described her as an "ageless spinster resembling an angry and efficient canary" and noted that she used profanity. Cason was upset, and she sought damages of one hundred thousand dollars.[3]

Angry and insulted, these people could have done any number of things. On seeing her picture in the *Saturday Evening Post*, Muriel Peay could have gone home and cried. Perhaps she did. The unwilling subjects of the Sponsored Stories program could have boycotted Facebook—perhaps they did, too. But these individuals also chose to sue. In the past hundred years, in increasing numbers, Americans have turned to the law to help them defend and control their public images. The twentieth century saw the creation of what I describe as a *law of public image*, and the phenomenon of *personal image litigation*.

Under these laws of image, you can sue if you've been depicted in an embarrassing manner, even if no one thinks less of you for it. If a newspaper or website publishes your picture in a way you find offensive, you can, under certain circumstances, receive monetary damages for your sense of affront—for the outrage that someone has taken liberties with your public image and interfered with the way you want to be known to others. *One's image* or *public image* is one's public face or persona, the impression one makes on the world. One's deeds, dress, gestures, speech, looks, even one's online presence—all are elements of public image. An image is something that one has, and that one creates: most of us, in some form or another, are trying to project a particular image of ourselves, an image that we hope will stick with others. Reputation, as we will see, is an aspect of public image, a dimension of one's public persona. The laws of image protect the right to control one's public image, to defend one's image, and to feel good about one's image and public presentation of self. These image laws consist of the tort actions, or civil legal actions, for invasion of privacy, libel, and intentional infliction of emotional distress.

Why does the law in the United States acknowledge rights to control one's public image? Why does the American legal system permit recovery for tarnished images and hurt feelings? Why have so many mobilized the law to defend their public images? This book explains how and why these laws of image came to be. It is not a history of the law alone; it is a story about the interrelationship of law and culture—how these laws were shaped by cultural forces, and what they tell us about American society and its values, beliefs, and preoccupations. The development of image law is part of a broader saga about how Americans became fascinated with, perhaps even obsessed with their personal images.

Since the turn of the twentieth century if not earlier, the United States has been an *image society*. Images surround and besiege us—in advertisements, in newspapers and magazines, on billboards, throughout the cultural landscape. We are highly attuned to looks, impressions, and surface appearances. Perhaps no image is more seductive to us than our own image. In 1961, the historian Daniel Boorstin observed that when people talk about themselves, they talk about their images.[4] If the flourishing industries of image management—fashion, cosmetics, photography, press agentry, and so on—are any indication, we are indeed deeply concerned with our looks, social appearances, and the impressions that we make.

Our celebrity sagas and rags-to-riches stories describe people catapulted to wealth and fame because of their images. We have invested billions of dollars and many hours in our images and have burdened them with great emotional and psychological weight. In the stories we tell about happiness and achievement, images are the key to prosperity, social acceptance, and personal well-being.

The laws of image, I argue, are a manifestation of this *image-conscious sensibility*. They reflect a focus on images that has been, for over a hundred years, essential to our visions of self and personal identity. This book will illustrate how the laws of image are the expression of a people who have become so publicity-conscious and self-focused that they believe they have a right to control their public images, to manage and spin them like actors, politicians, and rock stars.

~

The story begins in urban America in the late nineteenth century, a time of profound social, cultural, and technological transformation. In contrast to small towns, where people knew each other intimately, newcomers to the burgeoning cities found themselves strangers, often known to each other only as superficial images: through newspaper stories, photographs, quick glances on the street. Urban dwellers began to conceptualize their social identities in terms of images and surface appearances, and sought to make positive first impressions on others through careful manipulation of their looks and behavior. They also became sensitive to threats to their public images, particularly from the new mass-market press. Beginning in the 1880s, in what would become a long and venerable tradition, the popular press began to trade in "gossip" and other intimate accounts of personal life. The press was becoming an industry of counterimage, devoted to undermining people's public images and social facades. In unprecedented numbers, the subjects of undesirable media coverage sued the press for libel, the law's traditional, age-old remedy for injuries to reputation.

The tort of libel dealt with false statements that lowered one's standing among one's peers, statements that caused a person to be scorned or shunned by his community. Libel did not always or adequately address the problem of media gossip— the publication of facts that were often true, and that did not necessarily injure one's reputation, but nonetheless caused humiliation and distress. In many cases, the subjects of gossip were upset not only by the embarrassing depictions, but even more by the fact that they had lost control of their images, that the media had taken from them their prerogative to determine how they would be known to the world. The search for legal remedies for the gossip problem led to the invention of the "right to privacy." Proposed in 1890, the right to privacy was a right to not have one's picture or personal information displayed to the public against one's will, in a humiliating or upsetting manner. Long before it offered protection against unauthorized data collection, government spying, or intrusions into one's private space, the right to privacy was the right to control one's public image, and to be compensated for emotional distress when the media interfered with one's own, desired public persona. The right to privacy was an expression of the nascent image-conscious sensibility.

By the mid-twentieth century, a legally enforceable right to privacy had been accepted in most American jurisdictions. It was part of a larger body of image law that had come into being, as courts and legislatures sought to give people greater control and protection of their public images in an age of proliferating mass communications. Plaintiffs could bring suit under the new tort of intentional infliction of emotional distress to compensate their hurt feelings when they were publicly depicted in an embarrassing fashion. Statutes imposed liability for the use of people's visual images without consent. In a historic shift, libel law was expanding to remedy not only harms to reputation but injuries to one's feelings when the media portrayed a person in a manner he found upsetting, even if the depiction was benign in others' eyes. The volume of lawsuits brought under these image torts rose steadily, and personal image litigation became a fixture of the legal landscape. Courts and commentators described the ability to control one's public image as an important personal right, linked to cultural ideals of freedom and self-determination.

The rise of these image torts and personal image litigation tracked mounting concerns with images, social appearances, and self-presentation in public. By the postwar era, cultural forces such as advertising, celebrity, the fashion industry, and popular psychology encouraged people to view their public images as the expression and summation of their inner selves. Controlling and perfecting one's public image was described as the key to personal, social, and material success. Critics observed an "other-directed" self—a personality type consumed with one's image and the act of constructing a pleasing public facade. By the 1990s, plastic surgeons, personal image consultants, and "reputation managers" were in high demand in a world where, to quote a 1990 ad campaign, "image is everything." In recognizing injuries to public image as worthy of legal attention, and in some cases monetary judgments, the law contributed to the cultural focus on images and the construction of the modern image-conscious self.

And yet, American laws do not protect the right to one's public image and persona as extensively as in other parts of the world.[5] In some European countries, under certain conditions, newspapers or websites can be forbidden from publishing ostensibly newsworthy pictures of people, or facts in the public record, without the subject's authorization.[6] This broad protection of public image would be unimaginable in the United States. Since the 1940s, the image torts have been substantially constrained by freedom of speech and press, and it is difficult to recover under them. Despite this, the laws of image remain alive, not only on court dockets but in legal culture—in Americans' beliefs about the law, the legal system, and their legal rights and entitlements.[7]

The free speech restrictions on the image torts represent another dimension, perhaps the flip side, of modern image-consciousness. In a culture where images have been the currency of social exchange, where politics and social life have been mediated by images, the ability to freely disseminate images of people and public affairs has been linked to "free and robust" public debate and discussion, often described as one of the core values of the First Amendment. Expressive freedom in the United States has come to embody two competing ideals. It means the freedom to express oneself through one's public image—to create and define one's own public persona and social identity. At the same time, it is the freedom to make and distribute images of other people, even if caustic, embarrassing, or unflattering. The tension between these competing freedoms is a central theme in the history that follows. We want to control our own images, yet we want to be able to tear down other people's images, freely and without restriction.

∽

A social, cultural, and legal history of the laws of image and personal image litigation from the late nineteenth century to the late twentieth century, this book is novel in its conception. No book to date has envisioned this body of law as *image law*, oriented around the individual's interest in controlling, defending, manipulating, and perfecting his public image, an interest that grew from the social pressures and circumstances of the United States in the twentieth century.[8] There is a vast body of literature by legal scholars on the technicalities of libel and privacy law; critics and historians have also written a good deal on the significance of "images"—visual images, advertising, media images, celebrity images—in American cultural history; but no one has drawn the important connection between the two.

There are three key players in this story, and the narrative revolves around their competition, cooperation, and interaction. The first is the law and its formal architects, primarily courts and legislatures. I explain how the laws of image, principally libel and privacy law, developed over the twentieth century, and how the scope of these laws expanded to reach a range of perceived harms to people's public images and their feelings about their images. The extension of the law to address these sorts of injuries was historically significant; the law, for the most part, had not dealt with so-called intangible harms, injuries that were not to one's property or body. The creators and distributors of the mass media—newspapers, magazines, books, television, and film—also play a central role. These were the most common defendants in personal image lawsuits and in their own right important in the making of image law. The laws of image, in turn, substantially shaped media content.

The star of the story is the admittedly elusive "ordinary American," an individual who is not a celebrity, famous person, or public official. This work is a history of the *average person* and his struggles to preserve and control his public image. It attempts—as inevitably imprecise as the project may be—to track a sense of popular consciousness. Much attention has been given to celebrities and politicians, their public images, and their libel and privacy lawsuits, obscuring the image-consciousness of ordinary people and their efforts to use the law to defend their public images. Many libel and privacy cases in U.S. history have been brought by average citizens, not famous people, and often of quite humble background. A broad range of Americans have come to regard their public personas not only as social phenomena, to be negotiated through social interactions, but as legal entities, to be maintained and managed through the use of law and legal institutions. This legalization of personal image marks an important development in the history of the law and the modern history of the self.

A comprehensive account of America's image culture and image law would be a weighty tome. This work, instead, attempts a broad summary, a grand tour, an exploration of general trends as they have evolved since the late 1800s. Many interesting developments—the increasing litigiousness of celebrities and politicians, for example, or the evolving constitutional dimensions of libel law—can be touched on only briefly; citations and references are offered for those wishing to read further. In general, outside of law review pieces dealing with doctrinal developments in these areas of law, very little has been written on the history of the libel and privacy torts in modern America, especially their social and cultural implications.[9] As such, this book provides an opening foray into what will hopefully be an important line of sociolegal, historical research.

The first part of the book explores the foundations of image law and image litigation in the period from roughly 1880 to 1910. Chapter 1 looks at the rise of the popular mass media in the late nineteenth century and the subsequent defamation "explosion," in which ordinary people began to mobilize libel law in defense of their public images and reputations. Chapter 2 explores the origins of the image-conscious sensibility and one legal expression of that image-consciousness: the invention of the "right to privacy"—in its broadest sense, a right to control one's public image, a right that grew from the failure of libel law to address many of the injuries to the self and public persona inflicted by the emerging mass media. Chapter 3 narrates the popular and judicial acceptance of the right to privacy in cases involving the unauthorized publication of personal photographs in advertisements, a widespread form of Victorian-era "identity theft." Chapter 4 explains how a right to control one's public image was also being created and recognized in another, distinct context: in situations where people were misrepresented and humiliated in public places, such as theaters and railroad cars, injuring their public images and personal sensibilities.

The second half of the book moves into the twentieth century. In the 1920s, as Chapter 5 describes, the development of the mass media, the rise of a consumer culture, and the increasingly transitory nature of social relations heightened the emphasis on public images and the act of image-making. Chapters 6 and 7 discuss the significant development of the image torts in the mid-twentieth century and how these laws began to be limited and complicated by another image right: the media's right to make images of people, or the rights of free speech and press. Chapters 8 and 9 describe the cultural preoccupation with images in post-war America, the increase in personal image litigation, and the expansion of legal pathways to redress harms to one's public image and one's feelings about one's image.

The Conclusion briefly takes up the present day and the brave new world of images that lies before us. The internet has flooded the world with images and created a social universe structured around relationships mediated by superficial impressions and contacts. Our social identities are increasingly a function of the images and personas we present online. As the present outcry around online "privacy" suggests, many Americans believe there should be a legal right to control one's online image, however ephemeral that image might be. We eagerly use web technologies to create and disseminate images to an unprecedented mass audience, and many of us are not hesitant to mobilize the law when the internet's image-making properties are turned against us.

CHAPTER 1

Image and Reputation at the
Turn of the Century

Cedarville is a town near Plymouth, on Cape Cod. In the 1870s, it was a "strag-gling row of houses," where fishing and cranberry-picking were the primary means of livelihood. The town's schools were taught by educated, upper-class women who came from Boston, usually for a year or two. Around 1875, a young woman named Sarah Pratt McLean arrived in town. She took a teaching posi-tion and found herself amidst surroundings that "were full of strangeness. . . . The idioms of the people, their customs and traditions, impressed her with their novelty." When she left after five months, she began to jot down her memories. Eventually she had enough for a book, issued as *Cape Cod Folks* in 1881.[1]

The book purported to be an autobiography that described McLean's real-life adventures—in the classroom, living away from home, and becoming "the spec-tator of domestic squalls and village quarrels." She "wins admirers and lovers, and she actually gets one proposal." Although McLean changed the name of the town, she used the real names of the townspeople.[2]

Before long, the residents of Cedarville got hold of *Cape Cod Folks*. As they read, they recognized their "locality, their houses and their households, their social life and school system, and found even the indigenous modes of courtship graph-ically described."[3] When they realized that many of the characters were called by their actual names, outrage ensued. The result was a dramatic, highly publicized lawsuit. Dozens of characters in the book—nearly the whole town—sued the publisher for libel.

The late nineteenth century saw the significant expansion of libel law and litigation. Libel suits, in the words of one commentator, had become a "ruling passion among citizens."[4] In an important moment in the history of the law and the modern history of the self, both famous and ordinary people were bringing suit over false, embarrassing, and unflattering depictions in print. Once seen as something to be negotiated primarily through social interactions, in the rough-and-tumble of everyday life, reputations and public images were increasingly becoming legal entities, to be controlled and maintained through the use of law and legal institutions.

~

The story starts in the last two decades of the 1800s, an era that saw the flourishing of the printed word in the United States. Urbanization, an expanding audience for publications, and advances in publishing technology led to a massive volume of printed material. Paperbacks and other varieties of cheap books began to appear on the market. Mass-circulation magazines such as the *Ladies' Home Journal* debuted and became popular.[5] Total national circulation of monthly magazines rose from 18 million in 1890 to 64 million in 1905—nearly four magazines per American household.[6] Newspaper readership increased 400 percent between 1870 and 1900, and the number of newspapers doubled.[7] Perhaps more than any form of print, the daily newspaper became a consuming passion and the focal point of popular culture and social life.[8]

At the beginning of the century, the newspaper had been largely a local, small-scale affair. Most newspapers were "mercantile sheets" or political journals, directed towards educated men.[9] By the late 1800s, newspaper publishing had become a big business, aimed at a mass market. Major news publishing chains developed, including the Hearst, Scripps, and Pulitzer empires.[10] Urban newspapers increased in size and published up to six or seven editions a day. There was also a transformation in newspaper content. In the early 1800s, the typical subject of press coverage had been the activities of "public figures": politicians, public officials, captains of industry. Publishers eventually realized that "human interest" stories—"chatty little reports of tragic or comic incidents in the lives of the people"—attracted more readers than dry copy about the comings and goings of officials and statesmen. Crimes, love affairs, divorces, holidays, social outings, illnesses, births, deaths: these matters of ordinary existence were scooped out of neighborhoods by aggressive "roving reporters" and fed to a curious public.[11]

Personal lives, of both the poor and the rich, were dramatized and put on display. Newspapers published facts about ordinary people, obscure private citizens "with no claim to public mention."[12] "Here was a young, handsome woman . . .

suing a rich, fat, candy-making husband in Brooklyn for divorce," the novelist Theodore Dreiser wrote about a New York newspaper in the 1890s. A story about the vacationing of the Vanderbilts was juxtaposed to "a long, bright column . . . of the doings in the theatrical world," and "an interesting shooting affray on the mountains of Kentucky."[13] "The interest in other people's affairs in this country is almost measureless," observed *The Outlook* magazine in 1896. "The morning and evening papers make us feel as if we belonged to a great village and . . . as if our chief interest lay in what is going on at the other end of the street."[14]

In the 1890s, publishers took this to new heights with sensationalistic "yellow" journalism, rife with prominent illustrations, large type, and detailed coverage of murders and sexual affairs. Headlines were written in a breathless tone:

> A Regular Roarer. . . . Gone in the gloaming. A leading business man missing from his familiar haunts. He loved another man's wife too well. The veil lifted from a most remarkable condition of affairs. 'Tis the talk of the town. The people wonder how such naughtiness can exist. Overfond of wedding. A dapper dude with one wife in Pottsville, and another in Philadelphia. He has fallen into the consomme. In consequence a term in prison stared him in the face, holding the mirror up to nature. For sale by newsboys on the street. Only a nickel a copy. Don't miss it.[15]

Sometimes these accounts were true. Often they were faked. Publishers had few qualms about running stories that were exaggerated, distorted, unverified, or even wholly fabricated. The concept of journalistic ethics had not yet come into being.

With its dramatic stories about the secretly sensational lives of average people, the press tapped into a rich vein of popular interest and curiosity. Particularly in the cities, where people lived behind closed doors and were often strangers to each other, readers were interested in news about what their neighbors did and how the other classes lived. Information about the way ordinary people dressed, ate, worked, loved, and spent their leisure time offered newcomers to the city, both migrants from rural areas and foreign immigrants, critical details about the lifestyles and cultures of their new environment.[16] The popular press also served as a kind of connective tissue in a populace that was becoming diverse and heterogeneous. Although many of these publications were aimed at workers, their readership was not limited to a working-class audience.[17] Writes critic Janna Malamud Smith, "Stories [in the press] create[d] a shared culture, and their task was partly to replace the informal gossip of village life; it was impossible to whisper fast enough to pass important gossip to a whole city and few were inclined to whisper to strangers."[18]

Social elites, steeped in the virtues of modesty, gentility, and reticence, decried this effusive, sensationalistic, lowbrow filth. Newspapers were a "sewer" in which "the sins, the crimes, the misfortunes, and the weakness of our poor humanity" were chronicled, wrote critic Conde Benoist Pallen in 1886. "Here, spiced and fetid with all the filth of a degraded morale and an infamous taste . . . is served up the record of . . . murders, rapes, hangings . . . and all other abominations perpetrated by perverted humanity."[19] Particularly despised was the practice of bringing "unimportant persons to public notice."[20] Men and women who had done nothing but mind their own business found their reputations tarnished, sometimes irreparably, by untruthful and scandalous newspaper stories. "Unscrupulous newspapers, bent on entertaining their readers at any cost to happiness and truth," visited "terrible misery on inoffensive people," observed an 1889 article titled "Newspaper Brutality."[21] "Private reputations" were being destroyed "in order to make a salable and spicy paragraph."[22]

A man whose clandestine marriage was exposed in a gossip column, "elaborated . . . with sensational details," was so distraught by "the sudden gaze of a whole community" that he committed suicide.[23] Women who were falsely accused of indecent behavior and consorting with men lost opportunities for marriage and were shunned by others. In one incident that became the basis of a libel lawsuit, a Brooklyn newspaper, the *New York Recorder*, published an article about a woman named Ida Gates. According to the paper, she was a "dashing blonde, twenty years old, and . . . a concert-hall singer and dancer at Coney Island." Coney Island was regarded as a place of "evil report": "a resort for disorderly and disreputable persons." The article alleged that Gates had secretly married a seventy-five-year-old man who was "fond of pretty women." In reality, Ida Gates was a thirty-five-year-old schoolteacher who had recently moved from rural New York and "had never been on the stage in any capacity."[24] The publication was totally false, and her reputation was ruined. "It is high time for the American people to recognize that. . . . reputation is a valued possession," exhorted one writer. To rob a man of his reputation was "a crime against the community as well as against the individual," and it was "the duty of the community to punish it."[25]

Some critics proposed publicly shaming publishers as a means to crack down on the sensationalistic press. There were calls for newspaper boycotts.[26] In the 1880s and 1890s, several states proposed and passed laws providing for civil liability or criminal punishment for scandalous press content.[27] There was also a turn to the tort of libel. In unprecedented numbers, the victims of press gossip and sensationalism began to seek refuge in libel litigation.

~

For centuries, the twin torts of defamation—libel and slander—had protected reputations against scandalous falsehoods.[28] The tort of libel applies to defamatory material in print; and slander, spoken defamation. Libel and slander are civil actions between private parties for money damages. Although "malicious libel"—a libel directed against an individual with an intent to "breach the peace"— was a crime in most states in the nineteenth century, prosecutions for criminal libel were rare.[29] The laws of defamation are of old British vintage, dating back to pre-Norman times; defamation law was fashioned as a means to deter "blood feuds" and other forms of physical violence in defense of honor and reputation.[30] Libel and slander were transplanted to America with the rest of the English common law and had a rich life in American political culture. Libel suits had been typically brought by public officials over criticism in the press, while slander cases policed the excesses of gossip in small communities—chatter about people's crimes, misdeeds, and sexual affairs.[31]

In order to be legally actionable as a libel or slander, in most U.S. jurisdictions, a statement had to be both defamatory and false; there was thought to be no social value in a false fact. A defamatory statement was one that seriously lowered a person's esteem in his community: it exposed a person to "hatred" or "contempt," "injure[d] him in his profession or trade, [and] cause[d] him to be shunned or avoided by his neighbors."[32] The tort's protected domain is reputation, one's good name among one's peers. As a New York court explained in 1845 in *Cooper v. Greely & McElrath*, the "reputation of a person is the estimate in which he is held by the public in the place he is known."[33] Nineteenth-century America regarded reputation as a very serious matter. For merchants, professionals, and tradesmen, a reputation for honesty and good work was the key to success in the commercial marketplace. A woman's reputation for chastity determined her marriageability. A good reputation "makes friends . . . creates funds, . . . draws around [one] patronage and support, and opens . . . a sure and easy way to wealth, to honor, and happiness," one writer observed.[34] Reputation typically had a moral dimension. Accusations of having committed a crime, engaging in professional incompetence, or having a promiscuous tendency or "loathsome" illness—a venereal disease—were considered defamatory per se.[35]

Unlike status, which could be bought, or honor, which might be inherited, a good reputation, it was said, could only be had through individual effort. Reputation was thought to be the product of diligence and exertion, accrued through deeds over time, "slowly built up by integrity, honorable conduct, and right living."[36] Reputation was sometimes regarded as a form of quasi-property; a person was said to "own" his reputation, like one owned the fruits of one's labor. One's good name was "as truly the product of one's efforts as any physical possession."[37] To injure reputation was to thieve a man's most priceless asset. In Shakespeare's immortal words, "who steals my purse steals trash . . . but he that filches from me my good name robs me of that which not enriches him and makes me poor indeed."[38]

Because words are ambiguous and their meaning derived from context, there was often disagreement as to when a person had been defamed. It was the task of the jury to ascertain the "gist" of the disputed words. Interpretations varied by temperament and community. The word "pox" could mean "great calamity" or, alternatively, venereal disease. In one case, "hang him, he is full of pox," was held not to be libelous. "He caught the French pox" was said to be libelous, but "he caught the pox" was not.[39] "There is a great deal of the law of defamation which makes no sense," wrote the eminent torts scholar William Prosser. The law was filled with "anomalies and absurdities," and "no legal writer has ever had a kind word."[40]

The plaintiff in a libel case did not have to prove that the statement in question was false, or that his reputation had actually been harmed, in order to win damages for injury to his reputation. He needed only to present the derogatory statement and demonstrate that it could potentially hurt his reputation. The falsity of the statement was presumed; in most states, the publisher could exonerate itself by showing that the statement was true.[41] Libel was a strict liability tort— the publisher was responsible for his statements regardless of whether he published them innocently or maliciously. The only exception to these stringent rules involved statements about public officials and public affairs. In all of the states, there was a "fair comment" privilege that permitted publishers to make defamatory statements of opinion about public officials in their official capacity and about "matters of public concern," provided that they were issued fairly and with "an honest purpose."[42]

Although there were protections for freedom of the press within libel doctrine—the fair comment privilege and the defense of truth—nineteenth-century libel law on the whole prioritized personal reputation over the rights of the press. The legal prohibition or punishment of publications that had a "bad tendency," that offended people's sensibilities or had a "tendency" to create social unrest, was seen as a legitimate exercise of the state's police power that posed little if any constitutional difficulty. According to historian David Rabban, between 1870 and World War I, most courts employed some version of the bad tendency test.[43] The entire entry on freedom of the press in a 1901 encyclopedia stated that it "consists in the right to publish, with impunity, the truth, with good motives and for justifiable ends, whether it respects governments or individuals." It did not protect publications that "from their blasphemy, obscenity, or scandalous character, may be a public offense, or as by their falsehood and malice . . . may injuriously affect the standing, reputation, or pecuniary interests of individuals."[44] The law's purpose, it was said, was to protect society's order, harmony, and moral fabric by regulating the content of public expression. This restrictive position would eventually fall away in the twentieth century.

～

The rise of the sensationalistic press and "human interest" journalism led to a surge of libel lawsuits. As the *Albany Law Journal* wrote in 1895, "the number of actions for libel . . . seems to be increasing . . . [and] the feelings of men are becoming more and more sensitive to statements made in the newspapers."[45] In his study of tort litigation in turn-of-the-century New York, Randolph Bergstrom found that the number of defamation cases that appeared before the New York Supreme Court increased by over twenty times between 1870 and 1910.[46] Francis Laurent's study of a trial court in Wisconsin showed a significant increase in defamation cases between 1865 and 1914, most of them libel cases brought against local newspapers.[47] Between 1884 and 1895, the publishing trade journals *The Journalist* and *The Fourth Estate* reported increasing numbers of libel cases at the pretrial and trial levels.[48] Critic E. L. Godkin summarized the views of many when he wrote in 1880 that newspapers had become "simply instruments for the dissemination of libel."[49]

Editors and publishers complained loudly about the libel threat. In 1895, the editor of the *Denver Republican* declared that in fourteen years he had been sued for libel for a total of $1,200,000 and had been forced to hire a lawyer full-time to deal with libel cases.[50] Libel litigation was identified by the newly formed American Newspaper Publishers' Association as a major industry problem, and the ANPA engaged in numerous state and federal campaigns to liberalize libel law, under the rallying cry of freedom of the press.[51]

Not only were there more libel cases, but there was also a change in libel law's usual players. Historically, the typical libel case had involved politicians and public officials suing the press over political criticism.[52] In the late nineteenth century, as the press unveiled corruption and at times the seamy private affairs of public figures, political officials and other prominent people continued to bring a significant portion of the nation's libel suits. Writers, entertainers, and artists had also been somewhat litigious, and they remained so. Around the turn of the twentieth century, the famous Wild West entertainer Annie Oakley sued fifty-five Hearst newspapers for having written that she had stolen a man's trousers to get money to buy cocaine. Oakley traveled around the country for six years serving as a witness in her libel suits. It was the biggest libel lawsuit in U.S. history to that time.[53]

Yet many, if not the majority of libel lawsuits were brought by ordinary people, not public figures. A study of nearly 1,500 trial records of libel suits between 1884 and 1899 indicates that at least as many were brought by so-called private figures as by public figures.[54] My informal review of reported appellate cases between 1880 and the end of the nineteenth century shows a rise in libel cases brought by ordinary people against the mass-market press. The media's focus on "human interest" stories and everyday life spawned libel lawsuits by average citizens.[55] Libel plaintiffs came from all walks of life—they were students, workers, lawyers, writers, housewives, and schoolteachers.[56]

In the annals of libel history, this was a fairly novel phenomenon. Ordinary people had not been frequent subjects of press coverage before this time and thus had little reason or opportunity to sue for libel. In the instances where ordinary people did undertake legal action for reputational harm, the traditional vehicle was a suit for slander—oral defamation.[57] In small communities and towns, people were more likely to be defamed by spoken comments rather than printed material. The most common genre of slander cases involved sexual slander—allegations of female adultery or lack of chastity.[58] Slander lawsuits were infrequent, only an "occasional concern" of nineteenth-century courts.[59] They were difficult to win, because of various restrictions on the tort—in particular the rule that required plaintiffs to specifically demonstrate the economic losses or "special damages" they had suffered as a result of the slander, which could be hard to prove.[60] In small communities, reputational slights were typically worked out through informal methods, such as verbally or physically assaulting one's defamer—duels, yelling matches, fistfights.[61]

One of the most common genres of libel cases involved false and sensational accusations of crime. A man brought suit in 1885 when a newspaper article charged him with abusing his wife by taking away her child and not providing enough fuel to keep her warm.[62] A woman sued when she was falsely accused of running a "bawdy house."[63] Another sued over an article that said she had beaten a fruit-seller with a poker when he was trying to collect a bill.[64] A woman brought a libel claim when a newspaper made an unfounded statement that she was involved "with a sensational police court case" and that she had "a record well known to the police."[65]

As newspaper publishers used sexually tinged gossip about females to sensationalize copy and attract readers, women sued over accusations of unchaste conduct.[66] Allegations of sexual impropriety were taken very seriously in the culture of the time. In one case brought against the *Washington Evening Times*, an article stating that a woman working in a laundry "had been seen swinging out of a window in her night robe in a contest with another employee" and that she had "cursed the boss like a sailor [and] that she had thrown a cup of hot tea in the face of another employee" was held to be defamatory.[67] In an 1898 case, a young woman brought a libel suit against the *New York Morning Journal* over an article that described her as having engaged in a rowing contest with another girl over a handsome beau: "an aquatic love chase . . . for [a] Don Juan." The court held that the publication "gives rise to the suggestive suspicion that the woman guilty of such behavior was loose in conduct and ready for adventure, without regard to the becoming modesty of a woman," and was thus defamatory as a matter of law.[68]

～

New access to legal representation made these lawsuits possible. This era saw the development of the contingency fee agreement, in which a lawyer took a plaintiff's case without charge; when a settlement or judgment was achieved, the lawyer was to receive a portion of the damages, anywhere from 5 to 50 percent.[69] Such arrangements, which became common after the 1870s, opened up legal services to the public by allowing people to hire an attorney without paying fees up front. The rise of the contingent fee practice led to a wave of tort lawsuits in the late nineteenth century, often brought by injured people against large corporations, such as railroads.

Many libel plaintiffs were represented by contingent fee lawyers. Newspaper trade journals lamented that "people were tempted to try their luck on libel suits and there were too many hungry lawyers eager to aid them,"[70] and that libel suits were the product of "lower grade lawyers" who used them to "attend to the collection of debts due tradesmen."[71] Pressured by publishers, the Wisconsin legislature attempted to amend the state's libel law to bar all suits brought for a contingent fee.[72]

These "damage suit" lawyers were right to think that libel lawsuits might be lucrative. When they did succeed, private-figure libel plaintiffs could recover generously at trial.[73] There was no precise formula for the calculation of libel damages; awards were set by the jury, and plaintiffs were known to make large claims. Judgments in libel suits brought by private figures ranged from $500 to $45,000 (between $12,500 and $9 million in 2014 dollars).[74] Verdicts were comparable to and sometimes exceeded those in personal injury cases—the average plaintiff in a personal injury case in the late 1800s received between $1,000 and $2,000.[75] Injured reputations were in some cases regarded as seriously, if not more seriously than mangled arms and legs.

In justifying large judgments against publishers, courts noted the impact of reputational assaults delivered through mass communications, as compared to oral gossip. As a judge commented in an opinion upholding a $1,300 judgment against the press for having written about the alleged adultery of a local barber, the large damage award was justified because in contrast to spoken gossip, the injury caused by "defamation . . . through the columns of a newspaper" was great.[76] Whereas oral gossip was ephemeral—spoken in haste, and perhaps likely to be forgotten in haste—newspapers "are preserved for years and years," and "publication in the newspaper . . . gives the charge . . . a permanent lodgment in the memory of the living, and it may be reproduced when all else concerning the person has been forgotten."[77] When a person was defamed by others in a small community, he "could readily get rid of a damaged reputation by moving away a short distance." The popular press, with its vast circulation, had made it impossible for people to escape "public odium and contempt."[78]

Initiating a lawsuit was, inevitably, an assertion of rights. When plaintiffs commenced a libel lawsuit, they were claiming in effect that they had a legal entitlement to their reputations. There was nothing novel about this. In theory, the common law had always protected reputation. Yet the fact that more people were claiming the right—that men and women across the social spectrum, from the lowly to the celebrated, felt compelled to bring libel lawsuits—suggests not only that people saw their reputations and public personas as being especially imperiled, but also that those aspects of the self had become more valuable and treasured.

Middle-class Victorians, particularly professionals, placed great importance on their reputations, both personal and occupational.[79] A good reputation was a sign of moral virtue; it was also critical to social mobility in the late 1800s, a time of expanding economic and social opportunities. Reputation had meaning not only for those who sought to maintain their social positions, but for anyone who hoped to rise in status. There was another reason for this apparent protectiveness of reputation, as I suggest in the next chapter. Americans were becoming image-conscious—increasingly attuned to social appearances and the impressions they made in the eyes of others.

∽

As more libel cases were brought before the courts, there was a popular fascination with libel and libel litigation. Blow-by-blow accounts of sensational libel trials often appeared on the front pages and covers of newspapers and magazines, and cartoons, stories, plays, poems, and songs were written on libel-related themes. The idea of the ordinary person mobilizing the law against the big publisher—calling on the grand instrument of the judiciary to defend his name against an industry and institution seen as profit-hungry and even immoral—had great appeal at a time when Progressivism and the concept of corporate social responsibility were becoming matters of public interest and discussion.[80]

At the same time, the libel "explosion" raised eyebrows. Some commentators speculated that the public had become libel-happy, too eager to sue over what were, in some cases, minor slights. As one writer observed, "in years past the law of libel was thought to be somewhat oppressive. At the present day it tends to become ludicrous."[81] Writers spoke of the "recurrence of frivolous libel suits."[82] The average American was more than "eager to assume that [he] had been injured by . . . publication[s]"[83] and "happy in taking a chance at mulcting the press."[84] A magazine published this joke in 1887, when $250 was a significant sum:

> Lawyer (to client): You want to sue Robinson for five hundred dollars for libel, you say?
> Client: Yes; he has blasted my character forever.
> Lawyer: You think five hundred dollars the proper amount?
> Client: Well, make it two hundred and fifty dollars. I only want what's right.[85]

While many libel plaintiffs brought suit over serious accusations, other claims were arguably more trivial. In some cases, people were upset because they had been portrayed not in a manner that was objectively negative, but in a way that was simply displeasing to them, that clashed with how they wanted to present themselves to others. The *Kalamazoo Gazette* was sued for libel by a doctor for reporting that he had removed a "patty tuber" from a person's body. It was a typographical error; the passage should have read "fatty tumor." The doctor argued that the publication "held him up to ridicule."[86] A young woman successfully sued for libel over an ad published in the *Atlanta Constitution* that described her mother as having been bitten by a cat and subsequently developing the characteristics of a cat—purring, mewing, and so on.[87] In some cases it seemed that a libel was, to use the phrase of Jeremy Bentham, "anything published upon any matter of anybody which any one was pleased to dislike."[88]

But this was not the law's view. As a matter of formal legal doctrine, libel dealt with serious harms to one's good name in one's community, not mere slights to one's feelings. Reputation was a measure of self that was external and objective: how others saw a person, not how he viewed himself—nor his anxieties about how others would view him. Damages were awarded to compensate the plaintiff for a severe loss of social currency, not for mere embarrassment or chagrin at being made to look foolish. In the words of one legal treatise, defamation law did not compensate "spiritual grievances. . . . A mere injury to the feelings" without actual loss to social standing "cannot form an independent and substantive ground of proceeding."[89]

Yet some lawyers and legal commentators were beginning to argue that libel law should address these kinds of harms—not so much to one's actual reputation, but to one's feelings about one's public image. They believed that people should have a broad legal right to present themselves to the public on their own terms, to fashion their public personas as they wished. This was at the heart of the *Cape Cod Folks* lawsuit.

~

Sarah Pratt McLean's semiautobiographical novel from 1881, *Cape Cod Folks*, "written at the age of twenty-three by a diary keeping teacher who substituted for five months in a one-room school on the Cape," was one of the greatest literary hits of its time.[90] The book, which depicted the young woman's perspective on the residents of the sleepy, backward seaside town of Cedarville, "sold like wildfire," noted the *Chicago Tribune*.[91] Critics bestowed high praise on the author's skill at invoking the oddities, curiosities, and simple joys of rural village life. McLean's decision to use the real names of the townspeople in her story appears not to have been malicious, but naïve. "In the innocence of her heart," the author "neglected to substitute fictitious names for those of her friends in the village."[92]

McLean thought that the town was too far away from civilization to ever come into contact with her book. Yet a copy strayed into Cedarville. When the townspeople realized that many of the characters were called by their actual names, outrage ensued.

To be clear: there was nothing scandalous or libelous about the book itself. The book did not accuse anyone of crimes, adultery, of any kind of illicit or immoral behavior. There was nothing in it that was false. The residents of Cedarville knew that. What the book did do, however, was to publicize their folkways and make them look like foolish bumpkins. This was, apparently, intolerable to them. The residents began to write angry letters to the publisher.

A month after the book was released, the publisher, Alexander Williams & Co., issued a notice of apology, announcing that the names of the villagers would be changed in the next edition of the book. The new issue contained a disclaimer: "We distinctly deny having knowingly or otherwise misrepresented or caricatured any real persons, and deeply regret that the feelings of any one should be injured by the innocent fun contained in the book."[93] And yet the apology was not enough for the belittled community, which made a collective decision to sue for libel.

This was not entirely at their own initiation. According to the *Boston Globe*, "crowds" of plaintiffs' lawyers descended on the town and convinced the people to sue the publisher. A suit against the writer herself—a young woman with no assets—would be useless, but the publisher, an established Boston enterprise, might be profitably looted. The lawyers held a sort of "salon" in the front room of one of the villager's homes—"the novel serving tolerably well as a list for invitations"— and convinced them that there was a claim to be had, "dangl[ing] large verdicts before their eyes."[94]

Over forty residents sued Alexander Williams & Co. for libel, claiming over $50,000 in damages. The lawyers for the publishers began to receive personal letters from townspeople who sought damages for family members only casually mentioned in the book. "Dear Sir," one woman wrote, misspelled and scratched out in pencil, "I want you to settle with my to [two] sons that was made out fools in the cape cod folks." The publicity surrounding the libel suits increased sales of the book.[95]

Within two years, Alexander Williams had made settlements with almost all of the parties.[96] The damages paid ranged from $200 "down to a plug of tobacco, in proportion to the prominence of the character and the degree of the individual's indignation."[97] The settlements, it was rumored, nearly threw the publisher into bankruptcy. The only party that refused to settle was the man who was the romantic hero of the story, Lorenzo Nightingale.

～

Nightingale had been described in the first edition by his real name, Lorenzo Leonard Nightingale. In the second edition, the publisher changed his moniker to "Lute Cradlebow," aka "Bennie Leonard Cradlebow," "Bennie," "Ben," and "The Cradlebow."[98] In the story, Nightingale was the object of McLean's romantic attention. McLean described Nightingale as a handsome and valiant, albeit rustic, knight in shining armor. He was "tall, well-formed and sinewy, with black, curling hair, brownish mustache, and dark, penetrating eyes." At the time of the book's publishing, he was thirty-one, and many of the people described in the book were relatives.[99]

McLean had written that Nightingale had kissed her, and also that he was "the champion potato bugger and fiddler, whale-fisher, and cranberry picker of the neighborhood."[100] (A "potato bugger" was apparently one who shooed the insects off of potato plants.) Nightingale alleged that as a result of the book, "he ha[d] been pointed out when on the cars and at other places as the champion potato bugger and fiddler," and had been called "Cradlebow" in public."[101] Locally, he had "made some reputation as the 'young fellow who kissed the teacher.'" Over the summer, young Boston ladies of "culchah" went down to the Cape to gawk at him, to see the "Cradle-bow of Miss McLean's book." Nightingale alleged that "his own feelings and those of his family had been hurt"—to the tune of $10,000 (approximately $250,000 current value).[102]

The trial began on February 13, 1884, and was covered in national newspapers. The goal of the plaintiff's counsel was to show that the publication was false and defamatory, and that the "plaintiff was entitled to full compensation for being branded as one of the Cape Cod Folks and the gawky lover of Sarah Pratt McLean."[103] The offending parts of the book were read to the jury, including the passage that Nightingale most objected to: "stooping down, [he] kissed me, quite in a simple and audible manner on the cheek." Nightingale's lawyer claimed that this depiction was a "pack of lies." "Haven't you ever kissed any girl?" the judge asked Nightingale. "I might have," he hesitatingly admitted. It was "absolutely untrue," however, that he had kissed McLean. According to his testimony, "he never made love to the school-teacher, was not in love with her, and didn't know whether she was with him or not."[104]

The publisher's lawyer argued that the description of the Nightingale character was not defamatory in any way. There was no libel, he claimed, in being called a "potato bugger."[105] In fact, the lawyer argued, McLean had "made him a hero— had in fact created and extended but not injured his reputation."[106] While Nightingale might have been annoyed by the publicity, no one thought less of him for it. The defense noted that the book had not caused him to lose any work or the respect of his peers. In fact, not longer after the book's publication, he married.[107]

After two hours, a jury—of local Cape Cod folks—returned a verdict that was not surprising.[108] Although the material was technically not libelous, the jury nonetheless awarded Nightingale $1,095 in his suit against the publisher. The publisher appealed the case to the state's Supreme Court in October 1884, but before the Court rendered its opinion, the publisher settled with Nightingale for $500.[109]

~

The *Cape Cod Folks* lawsuit became a flash point of popular debate. Critics disparaged Nightingale for having brought a lawsuit over a publication that did not defame him and at worst annoyed him and made him look silly. As one writer summarized, "the general legal as well as popular opinion is that there is nothing legally libelous in this book—the only . . . claim is for the use of an actual name and the consequent annoyance—from ridicule and otherwise."[110] *The Independent* magazine observed that "there is nothing or very little in the book in the nature of censure or aspersion."[111] In the words of *The Literary World*, "We do not remember anything in the book . . . which would be deemed a libel in the popular sense." "The whole spirit is humorous, the situations are laughable, [and] the descriptions amiably satirical."[112]

According to the *New York Sun*, Nightingale was one of the new breed of "super sensitive folks" who had become the bane of the publishing industry. "Cape Cod is evidently a dangerous place for an imaginative young woman with a turn for satire," wrote the *Sun*. "We doubt whether there is any other part of this country where a young man would resent the charge of having kissed a pretty girl, particularly when her own narrative of the occurrence indicated that she rather liked it."[113] "If he considers himself libeled by the noble character he is represented as being, he must have a very high opinion of himself indeed."[114]

Some speculated that Nightingale's claim, like the rest of the suits, was motivated by money. As the publisher's lawyer told the *Boston Globe*, the townspeople "knew little of the book and cared less. Few had taken pains to read it. If there was any money in it for them, they wanted it, and that was all."[115] One writer who was familiar with the townspeople believed that they were suing because "they thought that they ought to have been paid for being put into the book, as the author was reputed to have made a great deal of money by it. . . . [F]inding that no money was coming to them, the next thing to suggest itself was a suit for damages."[116] The publishing world viewed the outcome with alarm. "Other satirical contemporaries should beware. I see innumerable checks for $1095 issuing from the offices of *Harpers' Weekly*, *Puck*, and *Life*," wrote one literary journal. If "Nightingale finds such ample redress for a little fun poked at him, what sums . . . may not some other song-birds who are turned to ridicule recover from their satirists?"[117]

Yet others praised the outcome in the case. Even though the matter might not have been technically defamatory, didn't Nightingale have a right to his public image, a right to be known to the world as he wished? "Lorenzo Leonard Nightingale . . . has won his suit for libel. It is well the action had this result. The financial success of the story had a tendency to open a new field for irresponsible and unscrupulous authors," wrote *The Current* magazine.[118] According to a commentator in the *Albany Law Journal*, "It would have a healthy restraining influence if verdicts were occasionally rendered against [writers] whose publications had no further effect than exposing the victims to ridicule."[119]

The thought of using the law to get money for this kind of injury to one's ego and feelings was appealing yet controversial. Many were scornful of the idea that harms to one's public image and personal sensibilities—without any real assault to "reputation"—were worthy of monetary compensation and the attention of public tribunals. But others were beginning to support the idea that people should have a broad right to determine how they were presented to the public, one that went beyond the narrow confines of the law of libel. It was this intuition that led to the "right to privacy."

CHAPTER 2

The Origins of the Right to Privacy

Around the time of the *Cape Cod Folks* lawsuit, another person whose public image had been tarnished by unfavorable publicity was mobilizing the law, in novel ways, in search of justice and vengeance. Samuel Warren was a member of the social elite in Boston who had graduated from Harvard Law School in 1878. At Harvard, Warren had befriended Louis Brandeis, a student from a Jewish merchant family in Louisville, Kentucky, who would go on to become a celebrated Supreme Court justice. After graduation, Warren and Brandeis founded their own law firm.[1]

In 1883, Warren married the daughter of Senator Thomas Francis Bayard. The new couple held social events at their home, which became rich fodder for the Boston society columns. Reporters attended their dinners and parties, disguised as waiters.[2] The details of Warren's social affairs—breathless accounts of weddings, banquets, and funerals—were spread out on the pages of local papers.[3] Warren was outraged at this unwanted publicity and turned to the more intellectual Brandeis, who channeled Warren's anger into an article titled "The Right to Privacy," published in the *Harvard Law Review* in 1890.[4] This important work established the practical and theoretical foundations of the tort action for "invasion of privacy."

Contrary to what is often assumed, Warren and Brandeis were not arguing for a broad "right to be let alone." Rather, as we shall see, what the famous article called for, more pointedly, was a legal right to control one's public image. Their proposed legal action for invasion of privacy would permit people to sue over the anguish that ensued when they were depicted before the public in an embarrassing, unfavorable, or otherwise displeasing manner, even though the material was not false or defamatory, as in Lorenzo Nightingale's case. By 1911, a handful of states had recognized such a "right to privacy."[5]

Like the surge in libel litigation, the development of the right to privacy was a response to the sensationalistic popular press. It also reflected a historic shift in the ways that Americans, particularly middle-class city dwellers, were conceptualizing their social identities and presenting themselves to others. The right to privacy was a response to an emerging *image-conscious sensibility* in the culture of the time. It was a reaction to a new sensitivity to personal image that grew from the demands of social life in an increasingly urban, commercial, mass-mediated society, where appearances, first impressions, and superficial images were becoming important foundations of social evaluation and judgment.

~

The image-conscious sensibility was in part a product of the city, and the late nineteenth century was the great Age of the City in the United States, when urbanization and the urban experience became a reality for millions. In 1860, only one-sixth of the population lived in cities; by 1900, a third of the population did.[6] Between 1860 and 1910, America's urban population increased sevenfold.[7] A demographer writing in 1874 noted that "the country is now but a suburb of the city."[8] Over 40 percent of the rural population was said to have "disappeared."[9]

The rise of the cities was a consequence of industrialization, vast immigration, and new modes of transportation and communication. The number of telephones grew from three thousand in 1876 to 1.3 million in 1900.[10] The number of post offices increased nearly threefold, the distance of telegraph wire by nine times, and the number of telegraph messages by seven times.[11] Skyscrapers, homes, and tenements were being constructed at a rapid pace, as were dry goods stores, department stores, and other consumer emporia.[12] In Chicago in 1889, railroad and "street car lines had been extended far out into the open country"; there were "miles and miles of streets," and "long blinking lines of gas lamps. . . . [and] narrow boardwalks" reached out as far as the eye could see.[13] Crowds of strangers in downtown streets, sprawling parks, electric theaters, department stores, and dizzying skyscrapers were testaments to the two great faiths of the Gilded Age: wealth and aspiration.

With this rapid move to the urban center came a profound personal decentering and disorientation. Sociologist Georg Simmel, in his 1903 essay "The Metropolis and Mental Life," described the way that "violent stimuli" in the cities—loud noises, bustling crowds, "the rapid telescoping of changing images"—created a new psychological state of mind, a kind of hyperawareness, in "contrast with the slower, more habitual, more smoothly flowing rhythm of the . . . small town and rural existence."[14] Nervous "diseases" like anxiety and neurasthenia were said to be the consequence of the fast pace of life in the city and "overstimulation." Not only were the senses being disarrayed, but established concepts of self and personal identity were coming undone. The environment of the cities was dizzyingly diverse; immigrant and native, black and white, rich and poor, young and old were thrown together in an unfamiliar social setting. Unmoored from the conventions, expectations, and restraints imposed by established communities and traditions, newcomers to the city often felt liberated to reinvent themselves, and began "to see themselves as architects of their own self-making."[15]

∼

In small towns and villages, a person's social identity had been largely a product of ongoing interactions with a known and familiar community. Various bits of information about people, gleaned from stories, gossip, conversations, and observations, were woven together into mental dossiers, as it were, "files" that grew thicker and more complex over time. While reputations and social identities were by no means unchangeable in the small town, they were somewhat fixed. The resident of a small community, one sociologist observed, "is constantly aware of being rated not only on present acts and appearances but those far back in life." The collective memory was often strong, and a person "knows better than to suppose that he can deceive [others] into thinking that he is something radically different from what he is."[16]

Urbanization unsettled this long-established way of creating a social self. In the cities, surrounded by strangers, one's social identity was more often a function of first impressions rather than ongoing contact—what observers might infer about a person based on chance encounters and glimpses on the streets, in theaters and stores, in railway cars, and the other public and commercial venues that made up the terrain of urban life. Simmel vividly captured this new social environment when he wrote that urban existence was comprised of arm's-length relationships and "impersonal cultural elements."[17] According to the urban planner Frederick

Law Olmsted, the anonymous city street was a reflection of the impersonal commercial marketplace, where individuals were surrounded by thousands of people daily yet had nothing in common with them.[18]

In small communities, there was relatively little need for an individual to carefully "signal" her identity—to display her background, beliefs, and social status—on the surface of her appearance. Ongoing interaction and a common culture made it fairly easy for the community to take stock of a person without resorting to elaborate signs and "performances." The more socially fluid and fragmented conditions of city life demanded that people externalize their identities. As Simmel wrote, the "brevity and rarity" of meetings between individuals on the streets and other urban venues created a desire to make "oneself noticeable" upon first glance, to distinguish oneself through one's manners, looks, and gestures.[19] In the cities, "we find ourselves reading off a whole personality from the gesture which a man uses to smooth down his hair. We glance at a set of clothing or the texture of the skin on a man's hand and read into it a class, an occupation, a whole way of life," observed anthropologist F. G. Bailey. There was, inevitably, a "jump from the small clue to the large judgment."[20]

The heightened importance of surfaces and first impressions led to increased attention to the presentation of self in public.[21] In the cities and large towns of the late nineteenth century, there was a new *image-consciousness*, a preoccupation with mastering and perfecting one's social appearance. "Impression management," to use sociologist Erving Goffman's phrase, became an important personal project and goal.[22] People began to speak of life in theatrical metaphors—of social existence as an "act" on a "stage." One "performed" one's identity, went out in public to "see and be seen."[23]

These "presentational performances" required proper costume, diction, and gestures. Advice and etiquette books with titles like *The Art of Pleasing, The Art of Good Manners, The Art of Good Behavior,* and *The Art of Speech and Deportment* streamed from the presses.[24] In these treatises were elaborate instructions on how to dress, how to greet people, when to smile, and what to say and not say in public. People with good manners did not "speak of private matters in general company," use slang, or fish for compliments.[25] Every gesture was to be plotted and scripted; behavior and speech were to be conducted formally, properly, and with dignified reserve. As one etiquette book commanded:

MISCELLANEOUS RULES

You should never scratch your head, pick your teeth, or clean your nails in company.

Never attract attention to yourself by talking or laughing loudly in public gatherings.

Never engage a person in private conversation in presence of others, nor make any mysterious allusions which no one else understands.

On entering a room, bow slightly, as a general salutation, before speaking to each of the persons there assembled.[26]

One of the most grievous social errors was to present oneself in a manner unsuited to a given social environment. Conduct before one's family was inappropriate before houseguests, and behavior suitable for one's parlor was not to be shared with strangers. Etiquette was highly gendered; respectable women were to convey, through demure dress, polite speech, and elegant gestures, signs of modesty and chastity, key female virtues of the time.[27]

This attention to appearances was strongest among the urban middle class, but it was not theirs exclusively. Although etiquette codes may have been "calculated . . . for the meridian of the city," they threw their "beams afar," and "something like a nationwide consensus of manners came about," according to historian Arthur Schlesinger. Rural Americans could not afford to be ignorant of city standards, for they might one day find themselves urban dwellers.[28]

Technological and industrial developments enhanced this attentiveness to self-presentation in public. Portrait photography was popular, and old technologies of looking were coming into greater use. Mirrors became a regular presence in middle-class bathrooms by the turn of the century.[29] Mass-produced clothing, ubiquitous by the 1890s, put a fashionable appearance within the reach of the ordinary consumer.[30] Advertisements encouraged people to scrutinize their appearances and to purchase items that would help them enhance their looks and images. People were becoming increasingly aware of, and sensitive to the visual impressions they created in the eyes of others. While public visibility had always been an essential part of life for the famous, the notion that "everyone could and should be looked at," writes critic Leo Braudy, was a novel, modern concept.[31]

By the late nineteenth century, individuals across the social spectrum were being encouraged to cultivate an attitude towards their bodies, appearances, and feelings that was strategic and instrumental. They were adopting an external perspective on themselves, considering how they might appear before strangers, and seeing themselves as *images* in the eyes of others. It was an accepted fact of life "that everyone employed 'fronts' when in public" and that all social appearances were, to some degree, constructed or contrived, observes historian Charles Ponce De Leon.[32] In the nineteenth-century commercial metropolis, the "immediate impressions people made upon each other" were coming to be seen as "the very basis of social existence."[33]

There was to be a reward for this scrupulous management of personal image—respect, upward mobility, and the possibility of social and material success. As the author of the treatise *American Etiquette and Rules of Politeness* summarized, in a man's social appearance lay his happiness, success, and fortune. "It does not matter in what work in life a man may be engaged, his chances for success are greatly increased by the cultivation" of good manners and a positive image. "The lawyer at the bar wins his jury oftentimes by his manner; the physician inspires confidence in his patients greatly by his manner; . . . the orator convinces by his delivery."[34] Especially in urban centers, where social hierarchies were particularly unstable, it was thought that the "self-made" man could create a new identity and advance socially by appearing more refined and genteel than he really was.

This is not to say that people always saw themselves as being "on stage" before audiences of distant and passive strangers. Even though city dwellers lived much of their daily lives in the impersonal public realm, they still preserved a sense of community in their families, neighborhoods, churches, and voluntary associations. In these contexts, intense personal connections and interdependent relationships were still important and functional.[35] Nor is it to imply that these practices were universal; emulating the manners and style of the bourgeoisie was not a possibility or perhaps even a wish for the millions who were excluded from "respectability" by virtue of their class, race, or ethnicity.

Nor still is it to suggest that appearances were being cultivated to the exclusion of morals. Middle-class Victorians put great emphasis on inner virtues such as sincerity, modesty, character, and self-restraint, qualities prized in an expanding industrial economy. The Protestant ethic of saving, self-denial, and deferred gratification was strong, and self-discipline and moderation were highly valued.[36] The idealized "man of character" was to cultivate these traits and manifest them in his social appearance—in the sincerity of his demeanor, the dignity of his dress, the trustworthiness of his handshake.

People were not becoming "superficial." We can see, nonetheless, a new attentiveness to public images, and to potential threats to those images. John Kasson, in his history of urban life and manners in the nineteenth century, has noted the great fear in this time of being discredited and exposed—that nosy neighbors, gossiping houseguests, and whispering coworkers might reveal the "truth" behind one's social facade.[37] The mass media were posing especially formidable threats to personal image, threats that the average citizen was seemingly helpless to control, manage, or defend against. With its vast circulation and sensational gossip about people's personal lives, the popular press had great power to undermine one's public persona and social performance.

❧

By the turn of the twentieth century, the mass-market press had become a vast industry of counterimage. Most papers ran regular features on politicians, businessmen, society leaders, and actors that offered readers a glimpse of their private lives and an appraisal of the subject's intimate habits and personality.[38] Reporters became notorious for climbing through open windows, peeping through keyholes, and assuming disguises.[39] The development of handheld Kodak cameras in the 1880s led to especially nefarious practices.[40] One New York newspaper employed a photographer to stand in the street and take snapshots of every person who appeared to be important.[41] The news value of such photos was not so much "that the photographs [were] of notabilities," but that they were candid and revealing, often "taken by stealth when the subjects were unconscious of the purpose of the person manipulating the camera."[42] Newspapers and magazines promised to go "behind the scenes" to allow readers to see whether individuals were the same in private life as in public. In this way, journalism played to the public's interest in the malleability of social identity and the constructed nature of public images. The more that personal identity was seen in terms of the presentation of facades and "fronts," the greater the public's interest in deconstructing other people's fronts.

Press outlets began to cover the home lives, even the romantic affairs, of high-ranking political officials. When President Grover Cleveland married while in office, journalists pursued the honeymooning couple, standing in the trees and shrubbery outside their residence and "distend[ing] their ears to catch every scrap of conversation."[43] Socialites were scrutinized; stage actors, the object of a burgeoning cult of celebrity, were also put under the looking glass. "One would think," a newspaper editorialized in 1888, "that actors and singers are the only people worth talking about in all this great, busy, active, pushing, enterprising world, and that newspapers are published for the express purpose of perpetuating the doings of actors in private life, rather than their endeavors upon the public stage."[44] Ordinary people's private lives were also exposed, often mercilessly. "Not only the private affairs of persons holding public relations are pried into. . . . but those of persons who have no public functions whatsoever."[45]

The human toll of these exposés could be severe. A man committed crimes in his youth and went on to become a respectable member of his community. The newspaper "amplified the story" of his past life "in sensational style" and the man died under the stress of the exposure.[46] The media "have put an end to all human privacy," lamented one writer. "There is absolutely no shelter for the unlucky man or woman whose career or circumstances in any way furnish material for sensational report."[47] "The sheer, unmitigated brutality of this invasion of privacy is so constantly illustrated in the columns of many newspapers that a large part of the American people have come to acquiesce in it as one of the fixed conditions of modern life."[48]

~

In the late 1800s, privacy was beginning to emerge as a major social concern for the middle class. In this book, we will see many different invocations of "privacy" in different historical moments. Although the meaning of privacy changes over time, there are important continuities. At its core, privacy is about the exercise of autonomy and control over the self—one's identity, activities, and personal information.[49] Privacy became a concern in the late nineteenth century with the rise of an industrial urban society and the agents of authority and coercion that came with it—bureaucratic governments, mass media, large managed workplaces, corporations, police forces. There was a widely expressed feeling that the ability to define and to "own" oneself—to live freely as a self-choosing, self-directing individual—was being impinged upon by distant, large-scale institutional forces over which the ordinary person had no oversight or control.[50]

One of the most egregious, widely complained of "invasions of privacy" was the journalistic invasion of home life. The private residence was described as sacred, a "castle where, when we desire, we may be shut out from the world, and within whose sacred enclosure we may draw our longest breath, speak our frankest word, and be our freest, truest self, with no fear of being misunderstood."[51] The home was a private sanctuary and haven, presided over by wives and female caretakers, a protected zone where one could exercise autonomy over one's self and express one's innermost thoughts and feelings apart from the demands of the workplace and social life.[52] This public-private division, writes historian Karen Lystra, "was a basic organizing principle of nineteenth-century middle-class culture."[53] Activities that took place in the home were regarded as secret and not to be discussed with others. Those who divulged their domestic lives in public were seen as immodest and vulgar in their breach of the boundaries between public and private life.[54]

The home was not only a protected domain for intimate life, but also the "backstage" to one's public performance, a place where people could drop their social "fronts," step out of character, and reveal their true selves.[55] People were said to have distinct public and private selves, and an important part of "privacy" was the ability to maintain this divide. Journalistic forays into domestic affairs were decried because they brought a person's private self into public view, undermining or compromising his public persona. Every person, it was said, should have his or her own "zone of privacy" in the home, regardless of one's status in public life. Even the president had a right "to go home from the show and be protected" from media coverage "as he rides hobby horse with his son, plays bear with his children on his knees or rolls over the floor with the baby."[56]

Privacy thus involved a corollary right to self-chosen publicity, a right to choose and create one's public self, distinct from one's private self and persona. As such, one's "privacy" could be invaded not only when one's domestic activities were exposed, but when any material about an individual was made publicly visible in a way that clashed with his desired public image. People of this time spoke of "invasions of privacy" when they were publicized in a manner that was embarrassing or uncomfortable to them, even though what was disclosed was technically not secret and did not happen behind closed doors. It was said to be an invasion of privacy, for example, when the details of a person's wedding ceremony were published without consent, even though the event occurred in public. A person walked down the street in the view of others. This act was indisputably public. But if a photographer took a picture of the person and published it in a newspaper, it could be an invasion of privacy. The term "invasion of privacy" was being used to describe any kind of upsetting, unwanted, or unauthorized depiction of one's person or personal affairs to a public audience, even if the materials disclosed were not literally "private." As personal image and self-presentation in public became matters of great importance, such acts of unwanted publicity were described as serious "assaults" to the individual, more "formidable and painful than an actual bodily assault might be."[57]

~

The legal status of these invasions of privacy was problematic. In general, there was no legal remedy for being publicized against one's will, or for being embarrassed or made "the town talk," unless the publication was false and defamatory.[58] The law of libel was "ludicrously inadequate" in many cases involving the public exposure of personal life, observed one commentator.[59] "Some merely curious incident in a man's life may be seized upon by a reporter with the result that for the time being, he is the most conspicuous person in the country. Yet, according to our present notions of the law of libel no cause of action would accrue to him unless his character had been defamed," wrote the lawyer Elbridge Adams. "It makes no difference how much he may dislike the publicity, or how greatly he may be pained by it . . . the fact of publicity alone will give him no right of action."[60]

Around 1880, a well-known critic made a public call for a broad legal right to control one's public image, one that was far more expansive than the limited reputational rights protected by the law of libel. E. L. Godkin, editor of *The Nation*, was a noted essayist, and like so many of the architects of image law in this period, hailed from the intellectual and social elite.[61] In an essay, "Libel and Its Legal Remedy," published in the *Atlantic Monthly*, Godkin criticized libel law for being too concerned with the technicalities of "reputation" and not enough with "outraged feelings and sentiments." "When a man in good standing" finds embarrassing personal facts about himself published in a newspaper, "his pain [is] apt to be intense," Godkin wrote. Even if the publication does not cause others to think less of him, he nonetheless suffers shame and "mortification." He becomes anxious and self-conscious; "he fancies that everybody who knows him has read [the article] and has been deeply impressed by it. As he walks down the street he thinks that every eye is turned on him."[62] Godkin's solution was to expand the law of libel, much as Lorenzo Nightingale had tried to do in the *Cape Cod Folks* suit. He argued that published material should be legally actionable as a libel even if it was not false or defamatory, but simply portrayed a person in a way that embarrassed him, made him uneasy, or otherwise affronted his sense of self.[63]

Godkin repeated this idea ten years later in a very similar article in the highbrow literary journal *Scribner's Magazine.* In the 1890 piece titled "The Rights of the Citizen," subtitled "To His Own Reputation," Godkin again argued that the law should protect not only the reputations but the feelings of people who had been unwillingly publicized.[64] Godkin discussed the possibility of a legal "right to privacy"—distinct from libel—which he described as the individual's right to "decid[e] how much or how little the community shall see of him, or know of him," to determine "how much knowledge of . . . personal thought and feeling, and how much knowledge . . . of tastes and habits, of his own private doings and affairs . . . the public at large shall have." Under this right to privacy, a person could sue the press and recover damages for truthful and nonlibelous but nonetheless upsetting or humiliating depictions. Godkin characterized privacy as an inherent right of personhood, "as much . . . as [one's] right to decide how [one] shall eat and drink."[65]

Godkin's piece in *Scribner's* was widely read in intellectual circles. Among those it intrigued was Louis Brandeis, a brilliant member of the Boston bar, then in his thirties.[66] It inspired his writing, later that year, of one of the most noted legal articles in history, said to be the "most influential law review article" of all time.[67]

$\sim$

An attack on the popular press, so much in the spirit of the day, the 1890 *Harvard Law Review* article "The Right to Privacy," attributed to Warren and Brandeis but written largely by Brandeis, decried gossip columns and information about personal affairs "spread broadcast in the columns of the daily papers."[68] "The press," Warren and Brandeis pronounced, "is overstepping in every direction the obvious bounds of propriety and decency. Gossip is no longer the resource of the idle and of the vicious, but has become a trade, which is pursued with industry as well as effrontery." "Persons with whose affairs the community has no legitimate concerns" were "being dragged into an undesirable and undesired publicity."[69] To a dignified person seeking respect and status, having the details of one's personal life publicized in the press caused embarrassment and "mental pain and distress," "far greater than could be inflicted by mere bodily injury."[70]

The article accused the press of "invading privacy" when it revealed a person's emotions, activities, and personal idiosyncrasies before a public audience, even though such matters were not "private" in the sense of being secret or concealed. Newspapers could "invade privacy" when they published a person's photograph, even if it was taken at a public event, or when they described one's participation in social activities such as weddings or balls. The article discussed the recent case of *Manola v. Stevens*, involving flash photographs of an actress obtained without her permission as she appeared on the stage.[71] The description of a woman at a social gathering was technically not "private," nor were pictures of an actress performing in public. These publications were nonetheless said to invade privacy because, in presenting the subject out of context and before an audience not of her own choosing, they impaired her ability to create her own social identity, to define her public image as she wished.

Like Godkin, Warren and Brandeis proposed a common law cause of action that would allow the victims of such "invasions of privacy" to sue and recover monetary damages.[72] Unlike libel, their tort of invasion of privacy did not protect a person's esteem in the eyes of others so much as one's capacity to define his own public persona: "the right of determining . . . to what extent his thoughts, sentiments, and emotions shall be communicated to others."[73] The privacy action was aimed specifically at the press on the theory that printed matter, because of its permanence and mass circulation, could create deep and irreversible harms. Embarrassing facts communicated orally, as chitchat or rumors, would not be legally remediable; spoken gossip, fleeting and transitory, was a familiar albeit annoying aspect of daily life that could be dealt with through extralegal means, or if the comments were especially impertinent, the law of slander.[74] Their proposed "right to privacy" did not address such privacy invasions as physical intrusions into the home, or wiretapping and eavesdropping by government and private actors, acts that were becoming increasingly common and that were beginning to be addressed by various statutory and common law provisions.[75] Rather, their concern was with unwanted publicity, with public image. The right to privacy was the right to keep one's personal affairs out of the public eye, and more broadly, to determine one's own public image without undue interference from the media of mass communications.

The bulk of the article was concerned with making the technical legal argument for the right to privacy. For this, Warren and Brandeis drew on the laws of intellectual property— copyright, trademark, and trade secrets. Under these laws, one had a right to prevent the publication and circulation of personal photographs and letters. Warren and Brandeis interpreted these intellectual property rights as part of a broader right to prevent one's thoughts or likeness from being displayed to the public against one's will. Based on this precedent, they argued, it was not a leap for the common law to recognize a right to privacy that would make the press liable for publishing pictures of people or personal information without consent. "Political, social, and economic changes entail the recognition of new rights," they wrote, "and the common law, in its eternal youth, grows to meet the new demands of society."[76]

Under their proposed privacy tort, damages could be recovered for injury to one's pride and feelings. Warren and Brandeis emphasized the legal distinction between one's privacy and one's reputation. Reputation, one's good name and the material and social benefits that flowed from it, was a quasi-property interest, a matter of "substance," something that was measurable and potentially calculable in terms of dollars and cents. The interest in privacy, by contrast, was ethereal and intangible; it lay not in the opinions of others but in one's emotions and sense of personal dignity. Dignity—a belief in the "intrinsic value" of every individual—was an important cultural value in this time, particularly in the Northern states.[77] But dignity was in general not an interest protected by the common law, which for the most part focused only on "tangible" harms— injuries to the body or to property.[78] In Europe, by contrast, dignitary rights, including the right to privacy and the right to one's image, were strongly protected. In France, the publication by newspapers of facts related to "private life" could be punished as a criminal offense.[79] Germany had a similar right to privacy, based on the principle that each person has a distinct "personality" or essence, and that to interfere with one's ability to express his "personality" through his words, acts, and appearance constituted a serious dignitary harm.[80] Brandeis, brought up in a Germanic tradition, had been inspired by these continental laws.[81] Unlike European privacy laws, which were aimed principally at protecting the public images of public figures, the American right to privacy was to be a right for everyone. Wrote Warren and Brandeis, "the design of the law must be to protect . . . all persons, whatsoever their position or station, from having matters which they may properly prefer to keep private made public against their will."[82]

Privacy's domain was the lofty realm of dignity, the soul, and the "spirit."[83] Yet the right to privacy also had a more earthly, instrumental aspect. In the image-oriented culture of Gilded Age America, unwarranted, unfavorable, embarrassing depictions in the press were seen as damaging in that they undermined a person's ability to cultivate his own public image, and therefore to maximize his fortunes and social potential.[84] The success of the right to privacy, both as a popular concept and as a matter of formal law, was rooted in practical and material concerns with public image in American social life.

◇

In a climate of discontent and anxiety around the new media of mass exposure, the idea of a legally enforceable right to privacy struck a nerve. "The Right to Privacy" was dissected, discussed, and praised in popular and legal journals—remarkable for a law review article. As legal commentator John Gilmer Speed wrote in 1896, "the definite establishment of this right of privacy is at this time of the greatest possible moment."[85] There was a "general agreement" among the public that "the time and place were ripe for the invention of a legal theory for enforcement of the right to privacy."[86] "If a man may appear in public, or seclude himself, as he sees fit, there is no sound reason why he should not determine the circumstances under which his face shall be exhibited in the newspapers," opined no less a legal authority than Supreme Court Justice Henry Billings Brown.[87] The prerogative to determine how much of one's life and identity one "gave" to the public was an inherent right of personhood, "each individual's very own."[88]

Lawyers wasted no time mobilizing the concept on behalf of clients claiming to have been maligned, exposed, or misrepresented by photographers, newspapers, magazines, and literary authors. One of their first successes came in September 1891, when the intermediate appellate court of New York decided the case of *Schuyler v. Curtis*. The case involved a suit by the relatives of Mrs. Schuyler, a deceased philanthropist, to enjoin the display of a bust of her at the 1893 Columbian Exposition in Chicago. Citing the Warren and Brandeis article, the opinion concluded that Mrs. Schuyler, even after death, had a privacy right in her image—a right to not have her likeness displayed to the public without consent, in this case the consent of her family.[89] In *Marks v. Jaffa*, from 1893, a newspaper published as part of a circulation scheme a picture of two actors, with an invitation to readers to vote on which was the more popular of the two. The court enjoined the publication on the basis of an "invasion of privacy," concluding that "no newspaper or institution, no matter how worthy, has the right to use the name or picture of anyone for such a purpose without his consent."[90]

At the same time, this novel—and vague—legal concept raised doubts and criticisms. The common law had traditionally prohibited legal recovery for injuries to the emotions in the absence of another recognized legal interest, such as freedom from physical harm, and yet the Warren and Brandeis proposal asked for exactly that. "An invasion of privacy, however distasteful it may be, or however deeply it may wound [one's] feelings, is not the subject of an action, for the common law does not recognize mental anguish as a ground for damages," observed Herbert Spencer Hadley, a law professor, in an article in the *Northwestern Law Review*.[91] Wrote the *Atlantic Monthly*, "Surely it is impossible that the law, which we are accustomed to regard as an agency for protecting our lives and our pockets, with a perfect disregard of feelings, should stoop to concern itself with the privacy of the individual."[92] Critics also wondered how, as a practical matter, "invasions of privacy" could be translated into money damages. "Suppose a flashy and objectionable paper should print the portrait of a private gentleman's wife or daughter. Every refined person would concede that there had been damage," but how could that be measured in dollars and cents?[93]

There were also free speech concerns. Under the dominant "bad tendency" test, the privacy tort was, as a technical matter, constitutionally unproblematic.[94] In the words of the *Virginia Law Review*, freedom of the press "was not intended to confer a license without any limitation, to override the rights of others," including the right to be left alone.[95] Yet some believed that the right of privacy—which imposed liability for the publication of *true* facts—could "have no existence consistent with free speech."[96] Politicians and public officials could potentially use their "right to privacy" to quash truthful criticism or suppress reports of misdeed or corruption. "The right of friends, neighbors, casual acquaintances, and even of strangers, to speak of, talk about, and freely discuss a person's life, habits, and personality is concededly so extensive that . . . no right of action arises until something is said that is defamatory," wrote the legal journal *Case and Comment*.[97]

Warren and Brandeis had proposed a limited privilege for the publication of "matters of public or general interest." "Matters of public interest" were topics that served the "public interest" in the sense of the public welfare or common good. Mere trivia and gossip, though perhaps interesting, were not "matters of public interest." The lives of ordinary people were usually not matters of legitimate public interest, as the public had no interest in them outside of mere curiosity, but the doings of public figures might well be. A news report discussing a politician's personal traits—whether he had a stutter or if he could spell, for example—would potentially be a matter of public interest, as it illuminated his capacity for office. However, an account of a politician's romantic life would not be privileged, as it had "no legitimate connection with his fitness for a public office . . . [or] legitimate relation to . . . any act" done by him in a public context.[98] The public did not have a need to know or a "right to know" such intimate, personal details.

Although the "matters of public interest" privilege provided some latitude for the press, it still exerted a potentially "chilling effect" on publishing.[99] Publishers, not knowing what courts might find to be a subject of "public interest," could self-censor, inhibiting the publication of important news. A few courts rejected privacy claims on free speech grounds. In *Corliss v. Walker*, from 1893, the wife of a deceased inventor brought suit against the publisher of an unauthorized biographical article about her late husband, claiming an invasion of privacy. The court noted that the imposition of liability for the publication of his life story would be a "remarkable exception to liberty of the press." When a person became a "public figure," he consented to having his activities put before the spotlight.[100]

Other detractors mocked the right to privacy as a concession to the "super-sensitive." As one magazine observed in 1891, commenting on the Warren and Brandeis article, "people of sensitive respectability [felt] it . . . detrimental to their comfort, their reputation, and their best interests, to have their names in . . . newspapers." "The feelings of these thin-skinned Americans" were "doubtless at the bottom of an article in the December number of the *Harvard Law Review*, in which two members of the Boston bar have recorded the results of certain researches into the question of whether Americans do not possess a common law right of privacy which can be successfully defended in the courts."[101]

Indeed, what seemed curious to some was that although people were crying out for privacy, they also seemed to be clamoring for publicity. The popular press had given rise to the new phenomenon of the publicity hound, the person who tried to achieve fame by actively seeking out newspaper coverage. As the *Century Illustrated Magazine* observed in 1896, people were "smitten with a form of insanity which may be called, for want of a dictionary word, publicomania." This "craving for publicity is not satisfied with anything but a paragraph in the newspapers; then it wants a column; and finally it demands a whole page with illustrations."[102] In a world where people were increasingly known to each other as media images, and where mass communications were becoming the connective tissue of social life, media publicity was a marker of social success, and also a means to success. A new chapter in the history of the American Dream was unfolding: one could achieve respect, prominence, and social mobility simply by getting one's name in the papers.

In 1889, *The Nation* commented disdainfully on this new world in which status and power were contingent on media recognition. "Very few indeed feel themselves capable of great deeds with either sword or pen . . . but there is nobody who does not feel notoriety to be within his reach—that is, does not feel that, with a very small expenditure of effort, he may become the talk of the town, or of the State, or even of the Union." Before the advent of the mass-circulation press, fame was relatively hard to come by. "But it can now be had by jumping off a bridge, marrying a woman of the town, buying a large house, eating thirty successive quails in thirty successive days, keeping a fast trotter, writing an erotic book, fighting a duel, owning forty pairs of trousers. . . . By the aid of newspapers our streets swarm with men who have that one note of fame which consists in being recognized and talked about."[103]

This easy track to the top was criticized by the established elite, which resented the threat to its status and authority from the lowborn, newcomers, and parvenus. The possibility of sudden and widespread media visibility was undermining the traditional notion of fame as the reward for hard work and achievement. The wish of "private persons" to "be talked about and thought about and written about"—in some cases, to have their personal affairs publicly discussed—was seen as vulgar, uncouth, and even immoral, as it mocked the boundaries between public and private and the sanctity of private life. "Persons who are imbued with this belief (in the extreme blessedness of notoriety) find it very difficult to acknowledge that everybody else is not of their mind, and would not be gratified by being made conspicuous," wrote a critic in the *New York Times*. But there were "a good many persons left in the world . . . to whom notoriety is distasteful, and undeserved celebrity entirely repulsive."[104]

Yet this class of modest, reticent, and genteel persons who shunned the spotlight seemed to be diminishing. "It is quite obvious that many men, and not a few women, are not half satisfied unless they form the subjects of paragraphs in papers." Journalists "almost credit themselves with philanthropy for liberating a few human beings from the misfortune of common privacy."[105] Hardly shrinking violets, socialites, for example, could take offense if their activities failed to secure a place in the gossip columns. There was also a growing sector of the populace for whom publicity—including publicity of personal life—was becoming an occupational requirement. Actors and politicians were regularly employing press agents to spin positive images of them in magazines and newspapers.[106] One observer noted that the press agent was becoming a "necessary adjunct" to all lines of work, and that "financiers, politicians, business men and social aspirants appreciate the wisdom of having their affairs looked after by a man who can obtain desired publicity and can, at times, prevent the undesirable kind."[107] For those whose success was dependent on public favor, positive publicity was always worth something.[108]

What had yet to be realized was that privacy and publicity were really two sides of the same coin, both conditions of social existence in the image society.

Those individuals who wanted the most publicity were often those who also wanted the most "privacy"—to be able to conceal unfavorable personal facts, and to manage the terms of their self-presentation more generally. The more people sought publicity, they more they claimed a "right to privacy," a right to control their public images. The right to privacy was the right to selective publicity, and it was becoming critical not only for public figures, but for everyone who "performed" in daily life.

CHAPTER 3

The Crisis of the Circulating Portrait

Elizabeth Peck was a widow who lived in the small town of Mount Auburn, Iowa. In 1904, she had a photograph taken in a portrait studio. The photographer, without Peck's consent, sold the negatives to the makers of Duffy's Pure Malt Whisky, which used them in an ad touting its properties as a "health promoting" tonic. The ad was published in the *Chicago Tribune* and several other newspapers across the country. "Nurse and Patients Praise Duffy's. Mrs. A. Schuman, One of Chicago's Most Capable and Experienced Nurses, Pays an Eloquent Tribute to the Great Invigorating, Life-Giving, and Curative Properties of Duffy's Pure Malt Whisky," read the ad's headline.[1]

Under the headline appeared a photograph of Mrs. Peck with the caption, "Mrs. A. Schuman," with an address in Chicago. "After years of constant use of your Pure Malt Whisky, both by myself and as given to patients in my capacity as nurse, I have no hesitation in recommending it," read the testimonial below the portrait. Mrs. Peck was not a nurse, and was a total abstainer from alcohol. The advertiser had, negligently or willfully, run the image of Mrs. Peck next to this phony testimonial. Peck, outraged and humiliated, sued for libel and invasion of privacy.[2]

Despite its invention as a remedy for the victims of sensationalistic journalism, the tort of invasion of privacy was rarely used in that context, at least in its early years. As E. L. Godkin presciently summarized in *The Nation*, the "legal remedy would very closely resemble that old-fashioned cure for the headache caused by too much intoxicating drink—'the hair of the dog that bit you.' That is to say, the man who feels outraged" by the publication of humiliating gossip "will, in order to stop or punish it, have to expose himself to a great deal more publicity. In order to bring his persecutors to justice, he will have to go through a process which will result in an exposure of his private affairs tenfold greater than that originally made by the offending article."[3] The right to privacy instead took off in a different kind of violation of the right to one's image. At the turn of the twentieth century, the right to privacy was mobilized in cases where people were upset about having their visual likenesses presented to the public in an embarrassing, unflattering, misrepresentative, or otherwise displeasing manner.

In particular, individuals whose photographs had been used in advertisements without their consent brought suits for invasion of privacy. In what was not an uncommon occurrence at the time, ordinary men and women like Elizabeth Peck found their pictures, quite randomly, in ads for a variety of products—patent medicines, complexion beautifiers, 5-cent cigars.[4] At a time when advertising for consumer products was seen by many to be disreputable and even immoral, these acts of image appropriation were regarded as highly offensive. Few things were more insulting and degrading, it was said, than the "wanton and brutal publication for advertising purposes of the portrait of one who has not consented."[5] It was in this context that the "right to privacy" as a right to one's image began to be recognized in American law. The right to privacy was the right to recover for the emotional anguish caused by this unusual form of identity theft—having one's picture used, without authorization, in an embarrassing and undignified commercial context.[6]

≈

By the late nineteenth century, photographic portraits had become an important part of people's social identities. Portrait photography had been introduced in the United States in the 1840s, and by the Civil War inexpensive photography studios had sprung up across the country.[7] Having one's portrait taken became a periodic and ordinary event. "About once in three years," a writer noted in *Cosmopolitan* magazine, "the average man nerves himself up to the task of securing his likeness, and when finished photographs are finally sent, . . . he frequently and surreptitiously gazes at them with an almost childlike pride and pleasure."[8] Writes historian Alan Trachtenberg, the ubiquity of photographic portraits and the near universality of sitting for one's photograph created "a new regard for visibility, for one's own image as a medium of self-presentation."[9] At a time when the painted portrait was a luxury few could afford, the photograph "[let] virtually everyone establish a visible self-image," and as such became an "emblem of democracy."[10]

The photograph's verisimilitude was regarded with awe and fascination; pictures seemed more real than real. The photographic image was considered to be not only more accurate than hand drawings but also more "authentic." It was thought that the photographic portrait captured the "essence" of a person.[11] Professional photographers said that the "true artist" treated people's surface appearances as expressions of a deep inner reality.[12] Photographic portraits were not simply a record of appearance but "a symbol of the inner self," a "window into the soul."[13]

Just as they sought to dress fashionably, adopt genteel manners, and project the best possible face to the public, the socially conscious and upwardly mobile tried to create favorable photographic images of themselves and to strategically display them to their advantage. In this way, photography was perhaps the first American "social medium," a technology people used to depict and construct their social identities and communicate them to others. Photographic subjects attended carefully to every detail—clothing, poses, backdrops, expressions—to create images that indicated "this is how I look, this is what I do, this is who I am."[14] Portraits were typically commissioned for personal uses, and portraits of individuals and families were collected in albums or hung on the walls of homes.[15] *Cartes de visite*, portraits glued to a card with the individual's name printed on the back, were circulated among friends and acquaintances as "calling cards" of personal identity.[16] With great interest and care, individuals memorialized themselves with their photographs, circulated those images to desired audiences, and displayed them in contexts they wished to be seen in.

Despite their efforts to control their photographic images and the circulation of those images, people found their pictures appropriated for a variety of uses. The public's fascination with photographic images led to a tremendous market in photographs of all kinds.[17] Photographers sold negatives and portraits to printers who used them on greeting cards and other decorative items.[18] Often they were sold to dry goods stores and junk shops. In the 1890s, the *New York Tribune* reported that small shops peddled "the second hand stock of the cheapest East side photograph parlors . . . pictures of bridal couples in full regalia, stiff and unhappy looking family groups."[19] Pictures were dispensed from vending machines and even given away free in cigarette packs.[20] Collectors would purchase random pictures of people for as little as a penny a piece, and there were rooms in homes that were "papered with photographs."[21] In a practice that was widespread but may seem odd to the modern reader, photographers also made a business selling random portraits of ordinary people to the advertisers of consumer products.

∾

In the late nineteenth century, advertising was becoming a ubiquitous presence in American life. As innovations in technology led to the mass production of low-priced, packaged consumer items, standardized, inexpensive food products, clothing, toiletries, and other luxury and leisure products flooded the market. Manufacturers built large marketing and purchasing networks, and a spectrum of retail businesses, from dry goods stores to department stores, arose in both urban and rural areas across the country.[22] As the growth in productive capacity outpaced the needs of the population, commercial entrepreneurs became obsessed with creating demand for consumer products. The key agent in this project was advertising, especially visual advertising.[23] Attractive pictures would play to consumers' emotions and stimulate yearnings for products that they did not need but merely fancied.

In the mid-1800s, chromolithography, an elaborate method for reproducing hand-drawn images, had been used to illustrate print advertising.[24] Advertising chromolithography sent into the popular culture a cornucopia of images of fantasy and abundance: voluptuous women, doll-faced cherubs, lush harvests, copious quantities of food.[25] In the 1890s, with the development of the halftone process, which permitted black and white photos to be printed on pages alongside typeset copy, photography began to replace chromolithography as the technology of choice for advertising illustration.[26]

By 1900, photography suffused the advertising space in popular magazines. Advertisers especially coveted photographs of females because of women's association with respectability—women's photos would "succeed in appealing to the 'better' sorts of audiences of both genders," writes historian Pamela Laird.[27] Several commercial companies, particularly liquor and patent medicines, decided that their ads "ought to be 'brightened by pretty faces,' and they began to use photographs of beautiful women for this purpose."[28] "Pretty girls," it was said, "could . . . sell absolutely everything."[29]

But it was not easy to obtain photographs to use in ads. Photography required cumbersome studio equipment; handheld Kodak cameras and "roving camera-men" were only beginning to come into existence.[30] It was also difficult to find subjects who would consent to have their images in ads.[31] There was not yet a commercial modeling industry; the first modeling agency in the United States did not take off until the World War I era.[32] Stage actors had begun lending their names and images to a variety of products, ranging "from chocolates and cigars to dentifrice and patent medicine," but celebrity product endorsements were, by to-day's standards, relatively rare.[33] Associated with loose sexuality and the Bohemian underworld, actors and actresses were seen as disreputable among many sectors of the populace.[34] Modesty was a critical element of female virtue, and the essence of modesty was concealment of the body in public. Actresses who sold pictures of their faces and bodies to advertisers were condemned as dissolute, no better than prostitutes.[35]

In contrast to our modern worldview, the buying, selling, and advertising of commercial products carried negative moral associations. Although consumer habits were becoming widespread, there were still significant ethical reservations around material indulgence. The core values of the middle class had historically been anticonsumerist: plain living, perpetual work, self-control, and deferred gratification.[36] The proliferation of products and the advent of a consumer culture led to vociferous attacks on consumerism and predictions of moral decay.[37] In his *Theory of the Leisure Class* (1899), Thorstein Veblen lambasted "pecuniary emulation" and "conspicuous consumption" as overindulgent and morally bankrupt.[38] "The girl who spends her allowance in candy and matinee tickets is relaxing the moral fiber of her own character," wrote one magazine author.[39] The United States was becoming a "commodity civilization," it was feared, a culture of superficiality and materialism, "submerged beneath the surface allure of having and displaying possessions."[40]

The marketplace for goods was seen as a locus not only of forbidden desire, but of corruption, deceit, and trickery.[41] The selling of goods was still linked in the popular imagination to the street hawkers and "confidence men" of an earlier era,[42] and advertising pitches of this time were often exaggerated if not totally false.[43] Advertisements for questionable health remedies, get-rich-quick schemes, and other outrageous fakery filled the pages of newspapers and magazines.[44] The advertisers of consumer products were widely viewed as little more than "liars and crooks," "bearing an odor of snake oil."[45] Respectable people did not engage in the needless acquisition of consumer goods, let alone consent to appear in product advertisements.

Thus faced with significant difficulties obtaining pictures, advertisers often resorted to the "black market" in portraits, buying or even stealing images from photographers without the consent of the photographic subjects. Sometimes the portraits were of famous people. An 1895 article from the legal journal *Case and Comment* lamented the advertising exploitation of the images of politicians, philosophers, and other notabilities. "Must an outraged nation," it asked, suffer a "wretched caricature of the sad, sublime face of Abraham Lincoln . . . posted up everywhere to advertise 'Bloater's Bitters,' or 'Smart Cuss's Corn Cure'?"[46] More often, though, the appropriated images were of ordinary men and women, individuals whose images were fungible and ubiquitous, and who would be unlikely and perhaps unable to take action against the advertiser. The newspapers regularly reported stories of average people who quite literally woke up one morning to find their photographs emblazoned on ads for random food products, patent medicines, and beauty items.

Advertisers typically chose a person's portrait because of the feelings the image might invoke in potential consumers. Portraits were selected not because they represented a particular person or identity, but for their ability to generate emotions or associations that would enhance the product's marketability and appeal. Often the depicted individual represented idealized attributes, such as youth, beauty, innocence, or sophistication. Pictures of babies, stately grandmothers, and "pretty girls" were of particular value in this regard.[47] These images created a "vague sense of desire" towards the advertised items and offered consumers a fantasy of what they might become or how they might feel if they acquired and used them.[48] Images of slender young women, dapper gentlemen, and rosy-cheeked children acquired sudden value in the new connotative economy of mass advertising, an industry that traded in aspiration, emulation, and desire.

By 1890, advertisers' use of misappropriated photographs—the "misuse of the faces of private persons"—had generated a public outcry.[49] As one writer in the *Washington Post* lamented, it was "the extreme of impudence for a firm or company to take the photograph of any living person, and, without permission, use it as a label for their goods."[50] "Any likeness of anything that is in heaven above we may expect to see in these days on city walls, slabsided rocks, or country barn doors, as the sign or trademark of some quack medicine or shoddy merchandise," mourned one critic.[51] Attractive young women were "liable to the shock of seeing their [pictures] used [in an advertisement] to blazon the alleged merits of a certain brand of cigar or whiskey," and "prominent citizen[s]" were subjected to "the mortification of seeing their photographs in the advertising columns of a newspaper." No one was immune from "the humiliation of this unbridled license by commercial pirates."[52]

The subjects of these so-called circulating portraits expressed strong feelings of embarrassment and shame. They were appalled when they found that their images had been used in advertisements. The injury was all the more damaging when a photograph of one's face—an intensely intimate representation of self, the "window into the soul"—had been commercially exploited. Friends and acquaintances saw the ads and jeered at them, or were shocked to find that a person they had considered to be upstanding and respectable had willingly "sold her face" to an advertiser.

In 1904, a woman who found photographs of her displayed in a store alleged that the act "humiliated her," "made her nervous," and caused her to be laughed at by her peers.[53] The *New York Times* wrote in 1907 that a local beauty queen suffered "mental anguish" when her picture appeared in an ad without her consent. She began to notice that some of her friends were looking at her strangely.[54] "I had such a sweet photograph of myself taken the other day, which was in great demand by all my admirers," a woman complained to the editor of a popular magazine. "Imagine my intense disgust and horror at seeing it used as an advertisement."[55] The unauthorized use of one's photograph in an ad created a profound sense of "exposure and violation."[56]

~

It was not long before this problem attracted the attention of the legal world. The legal status of these appropriated photographs was murky. As a matter of law, it was not yet clear who "owned" the rights to these images. In the late 1800s, some victims of photographic misappropriation brought successful actions for breach of contract against photographers who made and circulated unauthorized reprints.[57] But the breach of contract action was not a viable remedy in every "cir-

culating portrait" case. It was only applicable when the advertiser had obtained
the image from the photographer, which was not always the case, and it permitted suit only against the photographer, not the advertiser, with whom the victim
had no contractual relationship. Moreover, damages were limited. Under contract
rules, damages could be had for pecuniary loss caused by the unauthorized use of
the image, but in most cases, unless an actor or other public figure was involved,
the individual's photo had no market value. Embarrassment and shame—the
principal injuries alleged—were not compensable.

Beginning in the 1890s, in response to public pressure, statutory measures
were proposed to deal with the crisis of the "circulating portrait." One law journal
in 1895 recommended that every state legislature pass a law: "It shall be a crime
for any person to post, print, publish, or in any way make use of any portrait,
likeness, or caricature of any other person, living or dead, as an advertisement
for any goods, wares, or articles of merchandise of any sort, without the written
consent of the person whom such picture represents, if he is living, or of his next
of kin if such person is dead." "For the penalty something less than death may do,
but it should be severe enough to be effectual," it quipped.[58] The publication of
the picture of Mrs. Grover Cleveland in an ad for patent medicine prompted the
introduction of a bill in Congress that would ban the exhibition of any photograph or likeness of a woman without her authorization.[59] Supporters of a similar
bill in New York noted the inexcusable "annoyance" that had been "inflicted upon
innocent and quiet people, especially upon women, whose lineaments had been
disfigured and presented in public prints without their consent."[60]

The victims of circulating portraits were also seeking remedies in court, under the common law, for their dignitary and reputational injuries. Some brought
suits for libel. The claim in these cases was that the unauthorized publication of
one's picture in an advertisement lowered his or her reputation in the community
because of its implication that the person was immoral, having "allowed his or
her name (or image) to be used for commercial gain."[61] By the turn of the century, plaintiffs from a variety of backgrounds and circumstances had also initiated
claims for interference with one's right to control one's public image, as an "invasion of privacy."

~

In the many libel claims that were brought over misappropriated portraits, plaintiffs alleged that the unauthorized use of their images in advertisements created an impression of them that was false and that cast them into disrepute. In a number of cases, the plaintiff argued that the advertisement was defamatory because it falsely associated her with a dubious product. In a 1909 libel case, the picture of a senator was published in an ad for a patent medicine called "Doan's Kidney Pills." The senator was not a user of the product and had not endorsed it. The court held that he had a cause of action for libel because patent medicines were known to be fraudulent.[62] Another genre of "libel by advertising" cases involved false testimonials, as in Mrs. Peck's case. In a common practice at the time, advertisers appropriated portraits and published them alongside a false statement endorsing the product, purportedly from the depicted individual.[63]

In most "libel by advertising" cases, the chief argument was that one's *very appearance in an ad* was defamatory, regardless of the product that was advertised or any words associated with it. It was not merely the public association with a commercial product that was humiliating, but the assumption that viewers would make when they saw the advertisement: that the plaintiff had consented to have her photo used for advertising purposes. Plaintiffs "were scandalized by the possibility that people would assume they actually endorsed commercialized products."[64] In a 1909 case, *Munden v. Harris*, a Missouri appeals court held that a boy whose portrait had been used in an ad for a jewelry store had a cause of action for libel. The use of the boy's image "as an advertising aid to business" led viewers to make false assumptions about his character, and the plaintiff suffered disgrace, "vexation and . . . ridicule."[65]

The claims of reputational injury were even stronger when the subject of the portrait was a seemingly respectable middle-class white woman, as the public display of a woman's face and body in a commercial context carried overtones of illicit sexuality.[66] In *Kunz v. Allen*, a dry goods store surreptitiously took a film of a woman and used it in an advertisement.[67] The Kansas Supreme Court observed that the unauthorized use of the woman's image would discredit her, as it would lead viewers to assume that she was a paid model, calling her morals into question. "No woman of ordinary refinement would fail to be humiliated by the unauthorized publication of her portrait" in an advertisement for goods, observed the author of one law review article. "No judge will do violence to legal principles . . . if he recognizes . . . that this inevitable humiliation which every woman must feel. . . . is sufficient to make [the publication] defamatory."[68]

This was the argument in *Peck v. Tribune*, involving the small-town widow and the fake whiskey ad. Elizabeth Peck alleged that the advertisement had subjected her—a woman of "spotless reputation and blameless life"—to humiliation and the "contempt, ridicule, and scorn" of her peers. A woman had a right to not have her face "'blown about the pendant world' before the eyes of millions of her countrymen to advertise a certain brand of whiskey, charging her at the same time with the twin falsehoods of holding herself out as a nurse and having for years used and advocated the use by others of intoxicating liquors," Peck's lawyers argued.[69] The ad was an assault on her character because it presented her as a person "who has loaned or sold her face for advertising purposes."[70]

In an opinion by Justice Oliver Wendell Holmes, the U.S. Supreme Court concluded that an "appreciable fraction" of the population could very well regard Mrs. Peck with contempt, both for appearing to have endorsed whiskey, a product that some might view as immoral, and for appearing to have sold her image for advertising purposes. While there were some people who might view posing for an ad as morally unproblematic, being associated with advertisements could very well "hurt [one's] standing with a considerable and respectable class in the community."[71] As the Seventh Circuit Court of Appeals had put it, Peck had "indisputably suffered a wrong" to her reputation. By "the publication of her picture in [an] advertisement, people who recognize the portrait [will] think she has loaned her face in a way a self-respecting person would not have consented to."[72]

∾

By 1900, it was widely agreed that the unauthorized use of a person's likeness in an ad could create reputational harm and be legally actionable as a libel. Such acts also injured one's ability to create one's own desired public image—one's "right to privacy." Warren and Brandeis, discussing the problem of the "circulating portrait," had declared that the right to prevent such "public portraiture" represented the "clearest case" for their proposed legal right. There was a "widespread feeling," they observed, that the law "must afford some remedy for the unautho-rized circulation of portraits of private persons."[73]

To social critics, the circulating portrait symbolized a broader, disturbing cul-tural trend. In the new consumer culture, people were no longer able to define their own values and identities, it seemed, but were instead being controlled by material yearnings and persuasive and seductive advertising.[74] Advertisements had become so pervasive and voluminous that they intruded on people's thoughts and consciousness. As Samuel Hopkins Adams warned in *Collier's* magazine, "there is no hour of waking life in which we are not besought, incited, or com-manded to buy something of somebody."[75] Acquisitive values had pervaded the most intimate domains of the home. Bedrooms, bathrooms, and parlors were filled with mass-produced foodstuffs, trinkets, appliances, and clothes. At a time when women were regarded as the guardians of the home, the commercial use of female images was considered the most egregious example of the intrusion of market forces into the sacred realm of private life. The ideal of the autonomous, self-defining, "self-made man" appeared to be besieged in a world where people were being exhorted to orient their lives around their purchases and possessions.[76]

The circulating portrait epitomized these fears of the commodification of the self and the human experience. The appropriated advertising image exploited the depicted individual by turning her photograph into an object and a spectacle. In these ads, the actual identity of the depicted subject was meaningless; the image was valuable insofar as it could evoke a particular mood, status, or feeling to ap-peal to consumers and sell products. Human likenesses were becoming empty, fungible symbols of desire, and individuality destroyed as living people were re-duced to being mere "labels for goods."[77] People who had in no way courted profit or publicity were being enslaved, their "physiognom[ies] . . . pirated to tout another person's business."[78] The "right to privacy" was envisioned as a means to prevent this sort of commercial exploitation—to preserve a terrain for the self that was "beyond the reach of market forces."[79]

In contrast to the latter twentieth century when courts would award plaintiffs lost profits from the unauthorized commercial use of their images, damages for the photographic "invasion of privacy," circa 1900, compensated humiliation and mental distress. Plaintiffs usually did not seek to recover pecuniary losses from the advertising use of their images. This was not only because most people's likenesses, apart from celebrities', had little if any commercial value. There was also moral resistance to the idea of people making money off their images. The idea of one's image as a form of property that could be bought and sold was repugnant to the genteel Victorian sensibility. Wrote one judge in 1902, "we may discard entirely the suggestion that a lady has any thing in the nature of a property right in her form or features that is invaded by the circulation of her picture against her will or without her consent. That would be altogether too coarse and too material a suggestion to apply to one of the noblest and most attractive gifts that providence has bestowed on the human race." "A woman's beauty, next to her virtues, is her earthly crown," and "it would be a degradation to hedge it about by rules and principles applicable to property in land or chattels."[80]

∽

Around the turn of the century, a number of cases appeared in state courts alleging a "right to privacy" in one's visual likeness. Most involved ordinary people whose photographs had been used without consent in advertisements for consumer goods. The injury alleged was "offense," "mortification," and indignity. In many of these cases—the rule against recovery for "freestanding" emotional injuries notwithstanding—courts awarded damages for mental anguish. In the 1909 case *Foster-Millburn v. Chinn*, the picture of a senator from Kentucky was published alongside a false testimonial in an ad for patent medicine. He suffered "mortification of feelings." The court held that "a person is entitled to the right of privacy as to his picture, and the publication of the picture of a person without his consent, as a part of an advertisement for the purpose of exploiting the publisher's business, is a violation of the right of privacy." While "it has become a custom in the press to publish the pictures of prominent public men," the court noted, "it is a very different thing for a manufacturer to use without authority such a man's picture to advertise his goods."[81]

The most sympathetic privacy plaintiffs were often women. In 1904, a young woman who claimed that her picture was used without her consent in a corset advertisement brought suit on the theory that such vulgar publicity was "the . . . violation of the right of a decent woman to privacy."[82] That year, the *New York Times* noted the efforts of a young woman from Rochester to prevent the continued use of her image in an ad for a beauty product. The image "represents a woman, of whom only the face and one arm are visible, parting the curtains of a circular screen standing in a bathtub, and looking out towards the spectator." The picture was one that "any decent woman would most strongly resent being publicly shown."[83] Because a woman's social fate depended so heavily on her ability to project an image of chastity and modesty, courts were especially solicitous of women's claims to have been injured by commercial publicity. Just as courts in libel cases recognized the vulnerability and fragility of women's reputations, they acknowledged that women had especially strong claims to "privacy"—to not be thrust before the public gaze in a brazen, indelicate, or sexually suggestive manner.[84]

The public outrage around the 1902 decision in *Roberson v. Rochester Folding Box* attests to the popular sentiment that the commercial exploitation of a woman's likeness constituted a severe affront to her reputation, public image, and sense of self. The image of a young woman, Abigail Roberson, had been used without her consent in an ad for Franklin Mills Flour. The ad was titled "The Flour of the Family" and showed a line drawing of Roberson's head and neck, viewed from the side. The drawing was made from a photograph of Roberson. Below the image appeared a drawing of flour sacks and boxes and the words "Franklin Mills Flour." Twenty-five thousand copies of the ad were made and "conspicuously posted" in various locations, including "stores, warehouses, and saloons." Because the drawing was so realistic, Roberson's friends were able to recognize her identity.[85]

When Roberson saw herself in the ad, she was humiliated. She suffered "scoffs and jeers of persons who have recognized her face" on the ad, and "suffered a severe nervous shock, was confined to her bed, and compelled to employ a physician." She brought suit against the advertiser, the Rochester Folding Box Company, on the theory that the advertisement invaded her "privacy." She sought damages of $15,000 and that the defendants be enjoined from the further publication or circulation of the ad.[86]

The trial court rejected the advertiser's motion to dismiss Roberson's claim, noting that "any modest and refined young woman might naturally be extremely shocked and wounded in seeing a lithographic likeness of herself posted in public places as an advertisement of some enterprising business firm."[87] The intermediate court of appeals affirmed, yet the highest court in New York, in a 4–3 decision, reversed. The court refused to recognize a right to privacy, suggesting that to do so would unleash a "vast field of litigation."[88] Roberson had no protection for her image other than under the law of libel. In a statement that proved highly controversial, the majority opined that there was nothing unflattering about the picture; the likeness that appeared in the ad was complimentary. Because of this, Abigail Roberson had not truly been injured. Instead of being humiliated, some women might consider having their images publicly displayed in an advertisement, particularly if the picture was desirable, to be pleasant and "agreeable."[89]

The *Roberson* decision spurred major public protest. Popular publications were flooded with letters and articles attacking it. One writer expressed the prevailing mood when he observed that it was "outrageous that modest women who in no way put themselves before the public" could "be dragged into notoriety by any adventurer who thinks he can fill his pockets by exploiting them."[90] An editorial in the *American Law Review* argued that "the decision under review shocks and wounds the ordinary sense of justice of mankind."[91] "The sweeping character of this decision greatly strengthens the claim, advanced by the sensational press of to-day, of a right to pry into and grossly display before the public matters of the most private and personal concern."[92] The court's suggestion that Roberson actually enjoyed the publicity was seen as an offensive and reprehensible attack on a modest and demure female. "The Court of Appeals has told the plaintiff in advance that her grievance is fantastic and illusory. If she should happen to pine away and die of shame on account of such exhibition of her in public, she will have the consolation of knowing that, in the opinion of that court, she ought to have taken the exposure rather as a compliment."[93]

In response to *Roberson*, in 1903 the New York state legislature passed a Civil Rights Law—a so-called privacy statute—that made it both a misdemeanor and a tort to use, without consent, a person's "name, portrait, or picture" for advertising or "trade" purposes.[94] Recovery could be had for the indignities caused when an advertiser "ma[d]e use of a portrait of a beautiful woman to attract attention to some article of trade"[95]—when one's picture "was unauthorizedly published or used . . . in connection with the advertisement of some patent medicine or some other commodity which the advertiser was interested in selling."[96] The law was not really a "privacy" statute, but was addressed narrowly to the problem of the "circulating portrait," to placate public anger over the *Roberson* decision.

Within the first decade of its existence, the constitutionality of the New York statute was twice unsuccessfully challenged. In *Moser v. Press Publishing*, from 1908, an appeals court held that the statute did not violate freedom of the press because it did not infringe on the publication of truthful facts; it only curtailed the use of images in advertising, a genre then considered outside the scope of free speech law.[97] The statute was also challenged as a deprivation of property without due process of law. The plaintiff in *Sperry & Hutchinson Co. v. Rhodes*, a twenty-three-year-old newlywed, sat for her photograph in a New York studio. After a suitable portrait was made, the photographer, a man named Sol Young, made an arrangement with the Sperry and Hutchinson Company, a maker and vendor of trading stamps, in which a set of photographs at Young's would be offered as a "prize" for trading stamp redemption. Young was to display examples of his photographs in the Sperry and Hutchinson office, as an advertisement. One of the pictures was of Aida Rhodes. Young had not obtained her permission to use the photo. Rhodes and her husband saw the picture on display, and she was ashamed and distressed, especially when she realized that thousands of people had viewed the picture, including many of her friends. She won $1,000 at trial.[98]

Sperry and Hutchinson appealed to New York's highest court, and eventually to the U.S. Supreme Court in 1911. Sperry and Hutchinson's lawyers argued that the photograph belonged to Young, the photographer, and that Mrs. Rhodes "had only a sentimental interest in [it], such as a model might have in a statue or a painting for which she posed." Forbidding Young to profit from his photographs by using them as advertisements, and preventing Sperry and Hutchinson from displaying those images commercially, was to deprive them of valuable property.[99]

The state's highest court rejected the argument that a person's likeness belonged to the photographer who captured it, and that the subject surrendered all rights to it. The legislature's decision to condemn the commercial appropriation of personal images did not deprive anyone of property, but was rather a "recognition by the lawmaking power of the very general sentiment which prevailed throughout the community against permitting advertisers to promote the sale of their wares by this method."[100] The Supreme Court of the United States affirmed the state court and upheld New York's privacy law.[101] "It was the height of absurdity" for the company "to contend . . . that one has a liberty to take another's picture of so sacred a character that the legislature may not abridge or destroy it," observed the journal *Law Notes*.[102] There was a "natural and widespread feeling that such use of . . . portraits, in the absence of consent, was indefensible in morals, and ought to be prevented by law."[103]

~

In 1905, fifteen years after the publication of "The Right to Privacy," Georgia became the first state to recognize a cause of action for invasion of privacy under the common law. The landmark case *Pavesich v. New England Life Insurance* involved the unauthorized use of the photograph of Paolo Pavesich, an artist, in an ad for life insurance. Pavesich had posed for a portrait in a studio run by J. Quinton Adams, a commercial photographer in downtown Atlanta. Adams gave or sold a negative of Pavesich to Thomas Lumpkin, an Atlanta agent for the New England Life Insurance Company. The negative was made into a photo that was placed in an ad for the life insurance product next to a false testimonial that read, "In my healthy and productive period of life I bought insurance in the New England Mutual Life Insurance Co., of Boston, Mass., and to-day my family is protected and I am drawing an annual dividend on my paid-up policies." The ad ran in the *Atlanta Constitution*.[104]

The artist was not famous by any means. His picture was likely chosen because it suggested health, wisdom, and respectability; the robust, bespectacled Pavesich bore a resemblance to Theodore Roosevelt, who was president at the time. Pavesich did not own, let alone endorse the life insurance policy.

Pavesich brought a claim against the photographer Adams, the insurance agent Lumpkin, and the New England Life Insurance Company for libel, alleging reputational harm—that the ad brought him "into ridicule before the world." He also alleged mental distress and an invasion of his "right to privacy." Pavesich demanded what was then the tremendous sum of $25,000 for his reputational and emotional injuries.[105]

The Georgia Supreme Court held that Pavesich had a valid claim for libel because the publication created an impression of him that was false and that lowered his esteem among his peers. His acquaintances would likely conclude that he had accepted money to make statements about a policy he did not own; that he "lied for a consideration," making him "odious to every decent individual."[106] The court also concluded that he had a claim for invasion of privacy. It described the "legal wrong. . . . perpetrated by the unauthorized use of . . . pictures for advertising purposes." Pavesich suffered the embarrassment and indignity of "having his picture displayed in places where he would never go to be gazed upon, at times when and under circumstances where if he were personally present the sensibilities of his nature would be severely shocked." The ad could be posted "upon the streets . . . [above] the bar of the saloon keeper, or . . . [on] the walls of a brothel."[107]

The advertiser had not only deprived Pavesich of his ability to control his image, but dehumanized him by commercializing his persona. Like a consumer product, Pavesich's photograph had become a fungible commodity that could be circulated wantonly in the marketplace. To the advertiser and the readers who saw his image, Pavesich's unique identity as a human was irrelevant. Such degradation caused harms to the spirit "which are irreparable in their nature," the court determined. "The knowledge that one's features and form are being used for such a purpose, and displayed in such places as such advertisements are often liable to be found, brings not only the person of an extremely sensitive nature, but even the individual of ordinary sensibility, to a realization that his liberty has been taken away from him." "So thoroughly satisfied are we that the law recognizes . . . the right of privacy," the court concluded, "that we venture to predict that the day will come that the American bar will marvel that a contrary view was ever entertained by judges of eminence and ability."[108]

The *Pavesich* decision was celebrated nationally. The case stood for the laudable proposition, wrote the *Los Angeles Times*, that "personal liberty embraced the right of publicity—of freely appearing before the public" as one wished—"and therefore as a correlative matter, also encompassed a right to privacy."[109] Noting the "great regret" that had been expressed over the *Roberson* decision, the *American Law Register* observed that it was "gratifying" to see a contrary holding. The Georgia Supreme Court had "shown itself a more trustworthy organ of civilization" than New York's highest tribunal.[110] The case was a necessary response to the "unprecedented development in our times of the apparatus of publicity [that] has rendered it immensely more formidable than it was before to persons to whom publicity is abhorrent."[111]

By 1911, a handful of states had recognized a cause of action for "invasion of privacy" in cases involving people's likenesses used without consent in advertisements.[112] States were also beginning to recognize a privacy right to one's visual image outside of the advertising context. The Louisiana Supreme Court barred the police from displaying in the "rogue's gallery" pictures of people who had been accused but not convicted of a crime, under the theory of a "right to privacy."[113] The Kentucky Supreme Court held that a photographer who had sold pictures of two conjoined twins, who later died, violated the parents' right of privacy.[114] The idea of a right to privacy in one's visual image—a right to control the uses and display of one's likeness and persona—was beginning to command interest and support, both as a matter of formal law and in the popular imagination.

CHAPTER 4

Insult and Image

On the morning after the first Christmas of the twentieth century, Elizabeth Gillespie dressed, packed her bags, and got on a streetcar. One of relatively few practicing women doctors in New York City, Gillespie alighted an electrically operated trolley, the Brooklyn Heights Railroad. A few minutes after she boarded the car, the conductor came to collect the fare—a nickel. Gillespie gave him a quarter and asked for her change and a transfer.[1]

The conductor became distracted by another passenger. Gillespie again asked him for her change. The conductor denied that he owed her anything. He became gruff, and put his hands in his pocket and pulled out a handful of coins, saying, "Do you see any twenty-five cents there?"[2]

"You didn't give me twenty-five cents," he repeated. "It is the likes of ye -- you are a deadbeat; you are a swindler. I know the likes of ye."[3]

The conductor continued to insist that Gillespie was a "deadbeat," and that such swindlers were traveling every day on streetcars. Two men got on the car, and the conductor went out of his way to tell them that she was a cheat and that "she can't beat me." The entire carful of passengers was listening to this tirade against Gillespie.[4]

Gillespie was humiliated. She was so upset by this act of public shaming that she became sick and was confined to her bed for two days. She successfully sued the railroad for injury to her feelings and public image caused by insulting remarks made in the presence of others.[5]

∽

We have seen how the "old" tort of libel and the "new" tort of invasion of privacy were being mobilized to deal with assaults to public image from the popular press and advertisers. These were not the only threats to image in turn-of-the-century urban America. Commercial institutions such as railroads, department stores, and theaters were also posing dangers to people's reputations, public images, and social identities. In an era before courtesy and deference to customers were standard practice in service occupations, patrons like Elizabeth Gillespie suffered acts of insult, humiliation, and shaming at the hands of train conductors, theater ushers, hotel clerks, security guards, and other commercial personnel.

The victims of these affronts successfully took these wrongs to court. By the early twentieth century, courts had devised a tort action—a tort of "institutional insult," as I call it—that would permit people to recover damages for emotional distress caused by insults, epithets, and false accusations delivered by commercial employees in public places. This law of institutional insult, the forerunner of the modern tort of intentional infliction of emotional distress, was an important component of the developing laws of image. Like the right to privacy, it was a right to legal redress for injuries to a person's public image and one's feelings about one's image.

~

The story of the emergence of the tort of institutional insult is a story about innovations in the common law—and also about trains. We will start with the law. As we've seen, the common law had traditionally disfavored legal recovery for emotional injuries. With the exception of the privacy cases, a departure from the established rule, damage awards for mental distress could be recovered only when another legally recognized interest had been invaded, as when one experienced bodily harm.[6] At a time when the fields of psychology and psychiatry were yet undeveloped, it was thought that claims for emotional distress could be easily faked; they were "speculative" and hard to diagnose and prove.[7] Allowing people to recover for mere hurt feelings, it was said, would potentially unleash a flood of frivolous lawsuits and "open up a wide vista of litigation in the field of bad manners."[8] This strict position led courts to deny recovery for emotional injuries in what would seem to be quite deserving situations—for example, obvious cases of posttraumatic stress or "fright" stemming from near-miss accidents, or from witnessing loved ones injured or killed in rail accidents.[9]

Given this stance, there was, not surprisingly, no tort of insult in the United

States. One could not sue and recover for hurtful epithets that were not accompanied by physical injury or did not constitute an actionable libel or slander. This stood in contrast to Europe, which had a robust law of insult. In Germany, it could be both a tort and a crime to call a person a jerk, even if no one else heard the insult or thought less of the person because of it.[10]

The American rule on insult can be explained in part by the nation's democratic tradition, which lacks a feudal history. Aristocratic, highly stratified societies demand deference, courtesy, and politeness, but the United States has historically had a looser, more egalitarian character. This relative informality, writes legal historian James Whitman, produced a more rough-and-tumble emotional culture, in which people were expected to take it on the chin and absorb emotional slights, rather than resort to lawsuits.[11] Commentators juxtaposed American toughness, independence, and stoicism against hypersensitivity, huffiness, and litigiousness on the continent. As law professor Calvert Magruder wrote in the 1930s, "against a large part of the frictions and irritations and clashing of temperaments incident to participation in a community life, a certain toughening of the mental hide is better protection than the law could ever be."[12] The constitutional commitment to freedom of expression also disfavored a law of insult. "There is no occasion for the law to intervene with balm for wounded feelings in every case where a flood of billingsgate is loosed in an argument over a back fence," wrote torts scholars William Prosser and W. Page Keeton. People "must necessarily be expected and required to be hardened to a certain amount of rough language, and to acts that are definitely inconsiderate and unkind. There is still, in this country at least, such a thing as liberty to express an unflattering opinion of another, however wounding it may be to another's feelings."[13]

With this legal background in mind, let us get on the train.

$\backsim$

In the late 1800s, the railroads had become the preeminent form of transportation in the United States and central to the nation's economic and social life. Initially a series of separate lines, by 1890 American railroads had been woven into a national system with service to every region of the country.[14] Between 1881 and 1890, the number of passengers carried went from around 241 million to over 498 million.[15]

Because of their importance as a form of public transportation, railroads, although privately owned, were given the legal status of a public utility and regarded as a common carrier.[16] As a common carrier, the railroads were obligated to carry anyone who paid the fare. They also had to protect the safety and well-being of passengers. The railroad had to establish reasonable rules to guarantee the "comfort and convenience" of passengers; these could include rules about race, gender, and class segregation. If the rules were publicized and enforced consistently, the railroad could eject passengers who were noncompliant.[17]

The railroads were not only the most important form of public transportation but also an important social venue, a place where people sought to "see and be seen." Passengers worked hard to create favorable images for themselves through their dress, speech, and behavior. Sitting in the high-priced seats made a public statement.[18] The way one talked and carried oneself conveyed something about one's class and, potentially, one's character. So too did one's hat, shoes, and luggage. Conduct and appearance in the railroad car were seen as so critical to public image and social identity that entire treatises were written to guide passengers as they staged this particular social performance. There were guidelines on how to properly obtain a seat, and how to board elegantly while carrying a large suitcase. In 1874, the *New York Times* advised readers that in situations where "strangers are forced to sit beside each other in the cars, all conversation should be studiously avoided." It was also a breach of etiquette to bring on the train "an immense valise."[19] If one was displeased with another's conduct, the proper remedy was to scowl at them rather than lash out. "The scowl . . . is considered much more elegant."[20]

Crafting a favorable public image in this social environment was seen as especially important because of the way railroads threw people of diverse backgrounds together in an intimate and awkward public space. As historian Barbara Welke has written, "Everywhere the railroad went it brought the promise, values, and anxieties of modern, urban culture. . . . As on the urban street, strangers on the railway journey sat next to one another, brushed against each other in the aisles, and mingled in stations that in themselves became nodes of urbanity."[21] Like the city street, the railroad car was a site of identity slippage where strangers appeared before each other unmoored from their backgrounds, pasts, and usual social contexts. "Respectable ladies might travel beside women and men of a different class, race, or region. In a smoking car, businessmen from New York City could rub shoulders with country doctors or farmers," writes historian Amy Richter.[22] The instability of identity in this liminal space pushed people to vigorously assert their own claims to social identity.[23] Manners, fashion, and stylized gestures and conduct were critical signals of class, race, and status that socially separated the white middle class and aspiring middle class from their less privileged peers.

Railroad companies were aware of passengers' desire to maintain social appearances in this strange and disorienting public domain, and they parsed physical space in ways that reinforced socially salient distinctions. There were first-class cars, smoking cars for men, and separate ladies' cars to shield "respectable" white women, perceived to be vulnerable and helpless, from male rudeness and possible harassment.[24] Racial distinctions were also policed. In the South, railroads instituted racially separated accommodations, which became legally mandated under the rules of Jim Crow during the 1880s and 1890s.[25]

In the last decades of the nineteenth century, railroad companies attempted to train their workers in etiquette and required them to respect their customers' claims to status and identity by treating them with deference and good manners. There was a campaign to make railroad employees into "working class gentlemen."[26] Some railroad companies actually sent employees to "manners schools." As one conductor wrote in *Lippincott's Magazine* in 1886, although there were a "great many cranky and unreasonable people" on trains, the professional conductor did not lose his temper and "insult a passenger in the presence of others. We are paid to receive insults, not to give them."[27]

Yet acts of rudeness were common. Train personnel were notorious for their curt demeanor and rough conduct. "The nature of rail travel—the speed, the scale of operation, the rigid organization—often made the cars inhospitable to passengers' notions of courteousness, and the competing responsibilities of conductors compromised their ability to treat passengers politely," Richter writes.[28] "Every day and perhaps hundreds of times a day, [a conductor] must collect fares of fifty or a hundred persons in less time than he ought to have for ten," noted a writer in *Scribner's Magazine*.[29] After considering the "constant unceasing petty annoyances" routinely encountered on the job, a convention of passenger conductors asked, "Would it be singular if we became harsh in our manners and brusque in our speech?"[30]

Poorly paid and overworked, and dealing with a multitude of hurried customers, the male conductors, ticket-sellers, ticket-takers, engineers, and other personnel of local and interstate railroads often had little regard for the feelings, sensibilities, and social aspirations of the passengers they encountered. Exhorted by their employers to collect tickets from every passenger and to remove those customers who refused to pay their fare, train employees sometimes abandoned all semblance of politeness. There were apparently many acts of hostility. Railroad workers called passengers whom they perceived to be noncompliant "lunatics" and "deadbeats." They swore at them and made comments about their appearance. In one incident that became the basis of a lawsuit, a conductor shouted at a female passenger that "a big fat woman" like her had "no business sitting in front of the car."[31] Sometimes these epithets and accusations were shouted at the offending passenger as a prelude to expulsion from the train.

~

These outbursts spawned an entire body of legal cases. Between 1880 and 1920—the rule against emotional distress recovery notwithstanding—dozens of claims were brought over mental anguish caused by upsetting treatment on train cars. Sometimes passengers sued the railroad for failing to protect them against the verbal tirades of another passenger. More often, the claim was that a conductor, porter, or other train personnel had insulted and humiliated them with words that were abusive if not false. These "railroad insult" cases attest not only to the commonness of verbal roughness on the rails, but to the priority that patrons placed on maintaining their public images in this particular social venue. So many railroad insult cases were brought in this era that they yielded a body of case law that was recognized by the first *Restatement of Torts* in 1934.[32] In these cases, the essence of the harm was both *insult* and *shame*. The plaintiff was affronted in his sense of personal dignity, and also ashamed before others—concerned that fellow passengers would think less of him because of the employee's harsh actions or words, in particular a false accusation that carried an immoral connotation.

Many of the "railroad insult" lawsuits stemmed from disputes over "fare-skipping," in which the passenger was falsely and aggressively accused, before other passengers, of trying to ride without a valid ticket. In an 1897 case from Kentucky, the conductor destroyed a twenty-trip ticket given to him by the plaintiff, claiming that it was invalid, and required him to pay a cash fare. "You are a pretty thing—trying to beat your way," he said.[33] The man was distressed and humiliated before a crowd. In another case, a woman boarding a train with her fifteen-year-old daughter and eight-year-old son was stopped by the conductor and told that she must have a ticket for the boy. She bought one and boarded the train. Later, when the conductor collected tickets, "in a loud, harsh, and insulting tone of voice and manner, in the hearing of her children and other passengers," he said to her, "The idea of a woman trying to board a train with her child without a ticket! You can go on this time, but don't undertake such a thing again." The language and manner of the conductor "humiliated and insulted her" before others.[34] Often these disputes resulted in removal from the train car. On one Colorado train, the plaintiff refused to bring the tickets for himself and his party to the front of the car on the demand of the conductor, and was publicly accused of not being a "gentleman" and being a "damn little cur" "in the presence of a large number of his fellow passengers" with "whom he daily met and associated with." He was subsequently ejected and suffered "ridicule, humiliation, and disgrace."[35]

Another set of cases, largely from the South, involved claims of racial misidentification: conductors' attempts to relocate passengers sitting in the whites-only train car to the Jim Crow car. Plaintiffs, who claimed to be white, had protested these efforts, resulting in epithets and altercations. The insulting words exchanged and the act of being publicly identified as black were said to be deeply humiliating. In one Georgia case, a working-class man who identified himself as white sat down in the car for whites and was ordered to the blacks-only car. "Haven't I seen you in colored company?" the conductor asked him before several other passengers. He sued for injury to his feelings.[36] In a series of cases in the late 1800s, middle-class black women protested exclusion from the whites-only "ladies' car," as a challenge to segregation. Alice Williams, "decently and becomingly dressed, and behaving in a modest, decent, and lady-like manner," unsuccessfully sought damages for "great shame, indignity, mortification, and disgrace" caused by being dragged from her seat in a ladies' car.[37] These plaintiffs described segregated accommodations as an affront to their dignity—to a woman's right to fashion an image for herself as a respectable lady, and to have that image respected by others.[38]

Perhaps the most common kind of railroad insult case involved assaults to white women's claims to sexual virtue. Maggie Lane, "a woman of good character," brought a lawsuit when a train conductor said to her before other passengers, "You are a good-looking old girl, and I would like to meet you when you get off." He then accused her publicly of being "nothing but a whore" who "would go out to the lake and throw herself out to the men there."[39] In another case from 1897, a woman buying a ticket for a train was accused by railroad personnel of being "indecent, and having undressed before men." The abusive language "continued . . . for some 10 minutes, so that persons on the platform heard the abusive and insulting language." The woman sued the railroad for this insult and the ensuing humiliation and distress.[40]

At a time when it was becoming popular to sue the railroads, the railroad insult represented a fertile field for litigation. Lawsuits against railroads expanded significantly in the last two decades of the nineteenth century as train accidents increased, and with the development of contingent fee practices. There was also great symbolic appeal to suing the railroads. As America's first national corporations, railroad companies were the embodiment of the modern industrial order, and the most prominent of the impersonal commercial entities that were coming to dominate economic and social life.[41]

~

The railroads were not the only commercial institution being sued for acts of insult and shaming. Many similar lawsuits were brought against the operators of retail stores and places of public amusement—vaudeville theaters, bathhouses, carnivals, circuses, department stores. Like the rail car, these spaces were important venues of sociability in the urban environment.[42] They were also highly regulated and monitored. Stores and theaters were policed by ushers, security guards, ticket-takers, and other personnel who made sure that admissions were paid, "undesirables" were kept out, and that no pickpocketing or brawls between customers ensued.[43] Rough treatment, false accusations, and at times downright discourteousness were common.[44]

As in the railroad cases, the insults often stemmed from disputes over not paying one's fare or having an improper ticket. Patrons were incorrectly accused of being thieves, line-jumpers, and cheats. The insults often occurred before large crowds of strangers. In an Alabama case from 1913, *Interstate Amusement Co. v. Martin*, the plaintiff, while attending the theater, was invited onto the stage by one of the performers; while there, the performer "addressed to him insulting and defamatory language."[45] In another case, a husband and wife purchased tickets for a circus performance. At the show, when the husband asked to be moved to a better seat, the usher became upset and "addressed insulting and profane language to him" and also "addressed profane language to the ladies of the party, in the presence of many others."[46] In the 1911 case *Aaron v. Ward*, a woman sought to recover damages for humiliation after being kicked out of the bathhouse at Coney Island following a dispute over her place in line.[47]

Many of the plaintiffs in these cases were females. Some were exposed to profanity. Others were subjected to attacks on their reputations for chastity. In a 1904 case, a security guard at an amusement park told a woman patron, "after staring her in the face in a rude and insolent manner," "you must leave these grounds." He imputed that the plaintiff "was a lewd and base woman, unfit to be or remain upon said grounds." In reality, the woman was not a prostitute as accused, but a "lady of refinement and respectability," according to the Washington Supreme Court. This accusation occurred "in the presence and hearing of a large group of people." The woman initiated a lawsuit.[48]

~

In several of these cases, plaintiffs succeeded in obtaining damage awards for humiliation, shame, and injury to their public images. The commercial institution—the railroad company, theater, or amusement park—was liable for the actions of its workers under the tort doctrine of *respondeat superior*. Judgments in these "institutional insult" cases ranged from $250 to $1,000, similar to sums awarded in accident and physical injury cases in this era.[49] Recovery did not depend on whether the accusation was false; truth was not a defense. Mere rudeness was remediable, if it was offensive "to a normal person of ordinary sensibility."[50] Damages could be enhanced on the basis of the degree of the employee's insolent "tone and general attitude."[51]

The definition of a legally cognizable insult reflected dominant racial, class, and gender stereotypes—the superiority of whites over blacks, the affluent over the poor, and the helplessness and vulnerability of white women. The law reified and validated these inequities. Courts considered it an insult for a conductor to falsely accuse a well-off white man of failing to pay his fare, implying that he was a cheat or too poor to buy a ticket. In a Texas case from 1888, a railroad conductor wrongly expelled a man and his family from the first-class car and forced them to sit in the second-class "smoker" car. The Texas Supreme Court upheld the decision in favor of the plaintiffs, finding that the conductor put the family "under circumstances calculated to humiliate and mortify the feelings of the appellee and his wife who, from the record, appear to have been people of refinement and intelligence."[52] A privileged white woman bearing all the signs of respectability was said to be deeply insulted when she was treated roughly by a worker, or publicly denounced as a woman of ill repute.[53]

White judges and juries, especially in the South, regarded with great sympathy the pleas of white passengers claiming to have been falsely identified as black. It was by definition "insulting to call a white man a negro" as the accusation implied the "odium of illegitimacy," a Georgia appeals court concluded in 1905.[54] Black passengers' claims to have been insulted by segregated accommodations, by contrast, were given little credence. Segregated facilities were allegedly equal, not inferior by the fact of their separation.[55] In an 1869 case in which a black hairdresser brought suit against a railroad for refusing her admission to the ladies' car, the railroad lawyer denigrated the woman's claims to respectability. "To take such liberty with so great an aristocrat as a colored hair dresser was indeed insulting," he said in a voice "heavy with sarcasm."[56] The right to be treated with dignity in public places—to create a respectable image without insult and interference—was a prerogative largely limited to whites.

We should stand back and appreciate the significance of these cases. In contravention of the long-standing rule, plaintiffs recovered for "pure" emotional harms—emotional distress without any accompanying physical injuries.[57] Although there may have been a legally actionable slander in some of these cases, particularly if one was accused of lack of chastity or a crime, the basis of recovery was not injury to reputation. Plaintiffs recovered for their sense of affront and shame, and their fear that others would think less of them, regardless of whether anyone's opinion was actually lowered.

As in so many cases where the law is bent in a way that is contrary to an established position, it is out of a perceived, pressing need. In these cases, courts emphasized that the humiliation transpired before a large audience. It was the visibility of the act that led courts to regard these attacks more seriously than the "traditional" insult exchanged between two parties in the midst of a contained, private dispute. In a culture that was becoming especially attuned to social appearances, attacking a person's public image with a rude and abusive public insult was a serious personal affront. The injuries suffered by the plaintiffs, in other words, were not seen as likely to be faked or trivial; in the mind-set of the time, "judges would readily believe that . . . few people would [experience] such [encounters] without definitely suffering," observed the *Kentucky Law Journal*.[58] Whereas people should be expected to "cultivate a minimum defense mechanism" for "private insults which reach no other ear but their own," "a person ha[d] an interest" in not having his public image unjustly tarnished—in not being embarrassed, disrespected, or discredited "in the presence of third parties."[59]

The courts were particularly sensitive to the imbalance of power between patrons and commercial employees. In the railroad situation, the individual was a captive on a moving vehicle; the railroad had "unusual power and opportunity . . . to wound the feelings of those entrusted to its care."[60] People could not protest by taking their business elsewhere, because the major railroads had a monopoly over public transportation in most parts of the country.[61] The opinions in many of these cases are righteous and hortatory; in some cases, punitive damages were awarded.[62] Courts seemed to want to teach the defendants a lesson: through a judgment for the plaintiff, the institution would recognize the significance of exhibiting politeness towards its customers and respecting patrons' assertions of status and social identity.

These institutional insult cases contradict stereotypes of late nineteenth-century courts as biased towards the interests of emerging industries and hostile towards the victims of industrialization.[63] Courts validated plaintiffs' injuries as legitimate and described the defendants' conduct as reprehensible and unjustified. On the whole, it seems, courts demonstrated greater sympathy for the victims of institutional insults than those of railroad and other industrial accidents in this era. In contrast to the accident cases, in which plaintiffs were typically workers, most of the victims of the insult cases were middle class, especially middle-class white females, to whom the law and culture afforded special deference. Judges, who often came from a similar class background and shared in the values and worldview of the complainants, may have seen these assaults to reputation and public image—critical social currency, particularly among the upwardly mobile— as potentially serious impediments to a plaintiff's life prospects. White, well-off women and their social and emotional injuries were favored over male industrial workers and their physical injuries.[64]

∼

We can see these outcomes as a reflection of the growing attunement to images and appearances; they might also be understood in terms of the culture's intense fear of shame. Indeed, it can be striking to the modern observer how the victims of these institutional insults—like the subjects of "invasions of privacy"— described their injuries: they suffered "humiliation," "mortification," "outrage," and above all, "shame." Shame was an emotion that was commonly experienced, and people went to great lengths to avoid it.

Shame is the internalized experience of social rejection. In contrast to guilt, a feeling that one has not lived up to one's own moral standards, "*shame* has an 'external' reference; the pain it inflicts comes by way of an 'audience,'" writes historian John Demos. "To be sure, the audience is sometimes imagined, not real; but the sense of being watched, of being exposed and unfavorably scrutinized, is central either way."[65] The anthropologist Ruth Benedict described shame as "a reaction to other people's criticism. A man is shamed either by being openly ridiculed . . . or by fantasying . . . that he has been made ridiculous"—that his social image is not worthy of other people's approval.[66]

Shame flourishes in societies that have intense moral and behavioral expectations of their citizens that are pervasive and widely expressed.[67] Nineteenth-century America was in many ways a shame society—conformist, morally rigid, status minded. Social acceptance and social praise were contingent on the public display of manners, propriety, the "Protestant ethic" of self-restraint, and particularly for women, sexual virtue. There has been an argument in the literature on the history of the emotions that while shame flourished as a mode of social control in the colonial era, Victorian America relied on guilt to regulate behavior. Guilt had strong appeal in a society that valued economic individualism, writes historian Peter Stearns; it replaced disciplinary functions that had once been performed by more authoritarian strains of religion.[68] There is no question that guilt became more of a concern in late Victorian America, but it did not replace shame as a key emotion.[69] Shame remained a powerfully animating force, one that both inhibited and compelled a good deal of conduct. Key aspects of middle-class life—"divorce-free families, intense nurturing of children, longtime job affiliations, regularized consumption, [and] communal worship," to quote critic James Twitchell—may have been motivated by fear of guilt, but they were also driven by a fear of shame, of moral stigmatization and ostracism.[70]

The institutional insult tort was an outgrowth of this shame orientation, this intense concern with the judgments of others. The tort punished those who abused the power of shame. Shame was favored as a sanction for socially transgressive conduct, but it was a potent force that could be misused. The institutional insult tort offered plaintiffs a remedy when institutions unfairly wielded their authority over them to publicly humiliate and degrade them. To subject someone to unwarranted shame was not only a serious assault to that person's dignity but also an affront to social norms seen as serious enough to merit legal attention.

The institutional insult tort was tied to another important social value of this time—honor, a particular concern with image that had especially great purchase on the cultural imagination of the American South. Most of the institutional insult cases were brought in the South, and popular and judicial sympathy towards plaintiffs was strongest in this region, where an intense interest in social appearances was part of the region's long-standing culture of honor.

∽

In the nineteenth and early twentieth centuries, the concept of honor was a central feature of Southern society. In the South, a white man's honor was measured not by what he thought of himself, but by what others thought of him.[71] In the words of historian Bertram Wyatt-Brown, honor was an "inner conviction of self-worth," then a "claim of that self-assessment before the public."[72] Respectable Southerners were expected to perform their honor through their public conduct—through their gestures, words, mannerisms, and expressions.[73]

The concept of honor was a reflection of the hierarchical, intensely stratified nature of Southern society, tied to the region's feudal history and based on sharp inequalities of race and class. A man's honor was breached when he was not

treated with the proper respect that should be given him based on his social standing, or when his female family members were not treated as respectable ladies.[74]
Honor was viewed as a particularly male quality, although women had their own
variety of honor, in the fabled ideal of Southern womanhood, which placed demands on socially elite women to comply with particular codes of behavior and
required that others treat them with politeness and deference.[75] This Southern
model of self and social identity was distinct from its Northern corollary. Although Northerners were concerned with social appearances and the judgments
of others, the Northern ideal had a moral dimension. One was respected for one's
virtue: what one did, how one lived, what one had accomplished. In the South,
a person commanded deference largely for his social status and the class to which
he was born.[76]

Under the Southern code of honor, the male subject of disrespect or insult
was obligated to clear his name and resume his social position by performing a
ritual of vengeance and status rehabilitation. Typically, this required acts of physical violence. Among elites, the preferred ritual was dueling.[77] A function of the
duel was to give both participants a chance to prove that they deserved honorable
reputations.[78] One's willingness to duel was seen, in its own right, as a sign of
conviction, integrity, and courage.[79]

Dueling had originated from the small-scale, agricultural, feudal society of
the premodern South; it was an effective means of vindicating honor in small
towns and villages, where the insulter and the insulted had personal ties, and
where a close-knit community was present to witness the act of vengeance. Such
acts of retribution fit less readily into the world of large-scale urban commerce
that the South was becoming in the late 1800s. Decades after it had transpired
in the North, urbanization and manufacturing began in the South.[80] The population of towns and villages in the South grew by five million between 1880 and
1910.[81] During the 1880s, railroad construction in the South matched or surpassed
railroad construction in the rest of the nation.[82] By the turn of the century, urban Southerners lived in an environment that was beginning to be dominated by
commercial institutions, much like their Northern counterparts.

Though not inconceivable, it was not entirely feasible for a gentleman affronted in a railroad car or theater to take up arms against the usher or conductor
who had offended or ejected him. Gentlemen usually did not duel with inferiors,

and any physical attack would, in its own right, justify the exclusion.[83] Neither could the victim of a railroad insult likely challenge its corporate head—a distant figure outside the community—to a duel or fisticuffs. As the *Century Magazine* wrote in 1890, "bankers, mill-owners, superintendents of factories and railways, do not work . . . in an environment which compels the use of the pistol-pocket."[84] Physical violence as a means of dispute resolution was beginning to fall out of favor, as it came to be seen as anathema to the practices and norms of modern commercial culture. "'Chivalry' and common sense, the duello and modern business,'" were "absolutely incompatible."[85]

We might see the "institutional insult" lawsuit as an accompaniment to, or perhaps substitute for dueling and other acts of physical violence in defense of honor and reputation. In this era, Southern lawmakers, concerned with the casualties of dueling and the impression of barbarism that the practice gave the region, tried to crack down on dueling and to encourage the law as a means of dispute resolution.[86] In several states, dueling was outlawed.[87] In an attempt to replace dueling with litigation, three Southern states passed "actionable words" statutes that permitted a cause of action for insulting words that would "lead to violence and breach of the peace."[88] As a Mississippi court explained the purpose of the statute, it was to "induce citizens who are maligned and whose honor is impugned to resort to the courts of the country for redress by money judgment rather than to the old-time method of 'pistols and coffee for two.'"[89] Libel law was also being advocated by Southern officials as a substitute to the duel, and there is some evidence that libel cases increased in the South in the late 1800s.[90] The institutional insult lawsuit tracked a more general increase in the use of the law in the South to protect reputation, honor, manners, and people's images and claims to social identity.

Steeped in the same culture of honor as the plaintiffs in these cases, Southern courts and juries empathized with their sense of outrage and affront. The majority of the nation's railroads were owned by large Northern corporations,[91] as were the manufacturing and retail outlets that settled in the urban South at the turn of the century. Although they may have come from the South, railroad workers were seen as "corporate men" whose allegiance was not to their region but to their company.[92] Many Southerners appear to have resented the encroachment of Northern industry and culture on local tradition, and this sentiment may well have encouraged recovery in the institutional insult cases.[93] Southern courts and juries were not hesitant to permit affronted ladies and gentlemen to vindicate their honor, reputations, and social images in the face of impersonal Northern commercial forces that threatened regional traditions and ways of life.

~

Rather than change the traditional rule against emotional distress recovery, there was a resort to a legal fiction. Courts justified judgments for plaintiffs in the institutional insult cases on the notion of an "implied contract" between the railroad and the patron, as part of the railroad's duties as a common carrier. Though no actual contract existed, the railroad had a duty, it was said, to protect any individual rightfully on its cars from harm and abuse, including verbal abuse. The implied contract rationale dated back to an 1823 case, *Chamberlain v. Chandler*, in which a federal district court had held that the passengers of a ship could recover against the shipmaster for ill treatment of and injury to them during the voyage. The court noted that the passengers' contract with the carrier "is not for mere shiproom and personal existence on board, but for reasonable food, comforts, necessaries, and kindness."[94] In the public amusement cases, where the common carrier rationale did not apply, courts sometimes referred to an "implied contract" for courteous service in the customer's ticket for entry—the insult breached the plaintiff's so-called "right to go to any public place, or visit a resort where the public is invited . . . and remain there, free from molestation . . . insult, personal indignities, or acts which subject him to humiliation and disgrace."[95] Of course, there is no real contractual agreement in a ticket for railroad carriage or for admission to a place of amusement that a patron will receive noninsulting treatment. In an ordinary breach of contract case, one cannot recover for emotional distress.[96]

Courts sought to compensate plaintiffs in the institutional insult cases, but they did not want to give the appearance of permitting "pure" emotional distress actions, which would potentially open the feared "floodgates of litigation." They had to tread carefully, for fear of setting precedent that could be used in the increasing number of near-miss railroad accident or "fright" cases that were reaching the courts in the late 1800s. The "implied contract" rationale became an excuse for recovery without having to recognize a freestanding cause of action for emotional distress.[97] In torts scholar William Prosser's words, "an implied contract to be polite" was the "crutch" that "timorous" courts used to justify recovery in these cases.[98]

Although they are still technically good law, the institutional insult cases are no longer important in their own right.[99] This genre of lawsuit, which crested in the period between 1890 and 1920, largely disappeared by the 1940s. In a 2008 article called "Why Torts Die," law professor Kyle Graham put the institutional insult cases in his dustbin of "dead torts," noting that there have been "only a smattering of decisions in the past half-century in which plaintiffs have recovered even a pittance" under an institutional insult theory.[100] One reason for the demise of these cases has to do with the decline of passenger rail traffic; by 1920, the middle class was relying heavily on private automobiles for transport.[101] Another reason is that commercial employees are now trained to be more polite to patrons.[102]

The enduring legacy of these institutional insult cases lies in the modern tort of intentional infliction of emotional distress. Relying in part on the precedent in the institutional insult cases, twentieth-century courts began to recognize an independent tort action for "pure" emotional distress—for extreme emotional anguish intentionally inflicted, "even though no demonstrable physical consequences actually ensue."[103] We will be exploring this tort in subsequent chapters. The intentional infliction of emotional distress tort is not limited to situations involving public humiliation and shaming. Nonetheless, as we will see, it has been used in the service of public image, to redress the anguish and embarrassment caused by another person's interference with one's desired image and social appearance.

~

Like the growth of libel law and the invention of the right to privacy in the late nineteenth century, the rise of the "institutional insult" tort was part of the expansion of tort law to address the social problems and dislocations caused by urbanization and industrialization. The late 1800s saw the invention of the negligence tort—accident or "personal injury" law—in response to physical injuries inflicted by railroads, streetcars, factories, and other industrial forces.[104] The development and mobilization of the image torts—privacy, defamation, and the institutional insult or emotional distress tort—should be seen in the same vein:

as a legal response to the increasing number of dignitary, emotional, and reputational injuries visited on private citizens by large commercial entities, such as newspapers, advertisers, retail commerce, and railroads. The laws of image are, in many ways, accident law's unexplored corollary. The law was recognizing rights to control and protect one's public image in a world where images were becoming increasingly intertwined with people's emotions, sense of self, and social identities, and where those images were being manipulated—reproduced, miscontexualized, misrepresented, and distorted—by distant, powerful, seemingly unassailable forces of mass commerce and communications.

CHAPTER 5

The Image Society

For the next stage in the story, we take a leap forward in time. The first few decades of the twentieth century were a time of profound and irrevocable social change, a period of critical transformation in American life. A world war took place, shattering the genteel idealism of the Victorian age. Movements for political and social liberation—socialism, sexual liberation, civil rights, women's enfranchisement—challenged entrenched social hierarchies. The populace continued to diversify as immigrants arrived on the nation's shores en masse and African Americans from the South migrated to Northern cities. A technological revolution was under way with the electrification of homes and cities, the invention of the automobile, airplane, and motion pictures, and industrial processes that flooded the market with new goods and gadgets.

In the first few decades of the twentieth century, the United States became an *image society*. The intensification of the social, cultural, technological, and demographic trends we have seen thus far—urbanization, innovations in communication and transport, social and geographic mobility—led to an escalating emphasis on images, surfaces, and social appearances. Americans were increasingly envisioning their social identities as images, entangled if not congruent with the impressions they made in the eyes of others.

An especially intense brand of image-consciousness took root in the 1920s, a decade that is often described by historians as the first "modern" decade in American history.[1] In an age when strict Victorian moralism was fading from the cultural scene, when consumer culture and mass entertainment assumed a central position in American life, and when advertising, fashion, celebrity, and the media became important arbiters of values and conduct, there was a heightened focus on buying and selling, getting and spending, and cultivating good looks and personal charm. The rise of white-collar occupations led to a new emphasis on "salesmanship," which hinged on pleasing appearances. The advertising industry, in conjunction with the new field of popular psychology, promised individuals that they could use conspicuous consumption and the strategic display of goods to achieve a stunning image, distinguish themselves from the crowd, and "win friends and influence people."[2] Novel visual technologies, such as motion pictures, accentuated the importance of appearances and created the sense of being constantly subjected to the critical gaze of others. Film stars, who exercised meticulous control of their images, became role models and icons, modal selves in a culture where more than ever the key to success was seen as the ability to create a pleasing public image to amuse and impress others.

This rise of this image-consciousness tracks broad, fundamental changes in concepts of the self and personal identity in the twentieth century. The concern with appearance that took hold of the popular imagination in this era was different from the anxieties around image that were beginning to be expressed in the late 1800s. When Americans of that time sought to create a desirable image for themselves through the management of their dress, speech, and behavior, many did so against the backdrop of the idea of a consistent, stable self. Although the face one presented to the public may have been contrived in certain dimensions, there was thought to be a "real self" that existed in the "backstage," a self that one became and retreated to in the intimate domains of private life. In contrast, in the emerging modern sensibility, there was less of a sense of a clear core of self, of an essence of being or identity. In the new model, more of the self inhered in the image: *who one was* was how one appeared before others, and that appearance was relatively fluid and malleable. The self lived on the surface and was continuously regenerated through managed acts of self-performance and self-display. The effect of this union of the external and the intimate, of the social and the personal, was to freight personal image with tremendous emotional and psychological weight. The purpose of self-presentation was not merely to impress others or to avoid social disapprobation, but to construct one's very self through one's appearance and public image.

This chapter focuses on these cultural changes: the rise of this new, modern image-consciousness, and with it the ascendance of a new model of self, the self as image. In later chapters, we will examine how this image-consciousness found expression in twentieth-century law. In its ongoing and expanding recognition of a right to control one's image, tort law served as a stage for, and participant in, the growing cultural preoccupation with personal image. The visions of personhood and identity articulated by the law in turn transformed popular understandings of the self.

~

In 1890, the frontier closed.[3] In 1920, the United States achieved another demographic watershed: the census registered, for the first time, over half the population living in cities.[4] By 1930, New York City's population reached 7 million.[5] Chicago's population soared, reaching almost 3.5 million by 1929.[6] The modern metropolis had come into being, complete with looming skyscrapers, electrically lit streets and marquees, streetcar and automobile traffic, tenements and apartment buildings, palatial consumer emporia, and a diverse and cosmopolitan populace hailing from around the nation and the globe.[7]

As sociologists Robert Park and Ernest Burgess wrote in their 1925 study *The City*, social relations had become sterile, detached, and impersonal. "A very large part of the population of great cities, including those who make their homes in tenements and apartment houses," met but did not know each other.[8] The contacts of the city might have been face-to-face, sociologist Louis Wirth observed, "but they were nevertheless superficial, transitory, and segmental."[9] The "art of life" was "largely reduced to skating on thin surfaces and a scrupulous study of style and manners."[10]

This perceived depersonalization of daily life, and the superficiality of social exchange, produced something of an existential crisis for Americans in the 1920s. The culture was preoccupied with the dilemma of personal distinction—the difficulty of standing out from the crowd. The image of the menacing, enveloping, self-annihilating crowd pervades cultural texts of this time. Films like *The Crowd* (1928), replete with wide-angle shots of stark skyscrapers and vast, menacing cityscapes, visualized the terror of losing one's identity to the faceless mass. Sociologist Everett Dean Martin, in his work *The Behavior of Crowds*, described mass conformity—"crowd formation" and "crowd thinking"—as a serious menace to civilization.[11] The popular fascination with the film close-up—the enlarged image of the human face—symbolized the critical significance that was being placed on the individual in a world where the possibility of human uniqueness was seen as imperiled.

How could one stand apart from others and preserve a sense of self amidst a sea of strangers? This was the pressing question of the day. In the words of cultural historian Warren Susman, "we live now constantly in a crowd; how can we distinguish ourselves from others in that crowd?"[12] In a mass culture, where goods, lifestyles, and ideas were being subjected to standardization, how did one remain unique and convey that distinctiveness to others? The answer posed by advertisers, personnel managers, psychologists, and other cultural arbiters lay in *personal image*—a distinctive appearance, "magnetic personality," and pleasing first impression. Image was a kind of "aura" comprising one's looks, demeanor, gestures, tone of voice, and various other signs and superficial attributes. One's image conveyed important social facts about a person—one's taste, status, and personality—in a compressed and even instantaneous manner. A successful image was one that was so stunning and unforgettable—so charismatic and appealing—as to secure for a person instant recognition. American culture's fascination with personal image reflected concerns with the problem of individuality in the modern world, and it became a focal point of tremendous attention and energy. As a practical matter, it was extremely lucrative: it sold billions of dollars' worth of films, books, and consumer goods.

&

The fantasy of achieving an attention-getting image soothed the lonely city dweller beset by feelings of anonymity and insignificance. It kept alive the hope that one could be somebody in a world of nobodies. As a practical matter, the cultivation of a positive image had application in many areas of life in which the rise of a mass society and constant interaction with strangers posed very real and tangible problems of distinction and recognition. One domain in which the positive image and first impression were coming to be seen as critical assets was the burgeoning white-collar sector of the economy—business, sales, and customer relations. Success in these areas, it was said, hinged on the ability to cultivate a pleasing image—on "salesmanship," "people skills," and "brand recognition."

By the 1920s, the producer economy of the nineteenth century, in which creative and psychic energy had been largely directed towards the production of goods, was supplanted by a consumer orientation—a focus on buying and selling goods.[13] Between 1880 and 1930, the number of salaried employees increased by

eight times, composing over 60 percent of the middle class.[14] The first two decades of the twentieth century saw the phenomenal growth of the sales and service
industries. Salesmen and saleswomen became key figures in the new retail economy. They explained products to potential customers, pressured people to make
purchases, and created a sense of "brand loyalty."[15]

This transformation in employment revolutionized the nature of daily social
interactions. Bureaucratic, sales, and service jobs removed workers from direct
involvement in the production process and demanded associations with people
rather than things. Work depended no longer on physical labor, but on what
sociologist Arlie Hochschild has called "emotional labor"—the management of
personal behavior and feelings in a way that would create an outward demeanor
which pleased, soothed, or persuaded others.[16] At every level in the white-collar
hierarchy, from the salesperson to the manager to the executive, success at work
required impression management: the careful manipulation of one's acts, looks,
and speech to meet the emotional and psychological demands of customers and
clients, managers, and coworkers. Jobs required "people skills," the ability to deal
effectively with strangers or near-strangers on a regular basis.

The key to survival in the white-collar world hinged on what was being described as "salesmanship." The skills of salesmanship were said to be critical to
success, whether one was shilling consumer goods, floating ideas before a client,
or promoting oneself to one's boss.[17] The premise of salesmanship was that the
salesperson had a lot of information—and a lot of emotion—to convey in a short
amount of time; he had to compete with an array of products, vendors, and pitch-
men vying for the customer's attention. The basis of effective selling was thus
the positive first impression—creating a desirable image of a product and, even
more, creating a positive image of the salesman himself. Salespeople were told to
sell the customer on themselves and their personalities as much as they touted the
properties of their goods and services. As the popular advice writer Orison Swett
Marden observed in his 1921 book *Masterful Personality*, the best salespeople had
"such a winning personality" that people would buy from them "because [they]
liked the seller." "Popularity" and "personal magnetism" translated into "customers, influence, [and] power."[18]

How to sell the image and "personality" of the seller became serious business
for companies in the 1920s. Department stores and other retail outlets undertook

efforts to produce "people-sensitive" employees with pleasing, controlled person-alities.[19] Personnel experts, backed by research from the new field of industrial psychology, were hired to create harmonious relations in the workplace.[20] A good first impression became a necessary prerequisite for securing employment in the first place. Despite objective credentials, including school grades, job interviews in the 1920s depended heavily on "personal presentations."[21] Job candidates stud-ied advice manuals and schooled themselves in interview techniques. In the busi-ness world, "never before has there been such a demand for personality," Marden wrote. "A man's business worth is not gauged by his ability alone, but by his persuasive force, his power to please people, to interest them, and to make them believe in him."[22]

Before long, the imperatives of the world of sales and service were applied to social relations more generally. The efforts of salespeople to sell products to skepti-cal customers became a metaphor for the social struggle waged by every person in an effort to distinguish herself in the modern world. In a relatively mobile society, many personal interactions were fleeting and unlikely to be repeated. Attracting the attention and positive regard of strangers, the basis of success in any pursuit, demanded that an individual put forth an ideal impression on the first try.

A cottage industry of personal guidebooks arose to teach Americans the skills of "personal salesmanship" and "impression management," skills that could be applied to virtually every area of one's life, both personal and professional. This nascent self-help industry merged the prescriptive style of the nineteenth-cen-tury etiquette literature, with its lists of instructions and "dos and don'ts," with a new vein of popular psychology, which understood human experience in terms of emotional and psychic states that existed within the control of every individual. According to these manuals, every person, regardless of her occupation or sta-tion in life, could tap into her mental and psychic resources—into the power of positive thinking—to create social success and personal distinction through the cultivation of a positive image, look, and "personality."

The premise of the advice literature was that most people were not born with a naturally appealing public persona and had to work hard to cultivate one. One's public image could always be "successfully . . . doctored, repaired, refurbished, and improved."[23] This was an arduous, detailed project that entailed meticulous control of one's physical appearance, speech, posture, and gestures. Exercise, nice clothes, fastidious grooming, and conversational skills were essential. As Susman writes, "everyone was expected to impress and influence with trained and effective speech. . . . In these books and articles exercise, proper breathing, sound eating habits, a good complexion, and grooming and beauty aids were all stressed."[24] The goal was to achieve "charming manners, a fascinating, magnetic presence, [and] courteous, winning ways."[25]

Above all, the key to the positive first impression was to develop a hypersensitivity to other people's feelings and judgments. One had to cultivate an external perspective on one's self, to see one's self and image through the critical eyes of others. This meant eliminating "the little personal whims, habits, [and] traits that make people dislike you."[26] The author of *Personality: How to Build It* (1916) advised his readers to be constantly attuned to the presence and judgments of others.[27] "So much of our success depends on what others think of us."[28]

Perhaps no figure contributed more to the cult of salesmanship and first impressions than Dale Carnegie, a former lecturer and traveling salesman who found success by tapping into Americans' desire for greater self-confidence and "people skills." His series of 1912 lectures on public speaking, later published in 1936 as the best-selling book *How to Win Friends and Influence People,* reinforced the idea that the key to success was to manipulate one's image in order to impress and manipulate others.[29] Carnegie held up as a model of success the stage performer who had plotted out every aspect of his routine: "everything [he] did, every gesture, every intonation, every lifting of an eyebrow had been carefully rehearsed in advance. . . . [his] actions were timed to split seconds." He thrilled the crowd with his ability to convey "personality" "before the footlights."[30] In the social drama of his own life, every individual should perform with equal charm, if not precision. This was critical to social advancement, "especially if you are a business man." Such performances were also important for the "housewife, architect, or engineer" seeking to maximize his or her popularity and social potential.[31]

These modern success manuals showed little concern with the cultivation of diligence and good morals, which had been emphasized in nineteenth-century advice literature. The point of self-presentation was not to project respectability, manners, and virtue, but rather to please and manipulate. With their advocacy of personal image as a means of controlling other people's attitudes and behaviors, these treatises were more overtly manipulative than the genteel Victorian etiquette books we have seen. As historian Christopher Lasch has observed, the advice manuals of the 1920s differed from earlier ones in their "lack of interest in the substance of success, and in the candor with which they insist that . . . 'winning images' . . . count for more than performance, ascription for more than achievement."[32] To use the terminology of sociologist David Riesman, the modern American was becoming an "other-directed" individual whose life was organized by keeping attuned to the impressions and opinions of his peers.[33]

~

This emphasis on surfaces was not only an instrumental response to the social and economic demands of an urban mass-consumer society. Rather, it reflected a deeper change, a more profound reorientation in understandings of the self. Even though social and demographic changes in the 1800s had begun to alter the concept of personal identity, unmooring it from its traditional foundations and anchors, a person's core self was nonetheless thought to be largely bounded by fixed external circumstances—familial background, class status, ethnicity, regional culture, and religion.

People continued to define themselves according to these established markers of social identity. Yet in an increasingly mobile and unsettled social environment, personal identity was becoming more malleable, open, and fluid. If we are to take the "salesmanship" and "personality" literature as a clue to deeper social realities, the self was coming to be seen as more fragmented and discontinuous—a set of shifting roles and "multiple personalities." Many, it seemed, were becoming open to the idea of freely altering their behavior, appearances, and images to meet the expectations of others and the social needs of the moment.

This manipulation of self and persona was not seen as dissimulation. Creating a positive image and personality did not mean concealing a true, authentic self behind a social mask. Rather, the ideal envisioned that one genuinely partook in the social personas one adopted. That is, in the process of looking charming and personable, one really became charming and personable. There was no sharp line between reality and facade; the self became the face or faces one projected to the world. Significant segments of the culture seemed to be jettisoning the idea of a stable self and accepting the idea of the self as a construction, an ongoing process of performance, manipulation, and regeneration. The idea of the bifurcated self—of sharply demarcated public and private selves—was ceding to a vision of a performing self, one that shifted demeanor and behavior to suit the situation at hand, all the while seeming personable, expressive, and authentic. The concept of the private home as a cloistered backstage to one's social performance was becoming somewhat obsolete in a world where people were metaphorically "on stage" all the time.

The notion that identity is a social invention assembled out of the various, shifting impressions one makes on others became a major theme in the sociology and social psychology of this era. As William James wrote in his *Principles of Psychology*, a person tended to show different sides of him or herself to different people, creating multiple impressions and multiple selves. One had "as many different social selves as there are distinct groups of persons about whose opinion he cares."[34] As the social psychologist Charles Horton Cooley explained in his concept of the "looking glass self," social identity existed in the interaction between the image of self one conveyed to the public and reactions of others to that projection. According to Cooley, the self comprised "the imagination of our appearance to the other person; the imagination of his judgment of that appearance, and some sort of self-feeling, such as pride or mortification."[35] The self was one's image and, even more, one's feelings about one's image, and *one's feelings about other people's feelings about one's image*. This frank acceptance of the instability of the self and its manufactured, fragmentary, and multiple nature marked the beginning of a new chapter in the history of personal identity in the United States.

❦

Insofar as it could be packaged, prepared, perfected, and "sold" to others, the self took on qualities of a consumer product. Like bread, soap, shoes, and the other mass-produced items that were rolling off the assembly lines, personal identity was being discussed as a marketable commodity. As the self was becoming more and more commodified, it was more often expressed through consumption.[36] Advertisers began to describe consumer products as critical assets in the project of impression management and in the cultivation and selling of the self to others.

World War I, with its brutality and the social upheaval that followed in its wake, shattered the prudishness and idealism of the Victorian era, with its faith in moral perfection through self-control, sensual repression, and the spiritually redemptive powers of the private home. In the 1920s there was a "revolution in manners and morals," in which emotional and sexual expression, once proscribed among the middle class, ceased to be taboo.[37] Feminists and so-called sex radicals had spoken out against the "conspiracy of silence" around sex and urged the frank discussion of birth control and other intimate matters. By the 1920s, many subjects formerly off-limits had been woven into the fabric of popular discourse. The earlier ideal of emotional suppression and self-disciplined individualism was eclipsed by a new emphasis on self-fulfillment, emotional freedom, and personal expression.[38] The strict boundaries between public and private life were dissolving as the open display of one's thoughts, needs, feelings, and desires was no longer regarded as unequivocally vulgar, but in some cases as a normal and healthy aspect of human existence.

Consumer indulgence was embraced, and a culture of consumption became entrenched in American society. As wages rose and work weeks decreased in the prosperous decade, shopping became a leisure activity, and luxury items such as fashionable clothing and home furnishings came within the reach and desire of more buyers. Household expenditures tripled between 1909 and 1929.[39] As sociologists Robert and Helen Lynd observed in their classic 1929 study *Middletown*, the residents of that small city strove to "keep up with the Joneses" and to outmatch the consumer spending of their peers.[40] They conceptualized their identities and life trajectories in terms of purchasing products and advancing socioeconomically. It is not fair to impute a consumerist mind-set to everyone; as historian Jackson Lears observes, not all conformed to the standards held out to them by national advertisers, as regional, religious, ethnic, and other traditions often influenced people's beliefs and attitudes more than the imperatives of mass culture.[41] Yet among many sectors of the populace, people began to seek happiness and fulfillment in the continued acquisition of goods.[42]

One institution that turned consumer products from mere objects into the bearers of emotional, spiritual, and psychological meaning was the advertising industry. Advertising gained new prestige in the twentieth century. In an effort to "refute lingering charges of charlatanism," advertising agents "began to reinvent themselves as . . . businessmen" and did away with the earlier patent medicine and "snake oil" schemes. "Truth in advertising" was the new motto.[43] By 1920, "admen" were regarded as white-collar professionals.[44] The industry's newfound respectability contributed to the credibility and persuasiveness of its messages. Advertisers took advantage of recent developments in mass communication—the development of film and radio, and the increased circulation of newspapers and magazines—to disseminate their pitches and slogans to a national audience. They also relied on ever more persuasive appeals, including slick and professional illustrations, both drawn and photographed. By the 1920s, the vast majority of advertisements included pictures.[45] Print advertising, with its enticing images of happy families, flawless women, and dapper gentlemen, became a pervasive aspect of the visual landscape and a touchstone of everyday life. Ads became the mural against which Americans began to envision their lives, identities, and aspirations. With words and pictures, advertisers linked consumer items to such coveted internal states as self-respect and freedom, and promised consumers personal fulfillment through the purchase and use of the right products.

Historian Daniel Boorstin described the rise of advertising as one of the most "momentous sign[s] of the rise of image-thinking" in the twentieth-century United States.[46] Advertisers heightened concerns with personal image; indeed, the mission of the ad agency was to create discomfort and dissatisfaction with one's image that could only be assuaged through the purchase of goods. Like the "personality" and "salesmanship" gurus, advertisers encouraged consumers to see themselves, particularly their physical appearances, from an external perspective—through the searching gaze of strangers who needed to be persuaded or impressed. Ads played upon popular insecurities with identity and appearance, and they reinforced the perception that images were essential to social advancement. They reiterated that one had to work to create one's own favorable identity in the face of the critical judgments of others.[47]

Ads reminded readers that they were on display in a world peopled by spectators, detractors, and voyeurs. "Critical eyes are sizing you up right now. Keep your face fresh, firm, fit," threatened the manufacturers of Williams' Shaving Cream.[48] Beginning in the 1920s, "the women in ads were constantly observing themselves, ever self-critical," notes historian Stuart Ewen. "A noticeable proportion of magazine ads directed at women depicted them looking into mirrors."[49] "Do you wonder, when you meet a casual friend, whether your nose is shiny? Do you anxiously consult store windows and vanity cases at every opportunity?"[50] As an ad for Woodbury's Soap warned: "Strangers' eyes, keen and critical—can you meet them proudly—confidently—without fear?"[51]

Advertisers generated new social hells of anxiety and embarrassment and pushed new kinds of products to stave off such traumas. In the social world depicted in 1920s ads, the potential for humiliation and social failure lurked everywhere. In an ad that appeared in *Collier's* magazine in 1929, a woman who had chosen a poor brand of car was humiliated when the car broke down while she was trying to take two friends home from a party. The manufacturers of Arrow Shirt Collars advertised that their products had "completely rescued young men from inappropriate sportswear in business."[52] "Does your morning shave last as long as you wish?" asked a shaving cream advertisement, which promised "no evening embarrassment."[53] The most fearsome kind of social shame tapped into taboos against uncleanliness and poor grooming; an entire industry of new self-care and cleanliness products mushroomed in the wake of this manufactured hygiene panic. Ads for "halitosis" pervaded 1920s magazine copy.[54]

Historian Roland Marchand has described this advertising approach as the "parable of the first impression."[55] The moral of the story was eternal vigilance: letting down your guard and allowing others to see you when you were not at your best, even for a moment, had disastrous consequences. From no other cultural source "did people receive such frequent reminders that other people were constantly sizing them up and whispering about them behind their backs, or that they had so many possible reasons to feel a sense of social shame," Marchand writes.[56] Clearly many of the scenarios depicted in advertisements were fantastic; then as now, advertising was a funhouse mirror of sorts, exaggerating social conditions and anxieties in the quest for sales and profit. Yet the parable of the first impression, for all its dramatics, had a basis in the real social dynamics of modern urban life. The men who worked in the advertising industry knew from personal experience that in the business world first impressions did make a difference. They knew that externals were significant in a mobile, impersonal society, an age of "shifting relationships." "The parable of the first impression dramatized popular apprehensions about a society moving towards depersonalization," in Marchand's words. It stimulated the hope that people could triumph over the "unfair judgments of an anonymous society."[57]

The flip side of the social failure narrative was the saga of brilliant social triumph, and advertisements tantalized readers with these scenarios as well. Through consumer products, particularly fashion, grooming, and hygiene products, a person could not only correct peripheral weaknesses and minor flaws, but entirely reengineer his image. In the early twentieth century, the mass-market cosmetics industry became an important presence in women's lives, and cosmetics manufacturers promoted makeup as a means to personal transformation. The "before and after" trope was common. Just as they could follow the steps to effective "salesmanship" and achieve business success, they could follow manufacturers' beauty advice and tailor their image to brilliant precision. A booklet from the 1920s that advertised beauty aids depicted on its cover the slogan, "Your Masterpiece, Yourself." "Each portion of the body was to be viewed critically, as a potential bauble in a successful assemblage," Stuart Ewen writes.[58] Personal image was being described as a self-willed creation: something that could be plotted, designed, and manipulated through constant, concerted effort.

The allure of distinction was the psychic engine behind these advertising ploys. Advertisements promised consumers the fantasy of individuality—that one would not only secure the esteem and attention of others through the purchase of goods, but that one could use goods to achieve an inner sense of uniqueness and self-worth, a sense of being one's own person. As an ad for the E. V. Price Suit Company promised the middle-class male readers of *Collier's* magazine in 1929, "You can be months ahead in style. Our exclusive 'attitude method' of tailoring makes it possible not only to cut the suit to your measurements, but also to drape and balance it to your posture. It will be beautifully tailed for *you and you alone*."[59] Makeup manufacturers urged women to select rouge, powder, and eyeshadow suited to their own unique "type." Was she a seductive Cleopatra or Sheba type? A blond and aggressive Lorelei? The girl next door? Her "personality" dictated her cosmetics strategy.[60] Through the power of consumer choice, one could define one's own self and be *somebody*—not only in the eyes of others, but in one's own eyes.

Such gestures to autonomy and self-definition kept the spectre of the confidence man at bay. Image creation and impression management were said to be not merely about superficial transformations—about deceiving others—but about *inner transformation*, a prized goal in a culture that was becoming oriented around the goals and concerns of psychology and psychotherapy. In the 1920s,

"New Thought," "Mind Cure," and other strands of pop psychology were amalgamated with more academic strains of behaviorism and Freudianism and marketed to the public. As historian John Burnham writes, the "Age of Crowds" that witnessed a terror of losing one's individuality gave rise to a "strong sense of the urgency of finding one's self."[61] The 1920s saw the emergence of "psychological identities," concepts of self that were couched in terms of psychological issues, functions, and problems.[62] Popular self-help literature portrayed the individual psyche as marred and broken, and described the self as an evolving entity that could be continuously rehabilitated, perfected, and worked pure over time. In the beginnings of a "self-expression" ideal that would intensify over the twentieth century, it was said that a person could "actualize" only by externalizing and expressing the self. As historian Kathy Peiss observed in her study of the cosmetics industry, manufacturers in the 1920s promoted makeup as a tool for women to portray and create their individuality in a modern world. By choosing her own makeup style, by combining techniques and colors in her own customized fashion, she could "express herself" and in so doing achieve a feeling of emotional wholeness.[63]

Advertisements for clothing, food products, and even home appliances all employed this trope. In the modern social world, purchases were a language of self; one articulated one's identity through the car one had, the foods one consumed, the way one decorated one's house. Using goods as a means to authentic "self-expression" did not mean that one was locked forever into one's purchasing choices. A person could—indeed, was strongly encouraged to—change her image and personality through the constant acquisition and use of new products. These alterations were not false. A total makeover was not a betrayal of self. Indeed, if the new image more accurately reflected a person's inner feelings than the old image, then the transformation was healing. It was self-actualizing. Constantly changing how one presented oneself to others was part of the process of personal evolution and "growth." Commodity consumption could restore to individuals the sense of depth, substance, and personal meaning that had been undermined by cultural commodification itself.

The outer world and the inner life, the material and the spiritual, *public image* and *self-image* were merged in advertising's fantastic tableaux. Playing on instrumental concerns with social status and advancement, as well as deeper existential concerns with the nature of the self in a mass society, advertisers promised psychological and social regeneration through the continuous development of personal image, enabled by the programmatic acquisition of more and more prestigious goods. Ads preached that one of the most important things in life was to have a good image and to actively control and shape that image. Personal image was a calling card, the key that opened doors, the grease that smoothed the joints of social relations. Yet perhaps even more important than an objectively favorable image was a person's feelings about his or her image. It was critical not only that one looked good in the eyes of others, but that one's image reflected one's "self"— that it properly externalized the vision of self held in one's mind's eye. These were becoming preoccupations of the image-conscious society: having a good image, feeling good about that image, being the master of one's image.

~

Personal image was a constellation of nuances, associations, and impressions—the feelings and reactions one tried to invoke through the cut of one's clothes, the enthusiasm of one's gestures, the inflection of one's voice, and other cues that signified one's class, disposition, and demeanor. Not surprisingly, looks —visual appearances—were central to the modern concept of personal image. This was not only because physical appearances were the most obvious and visible means of distinction in the "crowd" setting. The emphasis on visual images of self can also be attributed to the overall priority that American culture began to place on looking—on gazing and being gazed upon—a pastime and phenomenon that was facilitated in large part by the advent and expansion of new visual technologies.

The period between 1900 and 1930 saw the rapid acceleration of the "visual revolution" that had begun in the late 1800s. Kodak cameras were in widespread use, and photographic and hand-drawn images populated the metropolis—on billboards, posters, marquees, window displays, and transit advertisements. The continued refinement of printing and photographic technologies, the growth of the cities, and the rise of advertising as a major source of revenue for publications led to an explosion of visually oriented print media, such as photojournalism and film. More than ever, daily life involved looking at images of people, and being looked at. On the streets, on subways, in department stores, and anywhere that crowds assembled, people experienced a sense of being gazed upon, of being scrutinized and sized up by others. The images—of faces, bodies, and candid expressions—that nineteenth-century America had characterized as deeply personal had become part of the public landscape, appearing on billboards, product packaging, and movie screens.

The growth of the visual media gave rise to a new, defining phenomenon of American society, perhaps the single greatest force behind the new culture of images—the entertainment celebrity. In the period between World War I and the 1930s, the United States became a "celebrity culture." We can understand the rise of celebrity in this period, particularly film celebrity, as the product of expanding modes of communication. The ascendance of the film star to the position of mass idol was also a response to American culture's need for new models of self in the image-based society. Film actors, who had seemingly mastered the art of impression management, became cultural heroes in the modern world of appearances and images. For their glamour, charisma, and dazzling looks, and their apparent ability to externalize their inner selves and personalities, they achieved recognition, success, and fortune. They were the antithesis of ordinariness; they stood out from the crowd. They had avoided in a remarkable and stunning manner what was seen as one of the chief burdens of modern society: the burden of being nobody.

❧

The history of the motion picture began at the dawn of the 1900s, when inventors learned to take and project photographic images in a way that created the illusion of motion. Initially, films consisted of disconnected views of still life—landscapes and city scenes—but before long, filmmakers had focused their gaze on people. This is what turned the movies from a mere technological novelty into a cultural fascination: the alluring close-up of the human face. The faces of actors, projected realistically and vividly on the large screen, seemed unusually lifelike. Audiences felt as if they were familiar with the actors depicted, which made them want to "know" them further—to learn about their personalities and personal lives.[64]

Beginning around 1912, the film studios, their publicity departments, and the media outlets they courted and fed, fueled this celebrity illusion by fleshing out the details. Newspapers and magazines described actors' habits, home lives, and personal activities, and through these facts turned stars into vivid, realistic-seeming "personalities" for the enjoyment of curious viewers and readers. Although film actors were still viewed with moral skepticism by some sectors of the populace, this was beginning to fade. The new worldview that embraced sensuality and self-display was finding respect and admiration for the performing professions. Seemingly personal stories about movie actors, popularized in the press, created emotional ties that would draw Americans deeper and deeper into the fantasy world of the stars. By the mid-1920s, movie actors had become household names and commanded public attention on par with presidents and world leaders.

Audiences were fascinated with the way film actors put themselves together—how they created a stunning image and constantly manipulated that image through the careful and strategic alteration of their appearance and style. Having arrived at a successful and attractive look for one role, they redid it for the next one. It was their ability to transform their images that led to their success—indeed, that got them the job in the first place. According to the famous Hollywood "rags to riches" success story, the aspiring celebrity, typically a person of humble origin, physically made herself over, and then "sold" her new image to a director or producer. Stars were described as the most canny salesmen of all, for they had mastered the art of selling themselves. They understood the relationship between personal image and success, and their life stories were object lessons in the importance of the meticulous management of first impressions.

Although the stock-in-trade of the film actress was her ability to rework her public appearance, the celebrity was not seen as deceptive or deceitful. Rather, as the film publicity departments preached, she merely "expressed herself" in each and every performance. She could not overtly dissimulate, for the movie camera with its searching gaze would ferret out and expose all falsity and inauthenticity. To be a star was thus not really to act, to put on masks or false fronts, but rather to perform one's self, albeit in many different guises. What made the star so enchanting was her ability to externalize her inner traits, to channel them into an image, and then to alter that image when the role required it, all the while keeping "true to herself." It was the polished and seemingly authentic nature of these self-performances that made the actor into a person worthy of celebration and set her apart from the crowd.

Personal life became the basis of modern fame. While nineteenth-century "public figures"—politicians, inventors, and captains of business—had been known for their productive achievements, modern fame more often celebrated a person's lifestyle and personal traits.[65] By 1927, the celebrity pantheon, as reflected in the content of a typical issue of the Sunday *New York Times*, included not only movie stars, but Broadway producers, poets, socialites, and athletes.[66] These icons were celebrated not so much for their accomplishments but for their interesting personalities and private activities. In this way, film stars and celebrity journalism played a critical role in the twentieth century's blurring of public and private life. In a consumer culture oriented around acquisition, leisure pursuits, and the elusive ideal of personal fulfillment, a desirable lifestyle came to be regarded as the pinnacle of public achievement. As the *New York Times* noted in 1920, the definition of a star was "one who only had to confine himself to one role—that of being himself."[67]

If stardom depended on looks and style, then anyone, in theory, could attain it. Fame was becoming an ideal, one seemingly within reach of the ordinary person. Even if one failed to make it to the big time, everyone could become a "star" of his own life by applying the image management strategies of celebrities to his everyday acts of self-presentation. As the celebrity literature preached, the props in the skilled self-performance were simple and mundane—cosmetics, hair dye, fresh breath, good posture, and so on. Cinematic and theatrical metaphors pervaded the era's cultural texts. "The woman in the home, the woman in business, in society, must make up for the part she is to play in life," preached one beauty writer. "The great moments of your life are 'close ups.'"[68]

The celebrity industry, the advertising industry, and the publishing industry worked together in an intimate partnership. Stars became product endorsers, paid to attest that particular goods, such as cosmetics and hygiene products, enabled them to achieve image perfection. Celebrity had become an immense source of economic value, and advertisers were regularly contracting with actors and other stars—sports stars, stage performers, and singers, among others—for the use of their images and endorsements in advertisements.[69] Actors wrote books and advice columns on beauty, etiquette, and the art of personal "salesmanship." Both on and off the screen, stars sold products, publications, and films. These allied industries of image came to constitute a huge sector of the economy. In 1929, annual expenditures on advertising reached over a billion dollars.[70] Sixty-five million movie tickets were being sold nationally each week in a population around twice that number.[71]

The industries of counterimage—the tabloids, gossip columns, and scandal publications that flourished in this era—were perhaps as critical to the new cult of image as the image-building industries. The illustrated news "tabloid" made its debut with New York's *Illustrated Daily News* in 1919, and scandal and confessional magazines with titles like *True Story* and *True Confessions* also became popular.[72] Most newspapers ran at least one, if not multiple gossip columns devoted to actors and other celebrities. With their seemingly privileged access to the stars, "gossip columnists" became cultural icons in their own right.[73]

As in the past, the raison d'etre of such publications was to deconstruct fronts, to go behind the celebrity facades and expose what stars were "really like." Gossip columnists and tabloids pounced on the actress who went to the grocery store without her makeup on, who let down her guard and was "too candid" with a reporter, who failed to recognize that she was under public scrutiny at all times. The consequence of not maintaining one's social performance could be severe. Newspapers in the 1920s teemed with stories about "star scandals," tales of actors who had failed to scrupulously conceal their personal activities—most often their sexual affairs—and paid the price with an embarrassing fall from public grace.

These plays of concealment and exposure were immensely fascinating to an image-conscious public. Americans followed with rapt attention the attempts of celebrities to invent and reinvent themselves and their public images, and the efforts of the media industry to deconstruct star identities by committing so-called invasions of privacy. For celebrities, participation in an "information game"—"a potentially infinite cycle of concealment, discovery, false revelation, and rediscovery," in sociologist Erving Goffman's words—was a basic occupational requirement.[74] This charade was said to represent the struggle, writ large, that every person would wage in her own efforts to create and perfect her public persona.

∼

The artifacts and incidents of American society in this era attest to the centrality and pervasiveness of this image-conscious thinking in the cultural imagination. The nation's entertainment and news media, its academic treatises, its art and literature, its selling appeals, and even its law evince a new and preeminent concern with the creation, expression, and management of public image—controlling it, defending it, perfecting it, feeling good about it.

There are few studies from this period that document the real, lived aspects of this image-consciousness, but the sociological evidence that we do have suggests that ordinary Americans were, in various ways, enacting the drama of "impression management" in their everyday lives. Studies of social behavior in universities from the 1920s demonstrate that college students who were socially conscious and upwardly mobile worked hard to display signs of good grooming and social etiquette.[75] Sociological research similarly shows that movie audiences were using actors as models in their own individual projects of fashioning a positive public image. In a massive study on "movies and conduct" led by sociologist Herbert Blumer in the late 1920s and early 1930s, a majority of young women audiences surveyed said they imitated movie stars' clothes, hair, and cosmetics.[76] They saw actors as icons of personal and social success, and they copied their styles and "personalities" assiduously. "After one of [Mary] Pickford's movies, I'd find myself walking up the aisle with that certain little bent knee, toe turning in walk," one movie fan told a sociologist in 1931. "I went so far as to dress up like Pickford's character . . . and have my picture taken."[77] The essence of creating a public identity was to perform and to be visible. In the image-conscious culture, the actor had become the modal self.

The concern with appearances and images that beset American culture in the 1920s and the fragmented and discontinuous nature of personal identity must not be overstated. Communities, familial bonds, and religious institutions continued to provide strong foundations of identity for many. A good portion of the populace still lived in small towns and villages, where relationships were more continuous and personal than in the city, and where a firm sense of identity was more strongly supported. There were large areas of life—the spiritual, the personal, the familiar—where image did not count for much. Most people undoubtedly conceived of themselves as more than assemblages of social facades and "stage effects."

Nonetheless, the uprooted and transient nature of an increasingly mobile urban society, and the imperatives and faiths of modern consumer culture, encouraged people to see themselves less in terms of enduring relationships, stable qualities, and moral visions, and more in terms of the various images one strategically created and projected to others. The self was coming to be regarded as more malleable and unstable, more thoroughly a matter of individual control and design, than in the past. The upshot of these developments was not only an increased consciousness of image, but also a feeling of entitlement to one's image. The more that a desirable image came to be regarded as essential to social status and advancement, and the more one's appearance before others was seen as coextensive with one's identity and "inner self," the deeper the public's commitment to a legal right to control one's public image: to transform it, manage it, shape it, publicize it, and reap its social and emotional rewards.

CHAPTER 6

The Laws of Image

Libel, Privacy, Emotional Distress

As the image-conscious sensibility gained purchase on the popular imagination, and the mass media proliferated, existing areas of law were expanded and new laws created to protect people's interests in managing, defending, and controlling their public images. In the 1930s and 1940s a number of states recognized the tort right to privacy, described as a right to avoid undesirable and "unwarranted publicity."[1] Libel claims increased, and courts were extending libel law to address a range of emotional and reputational harms. A new tort action remedied serious, intentionally inflicted injuries to people's feelings, including their feelings about their images. In several different contexts, courts were recognizing a right to one's image, and the *personal image lawsuit* became a fixture of American legal culture.

∾

In the period between the two world wars, the mass media suffused and transformed American life. Although the nation entered economic crisis in the 1930s—banks failed, companies went out of business, and unemployment rose to 25 percent—the consumption of newspapers, films, magazines, and radio skyrocketed. Daily newspaper circulation increased from 22.4 million copies in 1910 to 39.6 million copies in the 1930s.[2] Ninety percent of Americans were estimated to be newspaper readers.[3] Each year, 4,500 different periodicals were published.[4] By the end of the decade, half the homes in the United States contained at least two radios, which were on for about five hours a day.[5] By 1945, more homes and apartments had a radio than indoor plumbing or a telephone.[6]

Media consumption became ritualistic and the public dependent on mass communications as a source of news and entertainment.[7] The media not only served important informational functions—the public learned about economic affairs, the war, and national politics almost exclusively through the mass media—

but had become critical agents of acculturation, transmitting norms, lifestyles, and values to a vast populace. Newspapers, radio, magazines, and film created social bonds, allowing a culturally diverse and geographically scattered people to unite around shared images, impressions, and personalities. The instruments of mass communication were the key agents of a mass culture—a commercially produced culture created for profit and supported almost exclusively by advertising revenue. By World War II, mass-mediated images and ideals had become the focal point of popular culture and daily life.

Libel

With this proliferation of communication came more injuries to people's egos, images, and reputations. As soon as radio and motion pictures were popularized, their creators were sued for libel. These new media were treated the same under libel doctrine as print publications, although some argued that these especially vivid, intense, far-reaching modes of communication required special, more stringent rules of liability.[8] Because the voice was even more forceful and memorable than the written word, the circulation of a libel to "hundreds of thousands of listeners [via radio] causes far more harm than the appearance of the same statement in any newspaper outside metropolitan areas," wrote Harvard law professor Zechariah Chafee.[9] To be maligned in a film was potentially even more damning. "In the hands of a wrongdoer," motion picture technology had "untold possibility towards producing an effective libel," observed a New York appeals court in 1934.[10]

Though journalism had professionalized, adopting ethics codes, standards of objectivity and accuracy, and a "public service" mission,[11] newspapers and magazines still struggled with libel claims. Between 1910 and 1930, the *New York World* was faced with 220 libel claims totaling $17,600,168.[12] The *Graphic*, a notorious New York tabloid, faced libel suits totaling twelve million dollars in the 1920s.[13] Between 1923 and 1948, the *New York Times* was the defendant in 85 libel suits.[14] Publishing trade journals discussed the threat of libel; journalism schools offered specialized courses in libel; and defamation law handbooks were written.[15] Reporters and editors were given lists of taboo words and phrases; photographs, names, and other personal details about the subjects of news stories were cut to avoid possible libel suits.[16] Major newspapers, magazines, and book publishing houses retained libel lawyers for prepublication review,[17] and insurance organizations began writing libel and slander insurance for publishers and broadcasters.[18]

The problem was that publishers were disseminating more words and images than they could reasonably vet or process. The high volume of published material and the premium placed on fast reporting made it impossible to verify the accuracy of every statement.[19] Although editors and proofreaders were trained to identify and remove potentially libelous statements, defamatory comments still made it into print, often the result of careless mistakes. A brawl at a boarding house was reported by the *New York Telegram*: LANDLADY SLAYS HOST. The landlady sued; it turns out that a typographical error had changed "slaps" to "slays."[20] An article in the *Norfolk Post* described how a man was arrested in connection with a burglary in a neighborhood called Colonial Place. In reality, he was arrested for housebreaking in the neighborhood of Riverview. A judgment was entered for the plaintiff.[21] The rise of wire services such as the Associated Press led to new publishing dangers. A libelous story that originated with a wire service could appear in hundreds of publications, and every reprinting newspaper could be sued—a so-called chain libel suit.[22]

In some cases, publications were able to settle with complainants by offering cash payments, apologies, or retractions,[23] although a number of major publications, like the *New York Times* and the *New Yorker*, had a strict editorial policy of refusing to settle, as a way of discouraging so-called nuisance suits.[24] Editors and publishers described the "nightmare" of libel litigation.[25] One libel trial against a metropolitan newspaper extended over three months. The expense of trial preparation was estimated to be $200,000, and preparing evidence for the defense of truth occupied one attorney for more than three years.[26] One former member of the staff of the *New York World* speculated that the drain on the paper's resources from libel suits led to the demise of the newspaper in 1931.[27]

The author of a 1930 journalism textbook urged reporters to "lean over backwards" to avoid writing anything that "might possibly be construed as libelous," and to avoid "any words to which offense might be taken."[28] Other editors believed that "a paper which doesn't take chances is a dead paper. A too close attention to the absolute rules regarding libel . . . , result in a product which is flat, insipid, devoid of all those adornments of narrative, epithet, and description which make a great newspaper a living thing."[29] Some editors and publishers cowered in the face of libel.[30] Others took their chances. "There is scarcely an edition of a metropolitan daily newspaper that does not contain five or six potential libel suits. Its editors know it," observed an editor at the *New York Times* in 1940.[31] As an editor at the *New Yorker* wrote to one of its lawyers, "we don't doubt that it's full of libel, but would like to publish as much of it as you think we can get away with."[32]

~

The "libel climate" of the interwar period was one of increasing combativeness and bravado.[33] In an era of labor unrest, racial violence, and the rise of vocal dissenters on both the right and the left, libel litigation was a critical part of American political theater.[34] The intricate political battles involving libel in this period are many and complex; to do them justice requires detail beyond the scope of this story. In one of the most notable trends, politicians initiated "chain libel suits" against political columnists and broadcasters and the authors of so-called slander books— "spicy personal accounts of great public figures."[35] The author of the syndicated column *Washington Merry Go Round*, Drew Pearson, faced damage claims totaling more than one hundred million dollars.[36] As sociologist David Riesman observed in 1942, the public had become familiar with the "phenomenon of a maligned politician publicly announcing that he is consulting his lawyers and that he is filing a libel suit asking for six or seven figures in damages," a suit sometimes "allowed to drop when the incident blows over."[37] Defamation law's potential threat to free expression and public debate led to several academic studies; one of the most prominent was conducted by the Hutchins Commission on Freedom of the Press, an esteemed group of media scholars funded by *Time* magazine's Henry Luce and headed by Harvard's Zechariah Chafee. The challenge of modern libel law, the commission concluded, was to balance the continuing psychic and material importance of individual reputation with the public's need for timely news, commentary, and political criticism.[38]

Celebrities were also mobilizing libel lawsuits as a tool for coercion and strategic publicity. The powerful Hollywood studios, which controlled the careers and publicity of the most famous actors, used their influence over the nation's press to quash a good deal of potentially libelous or scandalous material. Defamatory comments nonetheless made it into print. Douglas Fairbanks and Mary Pickford threatened to sue a movie fan magazine over a rumor of estrangement.[39] The married actress Doris Keane brought suit against the tabloid the *New York Evening Graphic* over a publication that linked her romantically with another star.[40] The actor Ronald Colman instituted a libel suit over a statement about him in a New York paper that accused him of drunkenness.[41] Though hardly as litigious as their late twentieth-century counterparts, some celebrities were making the libel suit a part of their public relations repertoire, a way of promoting their desired public images by publicizing their version of the truth.

As in the past, average citizens appear to have brought the majority of libel suits. Libel litigation remained the bailiwick of the contingent fee practice. Publishing industry pundits claimed that there was a routine in "almost every large city"—a so-called libel racket—in which plaintiffs' lawyers read the newspapers with "an eye out for a chance to bring a libel suit."[42] Editor Neil MacNeil of the *New York Times* wrote in 1940 that "each edition is searched for libel actions, both by men and women who do not like the news and by lawyers looking for a case."[43] Juries were known to be sympathetic to libel plaintiffs, particularly private figure plaintiffs. Large jury verdicts were, in the opinion of a New York libel lawyer, a product of public "hostility" towards newspapers having to do with "unfair sensationalism" and "obviously flagrant invasions of privacy."[44]

One editor claimed that 75 percent of all libel suits were based on stories imputing some form of criminal activity; the rest were based on stories "relating in one form or another to . . . breach of the currently sanctioned moral code," such as adultery or divorce.[45] In a 1934 case, a couple sued for libel when a local gossip columnist wrote that they had a "rift in the lute," which the plaintiffs interpreted as an accusation that there was a breach in their marital relations.[46] A number of suits were brought over arguably less injurious comments. In *Walker v. Bee-News Publishing*, a man sued when a newspaper wrote about him, falsely, as having hosted a wrestling match. The newspaper had written that a boisterous wrestling match, which had given the audience a "swell time," was had in the barn of Tom Walker. The event had not occurred in the barn of Tom Walker, but rather in the barn of D. H. Walker, a few miles away. A court awarded damages. Tom Walker claimed that his reputation was injured, but the only party slighted may have been poor D. H.; as two lawyers quipped in their book on libel, "D.H. had been generous, his guests had a swell time, and Tom got all the credit and public acclaim for the entertainment."[47]

The number of libel suits was not high in any *absolute* sense. A 1937 study found that in Connecticut between 1919 and 1932 less than one percent of all litigation involved slander or libel.[48] The number of potentially libelous statements in newspapers and other publications was immense; the vast majority of those who had been maligned did not initiate or contemplate legal action. A libel lawsuit was a tedious and lengthy undertaking not for the faint of heart. Trials could drag on for years, during which time the allegedly libeled plaintiff was forced to suffer frustration, loss of time, and expense, not to mention ongoing publicity of the embarrassing accusations. Libel lawsuits were regarded as a last resort, when other options had been exhausted. Some victims of libelous statements in newspapers sought retractions, which were occasionally granted.[49] More direct methods of vengeance were also pursued. *Time* magazine reported in 1934 that when a gossip columnist reported a rumor about some local doctors engaged in potentially scandalous acts, one of the men who was implicated marched into the editor's office and "cracked him twice with a horsewhip."[50]

Despite the use of these extralegal methods of recourse, journalists, lawyers, and legal experts and scholars writing on libel described what they saw as increasing litigiousness around public image and reputation. The *New Yorker* did ongoing battle with both public and private figures who threatened to sue for libel, including parties who, according to one historian of the magazine, "fil[ed] one ridiculous claim after another, haul[ed] the magazine into court, and bombard[ed] its offices with bizarre correspondence and phone calls."[51] Editor Emile Gauvreau of the tabloid the *New York Daily Graphic* recalled that the paper was embroiled in libel suits by individuals who were not public figures or notables.[52] After Margaret Mitchell wrote *Gone with the Wind*, she was confronted with threats from people she had never heard of, alleging that they were the basis for her characters and that her descriptions had libeled them.[53] *Esquire* magazine in 1938 observed a trend towards "more frequent suits and threats of suits in libel."[54]

In 1933, an article by two lawyers in the *American Bar Association Journal* decried what they saw as people's expanding egos and their yearning for complete control over their public personas.[55] "With modern devices for the spread of individual influence, there appears a corresponding desire for wider and greater power over others. Less and less are we content to confine our reputation within family or neighborhood groups." "Our ego circles grow," they wrote.[56] As the average

American became more possessive of his public image, "more and more libel and slander" suits were "find[ing] their way into the court rooms." There was a "growing tendency to resort to the courts."[57]

∾

The law of libel was moving in contradictory directions in this era. Courts were extending greater protection to the press when it published on public figures and so-called matters of public concern. In some states, a conditional privilege within the common law of libel exempted false and defamatory statements of fact about public officials unless the plaintiff could show that the publication was made with malice, or reckless disregard of the truth. This was justified as protection for freedom of speech and press—the right of the press to engage in political criticism and the public's right to know about its leaders' acts and qualifications.[58] As the Kansas Supreme Court noted in its decision in *Coleman v. MacLennan*, adopting the privilege, "it is of the utmost consequence that the people should discuss the character and qualifications of candidates for their suffrages. The importance to the state and to society of such discussions is so vast and the advantages derived so great that they more than counterbalance. . . . injury to the reputations of individuals."[59] This privilege would later become a constitutional requirement in the landmark 1964 Supreme Court case *New York Times v. Sullivan*.[60]

Although courts were becoming less solicitous of the reputations and public images of public figures, they were at the same time expanding libel law's reach and scope. In the interwar years, some courts were broadening the definition of a defamatory publication. A defamatory publication was not only one that cast a person into disrepute. A publication could be defamatory if it tarnished a person's image *in his own eyes*, causing mental distress.[61] In 1936, the torts scholar Calvert Magruder noted libel cases where plaintiffs had won damages not for an objective loss of reputation but for "the sense of outrage and chagrin that the defendant should have made an attack upon his reputation."[62] A reflection, perhaps, of the image-conscious sensibility, courts were expanding libel's domain from external, interpersonal relations to include self-perception and one's feelings about one's public image.

A court held that a woman had a cause of action for libel when a newspaper said that she had been served with process while sitting in a bathtub—an accusation that did not impute immoral conduct or likely damage her reputation, but nonetheless embarrassed her.[63] In *Zbyszko v. New York American*, the newspaper in 1929 published an article on the theory of evolution. In one part of the article, the text read: "The Gorilla is probably closer to man, both in body and in brain, than any other species of ape now alive. The general physique of the Gorilla is closely similar to an athletic man of today, and the mind of a young gorilla is much like the mind of a human baby." Near that text appeared a photograph of the wrestler Stanislaus Zbyszko, in a wrestling pose, and under it a caption: "Stanislaus Zbyszko, the Wrestler, Not Fundamentally Different from the Gorilla in Physique."[64] He sued the *New York American* for $250,000. Though it was unlikely that anyone would think worse of the wrestler for the newspaper article, the jury sympathized with his sense of affront and awarded him $25,000.[65]

The key case in this trend was *Burton v. Crowell Publishing Co.*, from 1936.[66] In 1934, the Camel cigarette company published an ad featuring a color photograph of Crawford Burton, a stockbroker who was a famous amateur jockey, in riding costume, holding in front of him a saddle and girth. Camel's big ad campaign was celebrated in the trade as an "advertising sensation."[67] Burton had posed for the ad and had been paid $500 for the use of his testimonial and picture. In the ad, he is quoted as saying, "whether I'm tired from riding a hard race, or from a crowded business day, I feel refreshed and restored as soon as I get a chance to smoke a Camel."[68]

Two photographs were inserted in the ad. One was of Burton in riding shorts and breeches, seated with a cigarette in one hand and a cap and whip in the other. This ran with the caption, "Get a lift with a Camel," and "Have you tried this enjoyable way of heightening energy?" The second photo showed him coming from a race, carrying his saddle in front of him. Over the saddle at his middle a white girth fell loosely in a way that made it seem to be attached to Burton and not to the saddle. With this photo ran the caption, "when you feel all in"—that is, when you feel tired—smoke a Camel.[69] Burton alleged that the way the picture was shot made it appear that the objects he was holding were in fact his genitalia and that he was guilty of indecent exposure.[70] This configuration of Burton's physique and the equipment was almost surely accidental. The ad was published in a number of national publications, including *Life, Collier's Weekly*, the *New Yorker*, the *Literary Digest*, and the *New York Times*.[71]

Not long after the ad appeared, Burton returned to the floor of the stock exchange to be greeted by jibes from his colleagues. The smoking room of the exchange was filled with brokers on the day the picture first appeared. They peppered him with jokes about the allegedly "indecent" picture, asking him "how it felt" and "how much he made from renting it out." Burton said that the remarks upset him so much that he could not work and had to seclude himself at home for several days.[72]

Burton contacted a fancy, white-shoe law firm and filed suit for libel against the Manhattan advertising agency William Esty & Co., R. J. Reynolds Tobacco Co.—the makers of Camels—and a long list of publications, including *Time* magazine, and the Crowell Publishing Company's *Collier's* and the *American Magazine*. He claimed $200,000 in damages. Burton also sued a New York nightclub called Leon and Eddie's, arguing that one of the partners of the restaurant had superimposed a picture of his face in the place of Burton's and sent a copy of the picture to many of his friends.[73] The claim was that both the "saddle girth" photograph and the accompanying slogans were sexually explicit and defamatory and caused Burton "public ridicule, scandal, reproach, scorn, and indignity."[74] As Burton's lawyers wrote in their brief:

> plaintiff is prepared to show . . . that readers and observers connected the saddle-girth picture with the slogans, seeing the phrase "all in," [as] lewdly suggestive . . . followed with a similarly lewd meaning for the word "lift," as though . . . renewed virile potency were to be had from the proffered brand of cigarettes. . . . [M]any went on to read the subcaption in the advertisement, which speaks of "heightening energy" . . . in the same salacious vein as the flamboyant slogans themselves.[75]

A federal district court threw the suit out on the ground that the advertisement, albeit mirth-provoking, was "not libelous."[76] Burton appealed to the Second Circuit Court of Appeals. The Second Circuit overturned the lower court and held that Burton had a cause of action for libel.[77]

Judge Learned Hand observed that the vast majority of readers were not quite as dirty minded as Burton's stockbroker colleagues. Yet those seeking titillation, with a little imagination, might perhaps view the picture as a "fantastic and lewd deformity," "grotesque, monstrous, and obscene." The slogans, he admitted, added to the sense of lewdness—the "legends . . . reinforce the ribald interpreta-tion." The case was remanded for trial, and the jury found for Burton in the sum of $2,500.[78]

As the *Harvard Law Review* observed, *Burton v. Crowell* was the first major de-cision that held that "unintentionally causing widespread ridicule of the plaintiff" was libelous.[79] While libel plaintiffs, historically, could receive compensation for emotional distress if defamation had been shown, mental anguish in the absence of reputational harm had not been sufficient grounds for recovery.[80] Critics ob-served not only what they saw as the hypersensitivity of the plaintiff in *Burton*, but the absence of any real harm to his standing before others. As one writer commented, the injury was solely to the "plaintiff's feelings, on account of the mortification he suffered and irritation, perhaps, at the good-natured 'joshing' of his friends." "The laughter at his expense was not on account of anything in the publication tending to lower him in the esteem of others."[81] The decision extended "the law of libel to a situation where the plaintiff's reputation is not im-paired in the slightest."[82] It heralded the movement towards the extension of libel beyond the protection of "reputation," in the sense of the judgments of others, to a broader right to control one's public persona and protect oneself against "emo-tionally embarrassing situations."[83]

Emotional Distress

Libel law's turn towards the inner world of the feelings and sensibilities re-flected a new cultural sensitivity to the importance of the emotions. The old idea that emotional injuries were speculative and insignificant had become obsolete with the professionalization of psychology and the advent of the behavioral sci-ences, which produced a new appreciation of the psychic and emotional aspects of daily life.[84] As we have seen, psychology was popularized in the 1920s and psy-chological concepts became part of popular culture. The first popular psychology magazines began publication in that decade; numerous self-help books were re-leased, and newspapers carried daily columns of psychological advice. There was a "full-fledged pop psychological essence-and-identity industry" and people were encouraged to view themselves in distinctly psychological terms.[85]

The condition of a person's feelings was beginning to be seen as an important matter that affected one's behavior, body, and physical health. A 1922 writer in the

Michigan Law Review, noting the discoveries of "medical men and psychologists" about "emotion and its effect on the human body," observed that all emotions were connected to physical states and that feelings like fright and anger were more than just emotional matters.[86] "The mind of an individual, his feelings and mental processes, are as much a part of a person as his observable physical members. An injury, therefore, which affects the sensibilities is equally an injury to the person as an injury to the body would be."[87]

This awareness of the significance of the emotions and the mind-body connection was behind the expansion of legal recovery for emotional harms. By the 1930s, the notion that the law should focus only on tangible, material injuries had been largely discredited. Legal realists in the academy, who argued that formalistic legal doctrines should be adjusted to meet social needs and conditions, discussed the necessity of protection for the intangible, spiritual dimensions of the self.[88] Invoking the German concept of "rights of personality," Roscoe Pound distinguished "interests of substance"—"the individual economic life"—from "interests of personality"—"the individual physical and spiritual existence"—and called for greater recognition of the latter.[89] "Inasmuch as feelings and emotions have their basis in the body itself," wrote torts scholar Leon Green, it was "wholly unnecessary and impossible to separate the two." Green advocated the legal protection of such aspects of the self as one's "name, emotions, likeness and personal history."[90] Wrote professor Fowler Harper, "such dimensions of the persona could not be exposed or used by others without causing acute mental and emotional suffering."[91]

In law review pieces in the 1930s, William Prosser and Calvert Magruder, prominent and influential law professors, argued for a cause of action that would permit recovery for "pure" emotional distress—mental anguish in the absence of physical injuries. They claimed that the law, in actuality, already recognized such a tort, despite a formal position to the contrary. Among the cases they referred to were the "institutional insult" cases. Emotional distress damages had been awarded in these cases, even though the victims alleged no physical harm. The authors argued that courts should come forward and forthrightly recognize a tort for the intentional infliction of emotional distress rather than relying on "implied contract" rationales and other legal fictions.[92] The articles were subsequently cited by courts as justification for an independent tort action for intentional infliction of emotional distress, based on the principle "that one who, without just cause or excuse, and beyond all the bounds of decency, purposely causes a disturbance of another's mental and emotional tranquility of [an] acute nature . . . is subject to liability in damages for mental and emotional disturbance even though no demonstrable physical consequences actually ensue."[93] Emotional anguish included "all highly unpleasant mental reactions, such as fright, horror, grief, shame, humiliation, anger, embarrassment, chagrin, disappointment, worry, and nausea."[94] The intentional infliction of emotional distress tort permitted legal action against any person or entity, not only common carriers or commercial institutions, for seriously harming another's feelings. By 1936, twenty-one states allowed recovery for intentionally inflicted emotional distress in the absence of physical injury or an actionable assault or libel.[95] In 1948, the *Restatement of Torts*, a compilation of the law by a group of esteemed judges and lawyers under the aegis of the prestigious American Law Institute, recognized an independent tort action for intentional infliction of emotional distress.[96]

Many of the cases in which recovery was awarded for "pure" emotional distress did not involve shame or public embarrassment. In some states, a person could recover for the anguish caused by extremely upsetting acts committed by the defendant, regardless of whether anyone else witnessed them. Several cases involved the commission of a truly cruel or antisocial act, such as shooting a dog before the plaintiff, or a false report of the death of a loved one. The nature of the harm in these cases was shock and grief.[97]

However, a number of emotional distress cases were brought over acts of public shaming: false accusations of theft or cheating, imputations of unchaste conduct, and in one especially prominent genre in this time, aggressive and humiliating attempts at bill collection.[98] Shame had less purchase on the cultural psyche than it once did—the essence of shame was fear of moral disapprobation, a fear that diminished somewhat in the loosening moral climate of the twentieth century. But it was far from extinct as an animating emotion. Shame was commonly experienced around bodily issues—in particular, sexual shame—and also around poverty and debt, which were sensitive and morally charged, especially during the Great Depression.[99] In one case from 1934, a man won damages for shame and emotional distress from a collection agency that sent humiliating letters to his neighbors and employer announcing his unpaid debt.[100] A doctor brought a claim for emotional harm against the proprietor of an automobile garage who put in his window a large sign that read, "Dr. Morgan owes an account here of $49.67. And if promises would pay an account this account would be settled long ago."[101] In a few noted cases involving especially sympathetic plaintiffs, courts were also compensating a less serious kind of humiliation, namely, social embarrassment—when one was made to look foolish before others, but not for any morally culpable reason.

Carrie Nickerson, the plaintiff in the 1920 case *Nickerson v. Hodges*, was an unmarried forty-five-year-old woman, a former resident of an insane asylum, who lived near Shreveport, Louisiana. She came from a family that had, according to lore, buried a large amount of gold coin at an unidentified location. Nickerson was a traveling perfume saleswoman, and on one of her trips to the city, a "negro fortuneteller" told Nickerson that she knew where the fortune was buried. Nickerson proceeded to have a team dispatched to the divined location, a plot of land owned by the defendants, to dig up the gold. The crew spent several months digging with immense persistence. They dug all around the property—"around the roots of shade trees, the pillars of [the] house." The landowners, who had initially consented to the expedition, eventually tired of this.[102]

Disgusted, they buried a phony pot of gold for the explorers to find, as a practical joke. They took an old copper bucket, filled it with dirt and rocks, secured a lid to it, and then put a note on it, directing all heirs not to open it for three days. Nickerson found the pot and arranged for it to be shipped to a bank for safekeeping. It was her intent to open the treasure before a large crowd. Arrangements were made for the opening ceremony. At 11 AM on the scheduled day, the pot was taken out of the vault. In the words of the Supreme Court of Louisiana, "she was calm until the package was opened and the mocking earth and stones met her view." She became so enraged and violent that she had to be restrained.[103] Word of the hoax spread quickly throughout the area, adding to her humiliation.[104]

Nickerson brought suit against the landowners for $15,000. The case was delayed, and Nickerson died before judgment. The court permitted Nickerson's heirs to recover $500 for her emotional distress. In intentionally subjecting Nickerson to public humiliation, the landowners had transgressed norms of deference and respect towards a middle-class, middle-aged white woman. Vindication of Nickerson's embarrassment, the court concluded, was necessary to serve "the ends of justice."[105]

Privacy

The major development in image law was the growing judicial recognition of the tort of invasion of privacy. By 1940 the tort action for invasion of privacy, as a right to control one's public image, had been recognized in fifteen jurisdictions.[106] The *Restatement of Torts* acknowledged it in 1939: "a person who unreasonably and seriously interferes with another's interest in not having his affairs known to others or his likeness exhibited to the public is liable to the other," read its summation.[107] "In recent years the courts which have recognized the right of privacy for the first time have not felt obliged to indulge in lengthy apologia," observed the noted trial lawyer Louis Nizer in 1940. "This is the final stage in the acceptance of any new legal doctrine."[108]

Commentators described privacy, in all its meanings and senses, as assaulted, fragile, and under siege. As the *New York Times* lamented in 1931, privacy "belong[ed] on the museum shelf with the sorrowful relics of early Indian pottery and the statuary of the Greeks."[109] This was an era when the average person was getting used to both more and less privacy than in the past. Compared to life in the small towns of the nineteenth century, the city dweller had become accustomed to a substantial amount of isolation. He lived in close proximity to his neighbors, yet at the same time he was often a stranger to them. New communication technologies and the provision of social services by government institutions made it possible to function with a relative amount of anonymity, without deep involvement in, or dependence on, an intimate community. At the same time, those technologies and institutions enabled and even compelled people to expose large quantities of information about their private lives. Americans were becoming at the same time more private and more public; they simultaneously sought and shunned privacy and publicity, in contradictory, confusing, often inconsistent ways.

The modern bureaucratic state had been built on a mountain of personal data. Through the administration of the census, various surveys of economic and social conditions, and the income tax, the federal government was collecting vast quantities of personal information.[110] "If someone sees you in an automobile all he needs is the license number to find out you are the owner," complained a writer in the *Chicago Tribune*. "He can search the records and see what real estate you own . . . and personal taxes you pay."[111] As one writer noted in 1939, "the Federal Government last year sent out 135,000,000 questionnaires seeking exhaustive data on . . . the personal habits, condition, and conduct of citizens. . . . The government got intimate glimpses into the private lives of the other half by scanning the annual income-tax reports. . . . Each state, city, and county relief board . . . has snooped into tenement squalor to document the misery of millions of the nation's poor who are on relief."[112] In 1935, the Social Security program was created; an identification number was assigned to everyone, immediately spawning the problem of identity theft.[113]

Government and private employers were beginning to administer intelligence, personality, and vocational aptitude tests to potential employees, and new technologies posed formidable threats to one's right to be let alone. X-rays, polygraphs, hidden cameras, tiny recording devices, and other devices of detection and surveillance were coming into use, both for beneficial purposes—the prevention of crime and the arrest of disease—as well as for more nefarious aims, such as outright snooping. "The art of minding other's people business . . . has developed into a major industry, thanks to our modern mechanical equipment," quipped one journalist in 1932. "Diabolic invisible antennae now reach out everywhere to see and hear—almost to touch, taste, and smell—everything that goes on."[114] Courts were beginning to recognize a tort of "intrusion upon seclusion," a branch of the tort of invasion of privacy, which imposed liability for surreptitious information gathering and offensive intrusions into private spaces.[115]

But in an age before routine government wiretapping of private citizens—and before market research and consumer profiling turned private enterprise into major organs of surveillance—it was not government and industry, but the media that were seen as the greatest foe of personal privacy. "The newspaper dares rush in where government fears to tread," wrote critic Silas Bent. "The privacy of the home is safe from secret service invasion without warrant . . . ; but against reportorial invasion . . . there seems no adequate recourse."[116] "The klieg lights spare nobody, high or low."[117] The mass media were seen as particularly threatening to privacy and personal image, as they not only gathered large quantities of personal information but distributed that information far and wide, to the world's newsstands, theaters, breakfast tables, and living rooms.

∽

By the 1930s, the mass media had become a vast apparatus for the creation, dissemination, and display of personal images. The human interest style of journalism —the reporting of the news with a focus on personal life, as a "popular literature of true stories"—continued to flourish.[118] As the *North American Review* commented in 1937, there was great popular demand for "detailed, intimate information" about "who [people] are, . . . what they do," and especially "what they look like."[119] The period between the two world wars saw the tremendous expansion of the visual media. Photojournalism, or "pictorial journalism," was born in this era, and several significant national publications, including the popular magazines *Life* and *Look*, were devoted to reporting the news through pictures.[120] Almost all of the nation's approximately seventeen thousand movie theaters showed newsreels prior to the feature film.[121] By 1938, a third of an average daily newspaper's content consisted of pictures.[122] As a result of photojournalism and the newsreel, the "picture [was] more powerful than the word in the society of today."[123]

Handheld Kodak cameras had been in use since the early twentieth century, but in 1928 the "candid camera," a Kodak with a superfast shutter and flashbulb, was developed. The candid camera gave rise to a formidable paparazzi, notorious for its "hounding, spying, bribing, stealing, [and] camera-clicking."[124] Among some sectors of the press, the stalking of celebrities and other famous people became de rigueur.[125] Assigned to get a "pose" for a story, photographers were known to scrap any "code of ethical practice they may have had in their mind," observed one editor. "The photographer finds that he must be aggressive, sometimes offensively so."[126] During the notorious press coverage of famous aviator Charles Lindbergh in the early 1930s, reporters "descended upon [his] household, prying, spying, and trespassing in a ruthless stampede for news."[127] A photographer for the *New York Mirror*, intent on getting a picture of Lindbergh's son, forced off the road an automobile in which the child was a passenger. He got the picture, was praised, and won a bonus from his paper.[128]

Newspaper and film cameramen patrolled the city seeking interesting material: accidents, crimes, unusual faces. The staple of the movie newsreel was the ubiquitous street scene, in which unsuspecting subjects were photographed for display on the big screen, often in close-up. "No longer is it necessary to be spectacular in order to face the camera," observed the *New York Times* in 1931. "Now the newsreel companies search out their material, and youth, going for a stroll in the park, may suddenly find himself as part of a human interest sequence called 'Under a Lovers' Moon.'"[129] Media outlets seized on any public event or occurrence as an opportunity to publicize the "true stories" of the people involved in them. If a person assumed office or "built a better mousetrap than his neighbor," the media "will make newsreels of him and his wife in beach pajamas, it will discuss his diet and his health . . . it will publicize him, analyze him, photograph him, and make his life thoroughly miserable by feeding to the public [personal] details," noted the *American Mercury* in 1935.[130] While some publications had editorial rules against publishing facts about people only obliquely related to a newsworthy event—the *Brooklyn Eagle*, for example, did not print the names of the family members of criminals—others dragged even these tangential figures into the spotlight.[131] Across the media landscape, "instant celebrities" were being created every day, thrust before the public gaze, willingly or unwillingly.

What fueled this engine was curiosity about people and their personal lives, translated into circulation figures and dollars and cents. The more isolated Americans became from each other—secluded in their private residences, uprooted from traditional communities, and estranged from their neighbors—the more they sought to penetrate other people's privacy. As the *Washington Post* noted, readers were no longer as interested in finding out the president's stand on the tariff as they were "in knowing what he eats for breakfast and if he shaves himself."[132] A survey of national magazine articles written about actors, politicians, and other famous people in the 1940s observed that most of the stories focused not on their public accomplishments, but their personal activities.[133] Standard fare in these "human interest" publications, by today's standards, was relatively innocuous; although the marriages and divorces of public figures were reported, sexual affairs were generally off limits. Press outlets self-censored truly intimate details likely to offend readers' sensibilities in this still somewhat sheltered era.[134]

Audiences wanted to gawk, to peer in on others' lives, even to be voyeurs, but were upset when the gaze was turned back on them.[135] There was massive public criticism of media invasions of privacy—what one critic described as the "current doctrine . . . that the greatest good of the greatest number requires the immolation of a daily quota of private lives on the altar of publicity."[136] As one unwilling victim of publicity told a reporter: "I don't think it's fair, or good Americanism, to make snapshot pictures of unwilling persons and print them. I think that is stealing, just as much as stealing one's personal property. I think one's personal appearance is one's own, and I think that no one has a right to take that appearance in a picture without permission."[137] There were still people who "do not want to be dangled before the eyes of [the public] . . . or have their domestic affairs broadcast from coast to coast by glib radio gossips, or their names or pictures used to advertise candy, gum, toothpaste, or cigarettes."[138] The American Society of Newspaper Editors was so concerned by the outcry around privacy that it went on a public relations campaign, reminding readers that the profession, in its 1923 code of ethics, had pledged not to "invade private rights or feelings without sure warrant of public right as distinguished from public curiosity."[139] Editors justified invasions of privacy in the name of the public's right to know the news. "How can rotten government be exposed, or dirty business methods brought to light, without unfettered expression?" they asked. "If some innocent person gets hurt in the process, it is still for the public good."[140] These pronouncements failed to soothe public outrage.

To be clear, it was not total solitude, concealment, or anonymity that people wanted, but rather selective self-exposure. In an age when actors and other performers were seen as cultural heroes and models, celebrated for their personal lifestyles, publicity of one's private affairs was not always unwelcome, intrusive, or annoying. A writer in 1939 noted the "public eagerness to express opinions and pose for pictures for Inquiring Reporters who roam the large cities" and the "willingness of people to . . . surrender intimate secrets to radio personalities who exploit them on the air."[141] In a celebrity culture, a culture of exposure, being thrust into the spotlight for one's proverbial fifteen minutes of notoriety was, for some, an appealing possibility. "The pendulum has swung far since the hyper-reticent days of our grandmothers . . . the majority have lost all desire for privacy, either for themselves or for anyone else. They step eagerly into the range of every newspaper and movie camera, and send in their names by the thousand to have them announced over the radio," observed the *Atlantic Monthly* in 1932.[142] Many of the "gregarious millions" "crave to be lifted out of the morass of anonymity."[143] They believed that "any publicity, even though unfavorable, is better than none at all."[144] When the 1940 census added questions about income, educational level, and marital status, there was talk that this was an invasion of privacy. First Lady Eleanor Roosevelt defended the changes, noting that people no longer minded discussing their age, income, and whether they had been divorced.[145]

Regardless of whether one sought fame or was content in the confines of a narrower world, control over one's publicity and public image—the ability to put one's own "spin" on one's persona—was critical. People wanted to express themselves to others, to be publicly visible, and to create a public image, but on their own terms. Writers discussed the importance of a broad legal right to control one's image and the insufficiencies of the law of libel. "The whole force of the law of slander and libel is directed towards protecting the individual's reputation—a thing separate and apart from his personal feelings," noted the legal commentator Mitchell Dawson, writing in the *Atlantic*. "His reputation is the estimate which others have of him, and not the opinion which he has of himself. His good name, as a legal concept, has taken on an almost tangible character, and the subjective injury which may be done to him through spoken or written words, even though they shrivel his very soul, is of no particular moment in the eyes of the law." "If some unhappy person has a wart on the end of his nose, you may call attention to it in print or publish his photograph, wart and all, for circulation among a million readers, without any fear of liability for libel."[146] Defamation law was "hopelessly inadequate" to protect the individual's right to his image in the face of "multiplying hordes of newsmongers," and a right to privacy was essential.[147]

⌒

Although a number of cases in the 1930s and 1940s were brought over the exploitation of personal images in advertising, much of the action in privacy litigation in this time involved news and entertainment media—articles, books, newsreels, and films that published people's pictures and discussed their personalities, activities, and idiosyncrasies. A few involved the publication of deeply intimate, personal material. In 1939, *Time* magazine published an article titled "Starving Glutton" about a woman who had a metabolic disorder that led her to eat huge quantities without gaining weight. The picture published with the article, taken by a reporter over the woman's protests, showed Dorothy Barber in bed in a long-sleeved hospital gown. Captions under the picture read, "Insatiable Eater Barber, She Eats for Ten." Barber sued for invasion of privacy and won $3,000 at trial.

"Certainly if there is any right of privacy at all, it should include the right to obtain medical treatment at home or in a hospital for an individual personal condition . . . without personal publicity," the Missouri Supreme Court concluded, upholding the judgment.[148]

Yet the majority of privacy cases did not involve publications that were especially private. Truly intimate depictions—deeply personal gossip, explicit stories about people's romantic affairs, lurid photographs—were typically not the subject of lawsuits; the mainstream media for the most part did not trade in such matter, and legal action would only attract further attention to the sensitive, embarrassing material. Instead, most privacy cases involved situations where people had been presented in a manner they found unfavorable, misrepresentative, upsetting, or annoying, even though the activities portrayed were not especially scandalous, personal, or secret. A number of privacy suits, for example, involved photographs of a person taken on the street and published without consent. In these cases, the law of privacy had very little to do with "privacy." No exposure of "private life" had occurred. The right to privacy, plaintiffs claimed, was a right to not be depicted in a fashion that contradicted their desired self-presentation "under circumstances which are complimentary as well as those which are critical," as one court put it.[149] "Privacy" was about the right to choose one's own audiences, about shielding people from publicity that clashed with how they wanted to be known to others.

In the 1929 case *Jones v. Herald Post*, Lillian Jones witnessed her husband assaulted and stabbed to death on the street, and she tried to fight back against the attackers. She sued for invasion of privacy when the *Louisville Herald Post* published her picture with a truthful account of her heroic efforts. She claimed that the publication was offensive to her.[150] In *Hillman v. Star Publishing*, a young woman sued the *Seattle Star* for invasion of privacy when it ran her photo along with an article about her father's arrest for mail fraud. "Hillman Accused of Fraud. Warrant for Big Real Estate Shark. Federal Officials Are Hot on His Trail," read the headline. She claimed that this caused her "shame, humiliation, and a sense of disgrace."[151]

The plaintiff in *Blumenthal v. Picture Classics* was an elderly widow, a bread vendor, who sued over newsreel footage that depicted her selling her wares on the streets of the Lower East Side. The footage was a candid, unaltered street scene, part of a newsreel titled "Sight Seeing in New York with Nick and Tony." She was in the film for a total of six seconds. The woman complained that the portrayal was "foolish, unnatural, and undignified" and an invasion of privacy.[152] In *Sweenek v. Pathe*, from 1936, a woman claimed that unauthorized newsreel footage taken of her in an exercise course for overweight women was an invasion of privacy under the New York privacy statute because the footage was "for the purpose of trade" and was embarrassing.[153]

~

In 1926, author Edna Ferber, in her best-selling book *Show Boat*, had written about a character named Wayne Damron. Damron "opened the Black Diamond Saloon and on the day of the grand opening threw the keys into the waters of the river." Since that day the saloon had never been closed. A man named Wayne Damron, from a small town in Mississippi, filed a complaint against Ferber in 1927, claiming that his public image had been injured.[154] Damron alleged that he was a respectable citizen, a father, a member of a church, and had never been part of the saloon business. In the 398-page story, Damron's name was mentioned in one place.[155]

After an army plane crashed into the Empire State Building in 1945, a seventeen-year-old assistant pharmacist's mate in the Coast Guard, Donald Molony, evacuated victims from the burning building. Molony was awarded a Medal of Valor and featured in newspapers, newsreels, and magazines. In a magazine titled "Boy Comics," a series of cartoons showed Molony "procuring morphine, hypodermics, and first-aid kits from a drug store, giving first aid to an elevator girl who sustained severe burns, . . . and carrying out survivors." The depiction was celebratory, but Molony was upset. He claimed that there were inaccuracies in the illustration of his uniform, and that the comics were exaggerated in how they described some of his feats—suggesting, for example, that he had carried out two women at a time. These mistakes probably had no effect on the public's opinion of him, though they may have led to teasing by his friends. He sued for "invasion of privacy."[156]

Several years earlier, a radio operator, John Binns, had been involved in a shipwreck rescue. Binns's pioneering use of wireless telegraphy had saved hundreds of lives. Binns was celebrated in the major media outlets of the time. A newsreel company, in a staged reenactment of Binns's heroic deeds, used an actor to depict him. The depiction was not to his liking. Binns thought it was excessively dramatic and cartoonish, as it depicted him "in a ridiculous posture, smiling and smoking a cigarette, and winking and making grimaces for the amusement of the spectators." He sued for invasion of privacy, and a jury awarded $12,500 in damages.[157]

$\sim$

Some of these lawsuits—though certainly not all—could be described as fairly petty. Law professor Harry Kalven Jr. believed that most parties who came forward with privacy claims had "shabby, unseemly grievances and an interest in exploitation." "I suspect that fascination with the great Brandeis trade mark, excitement over the law at a point of growth, and appreciation of privacy as a key value have combined to dull the normal critical sense of judges and commentators and have caused them not to see the pettiness of the tort they have sponsored," he wrote in an article titled "Privacy in Tort Law—Were Warren and Brandeis Wrong?"[158]

Even the most seemingly "thin skinned" of these plaintiffs were not necessarily insincere or duplicitous, however. Although we can't know for sure, the men and women presented in an inaccurate or otherwise displeasing manner in various newsreels, comic strips, and articles may well have been hurt. Trial records, court opinions, and other documentary evidence from these lawsuits suggest that plaintiffs were indeed wounded and suffered embarrassment, insult, and distress.[159]

This sense of injury and affront is a testament to the image-consciousness of the time. Only in a culture where people feel deeply possessive and protective of their public images will such misrepresentations, even if objectively benign, be experienced as serious harms. Only in a culture that has invested great importance in images, that has freighted public images with such emotional and psychological weight, will the law recognize such harms and take them seriously. The law tracked the cultural focus on images, and in recognizing these "privacy" claims as worthy of judicial attention, and in some cases monetary judgments, courts validated, even heightened the image-conscious sensibility and contributed to the construction of the image-focused self.

~

Sympathetic to the importance of public image, and plaintiffs' interests in controlling and shaping their public personas, courts provided relief in a number of cases. Mrs. Blumenthal, the elderly bread vendor, and John Binns, the radio operator, mentioned above, won the sympathy of the judges and juries who heard their stories.[160] So did Louise Peed. Mrs. Peed was found unconscious in the apartment of a man who was not her husband, the victim of what the newspapers described as a "carelessly closed gas jet." The circumstances surrounding the incident are unclear. The *Washington Times* published a picture of Peed under the headline, "Two Gas Victims Recover Rapidly," along with a short story about the accident. Peed sued the newspaper; the defendant's motion to dismiss was rejected. "If the right to one's person is a right of complete immunity, to be let alone, then it would be seriously impaired if without his consent a picture of his person could be obtained by another and published in a newspaper," concluded the court. It mocked the newspaper's efforts to invoke freedom of the press as a defense: that liberty did not carry with it the "privilege of invading any . . . right of the citizen," including one's right to keep one's embarrassing misfortunes out of the papers.[161]

In 1948 the *Saturday Evening Post* ran an article titled "Never Give a Passenger a Break." The piece attacked the "haughty" cabbies of Washington, D.C., and accused them of cheating their customers. The story was filled with anecdotes about insulting, abusive, exploitative cabdrivers who took advantage of "poor trusting visitor[s]."[162] Several photographs ran with the article. One depicted a smiling, well-dressed woman talking to the article's author on the street. The caption read, "The lady cabby, by local standards, is unusually formal—[but] customers could guess from her cap that she drives a hack."[163] The caption did not explicitly name the woman, Muriel Peay, and the article did not refer to her. Peay had apparently posed for the photo but was not told how it would be used. She was offended at having her image exploited in this false and embarrassing context, and she sued for invasion of privacy.[164]

A federal district court held that Peay had a valid privacy claim. Innocent people like Muriel Peay, whose public image had been injured through no fault of their own, needed the law's protection against "undue and undesirable publicity." "When Brandeis and Warren wrote in 1890, it was the unseemly intrusions of a portion of the press into the privacy of the home that was emphasized as the main source of evil."[165] But "modern life with its accompanying increase in public media of communication, such as newspapers, monthly and weekly magazines, moving pictures, radio, and television, has created novel situations . . . [and] the potentialities" for invasions of privacy "are now greatly multiplied," the court observed.[166] It concluded that the publication of a photograph of a private person without consent violated the "privacy" right to one's public image.[167]

∽

Other privacy plaintiffs were unsuccessful. Wayne Damron, Donald Molony, Mrs. Sweenek, and Lillian Jones, mentioned above, all lost their lawsuits. At the same time that courts were recognizing a right to one's image which made embarrassing or distressing media representations legally actionable, they were also acknowledging another kind of image right: the right of publishers, writers, and filmmakers to depict people's likenesses and life stories, and the public's right to consume them.

Two ideals were coming into conflict. The law's increasing protection of people's public images, and popular support for a right to one's image, reflected a growing legal and cultural commitment to the ideal of self-expression. A right to express one's thoughts and beliefs—to publicly proclaim one's self and fashion one's own public identity and persona—was being recognized in various legal contexts in this time, including the constitutional law of religious freedom and freedom of speech. In a series of cases in the 1930s and 1940s, the Supreme Court invalidated the convictions of racial, political, and religious minorities who had been arrested under various state and municipal statutes for participating in communist meetings and rallies or distributing religious literature.[168] In *Cantwell v. Connecticut* (1940), the Court held that the arrest of a Jehovah's Witness for publicly playing a phonograph record with religious messages violated the man's right under the First and Fourteenth Amendments to freely communicate his beliefs and opinions.[169]

In the 1943 case *West Virginia State Board of Education v. Barnette*, the Court held a compulsory flag salute in a public school to be unconstitutional under the First Amendment, noting that "if there is any fixed star in our constitutional constellation, it is that no official, high or petty, can prescribe what shall be orthodox in politics, nationalism, religion, or other matters of opinion or force citizens to confess by word or act their faith therein."[170] Freedom of conscience and a right to profess one's self-chosen faith and identity were being cast as essential, constitutionally protected rights of personhood. Freedom of speech "became closely associated with the intertwined ideals of creative self-fulfillment (freedom to express oneself) and equality (freedom from discrimination or oppression)," writes historian G. Edward White. "Free democratic speech . . . signified the power of the human actor, liberated from the dominance of external forces, free to determine his or her individual destiny, required only to respect the freedoms of others."[171]

In tension with this right to express oneself and create one's own identity was a countervailing interest: people's right to make images of other people. In a culture where politics and social life were being transacted through images, where media images had become the common currency of social exchange, the ability to freely depict individuals and public affairs was said to be critical to the vigorous public discourse—the open exchange of ideas—that was beginning to be described as a central value of the First Amendment. We will be exploring this in greater depth in the next chapter. By the 1940s, imposing liability for truthful commentary about a person, even if deeply distressing to him, was coming to be seen as a form of state control over expression reminiscent of the totalitarian governments in Europe and Asia, against which the United States was at war.[172]

As in the libel context, courts were registering this free speech sensibility in the privacy law privilege for publishing "matters of public concern." As we've seen, Warren and Brandeis, and early courts adjudicating privacy cases, recognized a privilege that would exempt from liability the publication of "matters of public interest," or "matters of public concern." Before the 1930s, the definition of a "matter of public concern" had been narrow. Facts about "public figures"—politicians, public officials, actors—could be reported on so long as they bore directly on their professional duties and activities and were not "prurient" or "idle gossip" about their personal lives. Likewise, information about individuals involved in an important public event, such as a crime or a catastrophe, could be published so long as the details were pertinent to the event and did not constitute prying for curiosity's sake. What was a matter of "public concern" or "public interest" was not what actually *interested* the public—for then gossip and sensationalism might be immune—but rather what judges believed the public *should* know, in its own best interest.

In the 1930s and 1940s, courts began to expand the "matters of public interest" privilege. In the *Sweenek v. Pathe* case, the United States District Court for the Eastern District of New York held that newsreel footage of the overweight women's exercise course was a matter of legitimate "public interest," as it apparently interested—that is, piqued the curiosity—of its audiences. "It seems reasonably clear that pictures of a group of corpulent women attempting to reduce with the aid of some rather novel and unique apparatus" was a subject of "public interest," "at least so long as a large proportion of the female sex continues its concern about any increase in poundage," the court concluded.[173] Other sorts of purely entertaining, titillating material, such as a highly sensationalistic account of a criminal trial, tidbits in gossip columns, and dramatized accounts of crimes in detective magazines, were said to be matters of legitimate "public interest" that could be published freely, even if the individuals depicted in them were unwilling to be publicized.[174] For judges to create their own definition of "matters of public interest," one that overrode the media's publishing decisions and, implicitly, the public's consumption choices, was to some courts an impermissible censorship of the press.[175]

In a few decisions courts equated "matters of public interest" with "newsworthy" material and adopted an expansive definition of "the news." If something appeared in a newsreel, newspaper, or magazine—any publication that professed to be a "news" outlet—it was by definition a "newsworthy" "matter of public interest" and protected under the privilege. News, wrote a federal district court in 1936, included "all events and occurrences which have that indefinable quality of interest, which attracts public attention."[176] A report of a child custody proceeding, an article about a performer of "rope tricks," and a dramatized radio broadcast about a man's mysterious disappearance ten years earlier were all deemed to be "newsworthy."[177] As a New York trial court noted in the 1937 case *Lahiri v. Daily Mirror*, a right of privacy that imposed liability for "news items and articles of general public interest, educational and informative in character," implicated the rights of a "free press."[178]

Because there was great curiosity over public figures' private lives, their personal affairs were often "matters of public interest," said some courts. As such, public figures—defined as those who submitted themselves to "public approval"—had very little in the way of privacy. As the authors of the *Restatement of Torts* concluded, the public figure must "pay the price of even unwelcome publicity through reports upon his private life and photographic reproductions of himself and his family."[179] According to some courts, even ordinary people "waived" their right to privacy when they went into public places or were involved in "matters of public interest." "One who is not a recluse," according to the *Restatement*, must expect commentary on "the ordinary incidents of community life of which he is a part. These include comment upon his conduct, the more or less casual observation of his neighbors as to what he does upon his own land and the possibility that he may be photographed as a part of a street scene or a group of persons."[180] In *Jones v. Herald Post*, involving the woman who tried to attack her husband's murderer, the court concluded that the woman had, albeit unwillingly, become an "innocent actor in a great tragedy in which the public had a deep concern," and as such, it was not an invasion of privacy to publish her photograph.[181] In 1939, a California appeals court held that the husband of a woman who committed suicide by jumping off a building in downtown Los Angeles had no cause of action against the *Examiner* for publishing a photo of the suicide; the woman had willingly given up her right to privacy by virtue of killing herself in a public place.[182] Insofar as they generated public interest or curiosity, there was "no invasion of a right of privacy in the description of the ordinary goings and comings of a person or of weddings, even though intended to be entirely private."[183]

Not everyone in the legal world endorsed this expansive view of privileged material. To some, the public's interest in learning about people and public affairs, and the right of the press to convey that information, did not justify interfering with a person's public image when that interference created serious emotional or psychic harm. A battle was underway. The ideals of modern expressive freedom cut both ways: liberty meant the right to express oneself through one's image, and at the same time the freedom to make images of others. This tension would trouble courts, lawyers, legal theorists, and the public in the coming decades. When were the media justified in overriding people's right to create their own images? Could *the right to one's image* and *the freedom to image* be reconciled?

CHAPTER 7

The Freedom to Image

Sidis v. The New Yorker

In the years before World War I, William James Sidis was widely regarded as the most impressive child prodigy the world had ever seen. Sidis attended Harvard at eleven, spoke several languages, and was a mathematical genius. Between 1910 and 1920, he was an international celebrity, publicized in media around the world, and renowned for his intellectual feats. At the age of two and a half he could write both English and French on a typewriter. In grade school his mastery of complex mathematics approached the level of Harvard professors. It was speculated that his IQ was near 250. Headlines pronounced him a "boy wonder."

Yet as an adult, Sidis's life took a different turn. He neglected his mathematical talents and entirely retreated from public life. By the age of twenty, Sidis had become a recluse. At thirty-nine, he was an adding-machine operator living alone in a shabby Boston rooming house. Sidis was awkward and unkempt. He devoted his free time to collecting streetcar transfers and trivia about an obscure Native American tribe. The *New Yorker* tracked him down in his apartment, interviewed him, and wrote up his story in the magazine in 1937. The piece described his personal eccentricities in vivid detail. Humiliated and outraged, Sidis sued the *New Yorker* under the tort of invasion of privacy for the injuries to his feelings caused by the publication of true but embarrassing personal information.

Sidis sought to vindicate himself through the lawsuit. His admitted motive was to punish the *New Yorker* for interfering with his right to control his public image and "to be let alone." But in the hands of the magazine's lawyers, the case of William James Sidis versus *The New Yorker* became an important test case in an emerging battle between the right to privacy and freedom of speech. The case, filed in federal district court, was resolved in the Second Circuit Court of Appeals in 1940. The Second Circuit concluded that the magazine was not liable to Sidis, and that the tarnishing of Sidis's public image was an inevitable sacrifice to be made for the *New Yorker*'s right to publish freely and the public's "right to know" about the fate of a former celebrity. "Regrettably or not," the court wrote, "the misfortunes and frailties of neighbors and public figures" were subjects of "interest" to the public. As such, "it would be unwise for a court to bar their expression in the newspapers, books, and magazines of the day."[1]

This chapter tells the story of *Sidis v. F. R. Publishing*, a milestone in the history of privacy and personal image law in the United States. Fifty years after the "invention" of the privacy tort, *Sidis* was the first decision from a high federal court to imply that the right to privacy could be limited in the interest of freedom of speech. *Sidis* suggested that the right of the individual to control and express his own public image impinged on arguably more important rights: the right of publishers to make and circulate images of people, and the right of the public to consume those images.[2]

〜

William James Sidis was born on April 1, 1898—April Fools' Day, as he liked to say. His father, Boris Sidis, had emigrated to New York from the Ukraine in 1886 to escape political persecution; his mother, Sarah Mandelbaum Sidis, came to the United States in 1889. Boris Sidis earned his degrees at Harvard and taught psychology there, performing pioneering work in abnormal psychology. William was named after his godfather, Boris's friend and colleague, the American philosopher William James.[3]

Boris was a dedicated and prolific scholar. Almost as soon as William could talk, he became a subject for Boris's psychological investigations. Boris trained William to spell and read at a very young age. He could read the *New York Times* at eighteen months. Before he was five, he could recite all the hours and stations on a complex railroad timetable. Integral and infinitesimal calculus became his hobbies. When he was nine, he worked out a new system of logarithms based on twelve instead of ten. Boris published several papers in scientific journals describing his son's achievements and a book, *Philistine and Genius*, which used William's success story to praise homeschooling and critique the deficiencies of American public education.[4]

By the time *Philistine and Genius* was published in 1911, William was well known to the American public. Having got word of his amazing feats when the boy was only a small child, the press publicized him as "the most remarkable boy prodig[y] of whom there is record."[5] When he was three or four, he was featured in the popular magazine *North American Review*. At the age of six, when he was sent to a Brookline public school and went through seven years of schooling in six months, accounts of his activities were written up in the *Boston Transcript* and the *Boston Herald*. When he briefly attended high school, he was hounded by reporters. According to Sidis biographer Amy Wallace, "if [reporters] succeeded in finding him alone, one would pounce and hold him while another took his picture."[6]

What really brought William into the public eye was his enrollment at Harvard at the age of eleven. Sidis set a record in 1909 by becoming the youngest person to enroll at that university in its history. His story was splashed across the front pages of the nation's newspapers. The press offered predictions for a brilliant future, that the "boyish hand busily writing examination papers today at Harvard may well be ordained to push away the veil from some great fact or some mighty truth for which the world is waiting."[7] When young Sidis lectured an audience of professors at the Harvard mathematical club on his theory of four-dimensional bodies, he became a true celebrity. Newspapers across the country assigned reporters to cover "the Sidis case."[8]

The press was fascinated with the nature-nurture question: was Sidis naturally brilliant, or was his father's rigorous training behind his success? Many believed that Sidis was a testament to innovative child-rearing methods, that he was a "normal boy trained from his earliest years to think vigorously."[9] Several hundred newspaper editorials and educational articles between 1910 and 1912 used Sidis as evidence to show that public schools were "wasting time, fostering bad habits and in general doing more harm than good."[10] William's supporters went to great lengths to demonstrate that despite his genius, he was still a normal child. There were extensive discussions in the press of his personality and home life. "Apart from his marvelous brain and his extraordinary love of study," he was an average boy, explained one article. "There is no evidence that his studies have undermined his health. On the contrary, he seems to enjoy enviable bodily vigor."[11]

Yet others doubted the "rosy cheeks of the little Sidis boy."[12] While many observers predicted "wonderful achievements in the years to come," others feared that he would suffer "a breaking down physically and mentally." Critics described Sidis as the product of a brutal "scientific forcing experiment."[13] A 1911 article in

Science magazine, titled "Popular Misconceptions Concerning Precocity in Children," feared that false reports that William was well adjusted and had not been "robbed of [his] childhood" would lead to similar, and ultimately damaging efforts by parents to home-grow their own geniuses.[14]

These pessimistic assessments were probably more accurate. William was not a healthy boy. Even more destructive than the pressure from his father was the constant hounding by the press. Sidis sought refuge from the media attention in his hobbies and studies. Yet, as his biographer writes, the more he "hungered for privacy," "the more famous he became, and the more reporters hounded him."[15] The result was a nervous breakdown in 1910, not long after the famous Math Club lecture.[16]

The breakdown was widely publicized. Newspapers reported that William was seriously ill, and there were rumors that he would never return to Cambridge to complete his studies. Friends of the family asserted that "too great mental exertion" had a "great deal to do with the boy's sudden collapse."[17] His father was running a sanatorium in Portsmouth, New Hampshire, at the time, and William was rushed off there. When he finally came back to Harvard, he was retiring and shy. He could not lecture again, and he began to show a marked distrust of people and a fear of responsibility.[18]

But the media interest in Sidis did not relent. Shortly after his graduation from Harvard, he granted an interview to the *Boston Herald*. The interviewer went into depth on the subject of sixteen-year-old Sidis's sex life, and got Sidis to explain in detail his "solemn vow of celibacy."[19] The *New York Times* obtained the revealing interview, and before long other media outlets were commenting on his celibacy vow and joking about it.[20] After graduation, Sidis took a graduate student teaching position in mathematics at Rice University in Houston. News of his escapades in Texas—in particular his social blunders—was channeled back to the major East Coast papers. The *Boston Herald, New York Morning Telegraph,* and *New York Times,* among other outlets, ran stories about Sidis's bad manners, his awkwardness with women, and how he was mercilessly teased by his fellow students. Depressed, Sidis quit Rice and came back to Boston, where he enrolled at Harvard Law School. For unknown reasons he dropped out during his third year.[21]

Sidis fell out of the media spotlight briefly, until 1919, when he was arrested under the Espionage Act for participating in a socialist demonstration in which he had carried the hated red flag. He was sentenced to eighteen months in jail for inciting to riot and assault but was kept out of jail because of a deal that Boris struck with the prosecutor. The media covered the arrest and trial. "Evidently intellectual prodigy," quipped one journal, "is not always a moral prodigy." The publicity put Sidis back into his parents' sanatorium. In his early twenties, he emerged from their care and took up life on his own.[22]

Sidis drifted from city to city, working for subsistence wages as a clerk. In 1924 a reporter found him working in an office on Wall Street for twenty-three dollars a week, and the news made headlines.[23] The *New York Herald Tribune* exposed his identity in an article titled "Boy Brain Prodigy of 1909 Now $23 a Week Adding Machine Clerk." The reporter wrote of the "tragedy that young Sidis represents."[24] The article prompted a snide editorial in the *New York Times* called "Precocity Doesn't Wear Well": "the mental fires that burned so brightly have died down, to all appearances."[25] "Is It Too Bad If Your Child's a Prodigy?" was the title of an article that described Sidis's upbringing as a "sad mistake."[26] Sidis's rediscovery, according to the *Education Review*, led to a "perfect orgy of . . . triumph" by those who had criticized the overambitious parents of precocious children.[27]

After this first "rediscovery," Sidis plunged back into anonymity. In 1926, he published a book on his hobby of collecting streetcar transfers, titled "Notes on the Collection of Transfers," under a pseudonym, Frank Folupa. He continued to work as a clerk and boasted of his ability to operate an adding machine with great speed and accuracy. He had what biographer Wallace described as a "comfortable existence" out of the spotlight.[28] He wrote novels and pursued studies on a variety of unusual topics, including the Okamakammesset Native American tribe. From his rented room in a Boston boardinghouse, he gave lectures to friends on his various bizarre interests. He was well liked, though eccentric—unkempt, talkative, and graceless. He also demonstrated an extraordinary resentment of his genius past. When his father died in 1927, he did not attend the funeral. He refused whatsoever to talk about his childhood. When asked by acquaintances if he was the "boy genius," he barked at them angrily and ran out of the room.[29]

In August 1937, Sidis's "carefully built fortress of anonymity" came under siege when the *New Yorker* magazine published an article about him.[30] The story, titled "Where Are They Now? April Fool!" was presented as an intimate, firsthand account of Sidis as observed by a visitor to his apartment, a writer by the name of

"Jared Manley." As Judge Clark of the Second Circuit would later observe, the *New Yorker* article was entertaining, well written, and had "considerable popular news interest."[31] It was also snide, mocking, and condescending. But that was par for the course for the magazine, which advertised itself as sophisticated and witty, fashionably avant-garde, and "not meant for your old aunt in Dubuque."[32]

∿

In the 1930s, the *New Yorker* was a rising star in the world of popular publishing. Started in 1925, the magazine had become one of the nation's best-known magazines of literary and feature journalism, with a staff that included some of the most talented writers of the day. Between 1930 and 1940, it was experiencing rapid growth. In 1937, its circulation was 133,000; it would gain an additional 15,000 by 1940. Its stock-in-trade was literary profiles of famous people, lightweight feature articles, and "human interest" stories written with a cynical, caustic edge.[33]

In 1937 the magazine was running a "Where Are They Now?" series, profiles of "once famous front-page figures who had been lost to public view for considerable lengths of time."[34] The series played on the public's fascination with has-beens, the casualties of celebrity culture, and the fickleness of fame. A young and fairly unseasoned reporter, Barbara Linscott, interviewed Sidis in his apartment. Sidis had apparently consented to the interview but was unaware that it would be written up into a magazine article. Linscott wrote the initial draft of the article. James Thurber, the noted cartoonist, humorist, and essayist, did the rewrite, and the article bears his pen name, "Jared L. Manley." The famed writer and critic A. J. Liebling also contributed to the piece.[35]

As Thurber wrote, "William James Sidis lives today at the age of 39 in a hall bedroom of Boston's shabby South End."

> William Sidis at 39 is a large, heavy man, with a prominent jaw, thickish neck, and a reddish mustache. . . . He seems to have difficulty in finding the right words to express himself, but when he does, he speaks rapidly, nodding his head jerkily to emphasize his points, gesturing with his left hand, uttering occasionally a curious, gasping laugh. He seems to get a great and ironic enjoyment out of leading a life of wandering irresponsibility after a childhood of scrupulous regimentation. His visitor found in him a certain childlike charm.[36]

The piece noted that Sidis was employed as a clerk and that he sought such menial work because he refused to make use of his talents. "The very sight of a mathematical formula makes me physically ill," he had reportedly said. "All I want to do is run an adding machine." He said he never stayed long at any job because one of his fellow employees inevitably found out that he was the former "boy wonder," and he became so uncomfortable that he had to leave. When a person asked him "point-blank about his infant precocity, and insisted on a demonstration of his mathematical prowess, Sidis was restrained with difficulty from throwing him out of the room."[37] The article also lampooned his obsessions with streetcar transfers and the "history of the Okamakammesset tribe." "He has written some booklets on Okamakammesset lore and history, and if properly urged, will recite Okamakammesset poetry and even sing Okamakammesset songs. He admitted that his study of the Okamakammessets is an outgrowth of his interest in socialism." The reporter brought up the prediction of a professor at MIT in 1910 that Sidis would be a great mathematician and a famous leader in the world of science. "It's strange," he said with a grin, "but you know, I was born on April Fools' Day."[38]

Thurber claimed that he had wanted to use the article to make a point; he had hoped "that the piece would help to curb the great American thrusting of talented children into the glare of fame or notoriety, a procedure in so many cases disastrous to the later career and happiness of the exploited youngsters."[39] And yet the piece did exactly that—it thrust Sidis back into the spotlight—and in the process set off the fury of a man who thought he had the power to fight back.

◇

Sidis sued. Immediately after the article came out, Sidis contacted a lawyer and announced his intent to take the *New Yorker* to court. He did not want money, he asserted. Rather, he sought only vengeance: to punish the magazine for the unwanted and embarrassing publicity. To Sidis, the *New Yorker*'s act was the culmination of years of exploitation by the press. Sidis believed that a victorious lawsuit against the magazine would not only vindicate him personally, but make an important public statement condemning the abuses of the media, their exploitation of personal reputation and dignity in the pursuit of circulation and profit. Sidis saw the battle against the *New Yorker*, as he wrote to an old friend from his socialist days, as a possible "victory in my long fight against the principle of personal publicity."[40]

Sidis hired a Boston attorney, William Aronoff, who wrote to the *New Yorker* and warned them that Sidis was going to press a libel claim. Little is known about Aronoff or how Sidis chose him; what is known is that his tenure as Sidis's counsel was not long. Aronoff was one of a series of lawyers who would be summarily hired and fired by Sidis in his relentless pursuit of his "fight against . . . personal publicity." In early 1938, a meeting was arranged between Aronoff and the *New Yorker*'s counsel. The magazine's lawyers asked Aronoff to show how the article was false, and he would not. Aronoff left the office with threats of suit. Around the same time, Sidis also initiated a libel suit against the newspaper the *Boston American*, which published a piece in late 1938 based on the *New Yorker* article.[41]

Within months, Sidis had switched attorneys. He hired a small New York firm called Green and Russell, and Thomas Green met with the attorney for the *New Yorker*, Alexander Lindey. Green and company were clearly outmatched. Lindey was a seasoned entertainment and literary lawyer, perhaps one of the most experienced of his day. Shortly after the meeting, Sidis filed suit against the *New Yorker* in federal district court, in the Southern District of New York. He sued for $150,000, on two counts of invasion of privacy and one count of libel. Libel, of course, is a cause of action against false publications; privacy deals with true but embarrassing facts. In alleging both libel and privacy, Sidis claimed that the material was false but also admitted that it was true. This was a common strategy in suits against the press involving objectionable publications. The invasion of privacy claim was often used as a backup to the libel claim if the falsity of the material was contested. Sidis's lawyers knew well that what appeared in the article was true.[42]

The *New Yorker* had deeply offended Sidis—had "done a great injustice" to him, Green argued—by bringing him into the spotlight and interfering with his public image, effectively an image of "no image." According to Green's complaint, the publication had "deliberately and maliciously intruded on Sidis' right to privacy and had dragged him, against his will, into the cruel glare of publicity." Green told Lindey that Sidis wished not only to "even the score" with the *New Yorker*, "but to make an example of it, so that there would be no further inroads on his private life." If necessary, Green said, Sidis was "prepared to carry the case to the Supreme Court of the United States."[43] There was no reason for Lindey to believe that Sidis would not make good on his threats.

~

In 1938, Alexander Lindey was forty-three years old. A successful and well-known figure in the New York legal world, he had made his career defending free expression—the rights of journalists, novelists, playwrights, artists, and publishers both large and small. In particular, Lindey had made censorship his life's work, exposing it and destroying it wherever it existed. Even though the prudish sensibilities of the age of Queen Victoria were largely a thing of the past in American culture, censorship laws were still on the books in the 1930s. Several states had laws that required literature and films to be licensed before distribution, and licenses could be denied if the material was seen as "immoral" or as having a "tendency to corrupt" the audience.[44]

To Lindey, the idea that expression could be governed by a single moral standard was noxious to creativity and anathema to fundamental democratic principles. The idea that a chosen few could quash the rights of artists and writers to say what they wished, and the right of the public to choose what culture to consume, was a relic of the dark ages that had no place in a modern, pluralist American society. The more he looked, the more Lindey saw censorship lurking in many different areas of the law. Insofar as they prohibited certain kinds of publications, or imposed liability for publications based on their content, customs laws, postal regulations, and even the tort of libel were all forms of de facto censorship in Lindey's eyes. A free speech absolutist, Lindey wanted to eliminate nearly all legal restrictions on what people could write, read, and see.[45]

Lindey was a partner at Greenbaum, Wolff, and Ernst, a small and prestigious New York firm specializing in literary and free expression law. Founded in 1915 by the renowned civil liberties lawyer Morris Ernst, the firm's list of libel and intellectual property clients included many notables in the art and publishing world; among them, authors Edna Ferber and James Joyce. In the 1930s and 1940s, the firm was active in virtually every major lawsuit challenging literary and film censorship. Both Ernst and Lindey were counsel for the American Civil Liberties Union and founding members of a group called the National Council on Freedom from Censorship, an offshoot of the ACLU that had been started in 1931. As coauthors, they published a treatise against film and literary censorship titled *The Censor Marches On* (1940), and a book on the "chilling effects" of libel law called *Hold Your Tongue: Adventures in Libel and Slander* (1932).[46]

Greenbaum, Wolff, and Ernst had been the *New Yorker*'s in-house counsel since 1932. The firm was part of the growing group of legal practices specializing in media and First Amendment law. Most of the firm's work for the *New Yorker* involved protecting the magazine against libel claims. To stave off libel suits, the firm required writers to provide editors with the sources of their information, and the magazine established a highly organized and professional fact-checking department. In response to threatened libel suits, Greenbaum, Wolff, and Ernst developed a standard procedure: to notify the complainant that the magazine had not in fact libeled him, and to refuse to publish a retraction. The lawyers refused to settle, fearing that a reputation for easy settlement would invite libel claims. It was a point of pride at the *New Yorker* that it never once paid out cash to settle a libel suit. In virtually every case, the lawyers boasted, they had been able to use "explanation or persuasion" to convince the disgruntled to back down and abandon their claims.[47]

In early 1938, Sidis contacted the *New Yorker* reporter Barbara Linscott and allegedly threatened to do "dire things" to her unless she cooperated with him for the purpose of building up a case.[48] Lindey then dispatched an attorney to Boston to get Sidis to drop the suit in exchange for an "apology and small token payment for expenses occurred." Sidis—who Lindey believed was a "crackpot" with a "persecution phobia"—responded in a way that Lindey described as "downright screwy." He submitted to the lawyer a "written memorandum . . . with a long series of 'fines' to be paid" by the magazine if they mentioned his name again. Lindey properly interpreted this as a refusal. Lindey asked the *New Yorker*'s fact-checking department to check the accuracy of every statement in the article and obtained Linscott's notes. Recognizing that the "litigation may turn out to be a serious one," Lindey wrote his colleagues, it was extremely important that the case be "fully prepared."[49]

By the middle of 1938, it was beginning to seem highly unlikely that Sidis would drop the case. Sidis was becoming even more vengeful, embittered, and harassing. As the months progressed, Lindey became confident that the magazine would win. The fact-checking department was unearthing information about Sidis indicating that the facts in the article were true and that he had no basis for a claim for libel. Moreover, Lindey was convinced that Sidis had little legal ground to stand on with his invasion of privacy claim, as the published material could be described as a "matter of public concern." Lindey was also cognizant of the potential, serious conflict between the right to privacy and freedom of the press. To Lindey, the privacy tort, which permitted liability for the publication of truthful facts, seemed to be censorship in its purest form. As *New Yorker* editor Harold Ross observed, invasion of privacy suits, if successful, would theoretically put "all publications out of business, especially such publications as ours."[50] The *Sidis* case was thus of "great importance to writers and publishers," Lindey observed. "It involves the vexing question of the extent to which [personal matters] can be legitimately discussed in publications without contravening the right of privacy of such persons."[51]

As the case developed, Lindey began to see *Sidis* as potentially groundbreaking legal precedent. Lindey believed that the case posed a remarkable opportunity to have a federal court declare the privacy tort, at least as it applied to journalism and the publication of truthful facts, incompatible with emerging modern perspectives on freedom of speech and press. Lindey's legal strategy was to focus on the privacy claim, which he would try to defeat in a motion to dismiss in which he raised the free speech issue. Two decades earlier, such an argument might have fallen on deaf ears, but in the more liberal political and social climate of 1938, there was a good chance it could succeed.

~

When Warren and Brandeis wrote "The Right to Privacy," the law of freedom of speech had been governed for the most part by the "bad tendency" test, as we've seen. Legal prohibitions of speech that had a "bad tendency," that was said to offend private sensibilities or public morals, posed little if any constitutional difficulty; they were seen as legitimate exercises of the state's police power.

Beginning in the World War I era, a new generation of Progressive scholars and jurists challenged the "bad tendency" approach as inconsistent with ideals of participatory democracy. In this period, industrial workers, anarchists, socialists, and birth control advocates, among other activists, engaged in protests and acts of civil disobedience against this narrow view of expression rights. Laws that punished political dissent, they argued, contravened the constitutionally protected "freedom of public discussion"—the right of the people to express and to receive a multitude of viewpoints and opinions, and to govern themselves through free and open discussion of politics and public affairs. But theirs was a minority view, and it was not until the 1930s that this vision was realized in formal constitutional jurisprudence.[52]

In a series of cases involving criminal punishment of the controversial speech of socialists, communists, labor unionists, and other dissenters, the Supreme Court, beginning with *Near v. Minnesota* (1931), rejected the "bad tendency" rule and initiated the practice of heightened judicial scrutiny of state action abridging speech on politics and "matters of public concern," a broad domain that it defined as "all issues about which information is needed or appropriate to enable the members of society to cope with the exigencies of their period."[53] With the exception of material that posed a "clear and present danger" of imminent violence, prohibitions or impairments of expression on the basis of disfavored content or viewpoints were presumptively unconstitutional. Because free expression was "the matrix, the indispensable condition, of nearly every . . . form of freedom," as the Court wrote in 1937, freedom of speech occupied a "preferred position" in the scheme of constitutional liberties, and state actions restricting speech could not stand unless justified by a compelling government interest beyond mere disagreement with the views espoused.[54] Writes one constitutional historian, First Amendment rights came to occupy "a special constitutional and cultural place in America because of their intimate connection to the idea of democracy."[55]

In the liberal political climate of the New Deal era, with the rise of organized labor, a large immigrant population, and a vocal political left, freedom of speech and civil liberties were widely supported. The book burnings and violent repression of dissenters in Nazi Germany turned the public against the idea of state suppression of politics and culture. The destruction of a free press overseas strengthened Americans' commitment to press rights and open political criticism. Freedom of speech embodied principles of personal choice, self-determination, and self-expression. In the words of Supreme Court Justice William O. Douglas, the purpose of the First Amendment was to protect the right of the people to freely "pick and choose" what culture and information to consume "from the multitude of competing offerings," as "what seems to one to be trash may have for others fleeting or even enduring values."[56]

In this emerging view of free expression and democracy, the mass media played a crucial role. Courts were recognizing the importance of radio, film, and print publications in generating public discourse and disseminating news in a far-flung, geographically dispersed mass society. The mass media created social bonds and cultural connections within a vast, heterogeneous populace; few if any other cultural institutions had quite the same power to create this sense of a national public. Even gossip and human interest journalism served the function of maintaining social cohesion and social norms. By providing a diverse public with a set of common interests and shared knowledge, by sparking discussion and debate over social practices and values, such material served as the "printed folklore of the factory age."[57] Once seen as an enemy of the people—as a threat to the social order—the popular press was being recast by some courts as the representative of popular interests, as the agent of the people.[58] Insofar as the people subsidized the press with their dollars and cents, the press "gave the public what it wanted."[59]

In *Near v. Minnesota*, from 1931, which struck down a state law prohibiting the publication of a "scandal sheet," the Supreme Court noted the significance of the press—including tabloids and scandalous newspapers—in the workings of participatory democracy.[60] In *Grosjean v. American Press Co.* (1936), Justice Sutherland observed the significance of a free press in disseminating news and enabling the public to "unite for [its] . . . common good" as "members of an organized society."[61] Freedom of the press protected the public's interest in the "dissemination of news from as many . . . sources, and with as many different facets and colors as is possible," which was essential to "the vitality of our democratic government."[62]

At a time when First Amendment defenses were generally not raised in state tort actions, Lindey did not bring a formal constitutional argument. Rather, he brought his free speech claims within the "matters of public interest" or "matters of public concern" privilege to the privacy tort. In his motion to dismiss the privacy claim, he argued that the *New Yorker*'s publication about the tragic adult life of William Sidis was not a trivial or prurient matter but served the public's legitimate interest in learning about current events and "public affairs." The information about Sidis was not mere gossip, but a genuine "matter of public concern." The world was not so quaint and parochial as it had been in the days of Warren and Brandeis, and the public had come to accept a much broader range of material as having social meaning and value.[63]

The very premise of the privacy tort—the imposition of liability for truthful publications simply because they were offensive and upsetting to the individual depicted—was anathema to free and open "public discussion," Lindey argued. The right to privacy, as invoked by Sidis, would permit a person to effectively censor a news article simply because he did not like it. "We submit that the facts may be told about any person . . . without violating his right of privacy," Lindey argued in his brief. "It does not matter that he may object, preferring complete self-effacement and obscurity." "Freedom to speak the truth without restraint" was "one of the cornerstones of democracy." It was "more important that the truth be free than the plaintiff's sensibility should not be hurt."[64]

∼

Judge Henry Goddard at the U.S. District Court of the Southern District of New York heard Lindey's motion to dismiss Sidis's claim for invasion of privacy. Goddard was well versed in publishing law; over the years, given the court's location in New York City, the nation's publishing capital, Goddard had presided over hundreds of cases involving copyright, libel, obscenity, and other mass media issues. Recognizing the significance of the issues involved, Goddard kept the case under advisement for over two months.[65]

Goddard was extremely sympathetic to Sidis's plight. Sidis was a truly tragic figure. But he was not sympathetic to Sidis's legal argument, and he granted the motion to dismiss. Sidis had argued that the article was "unfavorable and harmful to [him]" and held him up to "scorn, ridicule and contempt." Not only was the piece highly offensive to his sensibilities, but the details of his personal life were private matters, not matters of public concern. Although he had been a public figure while he was a child prodigy, he had since faded from public view, and his affairs, once arguably of public significance, ceased to be matters of legitimate public interest. The public's fascination with his activities and lifestyle served only a lurid curiosity, an interest that was outweighed by his prerogative to seek anonymity, disappear from the spotlight, and be let alone.[66]

Goddard disagreed, concluding that the *New Yorker*'s discussion of Sidis was a legitimate matter of public concern, a matter of great "current interest." The details of his personal life, however banal, were "a matter in which the public is . . . concerned." Goddard's analysis was cryptic. He did not explain what he meant by "current interest," or why the public's "concern" with Sidis's private affairs was one that should be legally protected. In dicta, the judge suggested that the outcome in the case was dictated by "the right of free speech and freedom of the press."[67]

Undaunted, Sidis promptly appealed to the New York–based Second Circuit Court of Appeals. For the third time, he changed attorneys and was next represented by a small firm, Sapinsky, Lukas, and Santangelo. Lindey again tried to get Sidis to settle but insisted that "any money settlement was out of the question." He proposed that Sidis write a letter presenting his views, which would be printed in the magazine's corrections section, or that Sidis write an article for the *New Yorker* on "the collection of streetcar transfers," or "possibly on the subject of the vulnerability of the right of privacy of the individual in modern society." Sidis again refused. Claiming that his $17 weekly salary as an adding-machine clerk made the filing fees prohibitive, Sidis won a motion to file his papers with the court *in forma pauperis*. Edwin Lukas argued the case before the Second Circuit for Sidis.[68]

The *Sidis* case was heard in July 1940. The Second Circuit at that time was occupied by an especially distinguished lineup of judges, including Jerome Frank, Learned Hand, and Augustus Hand. The three-judge panel that heard the case consisted of Robert Patterson, Thomas Walter Swan, and Charles Edward Clark. Swan and Clark were former deans of the Yale Law School. Clark, who wrote the *Sidis* opinion, had been recently appointed by Franklin Roosevelt and was the principal author of the 1938 Federal Rules of Civil Procedure. Prior to taking up work in procedure, Clark had written on constitutional issues and had a particular interest in freedom of speech. As a law professor at Yale in the 1920s, Clark had written articles in the *Yale Law Journal* criticizing Supreme Court decisions that had upheld World War I–era convictions for dissident publications under the Espionage and Sedition Acts. The only hope for success of government by and for the people, he had written, was that "beliefs [be] formed without compulsion" and as a result of arguments tested in the marketplace of ideas.[69] Clark was "instinctive" in his "support of . . . free speech," a biographer observed.[70] Clark was quick to see the constitutional dimensions of the *Sidis* case. The case was one of the first to bring forward and test the argument that publishing intimate, revealing, or harmful facts about an individual could be actionable as a tort, consistent with modern free speech ideals.

At oral argument, Lindey maintained that the publication was a legitimate "matter of public interest" because it was instructive and educational; Sidis's later life was a "tragic illustration of the havoc caused by the ruthless parental exploitation of gifted children."[71] Lindey pressed hard on the constitutional issue. What was at stake in the case, he argued, was nothing less than the very meaning and future of freedom of speech and press. If Sidis's theory was upheld, publishers would self-censor to avoid liability, and "every time a publication printed the name or picture of a living person without his written consent, it would be inviting suit." The "bulk of contemporary nonfiction literature would have to go by the boards." "Biographical sketches such as those featured by every magazine of standing" and "discussions of prominent personalities" in such publications as the *New York Times* would be written out of existence. "Indeed, the circulation of all works dealing with the world we live in would be crippled."[72]

Sidis's lawyer reiterated his argument that the publication was not a privileged "matter of public interest" and that Sidis could not be considered to be a "public figure." According to Lukas, Sidis's fame had been tied to his childhood feats; with those events long passed, his affairs ceased to be of legitimate public interest, and he had a right to revert to the "unexciting life led by the great bulk of the community." The *New Yorker*'s lawyers mocked the notion that a public figure could ever "retire." "Society has an interest in free discussion," Lindey argued. "It would be an evil day for writers and publishers, and a worse one for the courts," when a public figure could "of his own volition withdraw from the public scene at any time," then "sue for breach of his right to privacy [when] he is subsequently written up."[73]

As in the lower court, there was great sympathy for Sidis. According to Lindey, Patterson brushed aside the *New Yorker*'s argument "rather angrily" and "said that . . . the article was cruel and unjustified."[74] Clark observed that the article was a "ruthless exposure" and "merciless in its dissection of intimate details of its subject's personal life . . . and the pitiable lengths to which he has gone in order to avoid public scrutiny."[75]

But the panel nonetheless affirmed the district court, holding that Sidis had not stated a cause of action under the common law right to privacy because Sidis was still a "public figure" and the story was a privileged "matter of public interest." "William James Sidis was once a public figure," Clark wrote. "As a child prodigy, he excited both admiration and curiosity. Of him great deeds were expected. In 1910, he was a person about whom the newspapers might display a legitimate intellectual interest, in the sense meant by Warren and Brandeis, as distinguished from a trivial and unseemly curiosity." "Since then," Clark continued, "Sidis has cloaked himself in obscurity." He had gone to "pitiable lengths" to seclude himself and separate himself from his painful past. Nonetheless, Sidis was still a "public figure," and his "subsequent history, containing as it did the answer to the question of whether or not he had fulfilled his early promise," was a privileged "matter of public concern."[76]

Why was the *New Yorker* article a "matter of public interest" or "matter of public concern"? Sidis's fate was a "matter of public interest," Clark concluded, because the public was "interested" in it; the story had "considerable popular news interest." How did Clark know that the public was interested in the *New Yorker* story? Because the article appeared in a popular magazine. The press, in Clark's view, was a barometer of popular tastes; editors' concerns with profit and circulation required them to stay abreast of current trends, interests, and "community mores."[77] Clark permitted the *New Yorker* to engage in what one law review writer at the time criticized as a "bootstrap-lifting venture." The *New Yorker* brought Sidis back into the spotlight, then pointed to the publicity and interest it had generated to argue that Sidis was a "public figure" and that the details of his private life were a "matter of public interest." This impermissibly "elastic interpretation" of the privileges, critics argued, rendered them "almost meaningless."[78]

Though Clark did not decide the case as a matter of constitutional law, the *Sidis* opinion, with its broad deference to editorial judgment and to popular tastes, reflected the emerging civil libertarian view of freedom of speech and press. A right to privacy that permitted public figures to throw a shield around their private lives and immunize themselves from comment and criticism, Clark suggested, violated democratic commitments to political transparency and accountability. A right to privacy that allowed courts to prohibit the publication of truthful information in the media constituted a potential judicial "censorship" of the press. While the *New Yorker* article may have been thoughtless, even crass, it was not the role of the court to enforce good taste. "Regrettably or not," Clark wrote, "the misfortunes and frailties of neighbors and public figures" were subjects of interest to the public, "and when such are the mores of the community it would be unwise for a court to bar their expression in the newspapers, books, and magazines of the day."[79]

~

As a testament to his wrath for the *New Yorker*, Sidis would not drop the case. After the decision, Sidis's lawyer, Edwin Lukas, wrote a scathing letter to the *New York Law Journal*, the preeminent journal of the legal profession, in which he attacked the court's conclusion that "the personal right of seclusion is held to be subservient to the dominant right of the press, in the 'public interest,' to disseminate 'information.'" "Apparently, by reason of the *Sidis* case, once a person has attention thrust upon him . . . his later life, private and deliberately secluded as it may be, for all time and for all purposes, can be exploited and made the subject of ruthless comment, if the truth be told." Lukas believed that the right to privacy encompassed a "right to be forgotten."[80]

Lukas then met with Alexander Lindey and notified him that Sidis planned to appeal the case to the U.S. Supreme Court. Sidis was "hyped" on the privacy claim, Lindey noted, and "this is going to be an important damn case if he goes through with the appeal."[81] After the Supreme Court denied certiorari in 1942, Sidis announced that he planned to pursue the original libel complaint. His new lawyer, Hobart S. Bird, argued that the *New Yorker* had caused the public to believe that Sidis was, among other things, "reprehensible, disloyal to his country, a criminal," "a loathsome and filthy person in his personal habits," "having suffered a mental breakdown," being a "neurotic person and having a deranged mind," and "one pretending extraordinary intellectual attainments and being a genius, yet in fact a fool, incapable of making a decent living and living in misery and poverty."[82] Sidis was determined to take the libel case to trial. "Certainly any ordinary plaintiff would have been discouraged long before this," Lindey wrote to Shuman. "It seems, however, that neither four court defeats nor the passage of time have served to dampen his ardor to press ahead."[83] Lindey asked Bird what Sidis really wanted, and the response was unexpected. Gone was the language of vindication, dignity, and justice—what Sidis wanted was money, "and $10,000 of it," Lindey wrote.[84]

On March 24, 1944, the case was put on calendar for trial. On April 3 and 4 of 1944, Sidis was called before Morris Ernst and deposed. In another attempt to get

Sidis to settle, Ernst offered him $1,000 "for any article you write of any length on any subject." "You will not have to use your own name," Ernst told him. "I will not disclose the fact that you are the author." Sidis again declined.[85] Afraid that a jury would find that Sidis had been libeled, the *New Yorker* offered Sidis a settlement in the amount of $600, which he accepted. It was the first time the magazine made a "straight money settlement."[86]

It's not clear why Sidis finally agreed to the *New Yorker*'s deal. An award of a mere $600 was a far cry from the substantial sums he had initially hoped to extract from the magazine. By 1944, however, Sidis could take satisfaction in the great cost and hassle the *New Yorker* had endured in the lengthy litigation. Sidis had not only punished the magazine in this way, but been vindicated in the process. Public opinion was on his side. Though the law was formally not in his favor, the judges had been demonstrably sympathetic. And Sidis had secured from the magazine, through the token settlement, what he saw as an admission of guilt. There was another reason for Sidis to settle: he was quite ill, and he needed whatever money he could get. The ongoing lawsuit had taken a serious toll on his emotional and physical health.[87]

The *New Yorker* considered itself victorious, regarding the small payout as negligible. But Sidis felt that he had triumphed in the case. As Sidis's biographer concluded, it was a sweet victory for William, who had been victimized by the press since his birth.[88]

∼

Sidis v. F. R. Publishing was the first pronouncement from a federal appeals court that the "privacy" right to a person's image could be broadly limited in the interest of freedom of the press. *Sidis* did not declare the privacy tort unconstitutional, although by refracting it through a modern constitutional lens, it threw into question its foundational premises and assumptions. As in so many legal cases, the significance of *Sidis* was not so much what the court actually decided as how it defined the contested issues. Adopting Lindey's stance, the Second Circuit described the conflict in *Sidis* as a clash of two competing and potentially irreconcilable rights: the privacy and image rights of individuals versus the free expression rights of the press and the public that it was said to serve. Contrary to the formulation of Warren and Brandeis, in which privacy was seen as protecting social interests, Lindey and the Second Circuit characterized the right to privacy as essentially antisocial: insofar as it deterred publishers from printing private but arguably important and interesting facts, the privacy tort took material out of the public domain that the public had a "right to know." This framing of the privacy tort as a threat to freedom of speech and to the "public's interest" in access to information was perhaps the most enduring legacy of the case.

The *Sidis* decision did not entirely foreclose liability for media interference with one's public image. Judge Clark left open the possibility that under extreme circumstances, a court might find a particular publication so offensive and out of step with "community mores" that it was not a "matter of public interest." As Clark wrote, "revelations may be so intimate and so unwarranted in view of the victim's position as to outrage the community's notions of decency." Recovery for invasion of privacy would be warranted if a publication went beyond all bounds of "legitimate interest" in a person's private life and catered only to a truly "trivial and unseemly curiosity." The media did not have free rein to publish private information—a line must be drawn somewhere, although "it was a difficult one to draw."[89]

Sidis was not binding on state courts, which were free to adopt whatever rules of liability they wanted. And in many states, as we will see, the right to privacy would provide broad protection for personal image so expansive that even Sidis might have recovered under it. Nonetheless, *Sidis* was extremely influential. *Sidis* came to stand for the maxim that in determining whether an item is a privileged "matter of public interest," "courts cannot impose their own views about what should interest the community." The ambit of "legitimate public interest" was to be construed broadly, perhaps as broadly as the content of the popular media itself.

∽

At a time of widespread concerns with privacy and personal image, the *Sidis* case became the focus of much discussion and debate. Sidis's legal battles were widely publicized; popular, academic, and professional legal publications discussed the case, commented on it, and generally lamented it. Despite apparent public interest in the *New Yorker* article, the overwhelming popular sentiment was that the reclusive genius had been badly wronged. The *New Yorker* article and the Second Circuit decision were criticized for having interfered with Sidis's right to self-reinvention and transformation, and what was being described as a core aspect of the right to one's image: one's *right to be forgotten*.

Critics were less upset by the initial publicity given to Sidis during his childhood than by the *New Yorker*'s attempt to revive interest in him. The magazine had, in their eyes, interfered with society's established customs and practices for putting people on and taking them off the public stage. As one writer noted in 1941, criticizing the decision, "in our modern civilization, many persons, such as criminals, stage and screen stars, and others who were in the public eye in past years are entirely forgotten today." The public's interest was transient and fickle, as evidenced by the often meteoric rise and fall of movie stars. By thrusting Sidis back into the limelight, the *New Yorker* had meddled with what was described as the natural social process of forgetting.[90]

The *New Yorker* article and the Second Circuit decision were also criticized for having interfered with Sidis's right to reinvent himself. By the 1930s, it was still possible to move to Texas, change one's name and appearance, and begin an entirely new existence. Yet as critics observed, popular journalism, which had discovered new ways to fill pages by rehashing old news, was creating a world where one could never escape one's past. As a legal commentator observed in the *American Mercury* in 1948, after *Sidis*, those whose "love affairs, marital troubles, and adventures in court or jail [were] rehashed in the Sunday magazines" could do nothing about it under the law. The moral of the *Sidis* case, he lamented, was "once news, always news."[91]

The law reviews and legal journals were highly critical of the Second Circuit's pronouncements and generally believed that *Sidis* was wrongly decided. *New Yorker* executive editor Ik Shuman mocked the "dissenting opinions of the law review writers," and Lindey quipped that "it is a lucky thing for us that judges and not law review writers sit on the bench."[92] All recognized the significance of the *Sidis* case as a milestone in the law of privacy and personal image. It was the first modern, authoritative ruling on what constitutes a "matter of public interest," and "how far into the public figure's life does the public's interest rightly extend."[93] After the Second Circuit decision, Lindey observed that there was a "tremendous interest in the case on the part of the legal profession" and that he had received "a number of requests for copies of the briefs from lawyers." In 1940, the case was the subject of the moot court at Yale Law School.[94]

Several legal commentators attacked the Second Circuit's interpretation of the "matters of public interest" privilege, which they saw as so deferential to the press that it was virtually meaningless. "According to this view the court looks to what people are 'interested in' in order to determine what can be written about other people's private lives. It hardly takes account of the human frailty to become more interested as the matter becomes more private."[95] "If 'public interest' is to be the touchstone, the phrase must be used with caution," wrote the *New York Law Review*. "Public interest may attach to an article in the sense that many persons are eager to read it. It will not follow from this that its publication, or the rule of law permitting its publication, will serve a public interest outweighing the individual distress it may cause."[96]

In contrast to civil libertarian strains of free speech thought, the sentiment from many of the academic, popular, and professional writers was that the courts had an affirmative duty to raise the moral standards of the public by imposing content-based limitations on popular literature and journalism. The Second Circuit abdicated "its duty to improve the mores of the community . . . by barring the expression of that which caters to . . . the less elevated tendencies of men."[97] "The courts are the final arbiters of what can be printed in magazines and newspapers," noted one critic. "Will they take upon themselves the burden of raising the standards of journalism and the mores of the community, or will they let the newspapers and magazines, prompted by a willing public curiosity, dictate to them the standards of what can be written about other people?"[98]

The public sympathy for Sidis only increased after his death not long after his settlement with the magazine. In 1944, Sidis had started another adding-machine job but was fired a few weeks into the position for what was described as negligence. In the summer of that year, his landlady found him collapsed in his room. He had suffered a massive brain hemorrhage. Sidis was taken to the hospital and died a few days later. It was widely believed that the stress of the lawsuit had killed him. The outpouring of pity in the newspapers and magazines was overwhelming.[99]

There were a few expressions of support for the Second Circuit decision. Judge Leon Yankwich, on the District Court for the Southern District of California, described the outcome in *Sidis* as a great advance for participatory democracy that like contemporaneous developments in libel law widened the "realm of public criticism" of public figures and public officials.[100] The publishing industry, naturally, was behind the decision. The trade journal *Publishers' Weekly* followed the case closely as it wound its way through the courts, and publishing industry lawyers celebrated the Second Circuit's opinion as a victory for freedom of the press and the free flow of information. Morris Ernst took great satisfaction in the outcome, both on free speech grounds and as a personal matter—he had grown to hate Sidis. Reflecting many years later on the case, he wrote that although "human sympathy was all in Sidis' corner," it was necessary for the court to "hurt Sidis" in the name "of the greater good."[101]

But these favorable opinions were in the minority. The evolving law of privacy and public sentiments about privacy were clearly not aligned. Nor were public attitudes towards privacy consistent. While the public appeared to embrace the broad civil libertarian principles then emerging in free speech doctrine, at the same time many seemed to support the imposition of liability for publications that were personally degrading and humiliating, that contradicted the way a person wanted to be known to the public. Freedom of speech, in this view, did not mean a blank check for the press to turn people into objects of public ridicule when they had done nothing to deserve it. The public reaction to *Sidis* exposed these contradictions. *Sidis* reaffirmed the public's belief in a right to privacy and a right to one's image in the midst of a culture increasingly committed to freedom of speech, the culture of celebrity, and massive public exposure.

CHAPTER 8

"An Age of Images"

By the 1950s, the laws of image were well established in American law and legal culture. The invasion of privacy and intentional infliction of emotional distress torts had been recognized in a majority of jurisdictions, and defamation law was extending to reach a broad spectrum of harms to people's public images and their feelings about their images. Both the famous and the unknown were asserting a sense of entitlement to control their public images and mobilizing the law to defend themselves against unwanted publicity and perceived distortions of their public personas. These developments were not uncontested. Both within and outside of the legal world, there were ongoing concerns with thin skins, faked lawsuits, and spurious claims, not to mention the potentially "chilling effects" on freedom of speech.

In the post–World War II era, courts imposed further limitations on the image torts in the name of freedom of speech and the public's "right to know." Despite this, the proliferation of the media, new communication technologies, and a cultural focus on personal images and "image management" led to the significant growth of image law and personal image litigation. There was deep cultural confusion around image laws and image rights. At the same time the laws of image were being narrowed, they expanded to accommodate people's increasing protectiveness of their public images in an image-saturated society, what was being described as an "age of images."[1]

∼

In postwar America, images—of affluence, desire, mobility, and fame— "reached . . . into every corner of our daily lives," observed historian Daniel Boorstin.[2] World War II had brought with it unprecedented prosperity, and the middle-class lifestyle came within reach for millions. Between 1947 and 1960, average incomes increased by as much as in the previous half century.[3] By the end of the 1950s, most families owned their homes, their cars, and a television set. A surfeit of new goods—frozen foods, toys, electric washers and dryers, stereos, Tupperware—became widely available for cash or for credit; the 1950s saw the popularization of the credit card. It was a culture of appearance and aspiration; advertising in glossy magazines and on television spread bright pictures of consumer products and their happy users for envy and emulation. Idealized images of coiffed housewives, well-fed children, and businessmen in "grey flannel suits" proffered marriage, family, and conspicuous consumption as the means to social inclusion and participation in the good life.[4]

These glittering images masked deep currents of anxiety—concerns with the soullessness of a materialistic culture, and Cold War fears of nuclear annihilation. They also concealed serious inequalities: persistent racism, sexual discrimination, widespread poverty. These social disparities, and the pressure to conform to the middle-class way of life, led to a cultural backlash: the civil rights, feminist, antiwar, counterculture, and other protest movements. These rebellions crested in the 1960s, although the stirrings of discontent started well before that decade. By 1950, critics had begun to challenge mainstream culture, with its emphasis on consumption and its seeming passivity, sterility, and complacency. *The Lonely Crowd*, by sociologist David Riesman, was one such expression.

Riesman wrote of the rise of a new personality type that was emerging as an influential minority in contemporary America, particularly among the urban upper middle class.[5] He called this the "other-directed" personality.[6] Riesman contrasted this with the "inner-directed" personality, epitomized by the nineteenth-century "man of character." The inner-directed individual was guided by an "inner gyroscope" of belief, tradition, and morals, "implanted early in life by . . . elders and directed towards generalized but nonetheless inescapably destined goals." By contrast, the other-directed individual—the product of an affluent, mobile, consumerist society—looked to his peers or to the mass media for response, affirmation, and guidance. Without a stable inner core or internal direction, he continually reinvented himself—his appearance and his image—in an effort to please others; to achieve social approval, psychological comfort, and status and material success. Riesman noted the manifestations of this other-directed orientation in various cultural practices and texts of the time, from children's novels to stories and ads in women's magazines that dealt with modes of manipulating the self in order to manipulate others, for the attainment of such "intangible assets" as prestige, acceptance, and affection.[7]

Riesman's book hit a nerve. *The Lonely Crowd* became the best-selling book by a sociologist in American history, with 1.4 million copies sold. The success of the book, critic Todd Gitlin notes, was its knack in "sympathetically expos[ing] the anxieties of a middle class that was rising with the postwar boom . . . busy availing itself of upgraded homes, machines, and status."[8] Although Riesman painted his description in somewhat stark terms, he captured what was being widely recognized as a new, modal American persona. The notion of the unstable, ungrounded, malleable self, motivated by the pursuit of peer approval and material gain, was echoed in a number of other popular and academic works of this time. William Whyte wrote of the "organization man"; Vance Packard described a nation of "status seekers"; and the sociologist Erving Goffman, in his *Presentation of Self in Everyday Life*, described social interaction as a series of elaborate choreographies of deception and self-interest.[9] These characterizations were not representative of the entire populace; many were untouched by the demands of the white-collar world, the exhortations of the mass media, and the enticements of consumer culture. Nonetheless, these critical descriptions do capture an unmistakable trend in the culture of the middle class and aspiring middle class—an orientation towards appearances, surfaces, packaging, glamour, the accoutrements of status, and perfecting and controlling one's image in the eyes of others.

This "other-direction" should be familiar by now, with its origins in the prewar era. However, significant developments in postwar culture escalated the emphasis on personal image and image management. By the 1950s, for the first time in U.S. history, there were more white-collar workers than blue-collar workers.[10] Labor power more than ever took the form of "personality" and "people skills." The burgeoning service occupations placed on their participants intense requirements for managed self-presentation—in Goffman's words, that "one give a perfectly homogeneous performance at every appointed time."[11] As the sociologist C. Wright Mills observed in 1951, the salesperson "in his work . . . often clashes with customer and superior, and must almost always be the standardized loser; he must smile and be personable, standing behind the counter, or waiting in the outer office." The sales floor had become the metaphor for all of middle-class life.[12] Advancement in the corporate "rat race" was being described as a series of postures, bluffs, and confidence games. An article in the *Saturday Evening Post* equated corporate success with being an "alibi artist" who believed it was more important to know the right people and impress others than to have real talent or ability.[13] The phrase "personal image" first entered popular culture in the 1960s. With will-power and focus, advised a 1962 business success manual titled *The Magic Power of Putting Yourself Over with People*, "you can have the kind of personal image you want," and through your image, "sell yourself" to others.[14]

The guiding theme of postwar advertising was that everyone and everything had an image that could be successfully marketed to anyone if presented convincingly enough. Advertising surged in the 1950s. By the mid-1950s, the United States was spending $9 billion to sell products—and people.[15] Politicians' increasing use of advertising techniques in their campaigns led the *New York Times Magazine* to dub the 1960 election cycle "The Year of the Image."[16] As ever, product advertisements encouraged consumers to view themselves with the critical gaze of spectators, as performers under the constant scrutiny of friends and strangers. A 1960 advertising campaign by Clairol featured a photograph of a model with beautiful hair. Over the photograph appeared the question, "Does she or doesn't she?" and underneath, "Hair color so natural only her hairdresser knows for sure."[17] The most skillful manipulators were those whose deceptions were undetectable.

Other "image industries" flourished. A majority of women used makeup; cosmetics were sold in a range of retail outlets; and beauty products began to be marketed towards and used by teenage girls.[18] Young women were spending $20 million a year on lipstick, $25 million on deodorants, and $9 million on home permanents. The cosmetics industry was selling over one billion dollars a year, and the garment industry was producing two billion dollars worth of goods annually.[19] The evolution of plastic and synthetic technologies opened up new possibilities for durable and stylish dress; high-fashion knock-offs were ubiquitous, and in the words of one clothing historian, fashion was "democratized."[20] Cosmetic surgery became popular, promising both men and women the possibility of perpetual youth.[21] The objective was to perfect one's public image, to be envied, to be looked at.

Television, introduced in the late 1940s, reinforced the intertwining of performance and reality and the idea of pleasing personal images as a source of success and approval. By the end of the 1950s, 88 percent of American households had a television set, and in the average household, the television was on for four or five hours a day.[22] Many Americans were "now living far from their families, in brand new suburbs where they barely knew their neighbors," observed 1950s chronicler David Halberstam. "Sometimes they felt closer to the people they watched on television than they did to their neighbors and distant families."[23] Television trained Americans from the youngest age to be spectators and consumers of images. Audiences learned to see themselves through the camera's gaze, envisioning how they might preen and present themselves to appear charismatic and "telegenic." Television also entrenched the culture and ethos of celebrity more deeply into the fabric of American life.

Celebrity culture flourished, and it spread beyond the realm of entertainment to virtually every other area of endeavor, including politics, science, and academics. The mass-mediated "superstar," a product of the postwar era, was emblematic of the age, obsessed as it was with images, entertainment, and fame. Celebrities knit together a national culture based on shared images—"Jackie's hairdo, Marilyn Monroe's pout, Marlon Brando's swagger."[24] As political campaigns were enacted through television, public office hinged on a candidate's "star quality." Richard Nixon's pale, awkward, sweaty appearance in a televised 1960 presidential debate against John F. Kennedy was said to have cost him the election. Political figures entered the celebrity pantheon, and the worlds of Hollywood and Washington merged. Kennedy was the first "electric president," whose life, career, and death were completely televised.[25]

As ever, the essence of celebrity remained style rather than substance. Modern celebrity rewarded those who had appealing lifestyles and personalities, and who could project those personalities in an alluring fashion. Since media attention— and little else—was the basis of fame, it remained an eminently democratic aspiration, one that burned bright in many ordinary hearts, from the waitress "who can sing" to small-town quarterbacks and beauty queens. Publicity and fame were seen as the pinnacle of achievement, the ultimate public benediction. As William Faulkner observed in 1955, it had become impossible "for any American to believe that anyone not hiding from the police would not want . . . his name and photograph in any printed organ."[26] Celebrities continued to serve as role models of successful self-presentation, and there was great fascination with the ways that stars publicized themselves, how they transformed, manipulated, and spun their images. The public was enthralled with backstages, with the activities of publicists and press agents, and the inner workings of Hollywood and other image-making "factories."[27]

In his widely acclaimed 1961 book *The Image: A Guide to Pseudo-Events in America*, Daniel Boorstin noted that the United States had entered an "age of images." Like Riesman, Boorstin lamented what he saw as the alienating effects of mass communication and mass consumption, the vaunting of surfaces over depth, and the centrality of simulated, vicarious experiences to cultural life.[28] Politics had become a form of shadow theater enacted through television clips, sound bytes, press conferences, and other staged "pseudo events," Boorstin wrote.[29] With actors such as Ronald Reagan becoming politicians, entertainment had conquered reality. A massive part of the national economy—the fashion, cosmetics, mass media, advertising, and public relations industries—was devoted to manipulating personal images for strategic advantage. It was becoming a matter of faith that the right image could "elect a President or sell an automobile, a religion, a cigarette, or a suit of clothes."[30] "Each of us hopes for a pleasing 'personality'—and our personality is the attention getting image of ourselves, our image of our behavior," wrote Boorstin.[31] Objectivity, originality, and other old-fashioned ideals were becoming obsolete. "Before the age of images, it was commoner to think of a conventional person as one who strove for an ideal of decency or respectability." Now one tried to "fit into the images found vividly all around him." "We have fallen in love with our own image, with images of our making, which turn out to be images of ourselves."[32]

~

The focus on personal image was part of an intensifying focus on the self. Never before had such attention been lavished on the individual—his rights, happiness, comfort, and physical and mental health. The prosperous postwar decades gave rise not only to an escalating sense of individual possibility and opportunity among the middle class, but to an unprecedented emphasis on what we now refer to as personal "well-being," especially emotional well-being. The era saw what has been described as a "therapeutic culture."[33] World War II had popularized psychology, and popular culture was suffused with psychological themes and concepts.[34] Between 1945 and 1970 the number of psychiatrists in the United States increased from 3,600 to 18,400.[35] Terms such as ego, inferiority complex, and self-esteem entered common parlance.[36] The critic Vance Packard estimated that a majority of the nation's largest advertising firms were writing their copy to appeal to the unconscious, a technique he called "mass psychoanalysis."[37] Public issues began to be framed through the lens of personal problems; social conflicts were described as consequences of people's hang-ups and neuroses, and emotional fulfillment and self-actualization were described as preconditions for happiness.[38] By the 1950s, writes one historian, "the quest for identity and self-fulfillment had become central preoccupations."[39] The belief that the individual's growth and perfection were among the most important goals in life led to a self-improvement industry, including psychotherapy, cosmetic surgery, and a booming diet industry.[40]

Essential to a healthy and functioning psyche, it was said, was the ability to express one's inner self in one's behavior and outward appearance. Self-expression was the antithesis of self-repression, which by the 1960s came to be associated with all things perceived to be traditional and authoritarian, including the nuclear family, established religion, and the state. By the late sixties, various political, social, and lifestyle movements—from the feminist to the civil rights movements, to the hippies and their imitators—had elevated self-expression into a form of rebellion, a political statement, and a fashionable style. Publicly airing one's feelings, desires, and private life came to be seen as a way of achieving authenticity, of validating the self and freeing it from stultifying social conventions.[41] "Never before had so many people tried to express how they really felt and rid themselves of their psychological 'baggage,'" writes one historian of America's therapy culture.[42] Salvation lay in "openness and communication," and "expressing feelings was akin to godliness."[43]

With sexual and family matters no longer considered exclusively private and off-limits to public discussion, and emotional life freighted with great importance and meaning, memoirs, talk show confessions, and other genres of self-indulgence and self-exposure became staples of popular culture.[44] As one writer for *Commonweal* magazine noted in 1957, "for large segments of our society the injunction 'know thyself' has been . . . replaced by the urge for self-revelation. No fact is too intimate or slight to be withheld from public circulation." "Journals, memoirs, and diaries" were "increasingly a part of the public diet." In almost every social group, there "are those who wish to stand in the spotlight of self-revelation and those who are eager to observe. And the best means of mass communication are used to bring them together."[45] In the hopes of achieving fame and public visibility, people willingly divulged their most intimate secrets before a mass audience.[46] The foundations of our twenty-first-century "oversharing" culture were in the making.

At some level, this exhortation to self-expression might appear to be a rejection of the formalities of self-presentation, self-monitoring, and self-manipulation that were central to the cultures of celebrity and consumption and the demands of modern bureaucracies, with their call for a standardized self and managed emotions. Yet the ideal of the expressive self also put great emphasis on self-presentation in public. The essence of expressive freedom was self-determination and the prerogative to express oneself through one's public persona. It was not to abandon control over self-presentation, but rather to exert it, fully, freely, and without hindrance. As historian Howard Brick writes, "one of the chief paradoxes of the 1960s was the coincidence of devotion to the ideal of authenticity"—to the "true self," free of social masks and conventions—and at the same time, fascination "with the ways of artifice, with the calculated techniques of image-making and the 'games people play.'"[47] While the counterculture may have widened the range of socially acceptable appearances and identities, the self-expression ideal nonetheless prized image management and the freedom to script one's own public performance.

"Personal choice"—whether choosing one's occupation, beliefs, life course, or public image—had become the signature value of the therapeutic, affluent society. America had become a "republic of choice," writes historian Lawrence Friedman, where the prerogative "to 'be oneself' [and] to choose oneself" was "placed in a special and privileged position."[48] At the core of being oneself and choosing oneself was choosing one's identity and how to present it to the public. More than ever, identity was regarded as a self-created construct, something that could be changed both through inner, psychological transformations and through superficial alterations to one's appearance and style. Social authorities lost their credibility in the wake of the upheavals of the 1960s, detaching people from familiar value commitments. Twenty percent of the population moved annually during most of the 1950s and 1960s; people were being unmoored from community at an unprecedented rate.[49] The modern self, wrote psychologist Robert Jay Lifton, was a "protean self," continuously adapting to changing circumstances, social demands, and trends.[50] The self was "ever evolving, constantly changing, on a never ending search for self-actualization and 'growth.'"[51] The widespread discussion of an "identity crisis" besieging Americans, beginning in the 1960s, revealed the prevailing belief that personal identity was unstable, shifting, and elusive, something to be perpetually manipulated and revised.[52] As Norman Mailer observed, "the first art work is the shaping of one's own personality."[53]

In this increasingly self-focused environment, attacks on one's ability to choose and create one's own public image were being cast as serious assaults not only to dignity, but to the psyche itself. To publicize someone against his will or in a distorted manner was a blow to his ego, a "debasement of his sense of himself as a person."[54] As a California appeals court judge opined, if a person's "serenity of mind is disturbed by . . . the publication in a newspaper or magazine of his picture, even though it be a complimentary likeness, he is entitled to redress."[55] Without a legal right to control one's public persona, how would an "individual remain an individual" in "our mass communication society"?[56] In a world of television, tabloid journalism, and a profusion of pictures in the visual environment, threats to public image were seemingly everywhere. The more intense the public's hunger for images and information, and the more sophisticated and complex the machineries of image-making, the more profound the possibilities for the tarnishing and fatal destabilization of one's public persona.

~

The affluent society consumed media images in unprecedented volume. Newspaper circulation reached historic highs; in 1950, the United States had 1,780 daily newspapers that ran about 55 million copies each day, and by 1960, there were 1.3 newspapers per American.[57] A paperback "revolution" made books available for only 25 cents, and between 1940 and 1960 book sales in the country increased by 450 percent.[58] During the 1950s, Americans were spending $18 billion annually on recreational pursuits, including books, magazines, and newspapers. New magazines like *TV Guide*, *Sports Illustrated*, *Mad*, *Playboy*, and the *National Enquirer* played to the cultural focus on sex, spectacle, and entertainment.[59]

The more that popular culture and social life revolved around mimicry and simulated experience, the greater the hunger for reality: a desire to see more and

more of real life, in all its intimate, mundane, and embarrassing forms, heightened, dramatized, and made larger than life, both in print and on the screen. One
of the most notable features of postwar journalism and popular culture, compared
to the pre–World War II media, were their realism and frankness. Old prohibitions against the discussion and depiction of graphic or intimate subjects—sex,
disease, violence—were fading away. Public tastes had "changed considerably
since the world war," leading to "a general relaxing of taboos," noted an editor
at the *Kansas City Times*.[60] Crime news took up more space in newspapers, and
tabloids and true-crime magazines with titles like *Official Detective Stories, Current Detective, Uncensored Detective*, and *Women in Crime* became popular.[61] The
National Enquirer was founded; the publisher came up with the idea by observing the way people gathered around auto accidents.[62] Pulp fiction flew off book-
shelves, and reality television became a fad. The popular television show *Candid
Camera* broadcast hidden camera footage of ordinary people being confronted
with unusual, often horribly embarrassing situations.[63] The game show *Queen for
a Day* featured housewives confessing their sad, true stories before a public audience; the saddest won prizes.[64]

Attracting audiences in this competitive market meant pushing the envelope.
Television news depended on excitement to hold audiences' fleeting attention,[65]
and critics lamented the trend towards "thrusting a microphone under the chin
of a woman who has watched her child being injured and urg[ing] her to tell the
viewers how she feels."[66] One commentator in the 1960s noted NBC's "remorse-
less focusing" on sustained close-ups of bleeding corpses and incidents in which
the family members of murder victims were pursued and assaulted by TV reporters. Descriptions of press conduct in a 1964 journalism text titled *The Press and
Its Problems* noted that reporters were using wiretaps and surreptitious recording
devices, closed-circuit TV and other miniaturized cameras, in addition to climbing fire escapes and posing "as detectives, coroners' assistants, or other public or
semi-public officials to gain access to places from which they otherwise would be
barred."[67] "Smile, You're on Candid Camera" became the catchphrase of a culture
that had become aware of the possibility of constant media surveillance.[68]

The continued growth of the psychological profession and the therapeutic
culture fueled the notion that a public figure—or anyone, for that matter—could
not be really known or understood without a searching investigation of his psyche

and private life. Deep exposés of personal lives became a staple of popular culture. As the vice president of *Look* magazine put it, "the press . . . has not only the right, but the duty, to publish facts pertaining to public figures, and in so doing, to examine them to see what makes them 'tick,' how they stack up on analysis, and what they are. . . . as persons."[69] Before World War II, the press had often concealed the more intimate private affairs of public officials, particularly their sexual affairs, as part of an unwritten agreement in which officials granted reporters access in return for suppressing scandal. Journalists were less likely to follow this agreement in the postwar era, particularly in light of journalism's new emphasis on investigative reporting.[70] The media's increasingly frank unveiling of the intimate and sexual, writes cultural critic Leo Braudy, reflected "a new eagerness" on the part of the media audience "to rip away the veil of official stories and discover the supposed real truth."[71] Sociologists observed an intensified public interest—"a particular and dangerous form of curiosity"—with "the privacies of personal life, especially sexual conduct among the socially prominent."[72] Observed sociologist Edward Shils, "the intimacies of other persons are 'interesting,' and whether they are degrading to the mighty or the great they are all the more acceptable." "The embarrassments of those who have discomfiting disclosures made about them are as attractive as a boxing match."[73]

∼

The state of image law and litigation reflected the growth of the media, its heightened sensationalism, and the image-consciousness in the culture of the time. Legal protections for people's public images and their feelings about their images increased in the postwar era, as did the use of the law to protect those interests. Libel assumed greater prominence in legal and popular culture, and privacy law and litigation expanded, as we will see in the next chapter. Given how much Americans invested in their public images—economically, psychologically, and emotionally—it was difficult for some to stand by idly and watch while those images were destroyed before a mass audience.

At its 1953 meeting, the American Newspaper Publishers' Association noted that libel claims against newspapers were on the rise. Arthur Hanson, counsel for the ANPA, claimed that the number of libel suits had grown by several hundred percent in the 1950s.[74] One experienced trial lawyer noted a surge of libel cases in the late 1950s and early 1960s; "the law of libel and slander has undergone a . . . revitalization, with a marked acceleration in the rate of institution of cases."[75] According to one torts treatise, libel suits had been far "more numerous" in the 1950s than in previous years.[76] The "climate for media libel suits in the United States" was "heating up."[77]

There was a great inflation in the size of judgments and claims; some plaintiffs were claiming that their reputations were worth millions.[78] Commentators observed the "vicarious satisfaction" of juries "in helping a libel case plaintiff to the pot of gold at the end of the rainbow."[79] As the famed plaintiffs' lawyer Melvin Belli noted, awards for libel, slander, and invasion of privacy were exceeding the value of the most horrible personal injury cases. "A man's reputation is worth more before a jury than his limbs—even his life."[80] To be clear, the press was not *losing* more libel cases. On the contrary, as one journalism trade journal remarked, there was increasing "judicial and legislative liberality in the matter of defenses," including the fair comment and truth defenses.[81] Wrote George Norris, libel lawyer for the *New York Times*, "It would seem that if anyone had an idea of getting rich quick, he would be better off looking for uranium than suing the *New York Times* for libel."[82] But media outlets seemed to be dealing with more libel cases than in the past, and when they did lose, they could lose big.

Newspapers that had not previously used lawyers for prepublication review took up the practice.[83] Literary houses were vigilant about screening manuscripts for libelous content; publishers vetted and routinely rejected literary works, both fictional and nonfictional, due to potential legal actions.[84] The *Saturday Review of Literature* noted in 1950 that the careful, pocketbook-conscious publisher "usually has every manuscript read by a libel expert before it is passed for manufacture." An error or lapse in this process could lead to an angry letter demanding satisfaction by the injured person, or by his lawyer, "who is either pressingly indignant or just pressing."[85] The former dean of the Columbia School of Journalism observed in 1952 that there was a new sensitivity towards libel among members of the press, and that libel training and "libel talks" were given at publishing conventions and seminars.[86] Journalism and publishing trade journals devoted increasing space to discussing libel liability and how to avoid it.[87] The public remained fascinated with libel and the possibility of suing for libel, as evidenced by the volume of popular entertainment on the subject, including the films *The Sweet Smell of Success* (1957), *Slander* (1957), and *Libel* (1959) about newspaper columnists and scandal magazines, their viciously defamatory attacks, and potential legal retribution.

According to some observers, politicians were becoming more aggressive in their use of libel litigation. Libel lawyer and journalism professor Harold Cross, writing in 1951, noted an increase in libel lawsuits in the field of politics. Cross speculated that the causes included more acerbic attacks on politicians by the press and the increasing sensitivity of politicians to assaults on their images, which had become critical assets in the age of televised campaigns and media spin.[88] McCarthyism and the postwar Red Scare led to a wave of lawsuits for libel and slander over accusations of communism. In one of the most high-profile suits in this vein, John Henry Faulk, a popular radio host and outspoken civil libertarian, sued AWARE, a right-wing group that blacklisted entertainment stars for alleged procommunist sympathies. Faulk was vindicated by a jury award of $3.5 million, the largest libel award in U.S. history to that time.[89] Ordinary people were also swept up in the anticommunist dragnet. In one noted 1951 case, a small-town, freethinking West Virginia schoolteacher named Luella Mundel was tagged by a member of the school board as a "poor security risk"; she lost her employment and subsequently sued for slander.[90] Allegations of communist involvement were considered so morally heinous as to be defamatory as a matter of law.[91]

Movie stars brought an increasing number of libel suits against broadcasters and publishers, especially the tabloid press. With the demise of the Hollywood studio system in the late 1940s, stars lost the protection for their images that the studios and their powerful publicity departments had once provided. Less able to defend their images against the attacks of gossip columnists and tabloids, they sought legal recourse. Suing for injuries to one's image became glamorous. In 1957, Frank Sinatra sued *Look* magazine over an article titled "The Life Story of Frank Sinatra, Talent, Tantrums and Torment."[92] Elizabeth Taylor filed six libel suits for over $7 million against various movie fan magazines over lurid headlines and revelations of allegedly "scandalous" sexual conduct.[93] The world paid attention to the stunning string of celebrity libel claims against *Confidential*, a sleazy gossip sheet that began circulation in 1952. *Confidential* magazine promised to go "where no publication had gone before" in exposing the private lives of celebrities. The publication was wildly successful—its July 1955 issue saw the biggest sales of any single magazine issue in history[94]—and it spawned a slew of competitors with titles like *Hush Hush, Uncensored, Exposed,* and *On the QT.*[95] Several Hollywood stars filed multimillion-dollar libel suits against *Confidential* over articles describing various acts of sexual misconduct. The state of California also brought criminal libel charges.[96] The publisher's attorney posed a novel defense: the publication was not false, but was merely revealing the truth that actors and their press agents were trying to conceal. The public was worshiping "false idols." The cases were eventually settled, the magazine went under, and the publisher killed himself.[97]

While public attention was fixed on these newsworthy lawsuits, ordinary people continued to mobilize the law of libel for vengeance, compensation, and reputational rehabilitation. In 1954, the *New Yorker* was sued over an article that told the story of a Nevada man named Joe who had been thrown off a freight train in front of a ranch house. The house belonged to a woman named Letty, described in the article as an "old coyote," who cared for Joe and then married him. Both the man and the woman sued the magazine for libel; the man claimed that the article implied that he had been illegally riding on the train, and the woman alleged that the epithet "old coyote" was defamatory. The *New Yorker*'s editors traveled to Nevada to research the case to prove the truth of their allegations. Such extensive efforts to defend libel claims were not unusual for the magazine in the 1950s.[98]

New media and media genres created new opportunities for libels and libel lawsuits. The publishers of pulp novels and true-crime magazines were frequent libel defendants. The new sexual frankness of the media produced a number of legal actions over allegations of perceived sexual transgressions. In a case from 1952, over four hundred salesmen and women at Neiman Marcus brought suit for $7,400,000 over a notorious book by two gossip columnists, called *USA Confidential*, in which the authors had written that "some models are call girls" and "most of the [male] staff are fairies too."[99] The advent of television broadcasting led to a new kind of defamation, defamation by broadcast, what one Georgia appeals court famously dubbed the "defamacast."[100] The makers of televised "reenactments" of historical or newsworthy events—the popular docudrama genre—inevitably offended the sensibilities of the real people they depicted. In 1919, a man had been convicted of a bank robbery, but was later pardoned. In 1952, NBC's *Big Story* series dramatized his ordeal. The man, who had tried to put his past life behind him, sued NBC, claiming that the actor who portrayed him resembled him, that his friends recognized him and became aware of his earlier life, and that he was deeply shamed.[101]

The vogue for "real life" and its depiction in memoirs, autobiographies, and other literary works led to libel and privacy lawsuits by the people depicted in these stories, or those who inspired lightly fictionalized characters. This was perhaps the fastest-growing area of image law. The *New York Times* noted a "rash of actions by plaintiffs who claim to have been damaged by movie, television, or book publicity that is distasteful to the plaintiff."[102] The popularity of biographies about living people led to a "surge of litigation . . . arising out of asserted rights of biographical subjects."[103] *Publishers' Weekly* warned fiction writers to change the physical appearance, occupation, or sex of any real person who was the basis of a character to avoid the danger of a libel suit.[104]

Some of the most famous literary works of the day were the subjects of libel claims. Grace Metalious, the author of the best-selling, scandalous 1956 book *Peyton Place*, about the seamy sexual affairs of a small New England town, was sued by her characters. Metalious had written about a virile school principal named Tomas Makris. Makris was the name of one of the author's husband's coworkers; he sued for libel, seeking $250,000, and eventually settled out of court for $60,000.[105] Frank Toscani, the American military governor of a small Sicilian town during World War II, who inspired a character in John Hersey's Pulitzer Prize-winning novel *A Bell for Adano*, sued the author for invasion of privacy and libel, claiming that the character's romance with an Italian woman depicted him falsely and was defamatory.[106] In 1950, an undertaker in a small town in Pennsylvania sued the author of *Miracle of the Bells*, a novel later made into a Hollywood film, for $750,000, claiming that readers of the book had identified him with "an unprincipled character in the novel" and that his standing in his community had been injured.[107]

In his novel *From Here to Eternity*, published in 1951, James Jones had written critically about the events in Hawaii surrounding the attack on Pearl Harbor. Jones had been stationed in the Schofield Barracks in Hawaii in 1940. As the lawyers for the publisher, Charles Scribner's Sons, had warned, the personnel who served at Schofield were still alive and could sue for libel. The threat in fact came to pass. Jones had written about a character named Angelo Maggio, a soldier who was depicted in the book as a hard-drinking gambler. In real life, a soldier named

Joseph Maggio had been in Jones's company. Claiming, without proof, that he was the inspiration for the character Angelo Maggio, and that he had been defamed by his depiction in the book, Joseph Maggio, then working as a postal clerk in Brooklyn, sued Scribner's for half a million dollars. The renowned copyright and literary lawyer Horace Manges represented Scribner's in a trial that became a crucible for literary realism. "The eyes of the book world are upon you," Manges told the jury. They voted 10–2 in favor of the defense.[108]

One might question whether *reputational* harm was really at issue in many of these cases. Historically, a person's reputation was an assessment of that person based on appraisals and judgments over time—the "estimate in which [one] is held by the public in the place he is known."[109] Reputation, in other words, depended on the existence of a consistent social group with whom a person regularly interacted. When a person was depicted in the mass media in an embarrassing manner, she might have been worried about her standing among her peers, but she was likely even more concerned with her *image*: the undesirable impression she made on a mass audience, faceless and unknown to her. The traditional concept of reputation, in the sense of the judgments of one's community, was becoming arguably less meaningful in a highly mobile, far-flung mass society where the very possibility of stable, intimate communities was increasingly precarious, if not remote.

～

To some critics, libel law was not enough. Repeating what was by then a familiar refrain, legal commentators argued that the complexities of libel doctrine, bogged down in the technicalities of the legal concept of "reputation," made the tort inadequate to redress the harms to the psyche and feelings caused by media misrepresentations. In 1962, the legal scholar Walter Probert argued that defamation should be reoriented to focus less on injury to reputation than on harm to one's self-image and emotions. The victims of defamatory statements suffered— even more than injury to their relationships—hurt feelings, low self-esteem, and "psychiatric concerns." It had become "an acceptable psychological notion that the individual's self-image is largely a reflection of the way he sees others reacting to him."[110] Such psychological factors, Probert wrote, "should weigh just as heavily" with judges "as does the inference of likelihood of harm to reputation."[111]

In the vein of *Burton v. Crowell*, the 1936 case over the optically illusive Camel cigarette advertisement, courts extended the definition of a defamatory publication to include representations that were not necessarily harmful to a person's social relations but that were nonetheless injurious to his sense of self and his feelings about his public image.[112] The law professor Edward Bloustein observed an "increasing tendency" among courts in defamation cases to go "beyond the traditional reaches" of the protection of reputation to protect plaintiffs against "personal humiliation and degradation."[113] Law professor John Wade noted that courts were expanding defamation law to include situations where there was no injury to the plaintiff's reputation but he was "subjected to mental disturbance."[114] In some jurisdictions, the actions for defamation and privacy were converging.[115]

The law moved even more squarely in that direction in the two decades following *New York Times v. Sullivan* in 1964. The famous *Sullivan* case grew out of news reporting on the civil rights movement. Sullivan, an elected city commissioner of Montgomery, Alabama, who supervised the police department, brought suit against the *New York Times*, claiming that he had been libeled by a full-page advertisement in the *Times*, created by a civil rights group, depicting violence against blacks by the Montgomery police. The ad contained errors, and the *Times* had published it without checking its accuracy. This was part of a string of libel actions against the Northern press by Southern opponents of the civil rights movement.[116] An Alabama trial court held that there had been a libel and the Alabama Supreme Court affirmed. The United States Supreme Court reversed the decision on First Amendment grounds, saying that the ad was protected by freedom of speech; even erroneous political criticism was protected, provided the errors were not made in "reckless disregard" of the truth.[117]

New York Times v. Sullivan, the first case in which the Supreme Court considered the First Amendment implications of the law of libel, constitutionalized the common law privilege we have seen, the conditional privilege for reports on public officials and "matters of public concern." After *Sullivan*, all libel plaintiffs who were public officials had to prove not only that the offending statement was false, but that it was published with reckless disregard of the truth.[118] In effect, the *Sullivan* decision immunized the publication of defamatory falsehoods made non-recklessly, leaving public figures with only a shred of reputational protection under the law of libel. The case, arguably the most important First Amendment decision of the twentieth century, was widely celebrated, famously described by one scholar as an "occasion for dancing in the streets."[119] It was the culmination of a feeling, both within and outside the courts, that the law of libel posed an important First Amendment issue, and that defamation litigation was being used to quash political criticism and debate. In the 1960s and 1970s, the Supreme Court decided a series of cases in which it extended the actual malice requirement to libel actions involving a broad category of "public figures," and also to "private figures" involved in "matters of public concern."[120]

One consequence of the *Sullivan* line of cases was the intensification of libel law's focus on self-image and emotional harms. In *Gertz v. Robert Welch* (1974), which added further First Amendment limitations to the defamation action, the Supreme Court held that compensatory damages in libel cases, including damages for emotional harm, could be awarded without demonstrating any injury to reputation. The plaintiff could simply show "personal humiliation and mental anguish and suffering."[121]

Nearly a hundred years after the *Cape Cod Folks* lawsuit of 1884, Lorenzo Nightingale, the much-maligned plaintiff in that case, was finally vindicated. By the late twentieth century, much of the money paid out in damage awards in defamation suits went to "compensate for psychic injury, rather than any objectively verifiable damage to one's reputation," observed law professor Rodney Smolla.[122] The focus of the action, in many instances, is the "decline in self-reputation" suffered by the plaintiff.[123] As libel scholar Randall Bezanson concluded, the tort's protected interest migrated from "extrinsic, community-based reputation" to "freedom from psychic or emotional harm to the individual."[124]

∼

In some cases, the libel lawsuit was in its own right a tool for image management. Plaintiffs rarely initiate libel suits just to obtain monetary relief; as Bezanson writes, those who sue for libel often "view the lawsuit as an instrument for self-help, regardless of its judicial outcome." Through the act of suing and asserting their own version of the truth, plaintiffs seek to correct what they view as falsity, exact vengeance, and rehabilitate their reputations and public images.[125] Whether they win or lose, the litigation process, particularly if it attracts media attention, offers a way for them to project their own desired images before a public audience.[126]

The use of the libel lawsuit as a strategic publicity mechanism can be seen vividly in the famous case *Cason v. Baskin*, which made its way through the Florida courts in the 1940s. The case involved the celebrity author Marjorie Kinnan Rawlings. Rawlings was the author of *The Yearling* (1938), a touching story about a twelve-year-old boy and a pet fawn. The best-selling book was hailed as a literary masterpiece and Rawlings was awarded the Pulitzer Prize for fiction. In 1942, she wrote a book called *Cross Creek*, an autobiographical depiction of her life in the Florida countryside. The book consisted of vignettes of Rawlings's interactions with colorful individuals in the local community. As in her previous writings, Rawlings—obsessed with chronicling "real life"—insisted on using her subjects' true names.[127]

One of the characters in the book was named Zelma. The character was based on a woman who was one of Rawlings's close friends, Zelma Cason. In real life, as in the book, Cason was a middle-aged social worker with a fiery temper. She was "mannish" for her time—she wore pants, owned a gun, and enjoyed watching boxing matches. She was notorious for her profanity. As one community member testified at trial, "you could hear Miss Cason cussing for a quarter of a mile." "She was very personable, and spicy as a whip." A local fish merchant testified that Cason tried to rent a fishing boat with the words, "I want to catch me some God damn fish."[128]

The description of Cason, in a chapter called "The Census," was highly complimentary, presenting her as a warm and caring individual who was dedicated to her clients and friends. However, there were a few passages that upset Cason. "Zelma is an ageless spinster resembling an angry and efficient canary," Rawlings had written. "She manages her orange grove and as much of the village and county as needs management or will submit to it. I cannot decide whether she should have been a man or a mother. She combines the more violent characteristics of both and those who ask for or accept her manifold ministrations think nothing of being cursed loudly at the very instant of being tenderly fed, clothed, nursed, or guided through their troubles."[129] In another passage, describing a trip into the countryside together, Rawlings wrote of Cason's commentary on country people who poached on the land: "My profane friend Zelma, the census taker, said, 'The b_____s killed the egrets for their plumage until the egrets gave out. They killed alligators for their hides until the alligators gave out. If the frogs ever give out, the sons of b_____s will starve to death.'"[130]

While working on *Cross Creek*, Rawlings had asked members of the community if they would mind being written up in the book. Many of the townspeople said they did not—they were even flattered. Some were "thrilled" at the thought of appearing in a book.[131] They considered it "an honor to be interesting enough to be written about."[132] Rawlings's care about making sure she had the consent of her subjects was the consequence of problems she had experienced with her earlier writings. Prior to finishing *Cross Creek*, Rawlings had written to her editor at Charles Scribner's Sons, Max Perkins, expressing concerns with potential libel suits. She wrote, "Now I have used true names in practically every instance. I have tried not to put things so that anyone's feelings would be hurt. These people are my friends and neighbors, and I would not be unkind for anything, and though they are simple folk, there is the possible libel danger to think of. What do you think of this aspect of the material?"[133] Perkins was unconcerned, believing that the "character of the people"—a largely rural community, not likely to be legally savvy—made a libel suit unlikely.[134]

Rawlings thought that Cason would be pleased by her appearance in the book. As she recalled, "I had no reason to believe she would object to brief mention. . . . [S]he is so vain, that I felt she would be immensely pleased by favorable mention, which I thought I was giving her in *Cross Creek*."[135] However, when Rawlings went to present Cason with an autographed book, she found her friend deeply upset. "You have made a hussy out of me," Cason hissed.[136] Cason claimed that she had received letters from all over the country asking about her; her coworkers teased her and called her "Cross Creek" and asked her to display her "famous profanity." She was so embarrassed that she ceased going out to eat at restaurants and instead would "drive up to a pig stand" and eat in her car.[137] In 1943, Cason contacted a lawyer, looking to sue for libel. The attorney urged Cason to sue for defamation and also for invasion of privacy, as a violation of Cason's right to avoid unwanted and unflattering publicity. The tort had not yet been recognized in Florida, and the lawyer believed that this could be an important test case.[138]

~

The problem between Cason and Rawlings could have been addressed without a lawsuit. A wood and steel bridge spanned "Cross Creek," the link between two nearby lakes. Feuding neighbors were encouraged to meet on the bridge and to settle their conflicts, while the rest of the community watched. No legal intervention was needed.[139] Such informal methods of dispute resolution were common in small communities at the time. As one anthropologist of the 1940s observed, "one gets the feeling that the law is dreaded and even hated" in some small towns. "Lawsuits are avoided as expensive and they are in no wise considered a safe or sure way to justice."[140] But a friendly handshake on the bridge would not yield the outcomes that Cason seemed to want.

Why Cason chose to initiate legal action over what was, for the most part, a favorable portrayal has been much debated by students and aficionados of this famous trial. Because of the prominence of the author, the case was chronicled extensively, and much of the correspondence around the case was preserved in Rawlings's personal archives at the University of Florida. We have a record of the personal feelings and motivations that led the parties to undertake this complex, lengthy, acrimonious case through numerous trials and appeals. A few possible motivations for the lawsuit stand out. Cason was driven to litigation, in part, by a desire for vengeance. There was a rumor in the community that Cason and Rawlings had quarreled a year earlier and that Cason was using the lawsuit to get back at her.[141] Cason also believed that she was being exploited by Rawlings, used as a "tool" for Rawlings's literary fame.[142] As Cason's lawyer wrote, Rawlings "betrayed her friend Zelma and exposed her to the jeers of the multitude for thirty pieces of silver."[143]

There is also some indication that Cason was in it for the money. Rawlings had become relatively wealthy from her writings, and Cason was reported to have told her friends, "I'm gonna get me some of that easy money." Cason sued Rawlings for $100,000. She allegedly promised her family some of the funds she thought she would make from the suit,[144] and told other characters in the book that if she won, "they could sue, too."[145] Rawlings mocked the idea of Cason's grievance as one of "delicate, crushed feelings," and described Cason's family as the "money-maddest folks you ever saw."[146]

Even more, it seems, Cason wanted to use the lawsuit to spin her own positive public image. Despite having attributes that were viewed as masculine at the time, Cason considered herself to be attractive and feminine, and she disliked the thought of being memorialized in a manner she thought to be vulgar and crude.[147] The image of Cason publicized in *Cross Creek* clashed with Cason's own self-image. A lawsuit—one that would be widely publicized because of Rawlings's prominence—would set the record straight. Cason hoped to use the litigation to perform her desired image before both the local community and also a national audience.

Libel defendants also use the litigation process to promote their own public images, and Rawlings embarked on a stunning performance, one that consumed her energies for over half a decade. She reacted violently to the accusations by Cason; to Rawlings, the lawsuit was a personal attack on her reputation as an author of integrity and literary merit. With the help of her lawyer, Rawlings masterfully authored her own account of the contested events. In legal documents, correspondence, and other writings, she portrayed Cason's attack on her as the result of spitefulness, vanity, and pettiness—"greed and unwarranted touchiness."[148] She publicized her version of the story to her famous colleagues in the literary world and rallied the support of fellow authors, including Margaret Mitchell, who praised Rawlings's efforts to "protect all writers against hi-jackers."[149] Fans rushed to her defense, writing letters of encouragement. A fan wrote of Rawlings's portrayal of Cason, "You painted her as a beautiful Florida wildflower and she turned out to be a poison ivy."[150]

Although Rawlings knew that the case could be settled for much less than it would cost to defend, she would not broach the possibility. She had a good name to vindicate; she did not want to go down in history as a libeler. "Millions for defense but not one cent for tribute," she declared.[151] She also saw her defense as a crusade for authors' rights. "A vital principle is involved: the right of anyone to write of his or her own life, where that necessarily involves mention of other people," Rawlings wrote in correspondence to *Time* magazine.[152] In a letter to her attorney Phil May, she said, "I could have bought off Zelma for a thousand, which would have given her a moral victory. . . . But I felt I could not stop short of complete vindication where so vital a principle was at stake."[153] She would have been "betraying all writers" if she took "the easy way out."[154]

The trial was covered extensively by the local and national press. The courtroom was packed with spectators—Cason's lawyer described it as a "Roman circus"; Rawlings's friend, author James Cabell, quipped that the proceedings were so spectacular as to have been "invented by Lewis Carroll at his top form."[155] Both Cason and Rawlings used the courtroom as a venue for strategic image performance. The gist of Cason's argument was that she had been horribly misrepresented; she was demure and feminine, not rough and profane. Rawlings's "clever and scathing verbal description" had inflicted a "gross indignity" on "a gentlewoman . . . of Georgia stock" to the "outrage of the finer sentiments of her nature and to the humiliation of her self-respect."[156] Cason, who wore a blue polka-dot dress with a fresh gardenia, testified that she had "never used the Lord's name in vain" in her life.[157] Rawlings thought this hilarious, coming from a woman who "cusses a blue streak in front of assorted people, and in a voice so loud that she is famous for its carrying quality."[158] Not only had Rawlings misrepresented Cason's character, Cason alleged, but she had thrust her on the public stage against her will, "invading her privacy." Before the book, Cason was a modest woman who "lived a quiet and private life, free from . . . the prying curiosity which accompanies either fame or notoriety . . . [and] withdrawn from the public gaze."[159] As the process of jury selection began, Cason pulled out her knitting and began to work on a blue sweater.[160] Various witnesses were called forth to proclaim that she was "essentially feminine."[161]

In court, Rawlings—in real life a tough-talking drinker and chain-smoker—also appeared demure and feminine, wearing pastel frocks, white beads, and matching pill-box hats.[162] In her testimony, she charmed the crowd, explaining to them her deep love of the community and her admiration for Cason; the description had been meant as a tribute to her independent spirit, not an attack or slur. When one of Cason's lawyers asked about the portrayal of Cason as "my profane friend," Rawlings said that "cussing is a matter of style." "Plain country cussin" was just a harmless local custom.[163] Rawlings and her lawyers obtained fifty-one of the people described in the book as witnesses. All testified that they enjoyed the publicity and that the description of Cason in the book was highly accurate.

Rawlings won the public image battle—the sympathies of the public and the press were clearly on the beloved author's side. In popular accounts of the trial, Cason came off looking shrewish, insincere, and litigious.[164] Her libel claim failed—the court concluded that none of the material about Cason was defamatory. As Rawlings's lawyer successfully argued, a fortyish unmarried woman could not be defamed by the term "ageless spinster," "nor could anyone short of a religious apostle be libeled by reference to his or her profanity." But Cason succeeded in other ways. Indeed, she achieved vengeance against Rawlings, who suffered greatly during the five years of the lawsuit. Rawlings spent a great deal of money defending herself in court. The emotional and physical toll on Rawlings was incalculable; her literary production dried up during the litigation, and the stress of the lawsuit seriously impacted her health.[165]

Cason also won her privacy claim. The Florida Supreme Court, in a groundbreaking decision, concluded that Cason's privacy had been invaded.[166] The court noted that the description of Cason was not objectively unfavorable. "The author speaks of appellant as 'my friend Zelma,' and, in spite of attributing to her the use of her own 'special brand of profanity,' on the whole she portrays plaintiff in a favorable light and evinces a real admiration for her. The quotations from the defendant's book, which appellant complains of, are on the whole complimentary and tend to create the impression that the author's friend Zelma was one who was worthy of her friendship—a fine, strong, rugged character—a highly intelligent and efficient person, with a kind and sympathetic heart, and a keen sense of humor." "Our conclusion is that, . . . considered as a whole, [the book] portrays the plaintiff as a fine and attractive personality."[167]

Nonetheless, the court concluded, the work was "a rather vivid and intimate character sketch," and as such "would make out a . . . case of an invasion of the right of privacy." "[T]here is a right of privacy, distinct in and of itself . . . for breach of which an action for damages will lie," the court declared.[168] For the first time in the state's history, the court recognized the tort of invasion of privacy.[169] Rawlings had harmed Cason's ability to control her own public image, and her feelings about her image, even if no one thought less of the "census taker" for her colorful literary persona. Like several others in this era, Florida's highest court deemed this injury worthy of recompense, part of the law's commitment to broad "protection for the person"—the individual's sense of self, his "mind and spirit," and his "emotions and feelings."[170]

CHAPTER 9

Privacy and the Image in Postwar America

One morning in 1952, Elizabeth Hill answered a knock at the back door of her home in the affluent Philadelphia suburb of Whitemarsh. She saw a strange unshaven man. Her husband, James Hill, the sales manager of a hosiery plant, was at work; the only members of the family who were at home were an eleven-year-old son and two four-year-old twins. Earlier in the day she had heard about three "desperate and vicious" bank robbers who had escaped the federal penitentiary in Lewisburg, Pennsylvania. "We're not going to hurt you—we just want your house for a day," the unshaven man said to her. Two other men appeared, pointing shotguns at Mrs. Hill. The men searched the house, and then said they would like breakfast. Mrs. Hill fixed them scrambled eggs, bacon, and coffee.[1]

The men bathed, shaved, used the family sewing machine to alter Mr. Hill's clothes, which they donned, ate copiously, and played poker. Two of the Hills' other children came home, as did Mr. Hill. The convicts treated the whole family courteously; there was no profanity or violence. After nineteen hours, they left in Mr. Hill's car and were later apprehended in an encounter with the police in which two of the convicts were killed.[2]

The incident was widely reported in the press. James Hill received several offers from magazines and television stations to dramatize the family's story, including a request to appear on the popular *Ed Sullivan Show*, but Hill was a "proper Philadelphian with a distaste for publicity," and he refused.[3] Rejecting a request for a paid interview, he wrote, "for the best interests of our children, we felt that it was best to avoid any course of action that might remind the children of our experience in September 1952."[4] The public's curiosity in the family eventually died out.

In 1954, a true-crime writer, Joseph Hayes, published a novel called *The Desperate Hours*. The story depicted a family of four held hostage by three escaped convicts. Prior to writing the novel, Hayes had clipped a large number of news articles about different hostage incidents that had recently occurred, including an article about the Hills. The novel was not based specifically on any of these incidents, Hayes alleged, but was a work of imagination shaped out of various elements of the different events.[5] Unlike the Hill family, the family in *The Desperate Hours*—named "the Hilliards"—suffer violence at the hands of the convicts; the father and the son are beaten, and the daughter is subjected to verbal sexual insults. The fictional Hilliards fight back; the son tries to get a message to the police, and the father attempts a daring rescue.[6] The book was made into a play, written by Hayes and also entitled *The Desperate Hours*.[7]

In 1955, *Life* magazine did a story on the play, titled "True Crime Inspires Tense Play," with the subtitle, "The ordeal of a family trapped by convicts gives Broadway a new thriller, 'The Desperate Hours.'"[8] *Life* was the nation's most popular magazine, a glossy photojournal that reached 21 percent of the entire population over ten years old.[9] Even though *Life*'s editors had evidence that the play was not exactly about the Hills' experience, the article described the play as a "reenactment" of the "ordeal of the James Hill family." *Life* photographed the play during its Philadelphia debut. The actors were taken to the actual house where the Hills had lived, and scenes from the play were performed on the site of the crime. *Life* ran several photographs that included an enactment of the son being roughed up by one of the convicts, and a picture of the actress who played the Hills' daughter biting the hand of a convict to make him drop a gun.[10]

The horrible incident again became a part of the Hills' lives. For two and a half years, the family had done everything possible to put the trauma behind them. "We wanted to forget it, individually and as a family," James Hill recalled. He felt that the publication had "wiped out in one minute" everything they had tried to achieve.[11] The Hills didn't understand how *Life* magazine could publish such an article "without . . . at least picking up the telephone to find out whether this was the truth or how we felt about it," James Hill said. "It was just like we didn't exist, like we were dirt, like they didn't care."[12]

James Hill "resisted his impulse to resort to the direct remedy of a simpler age—physical violence upon those whom he considered had perpetrated an outrage on his family," in the words of Supreme Court Justice Abe Fortas.[13] He instead picked up the phone. Hill called a Harvard classmate who was a senior law partner at a prestigious New York law firm. The firm's lawyers helped the Hills file suit for invasion of privacy.[14] Eleven years later, *Time, Inc v. Hill* reached the Supreme Court. It was the first case in which the Court addressed the "privacy" right to one's public image—whether, as a matter of formal constitutional law, civil liability for invasion of privacy could coexist with modern interpretations of freedom of speech. The Court's ultimately uneasy, tentative truce between privacy and free expression was emblematic of the culture of the time, which struggled to reconcile competing commitments to freedom: the freedom to determine one's own public persona, and the freedom to make images of people and public affairs. The case forced the Warren Court—the privacy Court and the free speech Court—to navigate between the two constitutional values it had championed and created.

~

In the 1950s, the privacy tort came into its own. The number of reported privacy cases more than doubled that of any previous decade.[15] By the 1960s, there were more than three hundred reported privacy cases, most of them involving the mass media.[16] Reported appellate cases were just the tip of the iceberg. "How many more [privacy cases] are settled in lower courts or out of court cannot even be estimated," wrote *Journalism Quarterly* in 1953. "The number of cases can be said to be definitely increasing."[17] By 1960, the invasion of privacy tort was "declared to exist by the overwhelming majority of American courts."[18]

Like the expansion of libel law and litigation, the increase in privacy cases can be attributed to the growing volume of media publications, their intimacy and sensationalism, and the sensitivity to personal image in the culture of the time. It was part of an expansion of tort liability and litigation more generally; encouraged by a newly organized, expanding plaintiffs' bar, courts and legislatures created new torts and eroded barriers to recovery within existing causes of action.[19] In the 1950s, the average tort award tripled in size, and it continued to expand through the rest of the century.[20] Tort litigation became big business; between 1950 and 1959, the amount paid into the tort system grew from $1.8 billion to $5.4 billion.[21] By the end of the 1950s, personal injury litigation had become a specialty of plaintiffs' lawyers.[22] While few plaintiffs' attorneys specialized in defamation and privacy law, those who worked on accident lawsuits sometimes included privacy and libel in their litigation repertoire.[23]

As in the past, privacy claims reflected the tenor of the media environment. Compared to the prewar era, many more cases involved graphic, even gritty material—gruesome photographs of dead bodies, women semiclad, detailed accounts of murders. In *Kelley v. Post Publishing* (1951), a newspaper published a picture of a girl killed in a car accident.[24] In *Waters v. Fleetwood*, a 1956 case from Georgia, a publication featured close-up photographs of the body of a murdered fourteen-year-old girl as it was recovered from a river.[25] Whether or not these cases succeeded depended on whether a court considered the material to be not "newsworthy," or to be highly "offensive." The gender of the plaintiff was often a significant factor in this determination. Courts were more likely to find an invasion of privacy when the plaintiff was female, and when the published material was of a bodily or sexual nature.

Despite great changes in the status of women since the early 1900s—women voted, drove, had entered the workforce in significant numbers, and even served in the military in limited capacity during the war—women's social fates still depended heavily on perceptions of their modesty and sexual virtue. Historian Wini Breines writes of the near-obsession with virginity and chastity in the middle-class culture of the 1950s.[26] Exposing a woman's body or personal affairs to the public, especially in a sexually suggestive manner, could have serious consequences for her reputation and social standing. Some judges still spoke in the language of the Victorian age, redolent with chivalry and paternalism. Steeped in long-standing stereotypes about women as creatures of special sensitivity and "delicate constitution," they regarded women's psyches as fragile; women's feelings and sensibilities, it was said, were more likely to be injured by unwanted publicity, particularly the "wrong" kind of publicity, than men's. In a number of cases in the postwar era, women were held to have valid privacy claims around intimate or suggestive publications when the same material might have been "newsworthy" about a man.

This gendered double standard dates back to the earliest history of privacy law.[27] In one of the most famous examples, *Melvin v. Reid* (1931), the California Supreme Court held that a rehabilitated former prostitute whose life story was made into a film could sue for invasion of privacy, even though her crimes were matters of public record. She claimed that the film caused her friends to learn "for the first time of the unsavory incidents of her early life" and that they subsequently "scorn[ed] and abandon[ed] her." The court concluded that the publication of these prior incidents "was not justified by any standard of morals or ethics known to us and was a direct invasion of her inalienable right guaranteed to her by our Constitution, to pursue and obtain happiness."[28] A number of cases we have seen in this book—among them, *Cason v. Baskin, Peed v. Washington Times,* and *Blumenthal v. Picture Classics,* all with female plaintiffs—concerned material that was either in the public record, had occurred in a public place, or would be a "matter of public concern" under any fair interpretation of the case law. *Cason,* it will be recalled, involved the "ageless canary" of *Cross Creek; Peed,* a truthful news report on an asphyxiated woman; and *Blumenthal,* a woman walking on the street who was depicted in an embarrassing manner in a newsreel. Plaintiffs survived defendants' motions to dismiss their privacy claims, and in some cases won favorable verdicts.[29]

Courts often applied a different—albeit informal and unspoken—set of rules and assumptions in privacy cases involving women, particularly older white women, seen as entitled to special deference and respect. Legal scholars have documented the existence of gender biases in tort law; assumptions about women's alleged mental and physical inferiority, and the systematic devaluation of women's perspectives and experiences, have been hardwired into many areas of tort doctrine.[30] Although ostensibly meant to privilege and protect women, the laws of privacy and public image, like laws that more overtly disadvantaged females, also reinforced gender inequalities. Insofar as they embodied, to use the words of historian Barbara Welke, a "debilitating image of women's nature"—of women as weak, vulnerable, and emotionally unstable—they exacted a toll on all women.[31] On the other hand, one might see this gendered double standard as discrimination against men: privacy law held males to a stringent, perhaps unreasonable standard of masculinity that denied the reality and significance of their emotional injuries. The upshot of this gendering of the law was that many of the most important twentieth-century cases recognizing a right to one's image involved female plaintiffs; women and their claimed emotional and dignitary injuries drove the development of modern privacy law.

The 1951 case *Leverton v. Curtis* involved a ten-year-old girl who was hit by a car. A photograph of her as she lay in the street right after the accident—depicting her face distorted in pain, her hair and clothing in disarray, and her legs exposed to the hips—appeared in a newspaper the next day, and later in a national magazine. A jury awarded damages, concluding that there was no legitimate public interest in the picture.[32] In 1961, a forty-four-year-old mother, Flora Bell Graham, the wife of a chicken farmer from rural Cullman County, Alabama, attended the county fair with her sons, and she went with them into a funhouse. As she left, her dress was blown up by air jets—part of the "fun." A photographer from the local paper got a snapshot, and the picture of the woman, shocked in her panties, ran on the front page. Even though the picture was taken in a public place, the trial court made an award of several thousand dollars, upheld by the state's Supreme Court. "Not only was th[e] photograph embarrassing to one of normal sensibilities," the court concluded, but was "offensive to modesty or decency" to the point of being "obscene."[33] The Seventh Circuit in 1962 held the publication of stories of the rape-murder of a young girl in a true-crime magazine to be an actionable invasion of privacy.[34] The *Miami Daily News* published an article that contained the statement, "Wanna hear a sexy telephone voice?" It gave instructions to call a particular phone number and to "ask for Louise." "Louise" filed suit, alleging that the article not only injured her public image, but led to "many hundreds of telephone calls by various and sundry persons seeking to talk to and listen to the plaintiff." A Florida appeals court denied the newspaper's motion to dismiss the privacy claim.[35]

It was not only suggestive or explicit portrayals that "invaded privacy." Postwar courts found invasions of privacy in all manner of media depictions that plaintiffs claimed to be embarrassing, offensive, or otherwise injurious to their sense of self and public image. Literary authors like Rawlings whose characters were based on, or resembled real people found themselves defendants in privacy cases.[36] Photographers were also sued; *American Photography* urged its readers to obtain releases from photographic subjects, as "a man's likeness" was in many circumstances legally "his own, and it is for him to determine and say just how far and to what extent it will be exposed to the public gaze."[37] The makers of motion pictures also faced privacy claims; the film industry was a real "target for invasion of privacy lawsuits," noted one publishing trade journal in 1953.[38] In 1949, the Marine Corps officer whose life story had been made into the famous Hollywood war film *The Sands of Iwo Jima* sued for invasion of privacy.[39] A California trial court issued a $290,000 judgment against the film company Loew's Inc. over a complaint by a woman who was the model for an army nurse in the film *They*

Were Expendable. The court found that depicting her romance with a navy lieu-
tenant on screen was an invasion of her privacy.[40]

Television stations also faced privacy suits over both live and recorded broad-
casts. Because television had a vast audience, was broadcast directly into the
home, and was often unedited, "an individual's right of privacy is more directly
invaded by the reproduction of a television program . . . than by a newspaper or
radio account," argued a law review writer in 1952.[41] Some feared that the increasingly ubiquitous presence of television cameras and live coverage of public events
would lead to the complete evisceration of privacy. "An employee reports that he
is ill and unable to come in for work. However, while viewing the telecast of the
afternoon baseball game the employer sees . . . [the] employee in the crowd at the
game. Has the employee any cause of action based on an invasion of his privacy?"
asked one legal commentator.[42] Despite television's possibilities for massive harm
to public image, courts judged invasions of privacy committed via television with
the same standards they used for print.[43] In a 1955 Florida case, *Jacova v. Southern
Radio and Television Co.*, a newscast depicted a man who had been arrested at a
cigar store as part of a police gambling raid. The man, who had stopped at the
store to buy a newspaper, was falsely accused of being a gangster, and the footage
depicted him being shoved up against a wall by the police. He sued for invasion
of privacy and lost; the material had "news value," according to the court.[44] Since
television served the important public function of delivering news and entertainment, the court concluded, it should be treated no differently under privacy law
than newspapers, magazines, and books.[45]

Privacy cases continued to be brought—and won—over publications that
were benign in most people's eyes, in some cases even complimentary, albeit displeasing to the subjects of publicity. In the early 1960s, Warren Spahn, the famous
baseball player, sued over an unauthorized biography that he claimed was too
flattering. The biography depicted him as a war hero who had been awarded the
Bronze Star. Spahn had served in the army, but had not been decorated. The book
also inaccurately portrayed his relationship with his father, who appeared in the
story as a kind mentor and coach, and it incorporated false, invented dialogue.
Spahn found all this to be offensive, sued for invasion of privacy under the New
York statute, and was successful at trial. Spahn later told an interviewer that he
was embarrassed at the way his military experience had been glorified and was

concerned that people would think he planted the account to make himself look heroic. He sued because he believed "it was simply wrong just to make up stories about someone."[46] The publication was enjoined and Spahn awarded damages.[47]

Fictionalizations like the Spahn case, whether drastic or mild, were the basis of a number of privacy claims.[48] In 1956, when a commercial flight from Honolulu to San Francisco developed engine trouble, a commander with the navy who was on board helped land the plane and evacuate several of the passengers. An NBC reenactment of the incident depicted him "praying during the course of the emergency landing . . . wearing a so-called Hawaiian shirt . . . [and] smoking a pipe and cigarettes." He did not smoke and had been uniformed during the event. This misleading depiction caused him "great mental pain and suffering." A federal judge concluded that a jury could find an "offensive invasion of privacy" in the distorted broadcast.[49] Torts scholar William Prosser, in a seminal 1960 law review article titled "Privacy," described these "false presentation" cases as actions for "false light" invasion of privacy, in contrast to cases involving the "public disclosure of private facts," where injury had been caused by the publication of truly intimate or personal material.[50]

Miscontextualized and mislabeled photographs also continued to provoke legal action. The celebrated photographer Henri Cartier-Bresson photographed a couple at an ice cream shop in the Farmers Market in Los Angeles. The picture showed the man and woman seated at a counter with the man's arm around the woman. The photo had been used in *Harper's Bazaar* to illustrate an article titled "And So the World Goes Round," a short commentary reaffirming "the poet's conviction that the world could not revolve without love." Observers thought the picture was attractive and pleasing. But the couple alleged that it misrepresented them, and they sued. The California Supreme Court in 1952 concluded that there had been an invasion of the couple's privacy. The majority concluded that their "amorous pose" was a personal, "private" matter, even though it had taken place in public.[51]

The "privacy" right to one's public image was widely supported, both in popular culture and in the legal world. The idea of a legal right to protect one's public image against unwanted or distorted media depictions resonated with cultural ideals of personal autonomy and self-invention. Just as one had a right to buy the car one wished, to pursue one's chosen career, or to move to San Francisco and put flowers in one's hair—or so said the arbiters of popular culture—every person had a right to construct his or her own social persona. Privacy was the individual's "rightful claim . . . to determine the extent to which he wishes to share himself with others," in the words of one legal scholar. Everyone had a right to "choose those portions of the individual which are to be made public."[52] In his 1967 work *Privacy and Freedom*, one of the many books on privacy published in the 1960s, legal scholar Alan Westin described privacy—the right "to determine when, how, and to what extent information about [oneself] is communicated to others"—as an essential instrument for "achieving individual goals of self-realization."[53] Scholars were urging a "right to biography"—people's lives "belonged" to them, therefore individuals should have a right to control what others wrote about them.[54] The essence of "privacy" was the protection of personal "independence," wrote law professor Edward Bloustein, and unwanted media depictions were a serious offense "against the right of the individual to be self-determining."[55] "In defamation a man is robbed of his reputation; in [privacy] cases it is his individuality which is lost."[56]

Support for the tort law of privacy, as a right to control one's public image, was underscored by growing legal protections for privacy more broadly, in response to a "privacy panic."[57] The expanding mass media, particularly the visual media, continued to pose perceived threats to privacy; there was "considerable indignation [throughout] the land concerning . . . photographic invasion[s] of privacy," noted one photographer in 1950.[58] There were also new, terrifying technological developments. Tiny listening bugs, microphones, miniaturized cameras, closed-circuit TV, telephoto lenses, and infrared light technology, developments of the World War II era, were being used by the government, the burgeoning private detective industry, and the news media.[59] Wiretapping and other methods of government surveillance surged during the McCarthy era, the civil rights movement, and the Vietnam War.[60] Large-scale data collection became a concern with the rise of the first primitive computers in the 1960s.[61] Tools for snooping and prying had become available to the average citizen; people could purchase a device that "picked up sound in rooms across the street" for $15, and $150 bought a TV camera "the size of a book that can spy on a room while you secretly watch on a distant monitor."[62] Mused the *New York Times* in 1966, "what has been described as an age of alienation is, in truth, an age in which no one can ever be sure he is alone."[63] Courts expanded the scope of the tort of "intrusion upon seclusion," a branch of the tort of invasion of privacy that imposed liability for unwarranted invasions of one's personal, physical space. In 1964, the New Hampshire Supreme Court held that it covered electronic eavesdropping.[64]

In the 1960s, in a number of different contexts, the Supreme Court recognized a constitutional right to privacy. As historian of privacy Frederick Lane notes, prior to the start of Chief Justice Earl Warren's term in 1953, the term "privacy" appeared in just 88 Supreme Court opinions. By contrast, the term appeared in 107 opinions during Warren's fifteen-year tenure.[65] Dominated by a liberal majority, the Supreme Court under Warren came to be regarded as the preeminent court protecting individual rights against encroachment by federal and state governments, and the "right to privacy" became the centerpiece of the Court's protection of individual autonomy, agency, and freedom.[66]

In *Mapp v. Ohio* (1961), the Court referred to the "freedom from unconscionable invasions of privacy"—unwarranted searches and seizures—as protected by the Fourth Amendment.[67] The Court recognized a right to "associational privacy" under the First Amendment in cases involving forced disclosures of group membership lists.[68] In *Griswold v. Connecticut* (1965), involving a statute that prohibited the dissemination of information about birth control, the Court held that various provisions of the Bill of Rights, "penumbras" and "emanations" of the First, Third, Fourth, and Fifth Amendments, protected privacy—marital privacy—as a core aspect of individual liberty.[69] This "discovery" of a right to privacy in the Constitution, and the Court's framing of privacy around principles of individuality, self-fulfillment, and a right to choose, were both cause and consequence of the self-focused ethos of the age, an era when, to use one sociologist's phrase, "anything that would violate our right to think for ourselves, judge for ourselves, [and] make our own decisions" was seen not only as morally wrong, but "sacrilegious."[70]

∾

In the 1950s and 1960s, the mass consumer and celebrity culture yielded another kind of "privacy" right to one's image. The right to privacy was extended to encompass a right to profit from the commercial exploitation of one's image—the right to sell one's image as personal property.

A good deal had changed since the early days of privacy law and the turn-of-the-century crisis of the "circulating portrait," in which individuals' likenesses were randomly appropriated for use in product advertisements. With the improvement of photographic technologies and the creation of systematic channels for producing and distributing advertising images, by the 1930s the black market in photographs of ordinary people had all but disappeared. The first two decades of the twentieth century saw the development of a commercial modeling industry.[71] Movie studios began licensing the names and images of stars to advertisers, and celebrity endorsers were treated by the public with the reverence afforded "aristocracy."[72] It was no longer considered shameful but prestigious and a sign of status to have one's image in an advertisement.[73] The ability to vend one's likeness for profit—to commodify one's self and one's image—meant that one had acquired the looks and charisma that were important cultural capital in the image society.

Though ordinary people occasionally brought suit over the unauthorized commercial use of their images,[74] after the 1920s public figures raised most of these "privacy" claims. In some cases, the injury claimed was emotional distress, and in others, lost profits. The results in these lawsuits were mixed. Some courts concluded that entertainment stars, who sought the spotlight and willingly exploited their images, could not claim emotional and dignitary injuries when their likenesses were publicized without consent. In *O'Brien v. Pabst Sales Company*, from 1941, Pabst, the beer brewer, had used the picture of one of the country's most famous football stars, Davey O'Brien, on its annual football calendar. On the calendar was a picture of a bottle of Pabst beer and some advertising text. O'Brien brought suit for invasion of privacy, claiming to be deeply affronted—he was a member of a religious group that opposed drinking. The court ruled that O'Brien was a "public figure" who had voluntarily sought publicity, and had no right to complain when he got more publicity than he wanted.[75] Yet, in other cases, courts permitted actors, sports stars, and other well-known individuals to recover for emotional harms and, in some instances, for the economic or "publicity" value of their images.[76]

In 1953, in the well-known case *Haelan v. Topps Chewing Gum,* a federal appeals court acknowledged a "right of publicity," "the right of each person to control and profit from the publicity values which he has created or purchased."[77]

The case involved a baseball card manufacturer that had used the likeness of a famous baseball player without payment or consent. Celebrity endorsements were big business; according to one firm that specialized in licensing celebrity images to advertisers, between 1945 and 1957, approximately 8,000 celebrities had been used to advertise 4,500 products.[78] The *Haelan* court made explicit what had been apparent for several decades: the act of commercializing one's persona, once viewed by some as so morally questionable as to be unworthy of the law's protection, no longer carried any stigma whatsoever.

Under this "right of publicity," damages would be computed in terms of economic loss, rather than the plaintiff's emotional injuries.[79] As the court observed, "It is common knowledge that many persons (especially actors and ball-players), far from having their feelings bruised through public exposure of their likenesses, would feel sorely deprived if they no longer received money for authorizing advertisements, [and] popularizing their countenances, displayed in newspapers, magazines, buses, trains, and subways."[80] There would be no "waiver" of the right by virtue of the plaintiff's celebrity. Wrote the entertainment lawyer Melville Nimmer in 1954, privacy law, "first developed to protect the sensibilities of nineteenth-century Brahmin Boston, is not adequate to meet the demands of the second half of the twentieth century."[81] Celebrities "do not seek the 'solitude and privacy' which Brandeis and Warren sought to protect. Indeed, privacy is the one thing they do 'not want, or need.'"[82]

By the 1970s, several states had adopted a "right of publicity" as a property-based interest. In some states, this was designated as a "branch" of the tort of invasion of privacy, the tort of "appropriation." The appropriation tort or right of publicity protected the "pecuniary interest in identity," with "identity" broadly defined as representations of one's "persona," including one's name, voice, and likeness. An oft-cited justification for a celebrity's right to recover the economic value of his image was that he had expended labor in its creation.[83] A celebrity's "identity, embodied in his name, likeness, statistics, and other characteristics, is the fruit of his labors and a kind of property."[84] Famous people brought suit under the right of publicity over the use of their images not only in advertisements, but in any kind of commercial use—their depiction in films, docudramas, biographical works, caricatures, and novels, as well as the use of their likenesses on merchandise and other consumer paraphernalia. Cary Grant sued *Esquire* magazine when it printed a photo of his head atop the torso of a model wearing a "cardigan sweater jacket" that was being featured by the magazine.[85] The actress Shirley Booth brought a lawsuit when Colgate used a cartoon character, "Hazel," popularly associated with Booth, to promote its laundry detergent without Booth's consent.[86]

Though celebrities were the greatest beneficiaries of the "right of publicity" or appropriation tort, the action was not limited to those who were famous. Courts held that ordinary people could obtain damages under the right of publicity as long as their images had any conceivable commercial value. In the 1950s, a veteran and his family were unable to find a house or apartment to rent because they had eight children. The man, Joseph Canessa, ran an advertisement in the "Lost and Found" section of a local newspaper, which said, "Lost the right to rent because of too many children." A salesman employed by a real estate company answered the ad and helped Canessa buy a house through the GI Bill. Canessa's story was publicized in the local newspaper. The real estate company used the news story, along with photos of Canessa, as part of its sales promotional materials. Canessa sued, and the New Jersey Supreme Court held that he could recover pecuniary losses. "People's names and likenesses belong to them. As such, they are property," it opined.[87] "However little or much plaintiff's likeness and name may be worth, defendant, who has appropriated them for his commercial benefit, should be made to pay for what he has taken whatever it may be worth."[88] Without embarrassment or moral hesitation, courts were concluding that everyone had a right to control their images, which included extracting from them commercial value.

∽

Privacy was not the only sacred ideal in postwar America. By the 1960s, freedom of speech had also become a core cultural and legal value. The student movement had begun with the famous Berkeley free speech protests, and the right to dissent, question authority, and challenge the status quo was a critical demand of the counterculture.[89] In the era of Vietnam, the Pentagon Papers, anticommunist purges, and the public revelation of extensive government spying, political criticism was being described as a public duty.[90] The "crusading journalist," risking punishment to expose injustice, was romanticized in the popular culture of the time.[91] The call for freedom of expression was not limited to the realm of political speech. Both within and outside official channels, dissenters sought to eliminate moral and legal proscriptions against the publication of pornography and other sexually themed matter, and to broaden the scope of artistic and cultural expression.[92]

The Supreme Court's protection of free speech was unprecedented. Between the end of World War II and the 1970s, the Court issued decisions that protected a wide range of previously proscribed material.[93] In *Winters v. New York* (1948), the Court struck down a New York statute prohibiting the publication of descriptions of "bloodshed, lust, and crime," which had been used to convict the seller of a true-crime magazine. The Court noted that freedom of speech encompassed publications that were offensive and had no literary merit; the "line between informing and entertaining is too elusive for the protection of that basic right."[94] In *Roth v. U.S.*, the Court narrowed the definition of constitutionally unprotected, obscene material.[95] In 1952, in *Burstyn v. Wilson*, the Court held film censorship to be an unconstitutional infringement on the public's right to consume art, entertainment, and culture of its own choosing.[96] *New York Times v. Sullivan* (1964) and *Garrison v. Louisiana* (1965) reduced libel liability for writings about public figures.[97] Almost three-fourths of the free speech cases that came before the Court in the 1950s and 1960s were decided in favor of free expression.[98] The Warren Court is widely regarded as the architect of modern free speech law.[99]

The Court's opinions described free expression as an important personal liberty, essential to self-fulfillment. The ability to freely express one's thoughts, beliefs, and personal identity was seen as essential to the growth and enhancement of the individual. Decisions also emphasized the importance of freedom of speech and press to democratic self-governance through "public discussion." As the Court wrote in *New York Times v. Sullivan*, "uninhibited, robust, and wide open" political debate was the cornerstone of participatory democracy.[100] With the public dependent on the mass media as a source of information about public affairs, "a broadly defined freedom of the press" was necessary for "the maintenance of our political system and an open society."[101] "Fear of large verdicts in damage suits" "present[ed] a grave hazard of discouraging the press from exercising its constitutional guarantees."[102]

In this free speech zeitgeist, courts often dismissed privacy suits against the media under the "matters of public interest" privilege, as in the *Sidis* case. Fearing a "judicial censorship" of the press, they continued to define the content of the popular media as synonymous with the "public interest."[103] If something appeared in the "press"—a film, novel, television episode, or even tabloid or detective magazine—by definition it was a matter of public interest and "newsworthy." "Some readers are attracted by shocking news. Others are titillated by sex in the news," observed the Third Circuit Court of Appeals. "This may be a disturbing commentary upon our civilization, but it is nonetheless a realistic picture of society which courts shaping new juristic concepts must take into account."[104] "In addition to the vast growth of the gossip columns," newspapers and magazines contained "detailed reports of the piquant facts in matrimonial litigation and the colorful escapades and didoes of well-known persons," noted one court. "We cannot undertake to pass judgment on those reading tastes."[105] The broad privilege was said to be necessary protection for the constitutional "right of the public to be informed," whether the information was material about a politician's home and family life or a sensationalistic article about a homicide in *Official Detective Stories* magazine.[106]

Public figures had no privacy, said some courts, having "waived" it by pursuing a career in the spotlight.[107] Celebrities assumed the risk of having their privacy invaded when they embarked on a path towards public recognition and fame. Insofar as the activities of public figures were almost always matters of public interest, virtually any media publication about them was immune from liability. NBC broadcast a conversation between Charlie Chaplin and a radio commentator that had been obtained by wiretapping. Chaplin was said to have waived his right of privacy over the phone conversation because he was a "prominent public figure whose activities are of general public interest."[108] So long as there was ongoing interest in the celebrity, the "waiver" of privacy was permanent. In 1949, a professional boxer who had retired from the ring to pursue a life of anonymity sued NBC over a radio broadcast that discussed his boxing career. The court held that no matter how much he wished to retreat from the public eye, he could not "draw himself like a snail into his shell" and retreat from public view at his "will and whim."[109]

In one noted case, a court held that famous people should have *some* kind of privacy. Walt Disney had invited Kirk Douglas and his two sons to his house for a private social visit, and Disney took home movies of them riding on Disney's toy train. Two years later, the movies were used on the nationally televised *Disneyland* show.[110] A California court permitted Douglas to proceed on his privacy claim against Disney, noting that "it is not enough to say that because he is a motion picture personality and a public character he has no private rights in the matter. Motion picture actors are not altogether 'goldfish in a bowl.'"[111] But this was the exception, not the rule. The right to privacy "does not exist where a person has become prominent or distinguished," asserted one federal judge. "By such prominence he has dedicated his life to the public and thereby waived his right to privacy."[112]

Every person, celebrity or not, surrendered his right to privacy by becoming part of an event that was a "newsworthy" matter of public concern, whether voluntarily or involuntarily, in the view of some courts.[113] A newspaper that ran a large picture of a murdered boy's decomposed body was not liable to the boy's parents. The court concluded that the boy, albeit unwillingly, became part of an event of "public interest" by virtue of being murdered, and waived his right to privacy.[114] In some cases, anyone connected to a public figure, however remotely, lost his privacy. As a teenager, a man married his girlfriend; the marriage was annulled, and the woman later became the actress Janet Leigh. The man sued for invasion of privacy when a gossip magazine recounted this many years later. The court dismissed the claim, noting that "people closely related to . . . public figures . . . lose their right to the privacy that one unconnected with the famous or notorious would have."[115] Likewise, given live television coverage, the paparazzi, and the increasing presence of cameras in public, people were said to assume the risk of unwanted publicity whenever they went outside their homes. While a person might have a cause of action for intrusion upon seclusion if a paparazzo broke down his door to get a picture, an individual in a public place was fair game.[116] The dominant rule was that "photographers on public property may take pictures of anyone they want to, objection or no[t]."[117]

A public so committed to privacy was at the same time remarkably sanguine about its loss. The culture seemed to crave privacy yet at the same time recognized the incompatibility of privacy with modern life, with its demands for disclosure and exposure. "Guarantee of the right of privacy is not a guarantee of hermitic seclusion," noted an Illinois appeals court in 1960. "Every election thrusts upon the shyest and most retiring citizen demands and obligations. A political campaign brings forth public insistence that he vote. Every television and radio program blares forth exigent calls to do or buy this or that. The census taker asks for the furnishing of private information. The mail brings importunities of every kind. The telephone serves a like purpose. Finally, the revenue collector pries into the very heart of what used to be a person's private affairs—how much he earned, how much he spent, how much he gave away."[118] Loss of one's privacy and control of one's public image was "one of the prices we pay for living in a free society—like taxes."[119] "Whether we like it or not, we have no more privacy than the proverbial goldfish. If we participate in any manner in the life of a community, we live in public."[120] "Exposure of the self to others in varying degrees is a concomitant of life in a civilized community," declared a Supreme Court opinion in 1967.[121] "The risk of this exposure is an essential incident of life in a society which places a primary value on freedom of speech and press."[122]

～

The tension between the right to control one's public image and the freedom to make images of others played out before a national audience in the milestone case *Time, Inc. v. Hill*, the first in which the Supreme Court addressed the First Amendment implications of tort liability for invasion of privacy. The *Hill* case came to the Court in 1965, a particularly charged moment in the histories of both privacy and free expression. The Supreme Court had just decided *Griswold v. Connecticut*, recognizing a constitutional right to privacy, and in 1964, *New York Times v. Sullivan*, expanding free speech protections under the law of libel. In the mid-1960s, the mass media was being attacked for its sensationalism and violence, yet at the same time, popular culture was celebrating the investigative journalist and his revealing exposés of social inequities and government corruption. The counterculture was under way; its rallying cry of autonomy and personal freedom encompassed both the right to privacy and the right to speak.

The *Hill* case had been brought under the New York privacy statute, which targeted the unauthorized use of people's names and likenesses for the purpose of commerce or "trade." This was the statute that had been passed in 1903 in the wake of the *Roberson* case. Under that law, if something was deemed to be "news," it could not be "trade" (even though, of course, news is commercial). If the material was false, or conveyed a false impression, it could not be "news"; therefore, if it was false (or fictionalized), it was "trade."[123] The Hills' lawyers argued that *Life* magazine falsely described the play *The Desperate Hours* as an account of the Hills' experience, even though *Life*'s editors had evidence to the contrary. The magazine knew that the play was not an accurate depiction of what happened to the Hills but claimed that it was a "re-enactment" in order to make the article more "newsy" and appealing.[124]

In 1962, a jury concluded that the New York privacy statute had been violated and made a large damage award to the Hills, even though the article and the play portrayed the family as noble and heroic. The Hills won $175,000 in compensatory and punitive damages, the largest invasion of privacy award in the state's history.[125] Several jurors had wanted to award as much as $500,000.[126] The decision was affirmed by the state's appeals courts, and *Life*'s publisher, Time Inc., appealed to the U.S. Supreme Court.[127]

The attorney for the Hills during the appeal was Richard Nixon—*the* Richard Nixon, who had been vice president under Eisenhower, unsuccessfully ran for president against John F. Kennedy in 1960, and then failed in his bid for governor of California in 1962. After his California defeat, Nixon, who had practiced law before his career in politics, went east and joined a Wall Street firm, which became Nixon, Mudge, Rose, Guthrie, and Alexander. Nixon saw his law practice as a way to rehabilitate his public image after the failed campaigns, and the *Hill* case was especially valuable in this regard. "The Hills were sympathetic clients—a normal middle-class mother and father who valued their privacy and their children's," observed colleague Leonard Garment.[128] In the *Hill* case, Nixon could be seen as a serious lawyer defending Americans' besieged privacy rights, not the spiteful politician who had bitterly attacked the press after his defeat in the California gubernatorial race, telling reporters, in his famous "last press conference," that they wouldn't have Richard Nixon to "kick around anymore."[129]

Nixon prepared meticulously, reading every law review article and every case on privacy and committing them to memory.[130] He filled yellow notepad upon notepad with comments on legal doctrines of privacy, the history of the New York privacy statute, and contemporary First Amendment theorists. The stakes were high for Nixon, who was hoping to make a political comeback. As Nixon wrote in a confidential memo to Garment, the publicity surrounding the case would help the firm in "bringing . . . more clients in the future" and—referring to his politi-

cal ambitions—also "in terms of other considerations which are broader than our
. . . commercial interests."[131]

Nixon argued that the magazine had created a fictionalized description of the
play as a "gimmick"—an advertisement to increase sales of the magazine—and
that the article was actionable as an unauthorized use of a person's identity for
the purpose of "trade." The Hills had been exploited to advance the pecuniary
interests of *Life* and the producers of *The Desperate Hours*. "The *Life* article was
a hoax executed with painstaking precision. It was based upon. . . . the use of
the Hills' former home and the cast of the *Desperate Hours* to create a 'newsy'
approach to coverage of the play," Nixon said in oral argument.[132] Were private
citizens, thrust into the spotlight against their will, to be exploited as "gimmicks
for commercial purposes in a falsified situation"? he asked.[133] "Our most fundamental position . . . is this: It is inconceivable that the law is powerless to protect
an individual from harmful exploitation through deliberate falsification such as
. . . in this case," Nixon wrote to his colleagues.[134] "I like my magazines newsy,
exciting, and stimulating, but not at [the] cost of invading [the] privacy of . . .
an ordinary middle class family by using their name in a fictionalized setting for
commercial gain."[135]

The magazine, represented by the elite law firm Cravath, Swaine, and Moore,
fired off the familiar defense: even though the facts may not have been completely
accurate, the article was "a subject of legitimate news interest," "a subject of general interest and of value and concern to the public." The members of the Hill
family were "public figures" who lost their right to privacy when they became
involved in a matter of public concern, albeit inadvertently.[136] Time Inc.'s lawyer,
Harold Medina Jr., a senior litigation partner at Cravath, argued that *Life* was actually doing the Hills a favor by making them look courageous and heroic.[137] This
outraged Nixon. As he wrote in a private memo to Garment, it was true that "*Life*
did not intend to hurt the Hills by its publication even though it did not show
them the courtesy of asking consent before using their names. *Life* just *didn't care*
about the Hills." The magazine was simply "using the Hills to help itself."[138] Even
"laudatory falsehoods," Nixon wrote, "affect what you think about yourself—a
man's self-respect."[139]

At the Court's first private conference on April 29, 1966, the vote was to affirm
judgment for the Hills. Six of the justices agreed that the article falsely portrayed

the Hills' experience and thus was a "trade" use and a violation of the privacy statute.[140] Chief Justice Warren assigned the drafting of the opinion to Justice Abe Fortas, who wrote a passionate defense of privacy and a scathing attack on the press.[141] Fortas not only was committed to privacy as a philosophical matter but, according to one of his clerks, "feared and loathed the press" due to his own unpleasant encounters with it, as well as those of his friend and benefactor, President Lyndon Johnson, who had appointed him to the bench. He wanted to narrow the scope of press freedom as set out in *New York Times v. Sullivan*.[142] "Wanton and deliberate injury of the sort inflicted by *Life*'s picture story is not an essential instrument of responsible journalism," he wrote. "The deliberate, callous invasion of the Hills' right to be let alone—this appropriation of a family's right to not be molested or have its name exploited and its quiet existence invaded—cannot be defended on the ground that it is within the purview of a constitutional guarantee designed to protect the free exchange of ideas and opinions."[143]

Justice Hugo Black, who had written some of the most important free speech and press decisions of the 1940s and 1950s, ultimately changed the Court's position. Black, a free speech "absolutist," believed that any restraint on press freedom was unconstitutional. As he wrote in a sixteen-page memo to the Court, hoping to sway the vote, "One does not have to be a prophet to foresee that judgments like the one . . . here . . . can frighten and punish the press so much that publishers will cease trying to report news in a lively and readable fashion as long as there is . . . doubt as to the complete accuracy of the newsworthy facts."[144] Black had a personal vendetta against Fortas dating back many years, and he saw this as an opportunity to attack his rival.[145] Black castigated Fortas's draft opinion as a profound threat to freedom of the press, and the worst First Amendment opinion he had seen during his time on the Court.[146] This entreaty proved persuasive; in the end, the vote was five to four for reversal.

∿

Time, Inc. v. Hill imported the *New York Times v. Sullivan* actual malice standard to the privacy domain. In the majority opinion by Justice Brennan, the Court held that the "constitutional protections for speech and press preclude the application of the New York statute to redress false reports of matters of public interest in the absence of proof that the defendant published the report with falsity or in reckless disregard of the truth." Henceforth, those claiming false representations under the New York privacy statute would have to show that the publisher ran the material knowing of its falsity or recklessly disregarding the fact that it might be false.[147]

The decision was narrow; it applied only to the New York privacy statute and had no bearing on the common law privacy tort. It did not declare the privacy tort unconstitutional. However, much as it had done in *New York Times v. Sullivan*, the Court reiterated that personal image law—in this case, one's "privacy" right to avoid unwanted public display in the media—raised free expression questions of constitutional stature. In dicta, the majority suggested that any legal restrictions on the publication of matters of public concern, broadly defined, encroached on First Amendment rights—that people's privacy and their right to their images could be breached for newsworthy purposes.[148] "The subject of the *Life* article, the opening of a new play linked to an actual incident," the *Hill* majority concluded, was a newsworthy, constitutionally protected "matter of public interest." The Court reversed the New York Court of Appeals and remanded the case for further proceedings.[149] Nixon, devastated, told colleagues that he "never want[ed] to hear about the Hill case again." By then, he was immersed in the 1968 presidential campaign.

The press, of course, saw the case as a victory, a major limitation on the privacy action that had become so problematic for the publishing industries. The president of Time Inc. issued a public statement praising the Court for upholding the "vital principle of a free press."[150] The *New York Times* ran the whole opinion under the headline, "Supreme Court Supports Press on a Privacy Issue."[151] In a shamelessly self-congratulatory move, *Time* magazine published a piece titled "A Vote for the Press over Privacy," in which it speculated that the ruling would probably eliminate many "nuisance" libel and privacy suits against the press.[152]

The decision was also widely criticized. If sympathetic plaintiffs like the Hills were not protected by the law of privacy, who would be? Garment believed that the decision offended many Americans, who were upset by "what they saw as the arrogance of journalists and intellectual elites in riding heedless over the interests and values of more ordinary folk."[153] As the legal scholar Willard Pedrick asked in a law review piece, "Are we here simply, or largely, as spectators, to be regaled and entertained by the misfortunes of our fellows as reported by the media of information, marvelous in their technological development? Are the tragedy and heartbreak of individuals, who have sought no role in the direction of our society, to be the stuff served up to beguile the rest of us?"[154] Wrote law professor Melville Nimmer, "The fact that what allegedly happened to the Hill family was news should not in the name of the First Amendment justify an obliteration of society's commitment to the values of privacy."[155] Fortas's dissent spoke of the "reckless and heedless" "assault" to the Hill family; Justice Harlan, concurring in part and dissenting in part, suggested that freedom of the press was being extended too far and noted the serious personal harms that could be caused by unwanted publicity.[156]

This was borne out in the aftermath of the case. At trial there had been testimony that the *Life* article had caused Mrs. Hill serious emotional injury. Two eminent psychiatrists said she had come through the original hostage incident well, but had "fallen apart when the *Life* article brought back her memories."[157] She was diagnosed with "severe reactive depression of psychotic proportions" and subjected to a course of electric shock treatment.[158] Mrs. Hill committed suicide four years after the Supreme Court's decision, in 1971.[159]

In the seventy years after the famous Warren and Brandeis invention, the legal action for invasion of privacy—as the right to one's public image—had developed, been recognized, and been seriously limited by courts that could not reconcile that right with American society's dependence on media images and its expanding commitment to freedom of expression. The *Hill* case captured the cultural and judicial confusion that defined, and that continues to define, this contested area of law. The history of American image law is a saga of simultaneous expansion and limitation: the increasing recognition of image rights, and at the same time their restriction by legal doctrines of freedom of speech. Much of the writing and scholarship in this area has focused exclusively on the latter, contractionary movement.[160] This book has looked hard at the expansionary trend, documenting why we have a law of image in the first place.

Conclusion

The Law and Personal Image in the Digital Age

The *Time, Inc. v. Hill* case marked the end of an era—the foundational period of the laws of image and the image society. By the 1970s, the basic doctrines of the tort laws of image had been established, as had American culture's image-conscious sensibility. As this book has illustrated, the twentieth century witnessed the rise of a cultural attitude or outlook, rooted in the middle class but not limited to it, in which the self is conceptualized in terms of images. Influenced by a variety of forces, from the "image industries" to celebrity culture to the mobile and fluid conditions of urban life, Americans became aware of having public images and *being* images: one's identity was embedded, at least in part, in the image or persona one strategically constructed and presented to others. In a world of crowds, surfaces, and distant and impersonal social relations, the ability to perfect and manage one's image came to be regarded as critical to social mobility, public recognition, and material success. In the therapeutic, individualistic culture of postwar America, it also became integral to ideals of personal liberation and psychological and emotional health. Individuals from a variety of backgrounds and circumstances asserted that they owned their images, that they had an entitlement to their images and a right to control them, and that this prerogative was critical to their ability to live and function as free and self-determining individuals, and to pursue the fabled American Dream.

The law both responded to and contributed to this focus on images and the rise of the image-conscious self. By the 1940s, a body of tort law—"image law"—protected the individual's public image, his ability to control his image, and his feelings about his image. These image torts consisted of a tort of intentional infliction of emotional distress, a tort of invasion of privacy, and a modernized defamation tort that addressed not only injuries to reputation, but slights to one's emotions and sense of self. We saw the expansion of litigation in these areas and, despite doubts and resistance among some sectors, widespread support for these laws—in the judiciary, among academics, and in the public at large. Tort law became a venue for, and participant in, Americans' concerns with personal image; the models of personhood and identity embedded in these laws in turn shaped cultural understandings of the self.

Personal image was *legalized*: images, and people's feelings about their images, came to be viewed as appropriate matters for legal intervention, regulation, and supervision. This is not to say that every person who was insulted, maligned, or misrepresented undertook legal action—far from it. Most libels, "invasions of privacy," and other image-based harms never made it to a lawyer, never made it to court. They were endured, or dealt with informally. I am not suggesting that Americans have been litigious around their reputations and public images in any absolute sense.[1] We can see, nonetheless, a growing "claims consciousness" around personal image.[2] As the law expanded its authority over image-based harms and emotional harms, as privacy and libel litigation gained publicity and apparent social approval, there was a popular awareness that affronts to one's public persona could be dealt with legally, if one chose—that legal recourse was one avenue, among many, that could be pursued, and perhaps should be pursued.

The effect of this legalization of image, I suggest, was to validate and reinforce the sense of possessiveness and protectiveness towards one's public image and persona. In acknowledging a right to control one's image and one's feelings about one's image, the law affirmed the image-conscious sensibility. As in so many other areas of conduct, the law marked out a terrain of normative, socially acceptable behavior and feeling through the reasonableness, or "reasonable person," standard. Particularly in the latter half of the twentieth century, courts and juries often defined the reasonable person with respect to image as an individual who was conscious of, and quite sensitive to his social appearance; who was likely to be hurt, perhaps deeply so, when publicized in a false, misleading, miscontextualized, or humiliating manner—or in any fashion that sharply clashed with his own self-image. While there was much disagreement as to the thickness of the normal person's skin, and the free speech limitations on image rights, the law recognized emotional distress as a reasonable response to a tarnished or distorted public persona, and deemed such injuries significant enough to merit recognition and recompense, although perhaps less so than some may have wished. This legal affirmation legitimated the seriousness towards personal image that was being cultivated and urged upon the public by the other cultural forces we have seen.

The law's intervention in the realm of image, and the public's perception of a legal entitlement to control aspects of one's public image, were part of a larger movement: the penetration of the law into virtually all areas of public and especially private life. By the 1970s, the law had made its presence known in a variety of domains previously untouched by it, including the intimate, familiar, intangible, and personal. Once viewed as matters to be dealt with privately, in one's community or family, or within one's personal conscience, domestic relations, sexual choices, and the problems and complexities of the emotions—one's psychic well-being and self-image—came to be viewed as properly legal affairs.[3] Free speech limitations notwithstanding, American culture embraced the idea of a legal right to be vindicated and compensated for image-based harms, part of a broader, fundamental right to possess and control the self.

∼

The tensions and trends described in this work persisted, and they continue in our digital, internet age. A nation saturated with mass communications, from print to cable TV to the internet, remains enthralled with consuming information about people—photos, films, trivia, titillating stories, tweets and Facebook posts. In a culture of consumerism and celebrity, a self-focused populace, more than ever, wants to manage, manipulate, and spin their personal images like actors and rock stars. While the public claims to resent the media's exploitation of personal reputation and privacy, it loves to watch people's images destroyed or dismantled before a mass audience. We want to reveal ourselves, to make ourselves public, to proclaim ourselves to the world, and with our blogs, smartphones, and webcams, we have the means to do it. But—as ever—we seek publicity on our own terms. This attitude is fitting for a culture that seems to want it all, and that has come to believe in many ways that it can have it all.

∼

The 1970s and 1980s were, in the view of some pundits, "the greatest age of individualism in American history." When the 1960s counterculture seemed to stall, many turned inward and sought to change themselves. Quipped journalist

Tom Wolfe, "let's talk about me" and "let's find the real me"; these were mantras of the time, dubbed the "Me Decades."[4] The ideal had become the "autonomous individual," seeking to choose his own life course according to his own "criterion of life-effectiveness," wrote sociologist Robert Bellah.[5] The person was the center of his own universe, and collective goals were subordinated to the pursuit of individual well-being, Bellah observed. Advertisers, ever in touch with the popular mood, noted that freedom of choice "came close to being sacred for Americans." "Have it your way," the pitch of an infamous 1970s Burger King ad campaign, summarized what seemed to be the spirit of the age.[6]

In the mobile, unstable social environments of the late twentieth century, marked by rapid population shifts and new technologies and besieged with information and fleeting media images, the modal self was a "pastiche personality," "a social chameleon, constantly borrowing bits and pieces of identity from whatever sources are available and constructing them as useful or desirable in a given situation," in the words of sociologist Kenneth Gergen.[7] There was no longer a "relatively coherent and unified sense of self," only "manifold and competing potentials."[8] Phrases like "makeover" and "radical self-transformation" entered the cultural lexicon in the 1980s, promoted by the multibillion-dollar image industries—advertising, cosmetics, fashion, psychotherapy, and the new industry of "personal image consulting."[9] By the late 1980s, a directory of "Personal Image Consultants" listed hundreds of "professionals nationwide who act as Pygmalions to their clients' public and private personas."[10] By 1991, Americans were spending more than $150 million annually on these image advisors, hoping to appear more "powerful and polished."[11] As one image consultant told the *New York Times*, "packaging people is like packaging products."[12]

Even before the internet, the most sacred and significant dimensions of personal and social life were memorialized, communicated, and conducted through images. Every phase and event of human existence, from birth to death, had seemingly become a "Kodak moment." Televangelists ministered to massive flocks beginning in the 1970s. Celebrity doctors and therapists discussed the intimacies of the body and psyche before primetime audiences and won national followings.[13] Political campaigns, whether at the local or national level, were almost entirely a product of media spin. The phrase "spin doctor" became popular in the 1980s, as did the concept of the "sound byte." Wrote one observer in 1997, describing a state of affairs well established by that time, "political campaigns, in search of the voter" had resorted "to the glitzy dumbed-down world of television. How is the marketing of a political candidate any different from the marketing of a new car or a hamburger?"[14] A celebrated ad campaign for Canon copiers in the 1990s proclaimed, "image is everything."[15] Coca-Cola parodied in a subsequent ad: "Image is nothing. Thirst is everything."[16]

"Self-expression" continued to be regarded as a key component of identity creation and emotional health—hence the freedom with which people aired their thoughts, feelings, and desires before others, both in the media and in everyday life and conversation. In the 1970s, Phil Donahue pioneered the talk show format and used television to "personalize public debate."[17] In the 1990s, Oprah Winfrey brought the psychological hang-ups, obsessions, and ordeals of ordinary people into the living rooms of America. Never before had people been so eager to watch other people's meltdowns, and to bare their own souls—their addictions, their weight struggles, their infidelities—to an audience of millions. In 1992, the *New York Times* noted aptly that the culture had become one of "staggering exhibitionism," where "individuals compete to reveal the most intimate and embarrassing aspects of their lives."[18] Shame had apparently ceased to motivate social behavior,[19] and the lines between public and private life had hopelessly blurred. Some wondered whether, in this culture of exposure, "privacy" had any meaning anymore. "Privacy has no longer been invaded; it's been eagerly surrendered," observed one critic in 1993, concluding that people no longer saw themselves as having private selves, as "private beings."[20]

In a media-driven, overstimulated, consumer-oriented society, where people competed to make themselves appealing to colleges, employers, and future mates, explicit metaphors of selling or marketing the self became ubiquitous. This acquired the label "personal branding" and, later, "reputation management."[21] Since the 1970s, with the publishing of historian Christopher Lasch's book *The Culture of Narcissism*, critics have routinely described America as a narcissistic society, a label not entirely without merit.[22] Wrote psychologist Philip Cushman in 1995, cynically but not inaccurately, many "middle-class white Americans were characterized by a sense of unconditional entitlement; they felt entitled to money, commodities, experiences, food, special treatment, respect (sometimes deference), speaking their mind, expressing their feelings, getting their way."[23] An array of cultural forces turned their energies to promoting and catering to the individual, his comfort, and his image—building self-esteem, offering "personalized attention," and "customized service." To many, it was "all about me."

Vast energies were poured into the construction of public images, and their systematic deconstruction. By the late 1980s, matters that publishers and producers would not have deigned to put before an audience even two decades earlier were deemed fit for public consumption. A milestone was set when the *Miami Herald* in 1987 reported that Gary Hart had spent the night with a woman who was not his wife, which seemed benign a decade later after the Bill Clinton affair.[24] *People* debuted in 1974 and acquired the largest audience of any American magazine.[25] The 1990s saw the beginning of tabloid television shows like *A Current Affair* and *Hard Copy*, and increasingly personal, voyeuristic media probes. The advent of cable news intensified the competition in the news and entertainment markets, leading to concerted efforts across the media spectrum to capture the interest of an increasingly desensitized public with a diminished attention span. Reality shows became a major TV genre, as did "hidden camera" exposés. The advent of the camcorder in the 1980s led to "home video" programs, in which audiences willingly submitted their most embarrassing personal videos for on-air disclosure in exchange for public visibility and the possibility of fame. As one journalist asked in the early 2000s, "If you are not on a reality show, or do not wish to be on one, or do not know someone who is on one or trying to be on one, do you exist"?[26]

By the new millennium, the sense of ownership of, and entitlement to one's personal image was never greater, as was the sense of the fragility of one's social identity, of one's image and persona under siege. Popular advice literature portrayed a cruel, unsympathetic world of detractors and "haters" seeking to tear down people's reputations, images, and personal "brands." Success in business and social life was characterized as a constant battle, a struggle to maintain a positive public image in the face of the critical judgments of others. Wrote a "personal reputation consultant," one of the most important laws of modern reputation was that "your Reputation WILL come under attack."[27]

❧

Personal image litigation remained a focal point of popular attention and a fixture of the legal landscape. Despite the constitutional limitations on libel law imposed by *New York Times v. Sullivan* and subsequent cases in the 1970s and 1980s, lawyers, journalists, and legal scholars observed what they described as a marked increase in libel litigation and a renewed "fascination with libel and privacy suits."[28] There was a "remarkable upsurge" in libel actions, accompanied by a "startling inflation of damage awards."[29] From 1964 to 1975, eleven hundred libel suits were filed against newspapers alone.[30] The 1980s saw the rise of the libel "megaverdict," a judgment of more than one million dollars.[31] By 1988, widely publicized statistics indicated that more libel cases were proceeding to trial, and that seven out of ten trials resulted in plaintiffs' judgments.[32]

As ever, celebrities and politicians were the most prominent and publicized libel litigants. In one landmark case from the 1980s, Carol Burnett won $300,000 in compensatory damages and $1.3 million in punitive damages against the *National Enquirer* for printing a story falsely alleging that she had been drunk and disorderly in a restaurant.[33] Celebrity libel lawsuits had seemingly become so voluminous—and in some cases, truly petty—that, as one commentator quipped, "apparently you're not an A-List celebrity unless you're involved in some sort of bogus defamation lawsuit."[34] But defamation remained an equal opportunity action. "Unknown, essentially anonymous individuals" were suing television hosts, newspapers, cartoonists, and novelists and their publishers over alleged libels, observed one former federal judge in 1987.[35] Commentators attributed this trend in part to media overconfidence—increasing sensationalism, carelessness, and envelope-pushing in the wake of the *New York Times v. Sullivan* decision.[36] In a 1990 book, law professor Rodney Smolla speculated that it was also an outgrowth of image-consciousness—American "attitudes about the importance of preserving personal tranquillity and the pertinence of one's public image in the battle for that preservation."[37]

Plaintiffs brought lawsuits for intentional infliction of emotional distress against the media with greater frequency beginning in the 1980s.[38] In one case, a woman sued a newspaper for emotional distress when it printed a photograph that made her appear stout.[39] Intentional infliction of emotional distress was alleged when a newspaper graphically described efforts to save the plaintiff's wife's life in an emergency room.[40] One claim resulted from plaintiffs being described as litigious in a newspaper article.[41] The tort of intentional infliction of emotional distress came of age when a panel of the U.S. Court of Appeals for the Second

Circuit affirmed a $200,000 judgment for the Reverend Jerry Falwell over the publication of a parody in *Hustler* magazine imputing to him outrageous sexual conduct. It was ultimately reversed by the U.S. Supreme Court in a 1988 decision, which applied the *New York Times* actual malice requirement to the emotional distress tort when it involved public officials and public figures.[42]

With the growing economic value of celebrity, and celebrity endorsements becoming a major source of income for stars, the number of right of publicity cases increased, and several states passed right of publicity statutes.[43] Both famous and ordinary people were asserting a right to profit from their images, however humble those images might be. A court held that a construction worker had stated a valid claim for commercial appropriation of identity when footage of him installing tile was used in a television commercial.[44] A woman brought suit for the value of her nude silhouette when a photographer took a picture of her while she was bathing naked in a stream with her child; the picture was subsequently used in an ad.[45] Though the right of publicity had been initially construed as protection for one's name and likeness, it was expanded to cover a variety of personal attributes, such as one's voice, gestures, and manner of dress, said to be aspects of one's "identity." Thus it was that Jackie Kennedy Onassis persuaded a court to block look-alike images of her in advertisements; the estate of Elvis Presley convinced a court to ban Elvis impersonators; and Bette Midler recovered for an imitation of her voice in a commercial.[46] Such was the logic of the image society—any invocation or use of an individual's looks or public persona, however superficial those attributes might be, constituted the exploitation of one's personal "identity."

Despite "a glut of publications and television programs devoted to the most intimate details of people's lives," there was a "rising tide of advocacy for personal privacy," observed the *New York Times* in 1992.[47] There was a "growing national sensitization to privacy," and it was resulting in "increased litigation."[48] The bar for recovery in cases against the media remained high.[49] Courts continued to defeat privacy claims on the basis of the newsworthiness or "matters of public concern" privilege, and to permit the media in many instances to essentially define the privilege. Items that have been held newsworthy have included the death of a child in a locked refrigerator, the identity of a woman who abandoned a newborn child, the extrication of a woman from a crashed car, and a sex-change operation.[50] But the privacy tort was not dead; the Supreme Court never declared it unconstitutional. Other than *Time, Inc. v. Hill*, the Court has said little about the First Amendment implications of tort liability for invasion of privacy.[51] In 1975 it had the opportunity to declare a categorical privilege for truthful publications, but it declined to take that course.[52]

In high-profile privacy cases in recent years, media defendants have suffered defeats or setbacks.[53] A former friend of the author of the 2003 best seller *The Red Hat Club* sued the author, claiming that a character in the book, depicted as a sleazy, "unrehabilitated alcoholic," had been based on her. A Georgia appeals court rejected the defendant's motion to dismiss the plaintiff's libel and privacy claims.[54] A federal district court in 1998 held that the entertainment stars Pamela Anderson Lee and Bret Michaels had a valid privacy claim when a video company obtained the couple's self-produced porn tape and distributed it without their consent.[55] In a case from 2006, a federal district court held that the publication of information about a woman's sex life in a newspaper gossip column was legally actionable as an invasion of privacy. "It is unlikely that a unmarried, professional woman in her 30s would want her private life about whom she had dated and had sexual relations revealed in the gossip column of a widely distributed newspaper," the court concluded. The public had no "legitimate concern" in such matters, which would cause "suffering, shame or humiliation to a person of ordinary sensibilities."[56] The tort of invasion of privacy, as a right to control one's public image, remains part of the twenty-first-century legal landscape.

～

The internet became popular, beginning in the late 1990s, because it fed our hunger for images and information. But it was not just another form of media; it was a participatory one that allowed users to partake in information's creation and circulation, including information about the self. Web technologies lent themselves to some of the culture's key ideals and aspirations—self-expression, self-transformation, careful "impression management." Through websites and blogs, people could design their very own, self-created social personas and publicize them to world. The concept of having a "public image" was revolutionized. The institutional mass media were no longer the exclusive bestowers of publicity and fame; mass visibility was within the reach of anyone with a computer and internet access.

Today users of online social networks like Facebook participate in forms of self-promotion that were once the preserve of politicians and stars—airbrushed photographs, strategically organized personal profiles, and carefully managed and staged social interactions.[57] Social networking profiles have become personal "billboards," venues for the performance and presentation of "one's managed, researched, well-crafted identity."[58] A study by the Pew Internet and American Life Project revealed that internet users, particularly young users, actively engage in "reputation management," carefully monitoring what appears about them online and taking steps to control their online identities.[59] As one recent magazine article exhorted its readers, "With the surge of social media, you have not only the ability, but you now have the need to manage your reputation, both online and in real life." "Why leave your . . . reputation to chance, when you can be your own PR guru and manage your image?"[60]

Online technologies permit the fantasy, if not reality, of total self-reinvention, allowing users to create a new public persona, or personas, for a variety of situations—a Facebook self, a professional identity, a "gaming self," and so on.[61] A testament to the self-expression ideal we have seen throughout this book, the construction of these online social selves often involves the revelation of intimate personal information. The quantity and depth of personal disclosures online is by any historical standard truly unprecedented. Blogs serve as personal diaries in which people describe their inner musings, bodily functions, and romantic lives, in amazing detail. Tweets allow people to become stars of their own lives, chronicling every movement for their "followers." Publicizing one's intimate, personal life has become for some a form of self-affirmation and self-validation; one's thoughts, activities, and very existence are not "real" unless one has blogged them, texted them, tweeted them, and posted them on Facebook. Commentators write aptly of a "privacy paradox": Americans are obsessed with privacy, yet exhibitionism is the norm.[62]

At the internet's inception, pundits predicted that the new medium would reinvigorate the public sphere, revitalize democracy, and lead to a flourishing of art, culture, discourse, and social relationships.[63] The web would be an accessible, largely uncensored, free forum for ideas, a true marketplace of thought. But the very properties that made the internet so conducive to communicative freedom—its anonymity, accessibility, and wide circulation—brought out quite often the worst in human nature and created untold potential for injury and abuse. With their power to disseminate gossip, falsehoods, and misrepresentations on a mass scale, online technologies represent perhaps the most potent threat to personal image in human history. As is well known, online communications have produced a proliferation of libels, invasions of privacy, and other, often very serious assaults to people's feelings, images, and reputations.[64] In recent years, there has been an outcry over online threats to privacy and reputation that surpasses that of the 1890s.

Some of this objectionable material is posted by the news media; much of it, by individual bloggers or social media users. Some appears for legitimately newsworthy or informative purposes; some, for malicious and nefarious ends. There is no need to catalog it—we all know about cyberbullying, revenge porn, and other forms of harassment, intimidation, and shaming. Yet interestingly, and perhaps revealingly, many of the vocal protests around assaults to online reputation and privacy do not concern slurs and misrepresentations by others, but rather the miscontextualization of self-posted material.

Cynthia Moreno, a high school student, wrote a critical poem about her hometown called "An Ode to Coalinga" and posted it on her MySpace web page. A reader, the school principal, submitted the ode to the local newspaper, and it was published in the Letters to the Editor section. It was attributed to Moreno, using her real name. She sued the newspaper for invasion of privacy, claiming that she intended the poem to be read only by her MySpace friends, not by a general audience, and that she had been humiliated and her public image injured.[65]

Facebook's sins in this regard are numerous. In 2006, Facebook introduced a "news feed" service. Under this service, an individual's Facebook activities were broadcast to all of his or her Facebook friends. This created a tremendous outcry. Facebook members wanted to limit their personal information to a selected group of friends, and the "news feed" dispersed it to a larger, unwanted audience.[66] Facebook was accused of invading its users' privacy. In another privacy gaffe, Facebook in 2011 introduced "Sponsored Stories," a system that enabled advertisers to use Facebook users' "likes" as product endorsements. If you "liked" Coca-Cola on Facebook, for example, Coke could then use your name and image in an advertisement. This sparked incidents reminiscent of the "circulating portrait" phenomenon of a hundred years ago. People who were unaware that their self-posted images, identities, and "likes" would be used in ads were humiliated and outraged at being unwilling product endorsers, and they sued Facebook. The company settled with the users for $20 million.[67]

How is it that people can willingly post personal information online, then complain when someone else presents that same information in another, albeit displeasing context? This is the continuation of the trend we have seen throughout this book: people want to expose themselves to the public—to create a public image, a visible public persona and presence—yet at the same time to manage and control those images. And this in part is what "privacy" has come to mean in the online world: a right to control the contexts and circumstances of our self-publicity.[68]

Distortions of our online images can have potentially very serious consequences—in the most extreme cases, threats to one's safety, one's employment, and one's hard-won reputation. At a purely psychic level, losing control of one's image can be very upsetting for a people deeply protective of their public personas and social appearances, particularly the "millennial" generation which came of age in the early 2000s, an admittedly self-focused bunch whom critics have described as being lost in a "narcissism epidemic."[69] The need for a stronger "right to privacy" in the digital world—a right to control one's online image—has been the subject of a good deal of campaigning and discussion.[70] The argument, which should be familiar to us, is that various sorts of online misrepresentations and miscontextualizations take from us our right to control our public identities and in so doing, diminish our very personhood. As the law professor Jeffrey Rosen wrote in the *New York Times* in 2010, "for some technology enthusiasts, the web was supposed to be the second flowering of the open frontier, and the ability to segment our identities with an endless supply of pseudonyms, avatars, and categories of friendship was supposed to let people present different sides of their personalities in different contexts." "What seemed within our grasp was a power that only Proteus possessed, perfect control over our shifting identities." But the dream of "perfect control," he lamented, proved to be a "myth."[71] The permanence of online information—the inability of online material to ever be fully deleted—is said to pose a profound threat to an important aspect of our image rights: our right to be forgotten.[72] "Information that was once scattered, forgettable, and localized is becoming permanent and searchable," observed law professor

Daniel Solove in his book *The Future of Reputation*. "These transformations pose threats to people's control over their reputations and their ability to be who they want to be."[73]

People seeking to regain control of their online images are now pursuing a number of different possibilities, including the use of "Reputation Defender," a paid service that will monitor one's online reputation and pressure websites to take down offending information. Reputation Defender will also bombard the web with positive information to "push down" negative information about a person in Google searches.[74] Another method is counterspeech: if you don't like what's been posted about you, post your own version of the truth. As in the past, legal solutions continue to be pursued. The number of libel suits against bloggers and users of social media is rising, as are lawsuits for invasion of privacy.[75]

In recent years, state legislatures have proposed and passed statutes that give people greater control over their online images, including a right to delete or erase embarrassing self-posted material. In 2013, California passed a law that gives youth the right to erase social media posts.[76] This so-called eraser law requires internet companies to provide a method for minors to permanently delete a posting or a picture from a website before it's transmitted to a third party. Other proposed privacy, reputation, and image protection laws are content-specific, prohibiting cyberbullying[77] or the transmission of sexually explicit photos of former lovers, so-called revenge porn.[78]

But what about free expression? In 1996, Congress passed Section 230 of the Communications Decency Act, which immunized websites from liability for statements posted by third parties. Part of the motivation behind the act was to keep the internet, then an emerging medium, a free and open domain for communication; if web-hosts feared being sued for every statement that appeared on their sites, it would have a "chilling effect" on speech and publication.[79] There seems to be great popular enthusiasm for a right to engage in free speech online, yet at the same time the public supports a right to be shielded from other people's expression.[80]

So we are back to where we began—or perhaps we never left it. An image-conscious populace attuned to threats to self-presentation, particularly mass-mediated threats, seeks legal recourse and intervention. Litigants assert a right to control their images, a right to reputation and privacy. What is different between today and a hundred years ago is that images have become even more critical to how we imagine ourselves, to our concepts of personhood and identity. The sense of possessiveness and entitlement to one's image is arguably much greater. With their power to humiliate and to destroy public images on a mass scale, digital-age threats are more profound than those in the newspaper age, as are the interests weighing against the right to one's image—the perceived social value of free expression.

I have not meant to critique Americans as hypersensitive, superficial, or litigious. I have not meant to trivialize or minimize the emotional and psychic harms that can be caused by humiliating, misleading, misrepresentative public depictions of individuals, particularly when they are circulated through the channels of mass communications. The point of this work is not to say whether image-consciousness is good or bad. It is merely to point out that it exists, that it has been present in our legal and social traditions for quite some time, and there appears to be no turning back.

Notes, Bibliography, and Index

Notes

Introduction

1. Steve Henn, "Facebook Users Question $20 Million Settlement over Ads," NPR, May 13, 2013. http://www.npr.org/blogs/alltechconsidered/2013/05/14/182861926/facebook-users-question-20-million-settlement-over-ads.

2. Peay v. Curtis, 78 F. Supp. 305 (D.D.C. 1948).

3. Cason v. Baskin, 155 Fla. 198, 201–202 (Fla. 1944).

4. See generally Daniel Boorstin, *The Image: A Guide to Pseudo-Events in America* (New York: Vintage Books, 1961).

5. See, e.g., Robin D. Barnes, *Outrageous Invasions: Celebrities' Private Lives, Media, and the Law* (New York: Oxford University Press, 2010); Andrew T. Kenyon and Megan Richardson, eds., *New Dimensions in Privacy Law: International and Comparative Perspectives* (Cambridge: Cambridge University Press, 2006); James Q. Whitman, "The Two Western Cultures of Privacy: Dignity Versus Liberty," *Yale Law Journal* 113 (2004).

6. Several European countries have broad prohibitions against the publication or distribution of people's visual images without consent. See Gert Bruggemier, Aurelia Colombi Ciacchi, and Patrick O'Callaghan, eds., *Personality Rights in European Tort Law* (Cambridge: Cambridge University Press, 2010). There is a "right to be forgotten" in France, Germany, Belgium, Finland, Italy, the Netherlands, and Switzerland; publications are forbidden from printing personal information about those who have been convicted of a crime and served their sentences. This right is said to serve the interest of the former criminal's rehabilitation and resocialization. See Bruggemier, Ciacchi, and O'Callaghan, *Personality Rights*, 204–205; Steven C. Bennett, "The 'Right to Be Forgotten': Reconciling EU and US Perspectives," *Berkeley Journal of International Law* 30 (2012): 162–163. A "right to be forgotten" that requires search engines to remove links to embarrassing or discrediting personal information upon demand was approved by the EU's highest court in 2014. David Streitfeld, "European Court Lets Users Erase Records on Web," *New York Times*, May 13, 2014.

7. Lawrence Friedman describes legal culture as the "ideas, values, expectations, and attitudes towards law and legal institutions, which some public or part of the public holds." See Lawrence Friedman, "The Concept of Legal Culture: A Reply," in *Comparing Legal Cultures*, edited by David Nelken (Aldershot: Dartmouth, 1997), 34.

8. Defamation law has been traditionally understood to protect reputational rights, and privacy law dignitary rights, or "rights of personality." The concept of "image law" encompasses these interests and extends them. In the twentieth century, I suggest, the torts of defamation and privacy came to protect the interest in managing and controlling one's public image, an interest that overlaps with yet is also distinct from dignity and reputation. On concepts of reputation in libel law, see, e.g., Robert Post, "The Social Foundations of Defamation Law: Reputation and the Constitution," *California Law Review* 74 (1986). For privacy law as protecting interests in dignity and "personality," see Samuel Warren and Louis Brandeis, "The Right to Privacy," *Harvard Law Review* 4 (1890): 193–220; Leon Green, "Relational Interests," *Illinois Law Review* 29 (1934): 460; Roscoe Pound, "Interests of Personality," *Harvard Law Review* 28 (1915); Edward Bloustein, "Privacy as an Aspect of Human Dignity: An Answer to Dean Prosser," *New York University Law Review* 39 (1964).

9. The most notable work on the social history of libel in the modern U.S., particularly political libel, is Norman Rosenberg, *Protecting the Best Men: An Interpretive History of the Law of Libel* (Chapel Hill: University of North Carolina Press, 1990). Lawrence M. Friedman, *Guarding Life's Dark Secrets: Legal and Social Controls over Reputation, Propriety, and Privacy* (Stanford: Stanford University Press, 2007), contains chapters on both libel and privacy in nineteenth- and twentieth-century U.S. history. For discussions of American libel law in its social contexts, see also David Rabban, *Free Speech in Its Forgotten Years, 1870–1920* (Cambridge: Cambridge University Press, 1997), 155–165; Morris L. Ernst and Alexander Lindey, *Hold Your Tongue: Adventures in Libel and Scandal* (New York: Abelard Press, 1932); Norman Rosenberg, "Taking a Look at 'The Distorted Shape of an Ugly Tree': Efforts at Policy-Surgery on the Law of Libel during the Decade of the 1940s," *Northern Kentucky Law Review* 11 (1988).

On the privacy tort's history, see Don R. Pember, *Privacy and the Press: The Law, the Mass Media, and the First Amendment* (Seattle: University of Washington Press, 1972); Randall Bezanson, "The Right to Privacy Revisited: Privacy, News, and Social Change, 1890–1990," *California Law Review* 80 (1992); Robert C. Post, "The Social Foundations of Privacy: Community and Self in the Common Law Tort," *California Law Review* 77 (1989); Dorothy J. Glancy, "The Invention of the Right to Privacy," *Arizona Law Review* 21 (1979); Samantha Barbas, "The Death of the Public Disclosure Tort: A Historical Perspective," *Yale Journal of Law and the Humanities* 22 (2010); Samantha Barbas, "Saving Privacy from History," *DePaul Law Review* 61 (2012); Samantha Barbas, "The Laws of Image," *New England Law Review* 47 (2012).

Chapter 1

1. Mary Elvira Elliot, et al., *Representative Women of New England* (Boston: New England Historical Publishing, 1904), 263; Sarah Pratt McLean, *Cape Cod Folks* (Boston: A. Williams, 1881); "Cape Cod Folks," *The Literary World*, September 10, 1881, 309.

2. "Cape Cod Folks," *The Literary World*, July 30, 1881, 255.

3. "A Novel Libel Suit," *The Literary World*, November 5, 1881, 392.

4. "Do Not Publish News of Libel Suits," *The Fourth Estate*, July 8, 1897.

5. Michael Winship, "The Rise of a National Book Trade System in the United States," in *A History of the Book in America, Volume 4*, edited by Carl F. Kaestle and Janice A. Radway (Chapel Hill: University of North Carolina Press, 2009), 57, 60–61; David Sumner, *The Magazine Century* (New York: Peter Lang, 2010), 16; Carl F. Kaestle and Janice A. Radway, "A Framework for the History of Publishing and Reading in the United States, 1880–1940," *History of the Book in America*, 10.

6. Richard Ohmann, "Diverging Paths, Books and Magazines in the Transition to Corporate Capitalism," *History of the Book in America*, 103.

7. Don R. Pember, *Privacy and the Press: The Law, the Mass Media, and the First Amendment* (Seattle: University of Washington Press, 1972), 10; David Copeland, *The Media's Role in Defining the Nation: The Active Voice* (New York: Peter Lang, 2010), 101.

8. Arthur Schlesinger, *A History of American Life: The Rise of the City, 1878–1898* (New York: Macmillan, 1948), 185.

9. Gunther Barth, *City People: The Rise of Modern City Culture in Nineteenth-Century America* (New York: Oxford University Press, 1980), 59; Hazel Dicken-Garcia, *Journalistic Standards in Nineteenth Century America* (Madison: University of Wisconsin Press, 1989), 30–32, 71–82.

10. John D. Stevens, *Sensationalism and the New York Press* (New York: Columbia University Press, 1991), 65.

11. Helen MacGill Hughes, "Human Interest Stories and Democracy," *Public Opinion Quarterly* 1 (1937): 80; Hughes, *News and the Human Interest Story* (1940; Westport: Greenwood Press, 1968), 12–13; Dicken-Garcia, *Journalistic Standards*, 64.

12. Chas Dudley Warner, "Newspapers and the Public," *Forum*, April 1890, 204.

13. Theodore Dreiser, *Sister Carrie* (1900; New York: Bantam Books, 1958), 274–275.

14. "The Passion for Publicity," *The Outlook*, April 25, 1896, 738.

15. Commonwealth v. Place, 153 Pa. 314, 319 (Pa. 1893).

16. Hughes, "Human Interest Stories and Democracy."

17. On Hearst's efforts to court a working-class readership, see Leonard Teel, *The Public Press, 1900–1945: The History of American Journalism* (Westport: Praeger, 2006), 7.

18. Janna Malamud Smith, *Private Matters: In Defense of the Personal Life* (Reading: Addison-Wesley, 1997), 86.

19. Conde Benoist Pallen, "Newspaperism," *Lippincott's Monthly Magazine*, November 1886, 473.

20. Richard Grant White, "The Manners and Morals of Journalism," *Galaxy* 8 (1869): 846, quoted in Dicken-Garcia, *Journalistic Standards*, 190.

21. "Newspaper Brutality," *Christian Union*, December 5, 1889, 708.

22. Warner, "Newspapers and the Public," 205.

23. "Newspaper Brutality," 708.

24. Gates v. New York Recorder Co., 155 N.Y. 228, 230–232 (N.Y. 1898).

25. "The Right to a Good Name," *The Outlook*, December 26, 1908, 891.

26. "Newspaper Brutality," 709.

27. Several states passed laws that prohibited the publication of "criminal news, police reports . . . or accounts of . . . bloodshed, lust, or crime." See Winters v. New York, 333 U.S. 507, 522 (1948).

28. On the pre-twentieth-century history of defamation, especially the law of libel, see Norman Rosenberg, *Protecting the Best Men: An Interpretive History of the Law of Libel* (Chapel Hill: University of North Carolina Press, 1990); Randall Bezanson, "The Libel Tort Today," *Washington and Lee Law Review* 45 (1988): 536–539; Robert Post, "The Social Foundations of Defamation Law: Reputation and the Constitution," *California Law Review* 74 (1986): 693–707; William Prosser, "Libel Per Quod," *Virginia Law Review* 46 (1960): 841–843; Stanley Ingber, "Defamation: A Conflict between Reason and Decency," *Virginia Law Review* 65 (1979): 796–801; Van Vechten Veeder, "The History and Theory of the Law of Defamation," *Columbia Law Review* 4 (1904); Roger Shuy, *The Language of Defamation Cases* (New York: Oxford University Press, 2010), 16–22.

29. "Developments in the Law of Defamation," *Harvard Law Review* 69 (1956): 945–946.

30. Shuy, *Language of Defamation Cases*, 16–17.

31. Rosenberg, *Protecting the Best Men*, ch. 1.

32. William Blake Odgers, *A Digest of the Law of Libel and Slander* (London: Stevens and Sons, 1896), 18.

33. Cooper v. Greely & McElrath, 1 Denio 347 (N.Y. Sup. Ct. 1845).

34. Joel Hawes, *Lectures Addressed to the Young Men of Hartford and New Haven*, 1828, quoted in Karen Haltunnen, *Confidence Men and Painted Women: A Study of Middle-Class Culture in America, 1830–1870* (New Haven: Yale University Press, 1986), 47.

35. Odgers, *Digest of the Law*, 32.

36. Veeder, "History and Theory," 33.

37. Post, "Social Foundations," 695.

38. William Shakespeare, *Othello*, III, iii, 8.

39. Morris L. Ernst and Alexander Lindey, *Hold Your Tongue: Adventures in Libel and Slander* (New York: Abelard Press, 1932), 33–34.

40. William Prosser, *Handbook of the Law of Torts* (St. Paul: West, 1971), 737, quoted in Post, "Social Foundations," 691.

41. Ibid.

42. Martin Newell, *The Law of Libel and Slander in Civil and Criminal Cases* (Chicago: Callaghan, 1898), 564.

43. David Rabban, *Free Speech in Its Forgotten Years* (Cambridge: Cambridge University Press, 1997), 2, 132; Michael Kent Curtis, *Free Speech, The People's Darling Privilege: Struggles for Freedom of Expression in American History* (Durham: Duke University Press, 2000), 385–395.

44. Stephen M. Feldman, *Free Expression and Democracy in America: A History* (Chicago: University of Chicago Press, 2008), 234.

45. "Current Topics," *Albany Law Journal*, July 6, 1895, 1.

46. Randolph Bergstrom, *Courting Danger: Injury and Law in New York City, 1870–1910* (Ithaca: Cornell University Press, 1992), 20.

47. Francis Laurent, *The Business of a Trial Court* (Madison: University of Wisconsin Press, 1959), 49, 164.

48. Timothy Gleason, "The Libel Climate of the Late Nineteenth Century: A Survey of Libel Litigation, 1884–1899," *Journalism and Mass Communication Quarterly* 70 (December 1993): 895.

49. E. L. Godkin, "Libel and Its Legal Remedy," *Atlantic Monthly*, December 1880, 730.

50. Edwin Emery, *History of the American Newspaper Publishers' Association* (1950; Westport: Greenwood Press, 1970), 49.

51. Ibid., 49–50.

52. Gleason, "Libel Climate," 895.

53. Louis Stotesbury, "Famous Annie Oakley Libel Suits," *American Lawyer* 13 (1905): 392.

54. Gleason, "Libel Climate," 895.

55. In the grand scheme of things, the libel lawsuit was still a relatively rare occurrence. Libel lawsuits were often regarded as a last resort, when extralegal solutions failed. Dueling with newspaper editors who printed libels was common in both the North and the South until the early twentieth century. See Ryan Chamberlain, *Pistols, Politics and the Press: Dueling in 19th Century American Journalism* (Jefferson: McFarland, 2009).

In 1879, when the *Chicago Times* criticized a burlesque troupe known as the Lydia Thompson British Blondes as "cheap tinsel" and "large limbed, beefy specimens of a heavy class of British barmaids," the head of the troupe, Lydia Thompson, stalked the publisher with a riding whip in her hands. When she found him, she struck him on the shoulders. She was fined $100. As she later told a reporter, "It was worth it. I could not break future engagements and return to Chicago to sue [the editor]. . . . It was worth it." See Justin E. Walsh, *To Print the News and Raise Hell: A Biography of Wilbur F. Storey* (Chapel Hill: University of North Carolina Press, 1968), 222.

56. Peter Karsten notes that about 12 percent of tort plaintiffs in the nineteenth century were professionals, proprietors, or their spouses; about 15 percent were skilled manual workers; about 25 percent semiskilled workers; and about 10 percent unskilled workers or domestics. Although the balance might have been slightly different in libel cases—more skewed towards the professional classes—my review of the reported appellate case law from this time indicates that libel plaintiffs represented a broad cross-section of the population. See Peter Karsten, "Enabling the Poor to Have Their Day in Court: The Sanctioning of Contingency Fee Contracts," *DePaul Law Review* 47 (1998): 231, 243; Randall Bezanson, "The Libel Tort Today," *Washington and Lee Law Review* 45 (1988): 539.

57. On actions for slander in the eighteenth and nineteenth centuries in the U.S., see Andrew J. King, "Constructing Gender: Sexual Slander in Nineteenth Century America," *Law and History Review* 13 (1995): 77 (noting that most nineteenth-century slander cases occurred in small rural communities); Rosenberg, *Protecting the Best Men*, 23–28; John Demos, "Shame and Guilt in Early New England," in *The Emotions: Social, Cultural and Biological Dimensions*, edited by Ron Harré and W. Gerrod Parrott (London: Sage, 1996), 75 (on slander in Puritan communities); Cornelia Dayton, *Women before the Bar: Gender, Law and Society in Connecticut* (Chapel Hill: University of North Carolina Press, 1995), 285–328.

58. See Lisa R. Pruitt, "Her Own Good Name: Two Centuries of Talk about Chastity," *Maryland Law Review* 63 (2004): 404.

59. Rosenberg, *Protecting the Best Men,* 27.

60. Newell, *Law of Libel and Slander,* 849–851. Accusations of criminality, inability to perform one's professional duties, lack of chastity, or having a sexually transmitted disease were actionable without a showing of special damages.

61. See, e.g., E. L. Godkin, "The Rights of the Citizen: IV—To His Own Reputation," *Scribner's Magazine*, July 1890, 61 (on dueling and other forms of violence as a means of defending reputation).

62. Republican Pub. Co. v. Mosman, 15 Colo. 399 (Colo. 1890).

63. Shelly v. Dampman, 4 Pa. D. 496 (Pa. Com. Pl. 1895).

64. Moore v. Leader Pub. Co., 8 Pa. Super. 152, 153 (Pa. Super. 1898).

65. Harriman v. New Nonpareil Co., 110 N.W. 33 (Iowa 1906).

66. Lawrence M. Friedman, *Guarding Life's Dark Secrets: Legal and Social Controls over Reputation, Propriety, and Privacy* (Stanford: Stanford University Press, 2007), 49–53.

67. Washington Times Co. v. Downey, 26 App. D.C. 258, 259 (D.C. Cir. 1905).

68. MacFadden v. Morning Journal Assn., 51 N.Y.S. 275, 280 (N.Y.A.D. 2 Dept. 1898).

69. Peter Karsten, *Heart Versus Head: Judge-Made Law in Nineteenth Century America* (Chapel Hill: University of North Carolina Press, 1997), 191.

70. "Do Not Publish News of Libel Suits," *The Fourth Estate*, July 8, 1897, 4.

71. Ibid.

72. "Current Events," *Central Law Journal*, March 22, 1889, 273.

73. Gleason, "Libel Climate," 899, 901. See also Brad Snyder, "Protecting the Media from Excessive Damages: The Nineteenth Century Origins of Remittitur and Its Modern Application in Food Lion," *Vermont Law Review* 24 (1999–2000): 309 (noting that "nineteenth-century judges rarely, if ever, interfered with jury-awarded damages in libel and defamation cases").

74. For the $45,000 figure, see Smith v. Times Pub. Co., 178 Pa. 481, 516 (Pa. 1897).

75. Bergstrom, *Courting Danger*, 159–166.

76. Jacksonville Journal Co. v. Beymer, 42 Ill. App. 443, 449 (Ill. App. 3 Dist. 1891).

77. Riley v. Lee, 11 S.W. 713, 715 (Ky. 1889).

78. Godkin, "Libel and Its Legal Remedy," 730–731.

79. Rosenberg, *Protecting the Best Men,* 189.

80. On Progressivism, see, e.g., Alan Dawley, *Struggles for Justice: Social Responsibility and the Liberal State* (Cambridge: Harvard University Press, 1993), 128–129.

81. "Comical Libel Suits," *The Independent,* November 24, 1881, 7.

82. "Current Topics," *Albany Law Journal,* March 21, 1896, 180.

83. "Libel News," *The Fourth Estate,* April 7, 1898.

84. "Do Not Publish News of Libel Suits," *The Fourth Estate,* July 8, 1897, 4.

85. Untitled, *Puck,* May 4, 1887, 169.

86. "Comical Libel Suits," 7.

87. Samuel Merrill, *Newspaper Libel* (Boston: Ticknor, 1888), 150–151.

88. Ibid., 39.

89. Thomas Starkie, *A Treatise on the Law of Slander, Libel, Scandalum Magnatum and False Rumors* (London: W. Clarke and Sons, 1818), 16. See also "Ridicule as Constituting a Cause of Action for Libel," *Western Reserve Law Journal* (January 1901): 199 (in order to be actionable, ridicule must "degrade or disgrace" the plaintiff. Being made "laughable" is not enough). Damages for emotional distress were "parasitic"— mental anguish was compensable under the law of libel, but only if the plaintiff had also suffered reputational harm. Bezanson, "Libel Tort Today," 539.

90. Arthur Hobson Quinn, *The Literature of the American People: An Historical and Critical Survey* (New York: Appleton Century Crofts, 1951), 659.

91. "Cape Cod Folks," *Chicago Daily Tribune,* August 8, 1887, 5.

92. Merrill, *Newspaper Libel,* 242.

93. "Cape Cod Folks," 5.

94. "Cape Cod Folks: The Numerous Libel Suits Almost All Settled," *Boston Globe,* April 14, 1884, 4.

95. Ibid.

96. "Cape Cod Folks," 5.

97. Merrill, *Newspaper Libel,* 242.

98. "Cape Cod Folks: The $10,000 Libel Suit of Lorenzo Nightingale," *Boston Globe,* February 13, 1884.

99. "An Angry Cape Cod Man," *New York Times,* February 14, 1884, 1.

100. "Is Potato Bugger a Libelous Term?" *Boston Globe,* October 22, 1884, 2.

101. "Angry Cape Cod Man," 1.

102. "A Novel in Court," *Boston Globe,* February 14, 1884, 2.

103. "Verdict for Cradle Bow," *New York Times,* February 15, 1884, 1.

104. "Angry Cape Cod Man," 1.

105. Ibid.

106. "The Cape Cod Folks Libel Suit," *New York Times,* April 3, 1885, 3.

107. "A Unique Verdict: Cape Cod Folks Adjudged as a Libelous Work," *Boston Globe,* February 15, 1884, 5.

108. "Verdict for Cradle Bow," 1.

109. Merrill, *Newspaper Libel*, 243.

110. "Cape Cod Folks: The Numerous Libel Suits Almost All Settled," 4.

111. "Comical Libel Suits," 7.

112. "A 'Novel' Libel Suit," *The Literary World*, November 5, 1881, 392.

113. "Super-Sensitive Folks," *New York Sun*, reprinted in *Publishers' Weekly*, February 23, 1884, 243.

114. "The Cape Cod Folks Libel Suit," *Boston Globe*, February 17, 1884, 4.

115. "Cape Cod Folks: The Numerous Libel Suits Almost All Settled," 4.

116. "The Talk of the Clubs," *New York Times*, February 17, 1884, 4.

117. "The Lounger," *The Critic and Good Literature*, March 1, 1884, 104.

118. "Untitled," *The Current: Politics, Literature, Science, and Art*, February 23, 1884, 148.

119. "Current Topics," *Albany Law Journal*, March 14, 1896, 164.

Chapter 2

1. Don R. Pember, *Privacy and the Press: The Law, the Mass Media, and the First Amendment* (Seattle: University of Washington Press, 1972), 21; Dorothy J. Glancy, "The Invention of the Right to Privacy," *Arizona Law Review* 21 (1979): 5.

2. Martin Burgess Green, *The Mount Vernon Street Warrens: A Boston Story, 1860–1910* (New York: Charles Scribner's Sons, 1989), 104.

3. Ibid.; Amy Gajda, "What if Samuel D. Warren Hadn't Married a Senator's Daughter? Uncovering the Press Coverage That Led to 'The Right to Privacy,'" *Michigan State Law Review* 1 (2008); see also Pember, *Privacy and the Press*, 24; James H. Barron, "Warren and Brandeis, The Right to Privacy: Demystifying a Landmark Citation," *Suffolk University Law Review* 13 (1979); William Prosser, "Privacy," *California Law Review* 48 (1960): 383; Alpheus Thomas Mason, *Brandeis: A Free Man's Life* (New York: Viking Press, 1956), 70.

4. Samuel D. Warren and Louis D. Brandeis, "The Right to Privacy," *Harvard Law Review* 4 (1890): 193.

5. Pavesich v. New Eng. Life Ins. Co., 50 S.E. 68 (Ga. 1905); Foster-Millburn Co. v. Chinn, 120 S.W. 364 (Ky. 1909); Munden v. Harris, 153 Mo. App 652 (Mo. Ct. App. 1911); Edison v. Edison Polyform & Mfg. Co., 73 N.J. Eq. 136 (N.J. Ch. 1907); N.Y. Civ. Rights Law § 50; Utah Code Ann. §§ 76-9-401 to -402; Va. Code Ann. § 8.01-40.

6. Walter I. Trattner, *From Poor Law to Welfare State, 6th Edition* (New York: Free Press, 1998), 164.

7. Richard Hofstadter, *The Age of Reform* (New York: Knopf, 1955), 173.

8. Quoted in Alan Trachtenberg, *The Incorporation of America: Culture and Society in the Gilded Age* (New York: Hill and Wang, 2007), 113.

9. Ibid., 114.

10. Charles William Calhoun, *The Gilded Age: Perspectives on the Origins of Modern America* (Lanham: Rowman & Littlefield, 2007), 2.

11. Burton J. Bledstein, *The Culture of Professionalism: The Middle Class and the Development of Higher Education in America* (New York: W. W. Norton, 1976), 47.

12. See Simon J. Bronner, *Consuming Visions: Accumulation and Display of Goods in America, 1880–1920* (New York: W. W. Norton, 1990).

13. Theodore Dreiser, *Sister Carrie* (1900; New York: Bantam Books, 1958), 12.

14. Georg Simmel, "The Metropolis and Mental Life" (1903), in *The Blackwell City Reader*, edited by Gary Bridge and Sophie Watson (Oxford and Malden: Wiley-Blackwell, 2002), 103–104.

15. Charles Ponce De Leon, *Self-Exposure: Human Interest Journalism and the Emergence of Celebrity in America, 1890–1940* (Chapel Hill: University of North Carolina Press, 2002), 26.

16. Albert Blumenthal, *Small-Town Stuff* (Chicago: University of Chicago Press, 1932), 144.

17. Simmel, "Metropolis and Mental Life," 110.

18. Trachtenberg, *Incorporation of America*, 110.

19. Simmel, "Metropolis and Mental Life," 109.

20. F. G. Bailey, *Gifts and Poison: The Politics of Reputation* (New York: Schocken Books, 1971), 10–11.

21. See Kasson, *Rudeness and Civility*, 112 ("The offering of the self to public scrutiny was one of the central adjustments of 19th century urban life").

22. Erving Goffman, *The Presentation of Self in Everyday Life* (New York: Doubleday, 1959).

23. On rituals of identity performance among elite New Yorkers in the 1800s, see David Scobey, "Anatomy of the Promenade: The Politics of Bourgeois Sociability in Nineteenth-Century New York," *Journal of Social History* 17 (1992): 213.

24. Arthur M. Schlesinger, *Learning How to Behave* (New York: Macmillan, 1946), 34–35.

25. Dana C. Elder, "A Rhetoric of Etiquette for the 'True Man' of the Gilded Age," *Rhetoric Review* 21 (2002): 157.

26. I. N. Reed, *The Ladies' Manual: A Guide to Women in Health and Sickness, from Youth to Advanced Age* (Chicago: I. N. Reed, 1883), 441–442.

27. See Karen Haltunnen, *Confidence Men and Painted Women: A Study of Middle-Class Culture in America, 1830–1870* (New Haven: Yale University Press, 1986).

28. Schlesinger, *Learning How to Behave*, 65–66.

29. Mark Pendergast, *Mirror, Mirror: A History of the Human Love Affair with Reflection* (New York: Basic Books, 2004), 249.

30. Rob Shorman, *Selling Style: Clothing and Social Change at the Turn of the Century* (Philadelphia: University of Pennsylvania Press, 2003), 5.

31. Leo Braudy, *The Frenzy of Renown: Fame and Its History* (New York: Vintage, 1997), 506.

32. Ponce De Leon, *Self-Exposure*, 29.

33. Richard Sennett, *The Fall of Public Man* (New York: Knopf, 1977), 151–152.

34. Walter Raleigh Houghton, *American Etiquette and Rules of Politeness* (Chicago: Rand, McNally, 1889), 27–28.

35. Thomas Bender, *Community and Social Change in America* (Baltimore: Johns Hopkins University Press, 1982), 117.

36. Friedman, *Life's Dark Secrets*, 37.

37. Kasson, *Rudeness and Civility*, 114–115.

38. Ponce De Leon, *Self-Exposure*, 55–57.

39. "He Was Wrong," *Life*, September 25, 1895, 204.

40. In 1888, George Eastman marketed his new Kodak camera, which was advertised as simple, light, and designed for taking surreptitious photographs of unwilling subjects. See Glancy, "The Other Miss M," 413; Robert Mensel, "Kodakers Lying in Wait: Amateur Photography and the Right of Privacy in New York, 1885–1915," *American Quarterly* 43 (March 1991).

41. "The Rights of Privacy," *New York Times*, July 19, 1896, 11.

42. Ibid.

43. Joseph B. Bishop, "Newspaper Espionage," *The Forum*, August 1886, 534.

44. *New York Daily Mirror*, December 22, 1888, 10, quoted in Benjamin McArthur, *Actors and American Culture, 1880–1920* (Philadelphia: Temple University Press, 1984), 151.

45. "The Right to Privacy," *Youth's Companion*, December 10, 1891, 641.

46. "Newspaper Brutality," 708.

47. Bradford Leavitt, "The Invasion of Privacy," *Pacific Unitarian,* May 1903, 262.

48. "The Passion for Publicity," *New Outlook*, April 25, 1896, 737.

49. See Gormley, "One Hundred Years of Privacy," 1336–1338. On changing meanings of privacy and demands for privacy in U.S. history, see Edward Shils, "Privacy: Its Constitution and Vicissitudes," *Law and Contemporary Problems* 31 (1966); Frederick S. Lane, *American Privacy: The 400-Year History of Our Most Contested Right* (Boston: Beacon Press, 2009); Rochelle Gurstein, *The Repeal of Reticence: America's Cultural and Legal Struggles over Free Speech, Obscenity, Sexual Liberation, and Modern Art* (New York: Hill and Wang, 1998).

50. Shils, "Privacy: Its Constitution and Vicissitudes," 291; Westin, *Privacy and Freedom*, 21 (noting the developments of modern societies that "work against the achievement of privacy": "density and crowding of populations, large bureaucratic organizational life . . . new instruments of physical, psychological, and data surveillance . . . and the modern state"). On attitudes towards privacy in Victorian America, see David Rosen and Aaron Santesso, "Inviolate Personality and the Literary Roots of the Right to Privacy," *Law and Literature* 23 (2011); Caroline Danielson, "The Gender of Privacy and the Embodied Self: Examining the Origins of the Right to Privacy in US Law," *Feminist Studies* 25 (1999).

51. "Ideal Homes," *The Unitarian*, August 1886, 211. See also Milette Shamir, "Hawthorne's Romance and the Right to Privacy," *American Quarterly* 49 (1997): 748–749 (noting the development of the concept of a right to privacy as a "middle-class

privilege" in the late nineteenth century, offering actual and symbolic protection to domestic life against "governmental and societal policing").

52. On the ideology of "separate spheres"—the domestic sphere as a protected space separate and distinct from the public sphere—see Barbara Welter, "The Cult of True Womanhood, 1820–1860," *American Quarterly* 18 (1966): 151–174; Karen Lystra, *Searching the Heart: Women, Men, and Romantic Love in Nineteenth Century America* (New York: Oxford University Press, 1989), 91–92.

53. Lystra, *Searching the Heart*, 17.

54. Only the uncouth displayed their feelings and private affairs in public and showed "the secrets of their homes, their social entertainments and aspirations to the world." "Old Principles Upheld," *New York Times*, June 8, 1897, 7.

55. See Haltunnen, *Confidence Men*, 104.

56. W. Archibald McLean, "The Right of Privacy," *The Green Bag* 15 (1903): 496.

57. Roberson v. Rochester Folding Box Co., 64 N.E. 442, 450 (N.Y. 1902) (Gray, J., dissenting).

58. Godkin, "Libel and Its Legal Remedy," 733.

59. "Newspaper Brutality," 709.

60. Elbridge Adams, "The Right of Privacy and Its Relation to the Law of Libel," *American Law Review* 39 (1905): 50.

61. On Godkin, see William Armstrong, *E. L. Godkin: A Biography* (Albany: State University of New York Press, 1978).

62. Godkin, "Libel and Its Legal Remedy," 732.

63. Ibid., 736.

64. E. L. Godkin, "The Right of the Citizen. IV. To His Own Reputation," *Scribner's Magazine*, July 1890, 66.

65. Godkin's view of privacy was elitist. The lower classes were too uncouth to appreciate the value of reticence, modesty, self-restraint, and cultivating a respectable image before the public, he wrote. Privacy was an interest of the cultured and "civilized." Godkin, "Rights of the Citizen," 66; Thomas, "Construction of Privacy in and around the Bostonians," 726.

66. "There is reason to believe that Godkin's *Scribner's* piece, as well as the famous editor's reputation among intellectuals, contributed to their thinking." Richard Hixson, *Privacy in a Public Society: Human Rights in Conflict* (New York: Oxford, 1987), 30.

67. Harry Kalven Jr., "Privacy in Tort Law—Were Warren and Brandeis Wrong?" *Law and Contemporary Problems* 31 (1966): 327.

68. Barron, "Warren and Brandeis, The Right to Privacy," 912; Warren and Brandeis, "Right to Privacy," 196.

69. Warren and Brandeis, "Right to Privacy," 196, 214.

70. Warren and Brandeis, "Right to Privacy," 196.

71. Dorothy J. Glancy, "Privacy and the Other Miss M," *Northern Illinois University Law Review* 10 (1990).

72. And under certain conditions, to obtain an injunction. See Warren and Brandeis, "Right to Privacy," 219.

73. Ibid., 198.

74. Ibid., 217. "The injury resulting from such oral communications would ordinarily be so trifling that the law might well, in the interest of free speech, disregard it altogether."

75. Even before Warren and Brandeis, a "right to privacy" existed in different areas of the law. The law of trespass and the constitutional rule against unreasonable search and seizure were described as protecting privacy interests. Eavesdropping, a common law crime, was prosecuted on the ground that "no man has a right . . . to pry into your secrecy in your own house." Anti-wiretapping laws were intended "to prevent the betrayal of private affairs . . . for the promotion of private gain or the gratification of idle gossip." See "The Right to Privacy in Nineteenth Century America," *Harvard Law Review* 94 (June 1981): 1895, 1901.

76. Warren and Brandeis, "Right to Privacy," 193.

77. On the concept of dignity in the nineteenth-century U.S., see Lawrence Friedman, *The Republic of Choice: Law, Authority, and Culture* (Cambridge: Harvard University Press, 1998), 41. See also Edward Ayers, *Vengeance and Justice: Crime and Punishment in the 19th Century American South* (New York: Oxford University Press, 1984), 19.

78. Damages for the violation of intangible interests—such as freedom from mental suffering—were recognized in areas of tort law, such as defamation, battery, false imprisonment, and malicious prosecution, but were only recoverable if another tangible interest, in the body or property, was injured. See William Prosser, "Intentional Infliction of Mental Suffering: A New Tort," *Michigan Law Review* 37 (1939): 880.

79. James Q. Whitman, "The Two Western Cultures of Privacy: Dignity Versus Liberty," *Yale Law Journal* 113 (2004): 1178–1179.

80. Whitman, "Two Western Cultures," 1180–1185.

81. On the influence of continental privacy concepts on Warren and Brandeis, see Whitman, "Two Western Cultures," 1204–1205. See also Paul M. Schwartz and Karl-Nikolaus Peifer, "Prosser's Privacy and the German Right of Personality: Are Four Privacy Torts Better than One Unitary Concept?" *California Law Review* 98 (2010): 1928, 1943 (noting the German roots of Brandeis's family and his study in Germany as a teenager).

82. Warren and Brandeis, "Right to Privacy," 214–215.

83. Ibid., 197.

84. On the "utilitarian individualism" running through the American tradition—the idea that one can achieve social and material success largely by one's own initiative—see Robert N. Bellah et al., *Habits of the Heart: Individualism and Commitment in American Life* (Berkeley: University of California Press, 1985), 33.

85. John Gilmer Speed, "The Right of Privacy," *North American Review* 158 (1896): 64.

86. Glancy, "Invention of the Right to Privacy," 7. See also Benjamin C. Bratman, "Brandeis and Warren's The Right to Privacy and the Birth of the Right to Privacy," *Tennessee Law Review* 69 (2002): 623, 650.

87. Henry Billings Brown, "The Liberty of the Press," *American Law Review* 24 (1900): 321, 329.

88. McLean, "Right of Privacy," 494.

89. Schuyler v. Curtis, 27 Abb. N. Cas. 387, 400 (N.Y. 1891). However, in 1895, the court of appeals reversed the decision in *Schuyler* on the grounds that the right to privacy did not survive a person's death. See Schuyler v. Curtis, 147 N.Y. 434 (N.Y. 1895).

90. Marks v. Jaffa, 6 Misc. 290, 26 N.Y.S. 908 (N.Y. Sup. Ct. 1893).

91. Herbert Spencer Hadley, "The Right to Privacy," *Northwestern Law Review* 3 (1894): 8.

92. "The Right to Be Let Alone," *Atlantic Monthly* 67 (March 1891): 428–429.

93. J. Gilmer Speed, "The Right of Privacy," *Saturday Evening Post*, cited in *Current Literature* 26 (September 1899): 220.

94. On the "bad tendency" test, see Paul Finkelman, ed., *Encyclopedia of American Civil Liberties, Volume 1* (New York: Routledge, 2006), 96–97; David M. Rabban, *Free Speech in Its Forgotten Years, 1870–1920* (New York: Cambridge University Press, 1997), 2, 132.

95. "The Right to Privacy," *Virginia Law Register* 12 (1906): 92.

96. "Rights in a Portrait," *Case and Comment* 9 (1902): 15.

97. "Actionable Publicity," *Case and Comment* 8 (1901): 194.

98. Warren and Brandeis, "Right to Privacy," 216.

99. For criticisms of the right to privacy from a free speech perspective, see "The Right to Privacy," *Liberty* 11 (1896): 2.

100. Corliss v. E. W. Walker Co., 57 F. 434, 435 (C.C. Mass. 1893).

101. From *Galveston Daily News*, referenced in the text of Lane, *American Privacy*, 63.

102. "The Craze for Publicity," *Century Illustrated Magazine*, February 1896, 631.

103. "Fame and Notoriety," *The Nation*, October 17, 1889, 306.

104. "The Right to Privacy," *New York Times*, June 23, 1891, 4.

105. "The Taste for Privacy and Publicity," *The Spectator*, June 9, 1888, 782.

106. W. Bob Holland, "The Passion for Publicity: Being an Account of the Ingenious Arts of the Press Agent," *Leslie's Monthly Magazine*, May–October 1904, 614.

107. Ibid.

108. Ibid.

Chapter 3

1. Peck v. Tribune, 214 U.S. 185 (1909).

2. Peck v. Tribune, 154 F. 330, 332–333 (7th Cir., 1907).

3. Godkin, "The Right to Privacy," *The Nation*, December 25, 1890, 496.

4. *Chicago Tribune*, July 29, 1907.

5. Burdett Rich, "What Invasions of Privacy Are Unlawful?" *Law Student's Helper* 18 (1910): 238.

6. See Samantha Barbas, "From Privacy to Publicity: The Tort of Appropriation in the Age of Mass Consumption," *Buffalo Law Review* 61 (2014).

7. Miles Orvell, *American Photography* (Oxford: Oxford University Press, 2003), 21.

8. Wilson Woodrow, "The Fascination of Being Photographed and the Improvement on Photography," *Cosmopolitan* 35 (1903): 683.

9. Alan Trachtenberg, *Reading American Photographs: Images as History, Matthew Brady to Walker Evans* (New York: Hill and Wang, 1990), 29.

10. Orvell, *American Photography*, 21.

11. Miles Orvell, *The Real Thing: Imitation and Authenticity in American Culture, 1880–1940* (Chapel Hill: University of North Carolina Press, 1989), 89; Mary Warner Marien, *Photography: A Cultural History, 2nd edition* (London: Laurence King, 2006), 74.

12. Trachtenberg, *Reading American Photographs,* 27.

13. Linda Haverty Rugg, *Picturing Ourselves: Photography and Autobiography* (Chicago: University of Chicago Press, 2007), 88.

14. Robert Hirsch, *Seizing the Light: A History of Photography* (Boston: McGraw-Hill, 2000), 79; Heinz Kurt Henisch, *The Photographic Experience: 1839–1914: Images and Attitudes* (University Park: Pennsylvania State University Press, 1994), 13.

15. Orvell, *Real Thing*, 73.

16. John Tagg, *The Burden of Representation: Essays on Photographies and Histories* (London: Macmillan, 1988), 50.

17. Robert E. Mensel, " 'Kodakers Lying in Wait': Amateur Photography and the Right of Privacy in New York, 1885–1915," *American Quarterly* 43 (1991): 32.

18. See, e.g., Moore v. Rugg, 46 N.W. 141 (Minn. 1890).

19. Mensel, "Kodakers Lying in Wait," 32.

20. Ibid.

21. Ibid.

22. Daniel Pope, *The Making of Modern Advertising* (New York: Basic Books, 1983), 32.

23. Ibid.

24. See Kevin G. Barnhurst and John C. Nerone, *The Form of News: A History* (New York: Guilford Press, 2002), 114–115 (on the difficulties of picture reproduction in the periodicals of the nineteenth century).

25. Pamela Walker Laird, *Advertising Progress: American Business and the Rise of Consumer Marketing* (Baltimore: Johns Hopkins University Press, 2001), 149.

26. Laird, *Advertising Progress*, 260–261; Orvell, *American Photography*, 184.

27. Laird, *Advertising Progress*, 266.

28. Lois W. Banner, *American Beauty* (New York: Knopf, 1983), 262.

29. Henisch, *Photographic Experience*, 232.

30. See generally Hirsch, *Seizing the Light*, ch. 2.

31. Elspeth H. Brown, *The Corporate Eye: Photography and the Rationalization of American Commercial Culture, 1884–1929* (Baltimore: Johns Hopkins University Press, 2001), 50.

32. See Scott Cross, *Beatrice Tonnesen: First Commercial Photographer and Artist*, http://www.beatricetonnesen.com/bio/; Brown, *Corporate Eye*, 51.

33. On celebrity endorsements in this era, see also Stuart Banner, *American Property: A History of How, Why, and What We Own* (Cambridge: Harvard University Press, 2011), 135–137.

34. See Benjamin McArthur, *Actors and American Culture, 1880–1920* (Iowa City: University of Iowa Press, 2000), 124–125, 130.

35. Erin Mack and Anita L. Allen, "How Privacy Got Its Gender," *Northern Illinois Law Review* 10 (1990): 441–444; Marlis Schweitzer, *When Broadway Was the Runway: Theater, Fashion, and American Culture* (Philadelphia: University of Pennsylvania Press, 2011), 101.

36. Lawrence Meir Friedman, *Guarding Life's Dark Secrets: Legal and Social Controls over Reputation, Propriety, and Privacy* (Stanford: Stanford University Press, 2007), 37.

37. Peter Stearns, "Stages of Consumerism: Recent Work on Issues of Periodization," *Journal of Modern History* 69 (1997): 103.

38. Thorstein Veblen, *The Theory of the Leisure Class; An Economic Study of Institutions* (1899; New York: Macmillan, 1912), 32, 75.

39. "Saving and Spending," *Harper's Bazaar*, June 1906, 573.

40. Simon Bronner, "Reading Consumer Culture," in *Consuming Visions: Accumulation and Display of Goods in America, 1880–1920*, edited by Simon Bronner (New York: W. W. Norton, 1989), 13.

41. T.J. Jackson Lears, *Fables of Abundance: A Cultural History of Advertising in America* (New York: Basic Books, 1995), 89.

42. Orvell, *Real Thing*, 53; Lears, *Fables of Abundance*, 94–95.

43. Pope, *Making of Modern Advertising*, 186–187.

44. Juliann Sivulka, *Soap, Sex, and Cigarettes: A Cultural History of American Advertising* (Boston: Wadsworth Cengage Learning, 2012), 34.

45. Stephen Fox, *The Mirror Makers: A History of American Advertising and Its Creators* (New York: William Morrow, 1984), 67.

46. "Advertising Brigands," *Case and Comment* 2 (1895): 4.

47. Richard Ohmann, *Selling Culture: Magazines, Markets, and Class at the Turn of the Century* (New York: Verso, 1996), 185.

48. Orvell, *American Photography*, 185.

49. "A Recent Instance," *Outlook*, October 4, 1902, 248.

50. "Untitled," *Washington Post*, September 14, 1902.

51. "Advertising Brigands," 3.

52. Petitioner's Brief at 7, Peck v. Tribune, 214 U.S. 185 (1909).

53. Rhodes v. Sperry & Hutchinson Co., 104 N.Y.S. 1102, 1103 (N.Y.A.D. 2 Dept. 1907).

54. "Medicine Boomed by Girl's Picture," *New York Times*, August 21, 1907, 7.

55. Belinda Briggs, "A Monstrous Outrage," *Puck*, February 27, 1884, 36.

56. Mensel, "Kodakers Lying in Wait," 31.

57. See, e.g., Moore v. Rugg, 46 N.W. 141 (Minn. 1890).

58. "Advertising Brigands," 4.

59. Frederick Lane, *American Privacy: The 400-Year History of Our Most Contested Right* (Boston: Beacon Press, 2010), 52.

60. "The Ellsworth Bill," *New York Times*, January 22, 1898, 6.

61. Rochelle Gurstein, *The Repeal of Reticence: America's Cultural and Legal Struggles over Free Speech, Obscenity, Sexual Liberation, and Modern Art* (New York: Hill and Wang, 1998), 163–164.

62. Foster-Milburn Co. v. Chinn, 120 S.W. 364, 365 (Ky. 1909). See also Martin v. The Picayune, 115 La. 979 (La. 1906); Mackenzie v. Soden Mineral Springs Co., 18 N.Y.S. 240 (Sup. Ct. 1891).

63. Ohmann, *Selling Culture*, 187.

64. Gurstein, *Repeal of Reticence*, 164.

65. Munden v. Harris, 134 S.W. 1076, 1079 (Mo. App. 1911).

66. Thomas Huff, "Thinking Clearly about Privacy," *Washington Law Review* 55 (1979): 785.

67. Kunz v. Allen, 102 Kan. 883 (Kan. 1918); see also Gerald Dickler, "Right of Privacy—A Proposed Redefinition," *United States Law Review* 70 (1936): 440–441.

68. Rich, "What Invasions of Privacy Are Unlawful?" 239.

69. Brief in Support of Petition for Writ of Certiorari at 3, Peck v. Tribune, 214 U.S. 185 (1909).

70. Reply Brief for Petitioner at 3, Peck v. Tribune, 214 U.S. 185 (1909).

71. Peck v. Tribune, 214 U.S. 185, 190 (1909).

72. Peck v. Tribune, 154 F. 330, 332 (7th. Cir. 1907).

73. Samuel D. Warren and Louis D. Brandeis, "The Right to Privacy," *Harvard Law Review* 4 (1890): 193, 195.

74. "As more and more people became enmeshed in the market's web of interdependence," writes historian Jackson Lears, liberal visions of "autonomous selfhood became ever more difficult to sustain." T.J. Jackson Lears, "From Salvation to Self-Realization: Advertising and the Therapeutic Roots of the Consumer Culture, 1880–1930," in *The Culture of Consumption: Critical Essays in American History, 1880–1980*, edited by Richard Wightman Fox and T.J. Jackson Lears (New York: Pantheon Books, 1983), 7.

75. Samuel Hopkins Adams, "The New World of Trade: The Art of Advertising," *Collier's*, May 22, 1901, 13.

76. Lears, *Fables of Abundance*, 37.

77. "Untitled," *Washington Post*, September 14, 1902.

78. Wilbur Larremore, "The Law of Privacy," *Columbia Law Review* 12 (1912): 695.

79. Jonathan Kahn, "Privacy as a Legal Principle of Identity Maintenance," *Seton Hall Law Review* 33 (2010): 371.

80. "The Right of Privacy," *Columbia Law Review* 2 (1902): 439.

81. Foster-Millburn Co. v. Chinn, 120 S.W. 364, 366 (Ky. App. 1909).

82. "The Right to Privacy," *New York Times*, April 3, 1904, 6.

83. Ibid.

84. On the gendered dimensions of privacy in nineteenth-century America, see Caroline Danielson, "The Gender of Privacy and the Embodied Self: Examining the Origins of the Right to Privacy in U.S. Law," *Feminist Studies* 25 (1999); Erin Mack and Anita Allen, "How Privacy Got Its Gender," *Northern Illinois University Law Review* 10 (1991); Karen Lystra, *Searching the Heart: Women, Men, and Romantic Love in Nineteenth Century America* (New York: Oxford University Press, 1989).

85. Roberson v. Rochester Folding Box Co., 171 N.Y. 538 (N.Y. 1902).

86. Roberson v. Rochester Folding Box Co., 32 Misc. 344, 345 (Sup. Ct. 1900).

87. Ibid., 347.

88. Roberson, 171 N.Y. at 545.

89. Ibid., 543.

90. "The Right of Privacy," *Los Angeles Times*, July 28, 1905, 4.

91. "Notes of Recent Decisions," *American Law Review* 636 (1902): 36.

92. "An Actionable Right of Privacy? Roberson v. Rochester Folding Box Co.," *Yale Law Journal* 12 (1902): 37–38.

93. "The Right of Privacy," *New York Times*, April 3, 1904, 6.

94. N.Y. Civ. Rights Law § 50 & 51.

95. Thompson v. Tillford, 152 App. Div. 928 (N.Y.A.D. 2 Dept. 1912).

96. Moser v. Press Pub., 109 N.Y.S. 963, 965–996 (Sup. Ct. 1908).

97. Ibid.

98. Sperry & Hutchinson Co. v. Rhodes, 220 U.S. 502 (1911).

99. Brief for Plaintiff in Error, 7, Sperry & Hutchinson Co. v. Rhodes, 220 U.S. 502 (1911).

100. Rhodes v. Sperry & Hutchinson Co., 193 N.Y. 223, 228 (N.Y. 1908).

101. Sperry & Hutchinson Co., 220 U.S. at 505.

102. "Statute Protecting Right of Privacy Constitutional," *Law Notes* 12 (1909): 184.

103. Rhodes, 193 N.Y. at 228.

104. See Anita Allen, "Natural Law, Slavery, and the Right to Privacy Tort," *Fordham Law Review* 81 (2012): 1187; Jefferson James Davis, "An Enforceable Right of Privacy: Enduring Legacy of the Georgia Supreme Court," *Journal of Southern Legal History* 3 (1994); Pavesich v. New Eng. Life Ins. Co., 50 S.E. 68, 69 (Ga. 1905).

105. Pavesich, 50 S.E. at 68.

106. Ibid., 81.

107. Ibid., 80.

108. Ibid., 80–81.

109. "The Right of Privacy," *Los Angeles Times*, July 28, 1905.

110. "The Right of Privacy," *New York Times*, April 23, 1905, 8.

111. Ibid.

112. Pavesich v. New Eng. Life Ins. Co., 50 S.E. 68 (Ga. 1905); Foster-Millburn Co. v. Chinn, 120 S.W. 364 (Ky. 1909); Munden v. Harris, 153 Mo. App 652 (Mo. Ct. App. 1911); Edison v. Edison Polyform & Mfg. Co., 73 N.J. Eq. 136 (N.J. Ch. 1907); N.Y. Civ. Rights Law § 50; Utah Code Ann. §§ 76-9-401 to -402; Va. Code Ann. § 8.01-40.

113. Itzkovitch v. Whitaker, 115 La. 479 (La. 1905).

114. Douglas v. Stokes, 149 S.W. 849 (Ky. App. 1912).

Chapter 4

1. Gillespie v. Brooklyn H. R. Co., 178 N.Y. 347, 348 (N.Y. 1904).

2. Ibid., 349.

3. Ibid., 349.

4. Ibid., 349.

5. Ibid., 350–351.

6. Calvert Magruder, "Mental and Emotional Disturbance in the Law of Torts," *Harvard Law Review* 49 (1936): 1035; Roscoe Pound, "Interests of Personality," *Harvard Law Review* 28 (February 1915): 359–360.

7. William L. Prosser, *Handbook of the Law of Torts* (St. Paul: West Publishing, 1971), 875–877; see also G. Edward White, *Tort Law in America* (New York: Oxford University Press, 2003), 103.

8. Magruder, "Emotional Disturbance," 1035.

9. See generally Martha Chamallas and Jennifer B. Wriggins, *The Measure of Injury: Race, Gender, and Law* (New York: New York University Press, 2010); Leon Green, "Fright Cases," *Illinois Law Review* 27 (1933); Martha Chamallas and Linda Kerber, "Women, Mothers, and the Law of Fright: A History," *Michigan Law Review* 88 (1990).

10. James Q. Whitman, "Enforcing Civility and Respect: Three Societies," *Yale Law Journal* 109 (2000): 1376–1378.

11. See generally Whitman, "Three Societies."

12. Magruder, "Emotional Disturbance," 1035.

13. William Prosser and W. Page Keeton, *Handbook on Torts* (St. Paul: West Publishing, 1984), 59.

14. Barbara Welke, *Recasting American Liberty: Gender, Race, Law and the Railroad Revolution* (Cambridge: Cambridge University Press, 2001), 15.

15. Ibid., 15.

16. See Stokes v. Saltonstall, 38 U.S. 181 (1839).

17. Welke, *Recasting American Liberty*, 324–325.

18. Ibid., 265.

19. "Railroad Manners," *New York Times*, May 27, 1874, 4.

20. Ibid.

21. Welke, *Recasting American Liberty*, 294.

22. Richter, *Home on the Rails*, 21.

23. Ibid., 55.

24. Roger Grant, *Railroads and the American People* (Bloomington: Indiana University Press, 2012), 25. See also Peter C. Baldwin, *In the Watches of the Night: Life in the Nocturnal City, 1820–1930* (Chicago: University of Chicago Press, 2012), 141.

25. See Welke, *Recasting American Liberty*, 255, 259–263; William G. Thomas, *Lawyering for the Railroad: Business, Law, and Power in the New South* (Baton Rouge: Louisiana State University Press, 1999), 129–130.

26. Richter, *Home on the Rails*, 112–127.

27. "My Experience as a Street-Car Conductor," *Lippincott's Monthly Magazine*, June 1886, 635.

28. Richter, *Home on the Rails*, 123; Thomas, *Lawyering for the Railroad*, 129–130.

29. B. B. Adams, "Everyday Life of Railroad Men," *Scribner's Magazine*, November 1888, cited in Richter, *Home on the Rails*, 123.

30. "Convention of Passenger Railway Conductors," quoted in Richter, *Home on the Rails*, 123.

31. Haile v. New Orleans Railroad and Light Co., 135 La. 229, 231 (La. 1914).

32. *Restatement of Torts* § 48 (1934).

33. Louisville & N.R. Co. v. Donaldson, 43 S.W. 439, 439 (Ky. 1897).

34. Texas & Pacific Railway Co. v. Tarkington, 27 Tex. Civ. App. 353, 354 (Tex. Civ. App. Dallas 1901).

35. Bleecker v. Colorado & Southern Railroad Co., 50 Colo. 140, 141–142 (Colo. 1911).

36. Wolfe v. Georgia Railway & Electric Co., 2 Ga. App. 499, 500–501 (Ga. Ct. App. 1907).

37. Alice Williams v. Jacksonville, Tampa, and Key West Railway Co., 26 Fla. 533, 534 (Fla. 1890); Welke, *Recasting American Liberty*, 303.

38. Welke, *Recasting American Liberty*, 302–303.

39. Knoxville Traction Co. v. Lane, 103 Tenn. 376, 380–381 (Tenn. 1899).

40. Texas & Pacific Railway Co., 39 S.W. 124, 124 (Tex. Civ. App. 1897).

41. Welke, *Recasting American Liberty*, 70, 267; Charles Postel, *The Populist Vision* (New York: Oxford University Press, 2007), 10–11.

42. On the importance of public recreation and amusements to late nineteenth-century urban social life, see Gunther Barth, *City People: The Rise of Modern City Culture in Nineteenth-Century America* (New York: Oxford University Press, 1980), 95.

43. On clerks, floorwalkers, and detectives in department stores, see Barth, *City*

People, 129–134; Elaine Abelson, *When Ladies Go A-Thieving: Middle-Class Shoplifters in the Victorian Department Store* (New York: Oxford University Press, 1992).

44. On the alleged rudeness of American shopkeepers and clerks in the nineteenth century, see John F. Kasson, *Rudeness and Civility: Manners in Nineteenth Century Urban America* (New York: Hill & Wang, 1990), 59 (noting that European travelers were often taken aback by the roughness of service personnel and advised etiquette manuals for shopkeepers).

45. Interstate Amusement Co. v. Martin, 8 Ala. App. 481, 483–484 (Ala. Ct. App. 1913).

46. Boswell v. Barnum & Bailey, 135 Tenn. 35, 36 (Tenn. 1916).

47. Aaron v. Ward, 203 N.Y. 351, 354 (N.Y. 1911).

48. Davis v. Tacoma Railway and Power Co., 35 Wash. 203, 205 (Wash. 1904).

49. Bergstrom, *Courting Danger*, 159–165 (noting that the average plaintiff in a personal injury case in the late nineteenth century received in the range of $1,000 to $2,000).

50. John W. Wade, "Tort Liability for Abusive and Insulting Language," *Vanderbilt Law Review* 63 (1950–1951): 68.

51. Ibid., 67.

52. St. Louis, Arkansas & Texas Railway Co. v. Mackie, 71 Tex. 491, 494–495 (Tex. 1888); Thomas, *Lawyering for the Railroad*, 130.

53. Knoxville Traction Co. v. Lane, 103 Tenn. 376, 53 SW 557, 558 (Tenn. 1899).

54. Wolfe v. Georgia Railway & Electric Co., 2 Ga. App. 499, 509 (Ga. Ct. App. 1907).

55. Welke, *Recasting American Liberty*, 338.

56. Ibid., 289.

57. Wade, "Tort Liability," 70 (noting that these cases are a "real anomaly"); Magruder, "Emotional Disturbance," 1050 ("apparent anomaly").

58. Reynolds C. Seitz, "Insults-Practical Jokes-Threats of Future Harm-How New as Torts?" *Kentucky Law Journal* 28 (1939–1940): 416.

59. Ibid., 418–419.

60. William L. Prosser, "Insult and Outrage," *California Law Review* 44 (1956): 60.

61. Welke, *Recasting American Liberty*, 169.

62. See, e.g., McNamara v. St. Louis Transit Co., 182 Mo. 676, 678 (Mo. 1904); Weber-Stair Co. v. Fisher, 119 S.W. 195, 196–197 (Ky. 1909).

63. See, e.g., Wex Malone, "The Formative Era of Contributory Negligence," *Illinois Law Review* 41 (July–August 1946): 151, 152. On the difficulty of industrial workers obtaining recovery for personal injuries, see Friedman, "Civil Wrongs," 351, 355, 357, 369; Bergstrom, *Courting Injury*, 74–75, 127.

64. On the paternalism and chivalry towards white middle-class women exhibited in the decisions in many personal injury cases in this time—in particular cases

involving physical injuries in and around railroads—see Barbara Welke, "Unreasonable Women: Gender and the Law of Accidental Injury, 1870–1920," *Law and Social Inquiry* 19 (1994); Margo Schlanger, "Injured Women before Common Law Courts, 1860–1920," *Harvard Women's Law Journal* 21 (1998).

65. John Demos, "Shame and Guilt in Early New England," in *The Emotions: Social, Cultural and Biological Dimensions*, ed. Ron Harré and W. Gerrod Parrott (London: Sage, 1996), 75.

66. Ruth Benedict, *The Chrysanthemum and the Sword: Patterns of Japanese Culture* (1946; New York: Houghton Mifflin, 1967), 223.

67. Toni M. Massaro, "Shame, Culture, and American Criminal Law," *Michigan Law Review* 89 (1991): 1916.

68. See Demos, "Shame and Guilt"; Peter N. Stearns, *Battleground of Desire: The Struggle for Self-Control in Modern America* (New York: New York University Press, 1999), 58.

69. Benedict suggests that shame and guilt coexisted in American culture: "A society that inculcates absolute standards of morality and relies on men's developing a conscience is a guilt culture by definition, but a man in such a society may, as in the United States, suffer in addition from shame when he accuses himself of gaucheries which are in no way sins." Benedict, *Chrysanthemum and the Sword*, 222.

70. James B. Twitchell, *For Shame: The Loss of Common Decency in American Culture* (New York: St. Martin's Press, 1997), 41.

71. Edward Ayers, *Vengeance and Justice: Crime and Punishment in the 19th Century American South* (New York: Oxford University Press, 1984), 19.

72. Bertram Wyatt-Brown, *Southern Honor: Ethics and Behavior in the Old South* (New York: Oxford University Press, 1982), 14; Alison L. LaCroix, "To Gain the Whole World and Lose His Own Soul: Nineteenth-Century American Dueling as Public Law and Private Code," *Hofstra Law Review* 501 (2004–2005): 503.

73. Brown, *Southern Honor*, 22.

74. Wyatt-Brown, *Shaping of Southern Culture*, 14.

75. On white Southern ideals of womanhood, see Anne Firor Scott, *The Southern Lady: From Pedestal to Politics, 1830–1930* (Chicago: University of Chicago Press, 1970); Elizabeth Fox-Genovese, *Inside the Plantation Household: Black and White Women of the Old South* (Chapel Hill: University of North Carolina Press, 1988).

76. Ayers, *Vengeance and Justice*, 19; Robert Post, "The Social Foundations of Defamation Law: Reputation and the Constitution," *California Law Review* 74 (1986): 701.

77. Charles Sydnor, "The Southerner and the Laws," *Journal of Southern History* 4 (1938): 17.

78. Harwell Wells, "The End of the Affair? Anti-Dueling Laws and Social Norms in Antebellum America," *Vanderbilt Law Review* 54 (2001): 1823; Warren F. Schwartz, Keith Baxter, and David Ryan, "The Duel: Can These Gentlemen Be Acting Efficiently?" *Journal of Legal Studies* 131 (1984): 325.

79. Parker, "Law, Honor, and Impunity," 319–320.

80. Edward Ayers, *The Promise of the New South: Life after Reconstruction* (New York: Oxford University Press, 1992), 21.

81. Ibid., 55.

82. Welke, *Recasting American Liberty*, 263.

83. Sydnor, "Southerner and the Laws," 17.

84. "The Lingering Duello," *Century Illustrated Monthly Magazine*, May 1890 to October 1890, 152.

85. Ibid., 153.

86. LaCroix, "Nineteenth-Century American Dueling," 556–557 (noting that the statute books of most states contained antidueling provisions by the mid-1800s).

87. Schwartz, Baxter, and Ryan, "Duel," 326, 328; Wells, "End of the Affair," 1825–1829.

88. Wade, "Tort Liability," 83.

89. Landrum v. Ellington, 120 So. 444, 445 (Miss. 1929).

90. Wells, "End of the Affair," 1829.

91. Welke, *Recasting American Liberty*, 169, 267.

92. Ibid., 268.

93. Trent A. Watts, *One Homogeneous People: Narratives of White Southern Identity, 1890–1920* (Knoxville: University of Tennessee Press, 2010), 131.

94. Chamberlain v. Chandler, 3 Mason 242 (C.C. Mass. 1823).

95. Interstate Amusement Co. v. Martin, 62 So. 404, 405 (Ala. Ct. App. 1913); Aaron v. Ward, 96 N.E. 736 (N.Y. 1911); see also De Wolf v. Ford, 86 N.E. 527, 530 (N.Y. 1908).

96. Prosser, "Intentional Infliction of Emotional Suffering: A New Tort," *Michigan Law Review* 37 (1938–1939): 882–883.

97. Ibid., 882.

98. Ibid.

99. Whitman, "Enforcing Civility," 1377.

100. Kyle Graham, "Why Torts Die," *Florida State University Law Review* 35 (2007): 372.

101. Ibid., 389.

102. See Michael A. DiSabatino, "Civil Liability for Insulting or Abusive Language," *American Law Reports 4th* 20 (1993): 773–812 (noting that "since few of these cases are of recent origins, it appears that the persons manning trains are more polite to passengers or passengers have become less sensitive").

103. Ibid.

104. White, *Tort Law in America*, 16; Friedman, "Civil Wrongs," 351; John Goldberg, "Twentieth Century Tort Theory," *Georgetown Law Journal* 91 (2003): 519.

Chapter 5

1. On the 1920s, see Lynn Dumenil, *The Modern Temper: American Culture and Society in the 1920s* (New York: Hill & Wang, 1995); Frederick Lewis Allen, *Only Yes-*

terday: An Informal History of the 1920s (New York: Harper & Brothers, 1931); David Kyvig, *Daily Life in the United States, 1920–1940* (Westport: Greenwood Press, 2002); William Leuchtenburg, *The Perils of Prosperity, 1914–1932* (Chicago: University of Chicago Press, 2010); Nathan Miller, *New World Coming: The 1920s and the Making of Modern America* (Cambridge: Da Capo Press, 2003); David J. Goldberg, *Discontented America: The United States in the 1920s* (Baltimore: Johns Hopkins University Press, 1999).

2. Dale Carnegie, *How to Win Friends and Influence People* (New York: Simon & Schuster, 1936).

3. See Frederick Jackson Turner, *The Frontier in American History* (New York: Henry Holt, 1921).

4. Herbert S. Klein, *A Population History of the United States* (Cambridge: Cambridge University Press, 2004), 151.

5. Richard Dennis, *Cities in Modernity: Representations and Productions of Metropolitan Space, 1840–1930* (Cambridge: Cambridge University Press, 2008), 21.

6. Arnold R. Hirsch and Raymond A. Mohl, eds., *Urban Policy in Twentieth-Century America* (New Brunswick: Rutgers University Press, 1993), 4.

7. As cultural historian Warren Susman summarized, "whether it is a change from a producer to a consumer society, an order of economic accumulation to disaccumulation, industrial capitalism to finance capitalism . . . it is clear that a new social order was emerging." "'Personality' and the Making of Twentieth-Century Culture," reprinted in Warren I. Susman, *Culture as History: The Transformation of American Society in the Twentieth Century* (New York: Pantheon Books, 1984), 275.

8. Robert Park and Ernest Burgess, *The City* (Chicago: University of Chicago Press, 1925), 40.

9. Louis Wirth, "Urbanism as a Way of Life," *American Journal of Sociology* 44 (1938): 12.

10. Park and Burgess, *City*, 40.

11. Everett Dean Martin, *The Behavior of Crowds: A Psychological Study* (New York: Harper & Brothers, 1920).

12. Susman, "'Personality' and the Making of Twentieth-Century Culture," 277.

13. On the rise of consumer culture in this era, see Roland Marchand, *Advertising the American Dream: Making Way for Modernity, 1920–1940* (Berkeley and Los Angeles: University of California Press, 1985); Stuart Ewen, *Captains of Consciousness: Advertising and the Social Roots of the Consumer Culture* (New York: Basic Books, 2001); Richard Wightman and T.J. Jackson Lears, eds., *The Culture of Consumption* (New York: Pantheon Books 1983); William Leach, *Land of Desire: Merchants, Power, and the Rise of a New American Culture* (New York: Vintage, 1994).

14. Lary May, *Screening Out the Past: The Birth of Mass Culture and the Motion Picture Industry* (Chicago: University of Chicago Press, 1983), 201.

15. Walter Friedman, *Birth of a Salesman* (Cambridge: Harvard University Press, 2004), 190–224; Olivier Zunz, *Making America Corporate, 1870–1920* (Chicago: University of Chicago Press, 1990), 184–196.

16. Arlie Russell Hochschild, *The Managed Heart: Commercialization of Human Feeling* (Berkeley and Los Angeles: University of California Press, 2003), 6–7.

17. See generally Friedman, *Birth of a Salesman*.

18. Orison Swett Marden, *Masterful Personality* (New York: Thomas Y. Crowell, 1921), 44.

19. Peter N. Stearns, *Battleground of Desire: The Struggle for Self-Control in Modern America* (New York: New York University Press, 1999), 154.

20. Ibid.

21. Kathy Peiss, *Hope in a Jar: The Making of America's Beauty Culture* (New York: Metropolitan Books, 1998), 192–194.

22. Marden, *Masterful Personality*, 41.

23. Daniel J. Boorstin, *The Image: A Guide to Pseudo-Events in America* (New York: Atheneum, 1962), 187.

24. Susman, *Culture as History*, 280.

25. Marden, *Masterful Personality*, 39.

26. Susman, *Culture as History*, 278, quoting B. C. Bean, *Power of Personality* (1920), 3.

27. H. Laurent, *Personality: How to Build It* (New York: Funk & Wagnalls, 1916).

28. Marden, *Masterful Personality*, 71.

29. Dale Carnegie, *How to Win Friends and Influence People* (1936; New York: Pocket Books, 1981).

30. Ibid., 56.

31. Ibid., xiv.

32. Christopher Lasch, *The Culture of Narcissism: American Life in an Age of Diminishing Expectations* (New York: W. W. Norton, 1979), 116.

33. David Riesman, Nathan Glazer, and Reuel Denney, *The Lonely Crowd: A Study of the Changing American Character* (New York: Doubleday, 1950).

34. William James, *Principles of Psychology*, Volume I (New York: Henry Holt, 1890), 294.

35. Charles Horton Cooley, *Human Nature and the Social Order* (New York: Charles Scribner's Sons, 1903), 152. See also Glenn Jacobs, *Charles Horton Cooley: Imagining Social Reality* (Amherst: University of Massachusetts Press, 2006), 68.

36. T.J. Jackson Lears, *No Place of Grace: Antimodernism and the Transformation of American Culture, 1880–1920* (Chicago: University of Chicago Press, 1981), 37.

37. Frederick Lewis Allen, *Only Yesterday: An Informal History of the 1920s* (New York: Harper & Row, 1931), 67.

38. See generally Susman, *Culture as History*; Robert S. Lynd and Helen Merrell Lynd, *Middletown: A Study in Contemporary American Culture* (New York: Harcourt, Brace, 1929); John D'Emilio and Estelle B. Freedman, *Intimate Matters: A History of Sexuality in America* (New York: Harper & Row, 1988), 240.

39. May, *Screening Out the Past*, 202.

40. Lynd and Lynd, *Middletown*, 81–82, 162.

41. T.J. Jackson Lears, *Fables of Abundance: A Cultural History of Advertising in America* (New York: Basic Books, 1994), 139.

42. Peter N. Stearns, "Stages of Consumerism: Recent Work on the Issues of Periodization," *Journal of Modern History* 69 (1997): 105.

43. Marlis Schweitzer and Marina Moskowitz, eds., *Testimonial Advertising in the American Marketplace: Emulation, Identity, Community* (New York: Palgrave Macmillan, 2009), 127.

44. Stephen R. Fox, *The Mirror Makers: A History of American Advertising and Its Creators* (Chicago: Illini Books, 1997), ch. 3; Mark Bartholomew, "Advertising and the Transformation of Trademark Law," *New Mexico Law Review* 38 (2008): 1 ("Often viewed with disapproval in the 1800s, advertisers were held in high regard throughout the first part of the 20th century").

45. Richard Ohmann, *Selling Culture: Magazines, Markets, and Class at the Turn of the Century* (New York: Verso Books, 1996), 176–180.

46. Boorstin, *Image*, 205.

47. Marchand, *American Dream*, 14.

48. Ad for Williams' Shaving Cream, *Collier's*, 1929.

49. Ewen, *Captains of Consciousness*, 177.

50. Peiss, *Hope in a Jar*, 142.

51. Ibid., 143.

52. Ad for Arrow Shirt Collars, *Collier's*, November 23, 1929.

53. Colgate's Rapid Shave Cream, *Collier's*, October 12, 1929.

54. Marchand, *American Dream*, 18.

55. Ibid., 208.

56. Ibid., 213.

57. Ibid.

58. Ewen, *Captains of Consciousness*, 47.

59. Ad for E. V. Price Suit Company, *Collier's*, 1929.

60. Peiss, *Hope in a Jar*, 146–148.

61. John C. Burnham, *Paths into American Culture: Psychology, Medicine, and Morals* (Philadelphia: Temple University Press, 1988), 77.

62. Joel Pfister, "Glamorizing the Psychological: The Politics of the Performances of Modern Psychological Identities," in Joel Pfister and Nancy Schnog, *Inventing the Psychological: Toward a Cultural History of Emotional Life in America* (New Haven: Yale University Press, 1997), 167.

63. Peiss, *Hope in a Jar*, 144.

64. On the early twentieth-century film cult of celebrity, see generally Samantha Barbas, *Movie Crazy: Fans, Stars and the Cult of Celebrity* (New York: Palgrave Macmillan, 2002); Robert Sklar, *Movie Made America: A Cultural History of American Movies* (New York: Random House, 1975); Richard DeCordova, *Picture Personalities: The Emergence of the Star System in America* (Urbana: University of Illinois Press, 1990).

65. Leo Lowenthal, "The Triumph of Mass Idols," in *Literature, Popular Culture, and Society* (Englewood Cliffs: Prentice Hall, 1961).

66. Charles Ponce de Leon, *Self-Exposure: Human-Interest Journalism and the Emergence of Celebrity in America, 1890–1940* (Chapel Hill: University of North Carolina Press, 2002), 47–48.

67. "Actors and Stars," *New York Times*, April 25, 1920, X4.

68. Peiss, *Hope in a Jar*, 143–144.

69. See Charles Eckert, "The Carole Lombard in the Macy's Window," in *Movies and Mass Culture*, John Belton, ed. (New Brunswick: Rutgers University Press, 1996), 95–118 ("The Hollywood studios, with their roster of contract stars, had come to occupy a privileged position in the advertising industry"). See also Michael Madow, "Private Ownership of Public Image: Popular Culture and Publicity Rights," *California Law Review* 81 (1993).

70. David Potter, *People of Plenty* (Chicago: University of Chicago Press, 1954), 169.

71. David E. Kyvig, *Daily Life in the United States*, 94.

72. Richard Schickel, *Intimate Strangers: The Culture of Celebrity* (Garden City: Doubleday, 1985), 50; Edwin Emery, *The Press and America: An Interpretive History of the Mass Media* (Englewood Cliffs: Prentice Hall, 1992), 281–283.

73. See generally Samantha Barbas, *The First Lady of Hollywood: A Biography of Louella Parsons* (Berkeley and Los Angeles: University of California Press, 2005).

74. Erving Goffman, *The Presentation of Self in Everyday Life* (Garden City: Anchor, 1959), 8.

75. See generally Lynd and Lynd, *Middletown*, 263–269, for a discussion of the influence of movies on youth in the 1920s.

76. Herbert Blumer, *Movies and Conduct* (New York: Macmillan, 1933); Peiss, *Hope in a Jar*, 191.

77. Barbas, *Movie Crazy*, 46.

Chapter 6

1. Sidis v. F-R Pub. Corp., 34 F. Supp. 19, 21 (S.D.N.Y. 1938).

2. Lynn Gorman and David McLean, *Media and Society into the 21st Century: A Historical Introduction* (Chichester: Wiley-Blackwell, 2009), 24.

3. For circulation figures, see Alfred McClung Lee, *The Daily Newspaper in America* (London: Routledge/Thoemmes Press, 1947), 731.

4. David E. Kyvig, *Daily Life in the United States, 1920–1940* (Chicago: Ivan R. Dee, 2004), 190–191.

5. Sean Cashman, *America in the Twenties and Thirties: The Olympian Age of Franklin Delano Roosevelt* (New York: New York University Press, 1989), 326.

6. James L. Baughman, *The Republic of Mass Culture: Journalism, Filmmaking, and Broadcasting in America since 1941* (Baltimore: Johns Hopkins University Press, 1992), 16.

7. For the "ritualistic" nature of media consumption in this era, see, e.g., Bernard Berelson, "What Missing the Newspaper Means," in *Communications Research: 1948–1949*, Paul Felix Lazarsfeld and Frank N. Stanton, ed. (New York: Harper & Brothers, 1949), 111–129.

8. Although the words were spoken, defamatory statements in broadcasting were considered libels rather than slanders because words disseminated over the radio, like written libels, were mass circulated and could potentially inflict serious damage to reputation. See Sorensen v. Wood, 123 Neb. 348 (Neb. 1932).

9. Zechariah Chafee, *Government and Mass Communications, Volume 1* (Chicago: University of Chicago Press, 1947), 79.

10. Brown v. Paramount Publix Corp., 240 A.D. 520, 522 (N.Y. App. Div. 1934).

11. At its first convention in April 1923, the American Society of Newspaper Editors adopted the first nationwide statement of journalistic ideals, which included objectivity, accuracy, impartiality, and "fair play." John D. Stevens, *Sensationalism and the New York Press* (New York: Columbia University Press, 1991), 115.

12. Frank Thayer, "The Changing Libel Scene," *Wisconsin Law Review* 1943 (1943): 333.

13. Emile Gauvreau, *My Last Million Readers* (New York: E. P. Dutton, 1941), 113.

14. George Norris to Godfrey Nelson, October 28, 1948, Arthur Hays Sulzberger Papers, Box 196, Folder 17, Manuscripts and Archives Division, New York Public Library.

15. On libel courses in journalism schools, see Betty Winfield, *Journalism—1908: Birth of a Profession* (Columbia: University of Missouri Press, 2008), 49.

16. Thayer, "Changing Libel Scene," 340.

17. In 1937, *Editor and Publisher* noted that half of the major New York papers used lawyers as "censors." M. Marvin Berger, "Detecting Libel Before It Appears," *Editor and Publisher*, May 29, 1937.

18. Thayer, "Changing Libel Scene," 340.

19. Ibid., 332.

20. "Libel, Contempt," *Time*, June 9, 1930, 60.

21. Norfolk Post Corp. v. Wright, 140 Va. 735, 737–738 (Va. 1924).

22. Thayer, "Changing Libel Scene," 331.

23. See James Kincaid, *Press Photography* (New York: American Photographic Publishing, 1936), 121 (noting that "few libel suits ever reach the litigation stage. If the newspaper sees it has little chance of winning a court battle, it will generally attempt to settle the case out of court with a cash award to the party damaged").

24. Burton Rascoe, "Libel's Lawyer," *Esquire*, August 1938, 103. Wrote *New York Times* publisher Adolph Ochs to the paper's lawyers in 1922: "You know my views about settling libel suits . . . I would never settle a libel suit to save a little money. . . . If we have damaged a person we are prepared to pay . . . and we accept the decision as part of the exigencies of our business." Adolph Ochs to Alfred A. Cook, May 9, 1922, Adolph Ochs Papers, Box 86, Folder 6, Manuscripts and Archives Division, New York

Public Library. On the *New Yorker*'s refusal to settle, see Kathy Roberts Forde, "Libel, Freedom of the Press, and the *New Yorker*," *American Journalism* 23 (2006): 76.

25. Stanley Walker, *City Editor* (Baltimore: Johns Hopkins University Press, 1999), 186. "The law of libel is the newspaper man's most constant nightmare." Robert Miller Neal, *Newspaper Desk Work* (New York: D. Appleton, 1933), 289.

26. Thayer, "Changing Libel Scene," 333.

27. William Findley Swindler, *Problems of Law in Newspapers* (New York: Macmillan Press, 1955), 99.

28. Nancy Barr Mavity, *The Modern Newspaper* (New York: H. Holt, 1930), 161.

29. Walker, *City Editor*, 186.

30. Kincaid, *Press Photography*, 117 (noting that "nothing is more feared in the newspaper world than libel. . . . Some things must be kept out of the newspaper because of that law which haunts the editor like a nightmare").

31. Neil MacNeil, *Without Fear or Favor* (New York: Harcourt, Brace, 1940), 337.

32. Forde, *Literary Journalism on Trial*, 94.

33. For the phrase "libel climate," see Timothy Gleason, "The Libel Climate of the Nineteenth Century: A Survey of Libel Litigation, 1884–1899," *Journalism and Mass Communication Quarterly* 70 (December 1993): 893–906.

34. See Norman Rosenberg, "Taking a Look at 'The Distorted Shape of an Ugly Tree': Efforts at Policy-Surgery on the Law of Libel during the Decade of the 1940s," *Northern Kentucky Law Review* 15 (1988): 19–29; V. F. Calverton, "The Libel Racket," *Current History*, May 1, 1938, 48.

35. "Slander Books," *Saturday Evening Post*, January 9, 1932, 24; "A Collect As You Go Tour of the Publisher's Chain," *Newsweek*, February 22, 1936, 50 (noting one politician's "touring legal circus" of suits against the Hearst papers).

36. See Rosenberg, *Protecting the Best Men*, 223.

37. David Riesman, "Democracy and Defamation: Fair Game and Fair Comment," *Columbia Law Review* 42 (1942): 1086.

38. Rosenberg, "Taking a Look at 'The Distorted Shape of an Ugly Tree,' " 41–47. See also The Commission on Freedom of the Press, *A Free and Responsible Press: A General Report on Mass Communication; Newspapers, Radio, Motion Pictures, Magazines, and Books* (Chicago: University of Chicago Press, 1947); Zechariah Chafee, *Government and Mass Communications* (Chicago: University of Chicago Press, 1947), 95–115. Reports and correspondence of the commission can be found in the Archives of the Hutchins Commission on Freedom of the Press, Special Collections, University of Washington.

39. According to some film industry commentators, the claim was a carefully plotted publicity stunt. Lynn Kear, *Evelyn Brent: The Life and Films of Hollywood's Lady Crook* (Jefferson: McFarland, 2009), 28.

40. Sydney v. MacFadden Newspaper Publishing Corp., 242 N.Y. 208, 210–211 (N.Y. 1926).

41. "Libel Suit Reply Made by Goldwyn," *Los Angeles Times*, November 11, 1932.

42. Walker, *City Editor*, 188.

43. MacNeil, *Without Fear*, 338.

44. Walker, *City Editor*, 189.

45. Ibid., 190.

46. Lyman v. New England Newspaper Co., 286 Mass. 258 (Mass. 1934).

47. Walker v. Bee-News Publishing, 122 Neb. 511 (Neb. 1932); Ernst and Lindey, *Hold Your Tongue*, 145.

48. See Charles Edward Clark and Harry Shulman, *A Study of Law Administration in Connecticut: A Report of an Investigation of the Activities of Certain Trial Courts of the State* (New Haven: Yale University Press, 1937), 12–13, 28, 31, 44. Of thirty-one cases, eighteen resulted in judgments for plaintiffs, and thirteen for defendants.

49. Thayer, "Changing Libel Scene," 342.

50. "Doctor & Duke," *Time*, January 15, 1934, 50.

51. Forde, *Literary Journalism on Trial*, 101.

52. Gauvreau, *My Last Million Readers*, 113.

53. Patricia Nassif Acton, *Invasion of Privacy: The Cross Creek Trial of Marjorie Kinnan Rawlings* (Gainesville: University of Florida Press, 1988), 76.

54. Rascoe, *Libel's Lawyer*, 100.

55. Morris L. Ernst and Alexander Lindey, "What Price Reputation?" *American Bar Association Journal* 103 (1933): 103.

56. Ibid.

57. Ibid.

58. Frederick Seaton Siebert, *The Rights and Privileges of the Press* (New York: D. Appleton-Century, 1934), 33–32; Snively v. Record Publishing Co., 185 Cal. 565 (Cal. 1921); Van Vechten Veeder, "Freedom of Public Discussion," *Harvard Law Review* 23 (1910): 416–417.

59. Coleman v. MacLennan, 98 P. 281, 286 (Kan. 1908).

60. New York Times Co. v. Sullivan, 376 U.S. 254 (U.S. 1964).

61. John Wade, "Defamation and the Right of Privacy," *Vanderbilt Law Review* 15 (1962): 1094.

62. Calvert Magruder, "Mental and Emotional Disturbance in the Law of Torts," *Harvard Law Review* 49 (1936): 1055.

63. Snyder v. N.Y. Press Co., 137 App. Div. 291 (1910); see also Enterprise Co. v. Ellis, 98 S.W. 2d 452 (Tex. Civ. App. 1936).

64. Zbyszko v. New York American, 228 A.D. 277 (N.Y. 1930); "Zbyszko v. Ape," *Time*, February 24, 1930, 72.

65. "A Collect As You Go Tour of the Publisher's Chain," *Newsweek*, February 22, 1936, 50.

66. Burton v. Crowell Publishing Co., 82 F. 2d 154 (2nd Cir. 1936).

67. "Camel Jockey," *Time*, January 18, 1937, 41.

68. Transcript of Record, Exhibit A, Burton v. Crowell Publishing Co., 82 F. 2d 154 (2nd Cir. 1936).

69. Ibid.

70. "Camel Jockey," 41.

71. Ibid.

72. Ibid.

73. "$22,250 Settlement in Burton Suit," *Editor and Publisher*, January 23, 1937, 12.

74. Complaint, Transcript of Record, 6, Burton v. Crowell Publishing Co.

75. Brief of Appellant, 7, Burton v. Crowell Publishing Co.

76. Transcript of Record, 25, Burton v. Crowell Publishing Co.

77. Burton, 82 F. 2d at 156.

78. "Gentleman Jockey Wins $2500 Award," *Editor and Publisher*, January 9, 1937, 27.

79. Recent Cases, "Libel and Slander—Liability for Publishing Photograph Which Created Optical Illusion Concerning Plaintiff," *Harvard Law Review* 49 (1936): 841.

80. See Kincaid, *Press Photography*, 120 ("ridicule is not libelous. Creating a laugh at someone's expense, regardless of how great the person's discomfort may be, will not support a libel suit").

81. Magruder, "Emotional Disturbance," 1056.

82. Ibid.

83. Nugent Shands, "Libel-Optical Illusion-Prima Facie Actionable," *Mississippi Law Journal* 9 (1937): 251.

84. G. Edward White, *Tort Law in America: An Intellectual History* (New York: Oxford University Press, 2003), 103.

85. Joel Pfister and Nancy Schnog, *Inventing the Psychological: Toward a Cultural History of Emotional Life in America* (New Haven: Yale University Press, 1997), 168.

86. Herbert F. Goodrich, "Emotional Disturbance as Legal Damage," *Michigan Law Review* 20 (1922): 497–498.

87. Reed v. Real Detective Pub. Co., 63 Ariz. 294, 306 (Ariz. 1945).

88. White, *Tort Law*, 75.

89. Roscoe Pound, "Interests of Personality," *Harvard Law Review* 28 (1915): 349.

90. Leon Green, "Right of Privacy," *Illinois Law Review* 27 (1934): 240.

91. Fowler V. Harper and Mary Coate McNeely, "A Re-Examination of the Basis of Liability for Emotional Distress," *Wisconsin Law Review* 426 (1938): 458.

92. William Prosser, "Intentional Infliction of Emotional Suffering: A New Tort," *Michigan Law Review* 37 (1938–1939); Calvert Magruder, "Mental and Emotional Disturbance in the Law of Torts," *Harvard Law Review* 49 (1936); White, *Tort Law*, 104.

93. Magruder, "Emotional Disturbance," 1058.

94. Prosser, "Insult and Outrage," 43.

95. White, *Tort Law*, 104.

96. *Restatement of the Law*, Supplement, Torts, S. 46 (1948).

97. Magruder, "Emotional Disturbance," 1042–1048, 1064–1066.

98. Walker v. Tucker, 220 Ky. 363 (Ky. 1927); La Salle Extension University v. Fogarty, 126 Neb. 457, 457–458 (Neb. 1934); Nickerson v. Hodges, 146 La. 735, 740–741 (La. 1920); Wallace v. Shoreham Hotel, 49 A. 2d. 81 (D.C. App. 1946).

99. Peter N. Stearns, *Battleground of Desire: The Struggle for Self-Control in Modern America* (New York: New York University Press, 1999), 258–259. On shame around poverty in the Great Depression, see Lawrence Levine, "American Culture and the Great Depression," in *The Unpredictable Past: Explorations in American Cultural History* (New York: Oxford University Press, 1993), 213–214.

100. La Salle Extension University v. Fogarty, 126 Neb. 457, 457–458 (Neb. 1934).

101. Brents v. Morgan, 221 Ky. 765, 766 (Ky. 1927).

102. Nickerson v. Hodges, 146 La. 735, 740–741 (La. 1920).

103. Ibid.

104. George W. Jarecke and Nancy K. Plant, *Seeking Civility: Common Courtesy and the Common Law* (Boston: Northeastern University Press, 2006), 3–6.

105. Nickerson, 146 La. at 740–741.

106. California, Colorado, Georgia, Illinois, Kansas, Kentucky, Louisiana, Missouri, New Jersey, North Carolina, Pennsylvania, South Carolina, New York, Virginia, Utah. See Louis Nizer, "The Right of Privacy: A Half Century's Developments," *Michigan Law Review* 39 (1940): 529–530. See also Basil Kacedan, "The Right of Privacy," *Boston University Law Review* 12 (1932); Gerald Dickler, "Right of Privacy—A Proposed Redefinition," *United States Law Review* 70 (1936); Roy Moreland, "Right of Privacy Today," *Kentucky Law Journal* 19 (1931); L. S. Clemons, "Right of Privacy in Relation to the Publication of Photographs," *Marquette Law Review* 14 (1930); Edward Doan, "The Newspaper and the Right of Privacy," *Journal of the Bar Association of Kansas* 5 (1937).

107. *Restatement (First) of Torts* § 867 (1939).

108. Nizer, "The Right of Privacy," 536.

109. Lewis Nichols, "Our Sacred Privacy Becomes a Memory," *New York Times Magazine*, October 11, 1931, Section 5, p. 8.

110. Frederick S. Lane, *American Privacy: The 400-year History of Our Most Contested Right* (New York: Beacon Press, 2011), 108–109.

111. Robert Floyd, "Privacy," *Chicago Sunday Tribune*, September 27, 1925, 8.

112. Meyer Berger, "Surrender of Privacy," *Scribner's Magazine*, April 1939, 16.

113. Lane, *American Privacy*, 108–111.

114. Mitchell Dawson, "Paul Pry and Privacy," *Atlantic Monthly*, October 1932, 385.

115. William L. Prosser, "Privacy," *California Law Review* 48 (1960): 389–392.

116. Silas Bent, *Ballyhoo: The Voice of the Press* (New York: Boni and Liveright, 1927), 54.

117. "The Passing of Privacy," *Washington Post*, June 30, 1936, 8.

118. A survey of news content in the *Philadelphia Evening Bulletin* in 1928 showed that the two most common kinds of stories were crime and "human interest" stories. See Mavity, *Modern Newspaper*, 36; Gerald W. Johnson, "Freedom of the Newspaper Press," *Annals of the American Academy of Political and Social Science* 200 (November 1938): 66–67.

119. Harry Shaw, "Pocket and Pictorial Journalism," *North American Review* 243 (1937): 303.

120. Berger, "Surrender of Privacy," 20.

121. Margaret Farrand Thorp, *America at the Movies* (New Haven: Yale University Press, 1939), 20.

122. William H. Young and Nancy K. Young, *The 1930s* (Westport: Greenwood Press, 2002), 163.

123. Shaw, "Pocket and Pictorial Journalism," 302.

124. H. L. Smith, "The News Camera on Trial," *Forum and Century* 5 (1937): 267–269; Leon R. Yankwich, "The Right of Privacy: Its Development, Scope and Limitations," *Notre Dame Lawyer* 27 (1952): 525.

125. Donald S. Baldwin, "If Your Photograph Were News," *Notre Dame Law Review* 4 (1929).

126. Walker, *City Editor*, 103–104.

127. Dawson, "Paul Pry and Privacy," 386.

128. John L. Hulteng, *The Messenger's Motives: Ethical Problems of the News Media* (Englewood Cliffs: Prentice Hall PTR, 1985), 169.

129. Nichols, "Our Sacred Privacy Becomes a Memory."

130. Newman Levy, "The Right to be Let Alone," *American Mercury*, June 1935, 197.

131. "Right of Privacy Undetermined," *Editor and Publisher*, April 25, 1936, 23.

132. Ed Streeter, "No Such Word as 'Privacy' in the Lexicon of Presidential Candidates," *Washington Post*, October 24, 1920, 61.

133. Leo Lowenthal, "The Triumph of Mass Idols," in *Literature, Popular Culture, and Society* (Englewood Cliffs: Prentice Hall, 1961).

134. See John H. Summers, "What Happened to Sex Scandals? Politics and Peccadilloes, Jefferson to Kennedy," *Journal of American History* (December 2000): 842–848.

135. As journalist Curtis MacDougall wrote in 1941, "One may resent having his own privacy invaded, but seldom objects to learning the 'low down' about motion picture stars, prominent athletes, officeholders, criminals, and of course, his neighbors." *Newsroom Problems and Policies* (New York: Macmillan, 1941), 328–329.

136. Dawson, "Paul Pry," 387.

137. Bent, *Ballyhoo*, 68.

138. Dawson, "Paul Pry," 387.

139. Walker, *City Editor*, 171.

140. Ibid., 206.

141. Berger, "Surrender of Privacy," 18.

142. Dawson, "Paul Pry," 387.

143. Ibid., 404.

144. George Ragland, "The Right of Privacy," *Kentucky Law Journal* 17 (1928): 87.

145. "First Lady Calls Census All Right," *New York Times*, March 19, 1940.

146. Dawson, "Paul Pry," 388.

147. Ibid.

148. Barber v. Time, 159 S.W. 2d 291, 295 (Mo. 1942).

149. Hull v. Curtis Pub. Co., 182 Pa. Super. 86, 99 (Pa. Super. 1956).

150. Jones v. Herald Post Co., 230 Ky. 227 (Ky. 1929).

151. Hillman v. Star Pub. Co., 64 Wash. 691–693 (Wash. 1911).

152. Blumenthal v. Picture Classics, 257 N.Y.S. 800, 801 (N.Y. App. Div. 1932).

153. Sweenek v. Pathe News, Inc., 16 F. Supp. 746, 748 (E.D.N.Y. 1936).

154. Morris Leopold Ernst, *So Far, So Good* (New York: Harper & Brothers, 1948), 54; Damron v. Doubleday Doran & Co., 231 N.Y.S. 444 (N.Y. Sup. 1928).

155. Levy, "Let Alone," 196.

156. Molony prevailed at trial, but the decision was reversed by an appeals court on the grounds that the publication was not sufficiently distorted to be "fictional," and therefore not actionable under New York's right of privacy statute. Molony v. Boy Comics Publishers, 98 N.Y.S.2d 119, 120–123 (N.Y. App. Div. 1950).

157. Binns v. Vitagraph Co. of America, 132 N.Y.S. 237, 238–239 (N.Y. App. Div. 1911).

158. Harry Kalven Jr., "Privacy in Tort Law—Were Warren and Brandeis Wrong?" *Law and Contemporary Problems* 31 (1966): 328.

159. See, e.g, the *Sidis* case, discussed in Chapter 7, and *Cason v. Baskin*, described in Chapter 8.

160. These cases were brought under the New York "privacy" statute, which prohibited uses of people's likenesses or identities for the purposes of advertising or "trade." Although the requirements of the New York privacy statute and the common law privacy tort were different in this regard (the common law tort was not limited to advertising or "trade" uses), New York privacy jurisprudence adopted many principles from common law privacy cases, and vice versa—in particular, on the question of what was a privileged "matter of public concern."

161. Peed v. Washington Times, 55 Wash. L. Rep 182–183 (DC 1927).

162. Peay v. Curtis Pub. Co., 78 F. Supp. 305, 309 (D.D.C. 1948).

163. James Brennan, "Never Give a Passenger a Break," *Saturday Evening Post*, February 28, 1948, 10.

164. In a companion case, Fowler v. Curtis Pub. Co., 78 F. Supp. 303 (D.D.C. 1948), sixty Washington cabdrivers sued the *Saturday Evening Post* for libel over the article.

165. Peay v. Curtis Pub. Co., 78 F. Supp. at 309, citing Hinish v. Meier & Frank Co., 166 Or. 482, 503 (Or. 1941).

166. Ibid.

167. Ibid.

168. See, e.g., De Jonge v. Oregon, 299 U.S. 353, 364–365 (1937); Stromberg v. California, 283 U.S. 359, 366–369 (1931); Martin v. Struthers, 319 U.S. 141 (1943); Lovell v. City of Griffin, 303 U.S. 444, 452 (1938); Feldman, *Free Expression*, 371–372.

169. Cantwell v. Connecticut, 310 U.S. 296 (1940).

170. W. Va. State Bd. of Educ. v. Barnette, 319 U.S. 624, 642 (U.S. 1943).

171.   G. Edward White, "The First Amendment Comes of Age: The Emergence of Free Speech in Twentieth Century America," *Michigan Law Review* 95 (1996): 331.

172.   Reuel E. Schiller, "Free Speech and Expertise: Administrative Censorship and the Birth of the Modern First Amendment," *Virginia Law Review* 86 (2000): 81.

173.   Sweenek, 16 F. Supp. at 747–748.

174.   See, e.g., Middleton v. News Syndicate Co., 162 Misc. 516 (N.Y. Sup. Ct. 1937); Elmhurst v. Pearson, 153 F.2d 467 (D.C. Cir. 1946). One New York trial court even described gossip about private individuals—"private social affairs and prevailing fashions involving individuals who make no bid for publicity"—as "public property," "where the apparent use is to convey information of interest and not mere advertising." Martin v. New Metropolitan Fiction, 139 Misc. 290, 292 (N.Y. Sup. Ct. 1931).

175.   See generally Samantha Barbas, "The Death of the Public Disclosure Tort: A Historical Perspective," *Yale Journal of Law and Humanities* 171 (2010): 182–189.

176.   Sweenek, 16 F. Supp. at 747, citing Associated Press v. INS, 245 F. 244, 248 (2nd. Cir. 1917).

177.   Berg v. Minneapolis Star & Tribune Co., 79 F. Supp. 957, 963 (D. Minn. 1948); Sarat Lahiri v. Daily Mirror, Inc., 162 Misc. 776, 783 (N.Y. Sup. Ct. 1937); Smith v. Doss, 251 Ala. 250, 253 (Ala. 1948).

178.   Sarat Lahiri, 162 Misc. at 782.

179.   *Restatement (First) of Torts* § 867 comment c. (1939).

180.   Ibid.

181.   Jones, 230 Ky. at 227.

182.   Metter v. Los Angeles Examiner, 35 Cal. App. 2d 305 (1939).

183.   *Restatement (First) of Torts* § 867 comment c. (1939).

Chapter 7

1.   Sidis v. F-R Publ'g Corp., 113 F.2d 806, 809 (2d Cir. 1940). Much of the material in this chapter is drawn from the New Yorker Archives, Manuscripts and Archives Division, New York Public Library.

2.   On the enduring significance of *Sidis*, see Amy Wallace, *The Prodigy: A Biography of William J. Sidis, America's Greatest Child Prodigy* (New York: E. P. Dutton, 1986), 236; Kim Lane Scheppele, *Legal Secrets: Equality and Efficiency in the Common Law* (Chicago: University of Chicago Press, 1988), 216–217; Emile Karafiol, "The Right to Privacy and the Sidis Case," *Georgia Law Review* 12 (1978). The story of William James Sidis is memorialized in popular culture; the 1998 film *Good Will Hunting* is said to have been based on his life. See also Samantha Barbas, "The *Sidis* Case and the Origins of Modern Privacy Law," *Columbia Journal of Law and the Arts* 36 (2012).

3.   Wallace, *Prodigy*, 1–20; Jared L. Manley, "Where Are They Now? April Fool!" *New Yorker*, August 14, 1937, 22.

4.   Wallace, *Prodigy*, 23; Manley, "Where Are They Now?" 22; Boris Sidis, *Philistine and Genius* (New York: Moffat, Yard, 1911).

5. Frank Fleischman, "A Boy Prodigy and the Fourth Dimension," *Harpers' Weekly*, January 15, 1910, 9.

6. Wallace, *Prodigy*, 35–38; "This Eight-Year-Old Boy Wonder Finds Mathematics Too Simple," *Washington Post*, December 2, 1906, A5.

7. "A Savant at Thirteen, Young Sidis on Entering Harvard Knows More Than Many on Leaving. A Scholar at Three," *New York Times*, October 17, 1907, SM9; see also "Boy Mathematician Astounds Educators," *Chicago Tribune*, January 7, 1910, 7; "Sidis Could Read at Two Years Old," *New York Times*, October 18, 1909, 7.

8. Wallace, *Prodigy*, 60; "Sidis Is Pythagoras," *Los Angeles Times*, June 17, 1910, 110.

9. "Sidis of Harvard," *New York Times*, October 18, 1909, 6.

10. H. Addington Bruce, "Intensive Child Culture," *Washington Post*, May 12, 1912, SM3; Frederic J. Haskin, "New Ideas in Education," *Washington Post*, February 23, 1910, 4.

11. "The Boy Prodigy of Harvard," *Current Literature* 48 (1910); "Wonderful Boys of History," *Washington Post*, January 23, 1910, M2; "Harvard's Quartet of Mental Prodigies: Unique Problem for Psychologists in Education of Young Sidis and His Three Companions," *New York Times*, January 16, 1910, SM11.

12. Wallace, *Prodigy*, 61.

13. Ibid., 53.

14. V. O'Shea, "Popular Misconceptions Concerning Precocity in Children," *Science* 34 (1911): 667–668; see also Joseph F. Kett, "Curing the Disease of Precocity," *American Journal of Sociology* 84 (1978): 183, 206.

15. Wallace, *Prodigy*, 55.

16. Ibid., 68–71.

17. "Fear Is Felt for Sidis," *New York Times*, January 28, 1910, 1.

18. Wallace, *Prodigy*, 53.

19. Ibid., 107.

20. "Harvard's Prodigy at Figures, Aged 17, Takes Vow of Celibacy," *Washington Post*, April 18, 1915, 9; "Prodigy of Harvard Vows Not to Wed—He's Only 17," *Chicago Tribune*, April 18, 1915, 1.

21. Wallace, *Prodigy*, 111–115, 135; see also Leon Guerard, *Personal Equation* (New York: W. W. Norton, 1948), 220. At Rice he was "treated like a two-headed calf. His boyish singularities were . . . mercilessly exposed and amplified. Because he blurted out that he had never kissed a girl, he was made the butt of endless practical jokes."

22. "Graduate of Harvard, Believer in the Soviet, Given Prison Sentence," *Atlanta Constitution*, May 14, 1919, 20; "Youngest Graduate of Harvard Is Sentenced," *New York Tribune*, May 14, 1919, 6; Manley, "Where Are They Now?" 25.

23. "Boy, Once Brain Wonder, Now a New York Clerk," *Washington Post*, January 11, 1924, 9.

24. Wallace, *Prodigy*, 170–171.

25. "Precocity Doesn't Wear Well," *New York Times*, January 11, 1924, 16.

26. "Is It Too Bad If Your Child's a Prodigy?" *Atlanta Constitution*, February 17, 1924, F3.

27. "Pathetic Fiction," *Education Review* 67 (June 1924): 158; see also "Sidis Hated His Father, Feels That He Was Treated Harshly as a Boy," *Boston Daily Globe,* January 11, 1924, 22A.

28. Wallace, *Prodigy,* 166.

29. Ibid., 166–167, 181–182; Manley, "Where Are They Now?" 25–26.

30. Ibid., 228.

31. Sidis v. F-R Publ'g Corp., 113 F.2d 806, 809 (2d Cir. 1940).

32. Kathy Roberts Forde, *Literary Journalism on Trial: Masson v. New Yorker and the First Amendment* (Amherst: University of Massachusetts Press, 2008), 9–10, 40–41; Wilfred Feinberg, "Recent Developments in the Law of Privacy," *Columbia Law Review* 48 (July 1948): 713, 718.

33. Ben Yagoda, *About Town: The New Yorker and the World It Made* (New York: Scribner, 2000), 96; see also David E. Sumner, *The Magazine Century: American Magazines since 1900* (New York: Peter Lang, 2010), 77.

34. James Thurber, *The Years with Ross* (New York: Harper Collins, 1959), 210.

35. Ik Shuman to Alexander Lindey, September 6, 1940, *The New Yorker* Archives, Manuscripts and Archives Division, New York Public Library; Shuman to Lindey, August 11, 1938; Shuman to Harriet Pilpel, August 22, 1938; Anthony Lewis, "The Right to Be Let Alone," in *Journalism and the Debate over Privacy* (Mahwah: Lawrence Erlbaum Associates, 2003), 61, 63.

36. Manley, "Where Are They Now?" 26.

37. Ibid., 26.

38. Ibid.

39. Thurber, *Years with Ross,* 212.

40. Wallace, *Prodigy,* 270.

41. *The New Yorker* to Barbara Linscott, January 24, 1938; Lindey to Shuman, September 14, 1938; Wallace, *Prodigy,* 225–228.

42. Lindey to Shuman, August 17, 1938; Brief for Defendant-Appellee, Sidis v. F-R Publ'g Corp., 113 F.2d 806 (2d Cir. 1940).

43. Lindey to Shuman, August 17, 1938.

44. See generally Paul Boyer, *Purity in Print: Book Censorship in America from the Gilded Age to the Computer Age* (Madison: University of Wisconsin Press, 2002), 203; Samantha Barbas, "How the Movies Became Speech," *Rutgers Law Review* 64 (2012).

45. "Alexander Lindey, 85, Lawyer and an Author of Textbooks," *New York Times,* November 12, 1981, D23; Boyer, *Purity in Print,* 203.

46. On Greenbaum, Wolff, and Ernst, see *The Irving Younger Collection: Wit and Wisdom from the Master of Trial Advocacy* (Chicago: American Bar Association Publishing, 2011), 492–496.

47. Thayer, "Changing Libel Scene," 338; Forde, *Literary Journalism on Trial,* 93–97.

48. *The New Yorker* to Barbara Linscott, January 24, 1938.

49. Shuman to Lindey, October 4, 1938; Shuman to Lindey, October 17, 1938; Lindey to Shuman, August 9, 1938.

50. Quoted in Kathy Roberts Forde, "Libel, Freedom of the Press, and the *New Yorker*," *American Journalism* 23 (2006): 81.

51. Brief for Defendant-Appellee at 12, Sidis v. F-R Publ'g Corp., 113 F.2d 806 (2d Cir. 1940).

52. On these free speech protests and the transformation of free speech law in this period, see generally David M. Rabban, *Free Speech in its Forgotten Years, 1870–1920* (Cambridge: Cambridge University Press, 1997); Stephen M. Feldman, *Free Expression and Democracy in America* (Chicago: University of Chicago Press, 2008), chs. 8–10; Mark A. Graber, *Transforming Free Speech: The Ambiguous Legacy of Civil Libertarianism* (Berkeley: University of California Press, 1991), chs. 2–4.

53. Near v. Minnesota, 283 U.S. 697, 708–722 (1931); Thornhill v. Alabama, 310 U.S. 88, 102 (1940).

54. Palko v. Connecticut, 302 U.S. 319, 327 (1937).

55. On the "preferred freedom" theory of the Court in this era, see Feldman, *Free Expression*, 371–372; G. Edward White, "The First Amendment Comes of Age: The Emergence of Free Speech in Twentieth Century America," *Michigan Law Review* 95 (1996): 299, 330.

56. Hannegan v. Esquire, 327 U.S. 146, 157–158 (1946); Reuel E. Schiller, "Free Speech and Expertise: Administrative Censorship and the Birth of the Modern First Amendment," *Virginia Law Review* 86 (2000): 1; White, "First Amendment," 331.

57. See Robert Park "News as a Form of Knowledge: A Chapter in the Sociology of Knowledge," *American Journal of Sociology* 45 (1940): 669, 679; John Dewey, *The Public and Its Problems* (Denver: A. Swallow, 1927), 98, 143, 213; Bernard Berelson, "What Missing the Newspaper Means," reprinted in *Mass Communications and American Social Thought: Key Texts, 1919–1968*, John Durham Peters, ed. (Lanham: Rowman & Littlefield, 2004), 254–262.

58. For sociological studies in this vein, see Helen MacGill Hughes, *News and the Human Interest Story: A Study of Popular Literature* (Chicago: University of Chicago Press, 1940), 13; Hughes, "Human Interest Stories and Democracy," *Public Opinion Quarterly* 1 (1937): 76–78.

59. Tom Goldstein, *Killing the Messenger: 100 Years of Media Criticism* (New York: Columbia University Press, 2007), 19 (noting the familiar defense of journalists, when criticized about content, that they were merely "giving the people what they want").

60. Near v. Minnesota, 283 U.S. 697, 708–722 (1931).

61. Grosjean v. American Press Co., 297 U.S. 233, 243 (1936).

62. Associated Press v. United States, 326 U.S. 1, 28, 29 (1945).

63. Brief for Defendant-Appellee, Sidis v. F-R Publ'g Corp., 113 F.2d 806 (2d Cir. 1940) (No. 400).

64. Ibid.

65. Lindey to Shuman, December 22, 1938.

66. Sidis v. F-R Publ'g Corp., 34 F. Supp. 19, 25 (S.D.N.Y. 1938).

67. Ibid.

68. Lindey to Shuman, November 30, 1939; Lindey to Shuman, April 6, 1940.

69. C.E.C., "Freedom of Speech, A Note on Professor Corwin's Article," *Yale Law Journal* 30 (1920): 68, 69–79.

70. Roger K. Newman, ed., *The Yale Biographical Dictionary of American Law* (New Haven: Yale University Press, 2009), 108. See also Fred Rodell, "For Charles E. Clark: A Brief and Belated but Fond Farewell," *Columbia Law Review* 65 (1965): 1323, 1324; Michael E. Smith, "Charles E. Clark and the Federal Rules of Civil Procedure," *Yale Law Journal* 85 (1976): 914, 915.

71. Lindey to Harold Ross, July 24, 1940.

72. Brief for Defendant-Appellee, Sidis v. F-R Publ'g Corp., 113 F.2d 806 (2d Cir. 1940) (No. 400).

73. Ibid.

74. Lindey to Harold Ross, July 24, 1940.

75. Sidis v. F-R Publ'g Corp., 113 F.2d 806, 807 (2d Cir. 1940).

76. Ibid. at 809.

77. Ibid.

78. Recent Decision, "Torts: Right of Privacy of Former Child Prodigy," *California Law Review* 29 (1940): 87, 88.

79. Sidis, 113 F. 2d. at 209.

80. Edwin J. Lukas, "Letter to the Editor," *New York Law Journal*, August 16, 1940.

81. Lindey to Shuman, December 2, 1940.

82. Wallace, *Prodigy*, 265.

83. Ibid.

84. Lindey to T. M. Brassel, December 21, 1943.

85. Frances Velie and Caroline Menuez, "Twilight of a Genius," *Coronet*, February 1945, 43.

86. Wallace, *Prodigy*, 269.

87. Ibid., 271–272.

88. Ibid., 269.

89. Sidis v. F-R Publ'g Corp., 113 F.2d 806, 809 (2d Cir. 1940).

90. "Torts—Right of Privacy—Matters of General or Public Interest," *Michigan Law Review* 39 (1941): 501, 503.

91. Mitchell Dawson, "Law and the Right of Privacy," *American Mercury*, October 1948, 401.

92. Lindey to Shuman, January 20, 1941; Shuman to Lindey, December 13, 1940, November 18, 1940.

93. Wilfred Feinberg, "Recent Developments in the Law of Privacy," 719.

94. Lindey to Shuman, November 18, 1940.

95. Fred Bartenstein Jr., "Recent Cases, Right of Privacy—Protection against the Publication of Newsworthy Information [Federal]," *Washington and Lee Law Review* 2 (1940–1941): 140.

96. "Notes and Comment, Limitations on the Right of Privacy of a Quondam Public Figure," *New York Law Review* 74 (1940): 423, 429, 430.

97. "Recent Decisions, Torts—Right of Privacy—Biographical Sketch of Former Child Prodigy as a Matter of Public Concern," *Fordham Law Review* 10 (1941): 108, 110–111.

98. Bartenstein, "Recent Cases," 141.

99. See, e.g., "Prodigy's Progress," *Washington Post*, July 23, 1944, B4 ("bright candle that he was, young Sidis was quickly burned out"); "Sidis, a 'Wonder' in Boyhood, Dies," *New York Times*, July 18, 1944, 21 ("The one-time 'boy wonder' was found seriously ill and in a coma Thursday night in his room in a Brookline boarding house, apparently destitute"); "Sidis, Noted Prodigy as a Child, Dies in Boston, Obscure," *Hartford Courant*, July 18, 1944; "The Hidden Genius," *New York Times*, July 19, 1944, 18.

100. Leon Yankwich, "The Protection of Newspaper Comment on Public Men and Public Matters," *Louisiana Law Review* 11 (1951): 327, 342.

101. Morris Leopold Ernst and Alan U. Schwartz, *Privacy: The Right to Be Let Alone* (New York: Macmillan, 1962), 186–187.

Chapter 8

1. Daniel L. Boorstin, *The Image: A Guide to Pseudo-Events in America* (New York: Vintage Books, 1961).

2. Ibid., 249.

3. Wini Breines, *Young, White and Miserable: Growing Up Female in the Fifties* (Chicago: University of Chicago Press, 2001), 3; see also William Chafe, *The Unfinished Journey: America since World War II* (Oxford: Oxford University Press, 2003); David Shi, *The Simple Life: Plain Living and High Thinking in American Culture* (Athens: University of Georgia Press, 1985); David Horowitz, *Anxieties of Affluence: Critiques of American Consumer Culture* (Amherst: University of Massachusetts Press, 2004), 49 ("By 1960, Americans ate, lived, drove, slept, dressed, and entertained themselves in ways that were dramatically different from those that prevailed in 1945").

4. David Farber, *The Age of Great Dreams: America in the 1960's* (New York: Hill and Wang, 1994), 9.

5. David Riesman et al., *The Lonely Crowd: A Study of the Changing American Character* (New York: Doubleday, 1950), 19.

6. Ibid.

7. Ibid., 83–108, 149–160.

8. See Todd Gitlin, foreword to *The Lonely Crowd*, by David Riesman (New Haven: Yale University Press, 2001), xiii.

9. See William Whyte, *The Organization Man* (New York: Simon & Schuster, 1956); Vance Packard, *The Status Seekers* (New York: David McKay, 1959); Erving Goffman, *The Presentation of Self in Everyday Life* (New York: Doubleday, 1959).

10. Paul Boyer et al., *The Enduring Vision: A History of the American People, Volume 2* (Boston: Wadsworth Cengage Learning, 2010), 841.

11. Goffman, *Presentation of Self in Everyday Life*, 56.

12. C. Wright Mills, *White Collar: The American Middle Classes* (Oxford: Oxford University Press, 1951), xvii.

13. Donald A. Laird, "Are You an Alibi Artist?" *Saturday Evening Post*, July 10, 1943, 80.

14. Arnold Stanley Norman, *The Magic Power of Putting Yourself Over with People* (Englewood Cliffs: Prentice Hall, 1962), xvii.

15. Eva S. Moskowitz, *In Therapy We Trust: America's Obsession with Self-Fulfillment* (Baltimore: Johns Hopkins University Press, 2001), 157.

16. David S. Broder, "Year of the Image," *New York Times*, May 8, 1960.

17. Quoted in Boorstin, *Image*, 225.

18. Kathy Peiss, *Hope in a Jar: The Making of America's Beauty Culture* (New York: Henry Holt, 1998), 245–247.

19. Breines, *Young, White, and Miserable*, 95; Herbert Koshetz, "Garment Industry Has No Complaint," *New York Times*, April 6, 1952, F1.

20. Susannah Handley, *Nylon: The Story of a Fashion Revolution* (Baltimore: Johns Hopkins University Press, 2000), 66.

21. Elizabeth Haiken, *Venus Envy: A History of Cosmetic Surgery* (Baltimore: Johns Hopkins University Press, 1999), 145.

22. Melvin DeFleur, "How Massive Are the Mass Media? Implications for Communications Education and Research," *Syracuse Scholar* 10 (1990): 24–25.

23. David Halberstam, *The Fifties* (New York: Villard Books, 1993), 195.

24. Farber, *Age of Great Dreams*, 49.

25. John David Ebert, *Dead Celebrities, Living Icons: Tragedy and Fame in the Age of the Multimedia Superstar* (Santa Barbara: Praeger, 2010), 75.

26. William Faulkner, "On Privacy: The American Dream: What Happened to It," *Harper's*, July 1955, 35.

27. Boorstin, *Image*, 194.

28. Richard H. Pells, *The Liberal Mind in the Conservative Age: American Intellectuals in the 1940s and 1950s* (Middletown: Wesleyan University Press, 1985), 225–226.

29. Boorstin, *Image*, 87.

30. Ibid., 183.

31. Ibid., 202.

32. Ibid., 192, 257.

33. Philip Rieff, *Triumph of the Therapeutic: Uses of Faith after Freud* (Chicago: University of Chicago Press, 1966); Moskowitz, *In Therapy We Trust*; Deborah Weinstein, *The Pathological Family: Postwar America and the Rise of Family Therapy* (Ithaca: Cornell University Press, 2013), 3–4.

34. See, e.g., Weinstein, *Pathological Family*, 3–4; Jonathan Metzl, *Prozac on the Couch: Prescribing Gender in the Era of Wonder Drugs* (Durham: Duke University Press, 2003); Eli Zaretsky, "Charisma or Rationalization? Domesticity and Psychoanalysis in the United States in the 1950s," *Critical Inquiry* 26 (2000).

35. Moskowitz, *In Therapy We Trust*, 217.

36. Ibid., 149.

37. Ibid., 157.

38. Jesse Battan, "'The New Narcissism' in 20th Century America: The Shadow and Substance of Social Change," *Journal of Social History* 17 (1983): 207.

39. Pells, *Liberal Mind in a Conservative Age*, 247.

40. Philip Cushman, *Constructing the Self, Constructing America: A Cultural History of Psychotherapy* (Reading: Addison-Wesley, 1995), 79; Haiken, *Venus Envy*; on dieting, see Hillel Schwartz, *Never Satisfied: A Cultural History of Diets, Fantasies, and Fat* (New York: Free Press, 1986).

41. Moskowitz, *In Therapy We Trust*, 219.

42. Ibid.

43. Ibid.

44. Christopher Lasch, *The Culture of Narcissism: American Life in the Age of Diminishing Expectations* (New York: W. W. Norton, 1991), 16–17.

45. "Expose Thyself," *Commonweal*, July 26, 1957, 411–412.

46. In the 1960s, Alan Westin noted studies that showed an increasing willingness to disclose personal information to pollsters and survey organizations. Westin, *Privacy and Freedom*, 53.

47. Howard Brick, *Age of Contradiction: American Thought and Culture in the 1960s* (Ithaca: Cornell University Press, 2000), 69, xvi.

48. Lawrence Meir Friedman, *The Republic of Choice: Law, Authority, and Culture* (Cambridge: Harvard University Press, 1990), 3.

49. Harold G. Vatter and John F. Walker, *History of the U.S. Economy since World War II* (Armonk: M. E. Sharpe, 1996), 81.

50. Robert Jay Lifton, *The Protean Self: Human Resilience in an Age of Fragmentation* (Chicago: University of Chicago Press, 1999).

51. Cushman, *Constructing the Self*, 77.

52. See James A. Dyal, "Images in the Lonely Crowd," *Vital Speeches of the Day* 31 (1965): 729.

53. Mailer quoted in Richard Poirer, *The Performing Self: Compositions and Decompositions in the Language of Everyday Life* (New Brunswick: Rutgers University Press, 1992), 103.

54. Edward Bloustein, "Privacy, Tort Law, and the Constitution: Is Warren and Brandeis' Tort Petty and Unconstitutional as Well?" *Texas Law Review* 46 (1968): 619.

55. Gill v. Hearst Pub. Co., 231 P. 2d 570, 571 (Cal. 1951).

56. This was a question asked by Richard Nixon in his capacity as plaintiff's lawyer in the oral argument in Time, Inc. v. Hill, 385 U.S. 374 (1967).

57. William H. Young, *The 1950s* (Westport: Greenwood Press, 2004), 153.

58. Lee Burress, *Battle of the Books: Literary Censorship in the Public Schools, 1950–1985* (Metuchen: Scarecrow Press, 1989), 73. John Tebbel, *A History of Book Publishing in the United States*, vol. 4 (New York: R. R. Bowker, 1978), 291, 308–350, 712.

59. David E. Sumner, *The Magazine Century: American Magazines since 1900* (New York: Peter Lang, 2010), 117.

60. See Curtis D. MacDougall, *The Press and Its Problems* (Dubuque: W. C. Brown, 1964), 119.

61. Gerhard Mueller, "Problems Posed by Publicity to Crime and Criminal Proceedings," *University of Pennsylvania Law Review* 110 (1961): 18–19.

62. Bill Sloan, *I Watched a Wild Hog Eat My Baby: A Colorful History of Tabloids and Their Cultural Impact* (Amherst: Prometheus Books, 2001).

63. Packard, *Status Seekers*, 217.

64. Amber Watts, "Queen for A Day: Remaking Consumer Culture, One Woman at a Time," in *The Great American Makeover: Television, History, Nation*, Dana A. Heller, ed. (New York: Palgrave Macmillan, 2006), 141, 154.

65. Wilbur Schramm and William Rivers, *Responsibility in Mass Communications* (New York: Harper & Row, 1969), 157.

66. Alan Westin, *Privacy and Freedom* (New York: Atheneum, 1967), 55–56.

67. See MacDougall, *Press and Its Problems*, 250; also James L. Aucoin, *The Evolution of American Investigative Journalism* (Columbia: University of Missouri Press, 2005), 78 (noting the development of portable tape recorders, wiretaps, and surveillance cameras).

68. Clay Calvert, *Voyeur Nation: Media, Privacy, and Peering in Modern Culture* (Boulder: Westview Press, 2004), 41–42.

69. "Sinatra Drops His Libel Suit for $2,300,000," *Los Angeles Times*, December 17, 1957, 4.

70. See Aucoin, *Evolution of American Investigative Journalism*, 51.

71. Leo Braudy, *The Frenzy of Renown: Fame and Its History* (New York: Vintage Books, 1997), 615.

72. Westin, *Privacy and Freedom*, 55.

73. See Edward Shils, "Privacy: Its Constitution and Vicissitudes," *Law and Contemporary Problems* 31 (1966): 302.

74. Norman Rosenberg, *Protecting the Best Men: An Interpretive History of the Law of Libel* (Chapel Hill: University of North Carolina Press, 1990), 247.

75. Francis Murnaghan, "From Figment to Fiction to Philosophy—the Requirement of Proof of Damages in Libel Actions," *Catholic University Law Review* 22 (1972): 4.

76. Vernon Miller, *Selected Essays on Torts* (Buffalo: Dennis, 1960), 191 n2.

77. Kathy Roberts Forde, "Libel, Freedom of the Press, and the *New Yorker*," *American Journalism* 23 (2006): 81

78. Rosenberg, *Protecting the Best Men*, 247. See also Kathy Roberts Forde, *Literary Journalism on Trial: Masson v. New Yorker and the First Amendment* (Amherst: University of Massachusetts Press, 2008), 113 (noting that "as the 1950s went on, libel complaints against the magazine began to include demands for large damage awards").

79. Murnaghan, "From Figment to Fiction," 4.

80. Melvin Belli, *Ready for the Plaintiff* (New York: Grosset & Dunlop, 1956), 160.

81. Harold Cross, "Current Libel Trends," *Nieman Reports*, January 5, 1951, 3.

82. Norris, "Forty Years," 10.

83. Bonnie Brennen, *For the Record: An Oral History of Rochester, New York, Newsworkers* (New York: Fordham University Press, 2001), 111.

84. See J. E. Smythe, "James Jones, Columbia Pictures, and the Historical Confrontations of From Here to Eternity," in *Why We Fought: America's Wars in Film and History*, Peter C. Rollins and John E. O'Connor, eds. (Lexington: University Press of Kentucky, 2008), 289.

85. "Publishers' Corner," *Saturday Review of Literature*, July 15, 1950, 26.

86. Cross, "Current Libel Trends," 2.

87. There was also a proliferation of publishing handbooks that discussed the law of libel. See, e.g., Swindler, *Problems of Law in Journalism*; Philip Wittenberg, *Dangerous Words: A Guide to the Law of Libel* (New York: Columbia University Press, 1947); Walter Allan Steigleman, *The Newspaper and the Law* (New York: W. C. Brown, 1950); Samuel Spring, *Risks and Rights in Publishing: Television, Radio, Motion Pictures, Advertising and the Theater* (New York: W. W. Norton, 1952).

88. Cross, "Current Libel Trends," 2–3.

89. Faulk v. Aware, 19 A.D. 2d 464, 470–471 (N.Y.A.D. 1963).

90. Charles H. McCormick, *This Nest of Vipers: McCarthyism and Higher Education in the Mundel Affair, 1951–52* (Chicago: University of Illinois Press, 1989); Floyd Abrams, *Speaking Freely: Trials of the First Amendment* (New York: Penguin Books, 2005), 153–187; "Precedent," *New Republic*, September 14, 1953, 5.

91. "Developments in the Law of Defamation," *Harvard Law Review* 69 (1956): 882 (noting that "to have called another a communist in 1939 would not have defamed him in some American communities, whereas the same charge would do so today"). See Frank E. Booker, "The Accusation of Communism as Slander Per Se," *Duke Bar Journal* 4 (Winter 1954): 1–15.

92. "Sinatra Charges 2,300,000 Libel," *New York Times*, May 8, 1957, 43.

93. "Elizabeth Taylor Files 6 Libel Suits," *New York Times*, December 1, 1960, 70.

94. Henry E. Scott, *Shocking True Story: The Rise and Fall of Confidential, America's Most Scandalous Scandal Magazine* (New York: Pantheon Books, 2010), 114.

95. See "The Press: Success in the Sewer," *Time*, July 11, 1955, 92.

96. Mary Desjardins, "Systematizing Scandal: Confidential Magazine, Stardom, and the State of California," in *Headline Hollywood: A Century of Film Scandal*, Adrienne L. McLean and David A. Cook, eds. (New Brunswick: Rutgers University Press, 2001), 206–231.

97. Ibid., 210.

98. Forde, *Literary Journalism on Trial*, 113, 110–114.

99. Neiman-Marcus Co. v. Lait, 107 F. Supp. 96, 102 (S.D.N.Y. 1952).

100. See R. Charles Ray, "Torts—Libel—Slander—Defamation by Broadcast—Defamacast Actionable Per Se," *Houston Law Review* 1 (1963–1964): 58; American Broadcasting-Paramount Theaters, Inc. v. Simpson, 106 Ga. App. 230, 126 S.E. 2d 873 (1962).

101. Bernstein v. NBC, 129 F. Supp. 817–818 (D.D.C. 1955). This was a privacy case, though similar facts also led to libel litigation.

102. Fred P. Graham, "Law: Rasputin a Test of Privacy," *New York Times*, October 24, 1965, E7.

103.   Lois Forer, *A Chilling Effect: The Mounting Threat of Libel and Invasion of Privacy Actions to the First Amendment* (New York: W. W. Norton, 1987), 210; see, e.g., Koussevitzky v. Allen, Towne & Heath, 188 Misc. 479 (Sup. Ct. 1947), aff'd, 272 A.D. 759 (App. Div. 1947).

104.   Samuel Spring, "Invasion of Privacy," *Publishers' Weekly*, February 2, 1952, 693.

105.   Emily Toth, *Inside Peyton Place: The Life of Grace Metalious* (New York: Doubleday, 1981), 174–175; "Libel Suit Is Settled," *New York Times*, November 27, 1958, 41.

106.   The privacy case went to trial, but the libel lawsuit was resolved when author Hersey complied with Toscani's demands to give his profits to charity. See Toscani v. Hersey, 271 A.D. 445 (N.Y. App. Div. 1946); Douglas Martin, "E. F. Toscani, 89, Dies; Model for Hero of 'Bell for Adano,'" *New York Times,* January 28, 2001, 30; "Libel Suit against Author of A Bell for Adano," *Publishers' Weekly,* March 23, 1946, 1740.

107.   "Miracle of the Bells Libel Suit Dismissed," *Publishers' Weekly*, February 11, 1950, 157.

108.   Dan Wakefield, "From Eternity to Brooklyn," *The Nation*, November 16, 1957, 339–341. Maggio also sued for invasion of privacy and lost. See People v. Scribner's Sons, 205 Misc. 818 (N.Y. City Magist. Ct. 1954).

109.   Cooper v. Greely & McElrath, 1 Denio 347 (N.Y. Sup. Ct. 1845).

110.   Walter Probert, "Defamation, A Camouflage of Psychic Interests: The Beginning of a Behavioral Analysis," *Vanderbilt Law Review* 15 (1962): 1182.

111.   Ibid., 1181.

112.   "Developments in the Law of Defamation," *Harvard Law Review* 69 (1956): 880–881. See Powers v. Durgin-Snow Publishing Co., Inc. 154 Me. 108 (1958); Moglen v. Varsity Pajamas, Inc. 213 N.Y.S. 2d 999, 1004 (N.Y.A.D. 1961) (dissenting opinion).

113.   Edward Bloustein, "Privacy as an Aspect of Human Dignity: An Answer to Dean Prosser," *New York University Law Review* 39 (1964): 993.

114.   John Wade, "Defamation and the Right of Privacy," *Vanderbilt Law Review* 15 (1962): 1094–1095.

115.   Harry Kalven Jr., "Privacy in Tort Law—Were Warren and Brandeis Wrong?" *Law and Contemporary Problems* 31 (1966): 332.

116.   Anthony Lewis, *Make No Law: The Sullivan Case and the First Amendment* (New York: Random House, 1991), 35.

117.   New York Times v. Sullivan, 376 U.S. 254, 280 (1964).

118.   Sullivan, 376 U.S. at 283.

119.   Harry Kalven Jr., "The New York Times Case: A Note on 'The Central Meaning of the First Amendment,'" *Supreme Court Review* 1 (1964): 221 n125 (quoting Alexander Meiklejohn).

120.   Curtis Publishing Co. v. Butts, 388 U.S. 130 (1967); Gertz v. Robert Welch, Inc., 418 U.S. 323, 348 (1974).

121.   Gertz v. Robert Welch, Inc., 418 U.S. 323, 350 (1974); Time, Inc. v. Firestone, 424 U.S. 448, 460 (1976); International Brotherhood of Electrical Workers v. Mayo,

281 Md. 475 (1977); Terrance C. Mead, "Suing the Media for Emotional Distress: A Multi-Method Analysis of Tort Law Evolution," *Washburn Law Journal* 23 (1983): 45–46.

122. Rodney Smolla, *Suing the Press: Libel, the Media, and Power* (New York: Oxford University Press, 1986), 24.

123. Robert D. Sack and Richard Tofel, "First Steps Down the Road Not Taken: Emerging Limitations on Libel Damages," *Dickinson Law Review* 90 (1985): 621.

124. Randall Bezanson, "The Libel Tort Today," *Washington and Lee Law Review* 45 (1988): 541.

125. Randall Bezanson, "The Libel Suit in Retrospect: What Plaintiffs Want and What Plaintiffs Get," *California Law Review* 74 (1986): 791. "The libel suit represents an official engagement of the judicial system on their behalf, and the act of suing represents a legitimation of their claims of falsehood. Indeed, many plaintiffs may believe they have no other means of recourse, and therefore feel that litigation is the only way to set the record straight."

126. Ibid. On the performative nature of libel suits for politicians and public figures, see David Riesman, "Democracy and Defamation: Fair Game and Fair Comment," *Columbia Law Review* (1942): 1086–1087.

127. Patricia Nassif Acton, *Invasion of Privacy: The Cross Creek Trial of Marjorie Kinnan Rawlings* (Gainesville: University Press of Florida, 1988).

128. Trial transcript, 225, Box 5, Folder 15, Cross Creek Trial Papers, Special and Area Studies Collections, George A. Smathers Libraries, University of Florida, Gainesville, Florida.

129. Marjorie Kinnan Rawlings, *Cross Creek* (New York: Charles Scribner's Sons, 1942), 48.

130. Rawlings, *Cross Creek*, 147.

131. Rawlings to May, February 5, 1943, in *Selected Letters of Marjorie Kinnan Rawlings*, Gordon E. Bigelow and Laura V. Monti, eds. (Gainesville: University Press of Florida, 1983), 234.

132. Ibid., 232.

133. Rawlings to Max Perkins, September 15, 1941, reprinted in *Letters*, 209–210, 235.

134. Acton, *Invasion of Privacy*, 17.

135. Rawlings to Phil May, February 27, 1945, reprinted in *Letters*, 259.

136. Trial Transcript, 63, 272, Box 5, Folder 15, Cross Creek Trial Papers.

137. Trial Transcript, 49–50, 55, Box 5, Folder 15, Cross Creek Trial Papers.

138. Acton, *Invasion of Privacy*, 57.

139. Ibid., 1.

140. James West, *Plainville, USA* (New York: Columbia University Press, 1945), 97.

141. Acton, *Invasion of Privacy*, 41–46.

142. Trial Transcript, 61, Box 5, Folder 15, Cross Creek Trial Papers.

143. Acton, *Invasion of Privacy,* 58.

144. Rawlings to Norton Baskin, August 4, 1943, reprinted in Roger L. Tarr, *The Private Marjorie: The Love Letters of Marjorie Kinnan Rawlings to Norton S. Baskin* (Gainesville: University Press of Florida, 2004), 106.

145. Rawlings to Maxwell Perkins (editor at Scribner's), June 4, 1946, reprinted in *Letters,* 287.

146. Rawlings to Norton Baskin, September 4, 1943, reprinted in *Private Marjorie,* 122.

147. See Trial Transcript, 68, Box 5, Folder 15, Cross Creek Trial Papers.

148. Rawlings to Philip May, February 5, 1943, reprinted in *Letters,* 232.

149. Acton, *Invasion of Privacy,* 76; Elizabeth Silverthorne, *Marjorie Kinnan Rawlings: Sojourner at Cross Creek* (New York: Overlook Press, 1988), 247.

150. Silverthorne, *Marjorie Kinnan Rawlings,* 247.

151. Acton, *Invasion of Privacy,* 74.

152. Silverthorne, *Marjorie Kinnan Rawlings,* 268.

153. Rawlings to Philip May, March 21, 1946, reprinted in *Letters,* 279.

154. Rawlings to Maxwell Perkins, June 5, 1946, reprinted in *Letters,* 285.

155. "Rawlings Cross Creek Praised by Witnesses," *Gainesville Sun,* May 23, 1946; Acton, *Invasion of Privacy,* 79. A writer in *Publishers' Weekly* described the litigation as "not unlike the legal battles in Dickens' novels." See Samuel Spring, "Invasion of Privacy," *Publishers' Weekly,* February 2, 1952, 689.

156. Declaration, Transcript of Record, 9, Box 5, Folder 14, Cross Creek Trial Papers.

157. Trial transcript, 73, Box 5, Folder 15, Cross Creek Trial Papers.

158. Rawlings to May, February 5, 1943, reprinted in *Letters,* 232.

159. Cason v. Baskin, 155 Fla. 198, 200 (Fla. 1944).

160. Acton, *Invasion of Privacy,* 80.

161. Trial Transcript, 124–37, Box 5, Folder 15, Cross Creek Trial Papers.

162. "Witness Says Cross Creek Is Literature," *Tampa Morning Tribune,* May 23, 1946; "Mrs. Rawlings Says She Is Worth $124,000," *Tampa Morning Tribune,* June 28, 1946.

163. Trial Transcript, 297, Box 5, Folder 15, Cross Creek Trial Papers.

164. For contemporary discussions of the case, see "Mammon in Cross Creek," *Cleveland Plain Dealer,* February 19, 1943; Spring, "Invasion of Privacy," 689–690; "Marjorie Kinnan Rawlings Wins Important Case in Florida Courts," June 29, 1946, *Publishers' Weekly,* 3328; *Time,* June 10, 1946, 42.

165. See *Letters,* 229–230.

166. Cason v. Baskin, 159 Fla. 31, 40–41 (Fla. 1947).

167. Cason v. Baskin, 155 Fla. 198, 205–207 (Fla. 1944).

168. Ibid., 212.

169. Ibid., 213. Rawlings's motion to dismiss the privacy claim was granted by the trial court on the grounds that the state did not recognize a right to privacy, and Cason appealed to the Florida Supreme Court. In 1944, the state Supreme Court,

recognizing an action for invasion of privacy, overturned the trial court's grant of the motion to dismiss and remanded the case to the trial court to permit Rawlings to show that the material was a "matter of public concern." Rawlings won at this trial, but Cason again appealed, and the Florida Supreme Court overturned the decision. Cason was awarded nominal damages for invasion of her privacy and attorneys' fees. The court concluded that only nominal damages could be had because Cason had not suffered mental anguish that seriously injured her health. Cason v. Baskin, 159 Fla. 31, 40–41 (Fla. 1947).

170. Cason v. Baskin, 155 Fla. 198, 213 (Fla. 1944).

Chapter 9

1. "House Party," *Time*, September 22, 1952, 30.

2. "Amateur Bank Robbers of Bronx Were 'Pros' Who Fled Lewisburg," *New York Times*, September 20, 1952, 1.

3. Fred Graham, "The Law," *New York Times*, December 12, 1965, E8.

4. Transcript of Record, Hill v. Hayes, 15 N.Y. 2d 986 (1965), 62.

5. Joseph Hayes, "Fiction out of Fact," *New York Times*, January 30, 1955, X1.

6. Leonard Garment, "Annals of Law, The Hill Case," *The New Yorker*, April 17, 1989, 91.

7. Joseph Hayes, *The Desperate Hours* (New York: Random House, 1954).

8. "True Crime Inspires Tense Play: The Ordeal of a Family Trapped by Convicts Gives Broadway a New Thriller, 'The Desperate Hours,'" *Life Magazine*, February 28, 1955, 75.

9. Erika Lee Doss, ed., *Looking at Life Magazine* (Washington, DC: Smithsonian Institution Press, 2001), 2.

10. "True Crime Inspires Tense Play."

11. Bernard Schwartz, *The Unpublished Opinions of the Warren Court* (Oxford: Oxford University Press, 1985), 249.

12. Ibid.

13. Ibid., 250.

14. Garment, "Annals of Law," 91.

15. Pember, *Privacy and the Press*, 147.

16. Harry Kalven Jr., "Privacy in Tort Law—Were Warren and Brandeis Wrong?" *Law and Contemporary Problems* 31 (1966): 327.

17. Norris Davis, "Invasion of Privacy, A Study in Contradictions," *Journalism Quarterly* 30 (Spring 1953): 187.

18. William L. Prosser, "Privacy," *California Law Review* 48 (1960): 389.

19. Lawrence M. Friedman, *American Law in the Twentieth Century* (New Haven: Yale University Press, 2002), 372–373; John Fabian Witt, *Patriots and Cosmopolitans: Hidden Histories of American Law* (Cambridge: Harvard University Press, 2007), 245.

20. Jed Handelsman Shugerman, *The People's Courts: Pursuing Judicial Independence in America* (Cambridge: Harvard University Press, 2012), 243.

21. Witt, *Patriots and Cosmopolitans*, 245.

22. Kenneth S. Abraham, *The Liability Century: Insurance and Tort Law from the Progressive Era to 9/11* (Cambridge: Harvard University Press, 2008), 83–85.

23. On the relative inexperience of plaintiffs' counsel in many libel cases—as compared to the well-trained and experienced media defense bar—see Norman Rosenberg, *Protecting the Best Men: An Interpretive History of the Law of Libel* (Chapel Hill: University of North Carolina Press, 1990), 225.

24. Kelley v. Post Publishing, 327 Mass. 275 (Mass. 1951).

25. Waters v. Fleetwood, 91 S.E. 2d. 344 (Ga. 1956).

26. Breines, *Young, White and Miserable*, 93.

27. See, e.g., Anita Allen, "How Privacy Got Its Gender," *Northern Illinois University Law Review* 10 (1989): 441; Caroline Danielson, "The Gender of Privacy and the Embodied Self: Examining the Origins of the Right to Privacy in U.S. Law," *Feminist Studies* 25 (Summer 1999).

28. Melvin v. Reid, 112 Cal. App. 285, 287, 298 (Cal. App. 1931).

29. Cason v. Baskin, 155 Fla. 198 (Fla. 1944); Peed v. Washington Times, 55 Wash. L. Rep. 182 (D.C. 1927); Blumenthal v. Picture Classics, 257 N.Y.S. 800, 801 (N.Y. App. Div. 1932). For other decisions that were also arguably influenced by the gender of the plaintiff, see Kunz v. Allen, 102 Kan. 883 (Kan. 1918); Barber v. Time, Inc., 348 Mo. 1199 (Mo. 1942); Kerby v. Hal Roach Studios, Inc., 53 Cal. App. 2d 207 (Cal. App. 1942); Peay v. Curtis Pub. Co., 78 F. Supp. 305 (D.D.C. 1948); Sutton v. Hearst Corp., 277 A.D. 155 (N.Y. App. Div. 1950).

30. See Martha Chamallas and Jennifer B. Wriggins, *The Measure of Injury: Race, Gender and Tort Law* (New York: New York University Press, 2010); Barbara Welke, *Recasting American Liberty: Gender, Race, Law and the Railroad Revolution* (Cambridge: Cambridge University Press, 2001); Barbara Welke, "Unreasonable Women: Gender and the Law of Accidental Injury, 1870–1920," *Law and Social Inquiry* 19 (1994).

31. Welke, "Unreasonable Women," 372.

32. Leverton v. Curtis Pub. Co., 97 F. Supp. 181 (E.D.Pa. 1951).

33. "County Fair Picture," *Editor and Publisher*, May 30, 1964; Daily Times Democrat v. Graham, 276 Ala. 380, 383 (Ala. 1964).

34. "Detective Magazines Fight Invasion of Privacy Ruling," *Chicago Tribune*, July 15, 1962.

35. Harms v. Miami Daily News, Inc., 127 So. 2d 715 (Fla. Dist. Ct. App. 1961).

36. Samuel Spring, "Invasion of Privacy," *Publishers' Weekly*, February 2, 1952, 690, 692–693.

37. Oliver Martin, "Legal Aspects of Photography," *American Photography*, January 1945, 22–24.

38. Davis, "Invasion of Privacy," 187.

39. Stryker v. Republic Pictures Corp., 238 P.2d 670, 671–673 (Cal. Dist. Ct. App. 1951).

40. Davis, "Invasion of Privacy," 187.

41. J. Joseph Cummings, "Television and the Right of Privacy," *Marquette Law Review* 36 (1952): 161.

42. Ibid.

43. Walter Allan Steigleman, *The Newspaperman and the Law* (Dubuque: W. C. Brown, 1950), 229; W. D. Oppenheimer, "Television and the Right of Privacy," *Journal of Broadcasting* 194 (1956): 1; Cummings, "Television and the Right of Privacy," 157.

44. Jacova v. Southern Radio & Television Co., 83 So. 2d 34, 37 (Fla. 1955). Spectators at sporting and other public events brought privacy claims over being depicted unwillingly on television, which often failed on the theory that the individual waived his right to privacy by virtue of entering a public space. See Cummings, "Television and the Right of Privacy," 161; Samuel Spring, *Rights and Risks in Publishing, Television, Radio, Motion Pictures, Advertising, and the Theatre* (New York: W. W. Norton, 1956), 292 ("By attending a public event, a spectator probably consents to the television use of his picture as part of the show") .

45. Jacova, 83 So. 2d at 40.

46. See Ray Yasser, "Warren Spahn's Legal Legacy: The Right to Be Free from False Praise," *Seton Hall Journal of Sports and Entertainment Law* 18 (2008): 49.

47. Spahn v. Julian Messner, Inc., 250 N.Y.S. 2d 529 (N.Y. Sup. Ct. 1964). On the torturous legal proceedings in this case, which involved three unsuccessful appeals to the U.S. Supreme Court, see Yasser, "Warren Spahn's Legal Legacy," 71–72.

48. See, e.g., Sutton v. Hearst Corp., 277 A.D. 155 (N.Y. App. Div. 1950); Jenkins v. Dell Pub. Co., 251 F.2d 447 (3d Cir. 1958).

49. Strickler v. NBC, 167 F. Supp. 68, 69, 71 (D.C. Cal. 1958).

50. Prosser, "Privacy," 389. The scholarly imprimatur offered by Prosser's article legitimized the privacy tort and hastened its recognition in a number of states. Neil Richards and Daniel Solove, "Prosser's Privacy Law: A Mixed Legacy," *California Law Review* 98 (2010): 1887, 1890.

51. Gill v. Hearst Pub. Co., 239 P. 2d 636, 638 (Cal. 1952). The decision was reversed on the grounds that the photo was not offensive and was "public" since it was taken in a public place. 253 P.2d 441, 444–445 (Cal. 1953).

52. Adam Carlyle Breckenridge, *The Right to Privacy* (Lincoln: University of Nebraska Press, 1970), 1–3.

53. Westin, *Privacy and Freedom*, 7, 39.

54. Lois Forer, *A Chilling Effect: The Mounting Threat of Libel and Invasion of Privacy Actions to the First Amendment* (New York: W. W. Norton, 1987), 208–209.

55. Bloustein, "Privacy, Tort Law, and the Constitution," 620.

56. Bloustein, "Privacy as an Aspect of Human Dignity," 981.

57. See Alan Westin, *Privacy and Freedom* (New York: Atheneum, 1967); Frederick S. Lane, *American Privacy: The 400-Year History of Our Most Contested Right* (Boston: Beacon Press, 2011).

58. Jacob Deschin, "The Candid Picture," *New York Times*, June 25, 1950, 83.

59. Westin, *Privacy and Freedom*, 67.

60. Lane, *American Privacy*, 133–135 (describing the 1950s as the "wiretapping decade").

61. Ibid., 143–145.

62. Ibid., 143.

63. Editorial, "Curbing Electronic Snoopers," *New York Times*, November 28, 1966, 38. See also Robert Kirsch, "Individual Privacy Loss: With Us Here, Now," *New York Times*, March 15, 1964, D18.

64. Hamberger v. Eastman, 206 A.2d 239 (N. H. 1964), involving surreptitious recording devices placed in a couple's bedroom.

65. Lane, *American Privacy*, 153.

66. Kermit Hall, *The Oxford Companion to the Supreme Court of the United States* (Oxford: Oxford University Press, 2005), 962.

67. Mapp v. Ohio, 367 U.S. 643, 657 (1961).

68. See NAACP v. Alabama, 357 U.S. 449 (1958); Shelton v. Tucker, 364 U.S. 479 (1960).

69. Griswold v. Connecticut, 381 U.S. 479, 484 (1965).

70. Robert N. Bellah, *Habits of the Heart: Individualism and Commitment in American Life* (Berkeley: University of California Press, 2008), 142. On privacy as a right to choose, see "Towards a Constitutional Theory of Individuality: The Privacy Opinions of Justice Douglas," *Yale Law Journal* 87 (July 1978): 1579.

71. Elspeth Brown, *The Corporate Eye: Photography and the Rationalization of American Commercial Culture, 1884–1929* (Baltimore: Johns Hopkins University Press, 2005), 261–270; Lois Banner, *American Beauty* (New York: Alfred A. Knopf, 1983), 261–270.

72. Jane M. Gaines, *Contested Culture: The Image, the Voice, and the Law* (Chapel Hill: University of North Carolina Press, 1991), 159.

73. Michael Madow, "Private Ownership of Public Image: Popular Culture and Publicity Rights," *California Law Review* 81 (1993): 164; George M. Armstrong Jr., "The Reification of Celebrity: Persona as Property," *Louisiana Law Review* 51 (1991): 459.

74. See Eick v. Perk Dog Food Co., 347 Ill. App. 293 (Ill. App. Ct. 1952); Bennett v. Gusdorf, 101 Mont. 39 (Mont. 1935).

75. O'Brien v. Pabst Sales Co., 124 F.2d 167 (5th Cir. 1941).

76. On recovery for pecuniary losses in advertising cases involving celebrities or well-known individuals, see Stuart Banner, *American Property: A History of How, Why, and What We Own* (Cambridge: Harvard University Press, 2011), 148–155; Eliot v. Jones, 120 N.Y.S. 989 (N.Y. Sup. 1910) (injunction issued); Loftus v. Greenwich Lithographing Co., 182 N.Y.S. 428 (App. Div. 1920); Lane v. F. W. Woolworth, 171 Misc. 66 (N.Y. Sup. 1939). These cases arose under the New York privacy statute. Under that statute, damages were technically to be awarded for emotional distress, but in a number of cases involving famous people, courts implied that damages could be had for pecuniary losses, although not explicitly stated in the opinions.

77. Haelan Laboratories, Inc. v. Topps Chewing Gum, Inc., 202 F.2d 866 (2d Cir. 1953); Melville B. Nimmer, "The Right of Publicity," *Law and Contemporary Problems* 19 (1954): 216.

78. Daniel L. Boorstin, *The Image: A Guide to Pseudo-Events in America* (New York: Vintage Books, 1961), 217.

79. Nimmer, "Right of Publicity"; Joseph Grodin, "The Right of Publicity: A Doctrinal Innovation," *Yale Law Journal* 62 (1953); Sheldon W. Halpern, "The Right of Publicity: Commercial Exploitation of the Associative Value of Personality," *Vanderbilt Law Review* 39 (1986): 1205–1207.

80. Haelan, 202 F.2d at 868.

81. Nimmer, "Right of Publicity," 203.

82. Ibid., 203–204.

83. Madow, "Private Ownership of Public Image," 175; Nimmer, "Right of Publicity," 216.

84. Uhlaender v. Henricksen, 316 F. Supp. 1277, 1282 (D. Minn. 1970).

85. Grant v. Esquire, 367 F. Supp. 876 (S.D.N.Y. 1973).

86. Booth v. Colgate-Palmolive Co., 362 F. Supp. 343 (S.D.N.Y 1973).

87. Canessa v. Kislak, 97 N.J. Super. 327, 351 (N.J. Super. Ct. 1967).

88. Ibid.

89. David Farber, *The Age of Great Dreams: America in the 1960's* (New York: Hill and Wang, 1994), 196–198.

90. See New York Times v. Sullivan, 376 U.S. 254, 283 (1964), noting the duty of the citizen to criticize government, no less than the official's duty to administer government.

91. See Amy Gajda, "Judging Journalism: The Turn Toward Privacy and Judicial Regulation of the Press," *California Law Review* 97 (2009): 1068.

92. Brick, *Age of Contradiction*, 196.

93. Nadine Strossen, "Freedom of Speech in the Warren Court," in *The Warren Court: A Retrospective*, Bernard Schwartz, ed. (New York: Oxford University Press, 1996), 71–72; Michael Kent Curtis, *Free Speech: "The People's Darling Privilege"* (Durham: Duke University Press, 2000), 400–404.

94. Winters v. New York, 333 U.S. 507, 510 (1948).

95. Roth v. United States, 354 U.S. 476 (1957).

96. Burstyn v. Wilson, 343 U.S. 495 (1952).

97. New York Times v. Sullivan, 376 U.S. 254 (1964); Garrison v. Louisiana, 379 U.S. 64 (1964).

98. Strossen, "Freedom of Speech in the Warren Court," 69.

99. See Harry Kalven Jr., "'Uninhibited, Robust, and Wide Open': A Note on Free Speech and the Warren Court," *Michigan Law Review* 67 (December 1968); Lucas A. Powe Jr., *The Warren Court and American Politics* (Cambridge: Belknap Press, 2002), 303–335.

100. New York Times v. Sullivan, 376 U.S. 254, 270 (1964).

101. Time, Inc. v. Hill, 385 U.S. 374, 389 (1967).

102. Ibid.

103. Aquino v. Bulletin, 190 Pa. Super. 528, 531 (Pa. Super. Ct. 1959).

104. Jenkins v. Dell Publishing, 251 F.2d 447, 451 (3rd Cir. 1958).

105. Goelet v. Confidential, Inc., 5 A.D.2d 226, 229 (N.Y. App. Div. 1958).

106. Kapellas v. Kofman, 459 P.2d 912, 923–924 (Cal. 1969); Blount v. T. D. Publishing, 423 P. 2d. 421 (N.M. 1966).

107. "As far as public performers are concerned, the right of privacy is nonexistent or has long since been waived. . . . Public performers who are currently in the public eye are in no position to claim injury to their mental interests." Harry P. Warner, *Radio and Television Rights* (Albany: Matthew Bender, 1948), 995–996.

108. Chaplin v. National Broadcasting Co., 15 F.R.D. 134, 139 (S.D.N.Y. 1953).

109. Cohen v. Marx, 94 Cal. App. 2d 704, 705 (Cal. App. 4th Dist. 1949).

110. "Walt Disney Sued by Kirk Douglas," *New York Times*, August 2, 1956, 49.

111. Douglas v. Disney, Calif. Superior Court for Los Angeles County, November 1956, cited in Harriet F. Pilpel and Theodora S. Zavin, *Rights and Writers: A Handbook of Literary and Entertainment Law* (New York: Dutton, 1960), 88–89.

112. Leon R. Yankwich, "The Right of Privacy: Its Development, Scope and Limitations," *Notre Dame Lawyer* 27 (1952): 519.

113. See, e.g., Samuel v. Curtis Pub. Co., 122 F. Supp. 327 (N.D. Cal. 1954); Abernathy v. Thornton, 263 Ala. 496 (Ala. 1955); Waters v. Fleetwood, 212 Ga. 161 (Ga. 1956); Rozhon v. Triangle Publications, 230 F.2d 359 (7th Cir. 1956); Jenkins v. Dell Pub. Co., 251 F.2d 447 (3d Cir. 1958); Frith v. Associated Press, 176 F. Supp. 671 (E.D.S.C. 1959); Bradley v. Cowles Magazines, Inc., 26 Ill. App. 2d 331 (Ill. App. Ct. 1960); Mahaffey v. Official Detective Stories, Inc., 210 F. Supp. 251 (W.D. La. 1962); Carlson v. Del Pub. Co., 65 Ill. App. 2d 209 (Ill. App. Ct. 1965); Cordell v. Detective Publications, Inc., 307 F. Supp. 1212 (E.D. Tenn. 1968).

114. Bremmer v. Journal-Tribune Pub. Co., 247 Iowa 817, 827 (1956).

115. Carlisle v. Fawcett Publications, Inc., 20 Cal. Rptr. 405, 415 (Cal. App. 5th Dist. 1962).

116. Westin, *Privacy and Freedom*, 70–73; Vance Packard, *The Naked Society* (New York: David McKay, 1964), 29–42.

117. "The Press: Freedom to Photograph," *Time*, August 9, 1954, 54.

118. Bradley v. Cowles Magazines, Inc., 26 Ill. App. 2d 331, 334 (Ill. App. Ct. 1960).

119. Harriet Pilpel, "But Can You Do That," *Publishers' Weekly*, April 9, 1963.

120. Yankwich, "The Right of Privacy," 526.

121. Time, Inc. v. Hill, 385 U.S. 374, 388 (1967).

122. Ibid.

123. Samantha Barbas, "The Death of the Public Disclosure Tort: A Historical Perspective," *Yale Journal of Law and the Humanities* 22 (2010): 207–208.

124. Time, Inc., 385 U.S. at 392, 394.

125. "$175,000 Awarded in Suit against Life," *New York Times*, April 19, 1962, 22;

Time, Inc. v. Hill, 385 U.S. 374, 379 (1967). A new trial on damages was ordered, and the court awarded $30,000 compensatory damages without punitive damages. Hill v. Hayes, 18 A.D. 2d 485 (N.Y.A.D. 1963).

126. Leonard Garment, *Crazy Rhythm: My Journey from Brooklyn, Jazz, and Wall Street to Nixon's White House, Watergate and Beyond* (New York: Times Books, 1997), 83.

127. Hill v. Hayes, 18 A.D. 2d 485 (N.Y.A.D. 1963); Hill v. Hayes, 15 N.Y. 2d 986 (N.Y. 1965).

128. Garment, "Annals of Law," 90–91.

129. Ibid., 91.

130. These are contained in the Wilderness Years Collection, Series VI, Legal Papers, Time. Inc. v. Hill, Nixon Presidential Library.

131. Richard Nixon to Leonard Garment, April 28, 1966, Box 16, Series VI, Legal Papers, Time, Inc. v. Hill, Nixon Presidential Library.

132. Garment, "Annals of Law," 103.

133. Ibid.

134. Untitled, Wilderness Years Collection, Box 14, Series VI, Legal Papers, Time, Inc. v. Hill, Nixon Presidential Library.

135. Untitled, Wilderness Years Collection, Box 14, Series VI, Legal Papers, Time, Inc. v. Hill, Nixon Presidential Library.

136. See Answer of Defendant, Transcript of Record, Hill v. Hayes, 15 N.Y. 2d 986 (N.Y. 1965).

137. Garment, "Annals of Law," 98.

138. Ibid.

139. Untitled, Box 14, Series VI, Legal Papers, Time, Inc. v. Hill, Nixon Presidential Library.

140. Memo, April 29, 1966, Box 1387, William O. Douglas Papers, Library of Congress.

141. Garment, "Annals of Law," 105.

142. Laura Kalman, *Abe Fortas: A Biography* (New Haven: Yale University Press, 1992), 262.

143. Schwartz, *Unpublished Opinions*, 249.

144. Ibid.

145. Garment, "Annals of Law," 93.

146. Ibid., 106.

147. Time, Inc., 385 U.S. at 388.

148. Harry Kalven Jr., "The Reasonable Man and the First Amendment: Hill, Butts, and Walker," *Supreme Court Review* (1967): 281.

149. Time, Inc., 385 U.S. at 378, 388. The Hills eventually settled with Time Inc., which agreed to pay $135,000 ($60,000 to Mrs. Hill, and $75,000 to James Hill). See Memorandum, Leonard Garment to Richard Nixon, May 18, 1967, Box 3, Series VI, Legal Papers, Nixon Presidential Library.

150. "Privacy and the Press," *Hartford Courant,* January 12, 1967.

151. Fred P. Graham, "Supreme Court Supports Press on a Privacy Issue," *New York Times,* January 10, 1967, 1.

152. "A Vote for the Press over Privacy," *Time,* January 20, 1967, 64.

153. Garment, *Crazy Rhythm,* 95.

154. Willard Pedrick, "Publicity and Privacy: Is It Any of Our Business," *University of Toronto Law Journal* 20 (1970): 402–403.

155. Melville Nimmer, "The Right to Speak from Times to Time: First Amendment Theory Applied to Libel and Misapplied to Privacy," *California Law Review* 5 (1968): 966. On the impact of the case, see Don R. Pember and Dwight L. Teeter Jr., "Privacy and the Press since *Time, Inc. v. Hill,*" *Washington Law Review* 50 (1974).

156. Time, Inc., 385 U.S. at 405–408, 411.

157. Garment, *Crazy Rhythm,* 82.

158. Transcript of Record, Hill v. Hayes, 15 N.Y.2d 986 (1965), 490–491.

159. Garment, "Annals of Law," 109.

160. There is a vast literature on this topic. Notable works include Harry Kalven Jr., "The New York Times Case: A Note on the 'Central Meaning of the First Amendment,'" *Supreme Court Review* (1964): 191; Lewis, *Make No Law*; Kermit L. Hall and Melvin I. Urofsky, *New York Times v. Sullivan, Civil Rights, Libel Law, and the Free Press* (Lawrence: University Press of Kansas, 2011); Lee Levine and Stephen Wermiel, *The Progeny: Justice William J. Brennan's Fight to Preserve the Legacy of New York Times v. Sullivan* (Chicago: American Bar Association, 2014); Diane Leenheer Zimmerman, "False Light Privacy: The Light That Failed," *New York University Law Review* 64 (1989): 364; Diane Leenheer Zimmerman, "Requiem for a Heavyweight: A Farewell to Warren and Brandeis's Privacy Tort," *Cornell Law Review* 68 (1983): 291; Robert C. Post, "The Social Foundations of Privacy: Community and Self in the Common Law Tort," *California Law Review* 77 (1989); Rodney Smolla, "Emotional Distress and the First Amendment: An Analysis of Hustler v. Falwell," *Arizona State Law Journal* 20 (1988): 423.

Conclusion

1. As many have pointed out, Americans are relatively nonlitigious when it comes to reputation, compared to the British, notorious for being "libel-happy." "A libeled American," wrote Zechariah Chafee, "prefers to vindicate himself by steadily pushing forward his career and not by hiring a lawyer to talk in a courtroom." Zechariah Chafee, *Government and Mass Communications, Volume 1* (Chicago: University of Chicago Press, 1947), 106–107.

2. On claims consciousness in privacy cases, see Harry Kalven Jr., "Privacy in Tort Law—Were Warren and Brandeis Wrong?" *Law and Contemporary Problems* 31 (1966): 338.

3. See generally Lawrence Friedman, *The Republic of Choice: Law, Authority and Culture* (Cambridge: Harvard University Press, 1990), 15.

4. Tom Wolfe, "The 'Me' Decade and the Third Great Awakening," *New York Magazine*, August 23, 1976, 26.

5. Robert Bellah, *Habits of the Heart: Individualism and Commitment in American Life* (Berkeley: University of California Press, 1985), 47.

6. Mary C. Waters, *Ethnic Options: Choosing Identities in America* (Berkeley: University of California Press, 1990), 150.

7. Kenneth Gergen, *The Saturated Self: Dilemmas of Identity in Contemporary Life* (New York: Basic Books, 1991), 150.

8. Gergen, *Saturated Self*, 80.

9. Patricia Leigh Brown, "Making Over an Image with an Expert's Help," *New York Times*, January 18, 1989, C1.

10. Laurel Graeber, "Image Inventors," *New York Times*, September 18, 1988, 22.

11. Nancy Marx Better, "The Executive Life; Image-Making, From Soup to Sales Pitch," *New York Times*, December 8, 1991, F29.

12. Better, "Image-Making."

13. Marni Jameson, "The Cult of Celebrity Doctors," *Los Angeles Times*, June 14, 2010.

14. "Image-Addicted Voters," *New York Times*, March 6, 1997, A22.

15. "At Home in Las Vegas with Tennis's Gaudiest Star," *New York Times*, October 29, 1990, C1.

16. "Coca Cola Is Introducing a Pithy New Campaign for Its Fast-Growing Sprite Soft Drink," *New York Times*, April 15, 1997, D9.

17. Eva S. Moskowitz, *In Therapy We Trust: America's Obsession with Self-Fulfillment* (Baltimore: Johns Hopkins University Press, 2001), 262.

18. Alex S. Jones, "News Media Torn Two Ways in Debate on Privacy," *New York Times*, April 30, 1992, B 11.

19. On the demise of shame in the late twentieth century, see James B. Twitchell, *For Shame: The Loss of Common Decency in American Culture* (New York: St. Martin's Press, 1997).

20. Roger Rosenblatt, "The Right to Know Everything About Everybody," *New York Times*, January 31, 1993, SM 24.

21. See, e.g., Peter Montoya and Tim Vandehey, *The Brand Called You: The Ultimate Brand-Building and Business Development Handbook to Transform Anyone into an Indispensable Personal Brand* (Personal Branding Press, 1999).

22. Christopher Lasch, *The Culture of Narcissism: American Life in the Age of Diminishing Expectations* (New York: W. W. Norton, 1979); see also Peter Marin, "The New Narcissism," *Harper's Magazine*, October 1975, 45–46; William K. Stevens, "Narcissism in the Me Decade," *New York Times*, November 30, 1977, 53; Jesse Battan, "The 'New Narcissism' in 20th Century America: The Shadow and Substance of Social Change," *Journal of Social History* 17 (Winter 1983): 199–207.

23. Philip Cushman, *Constructing the Self, Constructing America: A Cultural History of Psychotherapy* (Reading: Addison-Wesley, 1995), 221.

24. David Rosenbaum, "The President under Fire: The Overview," *New York Times*, January 29, 1998, A1; Jim McGee and Tom Fiedler, "Miami Woman Is Linked to Hart," *Miami Herald*, May 3, 1987, 1A.

25. David Sumner, *The Magazine Century: American Magazines since 1900* (New York: Peter Lang, 2010), 164–166.

26. Bill Carter, "A Reality TV Headcount," *New York Times*, November 29, 2009, WK3.

27. Andy Beal, "The 11 Unwritten Laws of Reputation Management," *Forbes*, January 4, 2011, http://www.forbes.com/sites/andybeal/2011/01/04/the-11-unwritten-laws-of-reputation-management/.

28. Rodney A. Smolla, *Suing the Press* (Oxford: Oxford University Press, 1986), 6.

29. Lois Forer, *A Chilling Effect: The Mounting Threat of Libel and Invasion of Privacy Actions to the First Amendment* (New York: W. W. Norton, 1987), 18; Anthony Lewis, *Make No Law: The Sullivan Case and the First Amendment* (New York: Random House, 1991), 200.

30. James Aucoin, *The Evolution of American Investigative Journalism* (Columbia: University of Missouri Press, 2005), 113.

31. Sack and Tofel, "First Steps," 610.

32. Alex S. Jones, "The Verdict Is Libel, and the Trend Is Up," *New York Times,* March 11, 1988, B11. Evidence suggests that libel litigation may have decreased since the 1980s. According to one source, there were 266 trials in the 1980s, 192 in the 1990s, and 124 in the 2000s. See John Koblin, "The End of Libel?" *New York Observer*, June 9, 2010.

33. Burnett v. Nat'l Enquirer, 144 Cal. App. 3d 991 (1983).

34. "Hot New Hollywood Trend: Crazy Defamation Lawsuits," *Hollywood Reporter*, August 23, 2011.

35. Forer, *Chilling Effect*, 23.

36. In 1972, a reporter/editor declared in a journalism trade publication that "the law of libel ha[d] been all but repealed" by *New York Times v. Sullivan*. See Aucoin, *American Investigative Journalism,* 70.

37. Smolla, *Suing the Press*, 16.

38. Drechsel, "Intentional Infliction of Emotional Distress," 339, 346; Jonathan L. Entin, "Privacy, Emotional Distress, and the Limits of Libel Law Reform," *Mercer Law Review* 38 (1987): 853.

39. McManamon v. Daily Freeman, 6 Media L. Rep. 2245 (N.Y. Sup. Ct. 1980). See also Loft v. Fuller, 408 So. 2d 619 (Fla. App. 1982); Hood v. Naeter Bros. Pub. Co., 562 S.W. 2d 770 (Mo. Ct. App. 1978); Fudge v. Penthouse Intern. Ltd., 840 F. 2d. 1012 (1st Cir. 1988); Grimsley v. Guccione, 703 F. Supp. 903 (M.D Ala. 1988).

40. Reichenbach v. Call-Chronicle, 9 Media L. Rep. 1438 (Common Pleas Pa. 1982).

41. Rutledge v. Phoenix Newspapers, Inc., 148 Ariz. 555 (Ariz. 1986).

42. Falwell v. Hustler, 485 U.S. 46 (1988).

43. Mark Bartholomew, "A Right Is Born: Celebrity, Property, and Postmodern Lawmaking," *Connecticut Law Review* 44 (2011): 316.

44. Ainsworth v. Century Supply Co., 295 Ill. App. 3d 644 (Ill. App. 2d. Dist. 1998).

45. Cohen v. Herbal Concepts, 100 A.D. 2d 175 (N.Y.A.D. 1984).

46. Onassis v. Christian Dior, 122 Misc. 2d 603 (N.Y. Sup. Ct. 1984); Estate of Presley v. Russen, 513 F. Supp. 1339 (D.N.J. 1981); Midler v. Ford Motor Co., 849 F. 2d. 460 (9th Cir. 1988).

47. Jones, "News Media Torn Two Ways in Debate over Privacy."

48. Deidre Carmody, "Right to Privacy vs. Right to Know Will Result in Clash, Editors Told," *New York Times*, April 12, 1978, B2. "False light" privacy cases increased almost four times between 1975 and 1981. James Lake, "Restraining False Light: Constitutional and Common Law Limits on a Troublesome Tort," *Federal Communications Law Journal* 61 (2008): 637.

49. From 1974 to 1984, plaintiffs prevailed in less than 7 percent of cases against the media involving the publication of private material. Randall Bezanson, Gilbert Cranberg, and John Soloski, *Libel Law and the Press* (New York: Free Press, 1987), 116.

50. Costlow v. Cusimano, 311 N.Y.S 2d 92 (N.Y. App. Div. 1970); Pasadena Star News v. Superior Ct., 203 Cal App. 3d 131 (Ct. App. 1988); Shulman v. Grp. W. Prods, Inc., 18 Cal. 4th 200, 955 P. 2d 469 (Cal. 1998); Schuler v. McGraw Hill Co., 989 F. Supp. 1377 (D.N.M. 1977).

51. In Cox Broad. Corp. v. Cohn, 420 U.S. 469 (1975), and Florida Star v. B.J.F., 491 U.S. 524 (1989), the Court addressed "privacy" claims brought against the media under state statutes that prohibited publishing the names of sexual offense victims. The media won in both cases on First Amendment grounds, but the holdings were limited to the particular factual contexts.

52. Cox, 420 U.S. 469. See also Bartnicki v. Vopper, 532 U.S. 514, 529 (2001) (noting the Court's "repeated refusal to answer categorically whether truthful publication may ever be punished consistent with the First Amendment").

53. See, e.g., Green v. Chicago Tribune Co., 286 Ill. App. 3d 1 (Ill. App. Ct. 1996); Gannett Co., Inc. v. Anderson, 947 So. 2d 1 (Fla. Dist. Ct. App. 2006); Conradt v. NBC Universal, Inc., 536 F. Supp. 2d 380 (S.D.N.Y. 2008); M.G. v. Time Warner, Inc., 107 Cal. Rptr. 2d 504 (Ct. App. 2001); Winstead v. Sweeney, 517 N.W. 2d 874 (Mich. Ct. App. 1994); Amy Gajda, "Judging Journalism: The Turn Toward Privacy and Judicial Regulation of the Press," *California Law Review* 97 (2009): 1069–1078.

54. Smith v. Stewart, 291 Ga. App. 86, 86–88 (2008).

55. Michaels v. Internet Entm't Grp., Inc., 5 F. Supp. 2d 823, 842 (C.D. Cal. 1998).

56. Benz v. Washington Newspaper Pub. Co., CIV A 05-1760 EGS, 2006 WL 2844896 (D.D.C. Sept. 29, 2006).

57. See Deborah Chambers, *Social Media and Personal Relationships: Online Intimacies and Networked Friendship* (Hampshire: Palgrave Macmillan, 2013).

58. Patricia Sanchez Abril, "A (My)Space of One's Own: On Privacy and On-

line Social Networks," *Northwestern Journal of Technology and Intellectual Property* 6 (2007): 83.

59. "Reputation management has now become a defining feature of online life for many internet users, especially the young." Mary Madden and Aaron Smith, "Reputation Management and Social Media," *Pew Research Internet Project*, May 26, 2010, http://www.pewinternet.org/2010/05/26/reputation-management-and-social-media/.

60. "The First Step to Building Your Personal Brand," *Forbes*, last modified February 14, 2012, http://www.forbes.com/sites/dailymuse/2012/02/14/the-first-step-to-building-your-personal-brand/.

61. Through their online activities, people "engage in multiple mini performances that . . . produce a presentation of the self that makes sense to multiple audiences, without sacrificing coherence and continuity." Zizi Papacharissi, ed., *A Networked Self: Identity, Community, and Culture on Social Network Sites* (New York: Routledge, 2011), 307.

62. See, e.g., Susan B. Barnes, "A Privacy Paradox: Social Networking in the United States," *First Monday* 11 (2006).

63. See John Harrigan, Kelly Garrett, and Paul Resnick, "The Internet and Democratic Debate," *Pew Research Internet Project*, October 27, 2004, http://www.pewtrusts.org/uploadedFiles/wwwpewtrustsorg/Reports/Society_and_the_Internet/Pew_Internet_political_info_report_1004.pdf.

64. Forty-nine percent of social network users have witnessed cruel behavior displayed by others. See "The Tone of Life on Social Networking Sites," *Pew Research Internet Project*, February 9, 2012, http://www.pewinternet.org/files/old-media/Files/Reports/2012/Pew_Social%20networking%20climate%202.9.12.pdf.

65. Moreno v. Hanford Sentinel, Inc., 172 Cal. App. 4th 1125, 1128 (Cal. App. 5th Dist., 2009).

66. Tracy Samantha Schmidt, "Inside the Backlash against Facebook," Time.com, September 6, 2006, http://content.time.com/time/nation/article/0,8599,1532225,00.html. See also Danah Boyd, "Facebook's Privacy Trainwreck," *Convergence: The International Journal of Research into New Media Technologies* 14 (2008): 13–14.

67. Steve Henn, "Facebook Users Question $20 Million Settlement over Ads," NPR, May 13, 2013, http://www.npr.org/blogs/alltechconsidered/2013/05/14/182861926/facebook-users-question-20-million-settlement-over-ads.

Facebook has committed a number of other "privacy" violations involving self-posted material. In 2009, it changed its site so that information that users designated as private, such as their Friends List, was made public. Facebook also told users they could restrict sharing of their personal data to limited audiences, but that turned out not to be true—their information was shared with third party applications their friends used. This caused an uproar, and it led to an FTC mandate requiring Facebook to seek permission from users before changing the terms of its service. Ashley Packard, *Digital Media Law* (Malden: Wiley-Blackwell, 2013), 204.

68. See Danah Michele Boyd, *Taken out of Context: American Teen Sociality in*

Networked Publics, Ph.D. dissertation, University of California Berkeley, 2008 (noting that privacy for teens is about "context and control"; "teens approach social media environments with a view of privacy that is primarily about having control over the situation"). See also Helen Nissenbaum, *Privacy in Context: Technology, Policy, and the Integrity of Social Life* (Stanford: Stanford University Press, 2009).

69. Jean M. Twenge, *The Narcissism Epidemic: Living in the Age of Entitlement* (New York: Atria Books, 2010): 270–281. In 2013, the "selfie"—a photo of oneself taken on a smartphone or webcam—was selected as the word of the year by the Oxford Dictionaries. Jenna Wortham, "Tech Terms Added to Dictionary," *New York Times*, September 2, 2013, B5.

70. With the approval of an online "right to be forgotten" in Europe in 2014, much of the discussion in the United States has centered on the need for a similar American right. See Eric Posner, "We All Have the Right to Be Forgotten," *Slate*, May 14, 2014, http://www.slate.com/articles/news_and_politics/view_from_chicago/2014/05/the_european_right_to_be_forgotten_is_just_what_the_internet_needs.html; Marc Randazza, "We Need a Right to Be Forgotten Online," CNN.com, May 15, 2014, http://www.cnn.com/2014/05/14/opinion/randazza-google-right-to-privacy/.

71. Jeffrey Rosen, "The Web Means the End of Forgetting," *New York Times*, July 25, 2010, MM30.

72. Victor Mayer Schonberger, *Delete: The Virtue of Forgetting in the Digital Age* (Princeton: Princeton University Press, 2009).

73. Daniel J. Solove, *The Future of Reputation: Gossip, Rumor and Privacy on the Internet* (New Haven: Yale University Press, 2007), 4.

74. Andy Greenberg, "Google-Proof PR?" *Forbes*, May 25, 2007, http://www.forbes.com/2007/05/24/google-search-reputation-cx-tech_ag_0525google.html.

75. Packard, *Digital Media Law*, 229; David Ardia, "Bloggers and Other Online Publishers Face Increasing Legal Threats," *Poynter*, March 4, 2011; David Ardia, "Freedom of Speech, Defamation and Injunctions," *William and Mary Law Review* 55 (2013) (noting that "bloggers, users of social media, and 'citizen journalists' are more often the target of defamation claims today, rather than institutional mass media"). For a compendium of defamation, invasion of privacy, and emotional distress cases related to internet-based activities, see the database maintained by the Citizen Media Law project, http://www.citmedialaw.org/database.

76. Cal Bus & Prof. Code 22580–22582; Somini Sengupta, "No U.S. Action, So States Move on Privacy Law," *New York Times*, October 30, 2013, A1; Jacob Gershman, "California Gives Teens a Do-Over," *Wall Street Journal*, September 25, 2013.

77. See "Cyberbullying," National Conference of State Legislatures, http://www.ncls.org/research/education/cyberbullying.aspx; Yamiche Alcindor, "States Look to Enact Cyberbullying Laws," *USA Today*, March 19, 2012.

78. Emily Shire, "Could Revenge Porn Bans Sweep the Nation?" *The Week*, October 10, 2013.

79. See Robert Cannon, "The Legislative History of Senator Exon's Communica-

tions Decency Act: Regulating Barbarians on the Information Superhighway," *Federal Communications Law Journal* 49 (1996); Anthony Ciolli, "Chilling Effects: The Communications Decency Act and the Online Marketplace of Ideas," *University of Miami Law Review* 63 (2008).

80. According to a survey by the Pew Internet Center, most Americans believe that existing laws are inadequate to protect privacy online. See Somini Sengupta, "Americans Go to Great Lengths to Mask Web Travels, Survey Finds," *New York Times*, September 5, 2013, B5.

Bibliography

Manuscript Collections

Cross Creek Trial Papers, Special and Area Studies Collections, George A. Smathers Libraries, University of Florida, Gainesville, Florida

William O. Douglas Papers, Library of Congress

New Yorker Archives, Manuscripts and Archives Division, New York Public Library

Adolph Ochs Papers, Manuscripts and Archives Division, New York Public Library

Arthur Hays Sulzberger Papers, Manuscripts and Archives Division, New York Public Library

Wilderness Years Collection, Nixon Presidential Library and Museum, Yorba Linda, California

Books and Articles

Abelson, Elaine. *When Ladies Go A-Thieving: Middle-Class Shoplifters in the Victorian Department Store*. New York: Oxford University Press, 1992.

Abraham, Kenneth S. *The Liability Century: Insurance and Tort Law from the Progressive Era to 9/11*. Cambridge: Harvard University Press, 2008.

Abrams, Floyd. *Speaking Freely: Trials of the First Amendment*. New York: Penguin Books, 2005.

Abril, Patricia Sanchez. "A (My)Space of One's Own: On Privacy and Online Social Networks." *Northwestern Journal of Technology and Intellectual Property* 6 (2007): 73–88.

"An Actionable Right of Privacy? Roberson v. Rochester Folding Box Co." *Yale Law Journal* 12 (1902): 35–41.

Acton, Patricia Nassif. *Invasion of Privacy: The Cross Creek Trial of Marjorie Kinnan Rawlings*. Gainesville: University of Florida Press, 1988.

Adams, B. B. "Everyday Life of Railroad Men." *Scribner's Magazine*, November 1888.

Adams, Elbridge. "The Right of Privacy and Its Relation to the Law of Libel." *American Law Review* 39 (1905): 37–58.

Adams, Samuel Hopkins. "The New World of Trade: The Art of Advertising." *Collier's*, May 22, 1901.

Allen, Anita. "Natural Law, Slavery, and the Right to Privacy Tort." *Fordham Law Review* 81 (2012): 1187–1216.

Allen, Frederick Lewis. *Only Yesterday: An Informal History of the 1920s*. New York: Harper & Row, 1931.

Ardia, David. "Freedom of Speech, Defamation and Injunctions." *William and Mary Law Review* 55 (2013): 1–84.

Armstrong Jr., George M. "The Reification of Celebrity: Persona as Property." *Louisiana Law Review* 51 (1991): 443–468.

Armstrong, William. *E. L. Godkin: A Biography*. Albany: State University of New York Press, 1978.

Aucoin, James L. *The Evolution of American Investigative Journalism*. Columbia: University of Missouri Press, 2005.

Ayers, Edward. *The Promise of the New South: Life after Reconstruction*. New York: Oxford University Press, 1992.

———. *Vengeance and Justice: Crime and Punishment in the 19th Century American South*. New York: Oxford University Press, 1984.

Bailey, F. G. *Gifts and Poison: The Politics of Reputation*. New York: Schocken Books, 1971.

Baldwin, Donald S. "If Your Photograph Were News." *Notre Dame Law Review* 4 (1929): 382–387.

Baldwin, Peter C. *In the Watches of the Night: Life in the Nocturnal City, 1820–1930*. Chicago: University of Chicago Press, 2012.

Banner, Lois W. *American Beauty*. New York: Alfred A. Knopf, 1983.

Banner, Stuart. *American Property: A History of How, Why, and What We Own*. Cambridge: Harvard University Press, 2011.

Barbas, Samantha. "The Death of the Public Disclosure Tort: A Historical Perspective." *Yale Journal of Law and the Humanities* 22 (2010): 171–216.

———. *The First Lady of Hollywood: A Biography of Louella Parsons*. Berkeley and Los Angeles: University of California Press, 2005.

———. "From Privacy to Publicity: The Tort of Appropriation in the Age of Mass Consumption." *Buffalo Law Review* 61 (2014): 1119–1190.

———. "How the Movies Became Speech." *Rutgers Law Review* 64 (2012): 665–746.

———. "The Laws of Image." *New England Law Review* 47 (2012): 23–92.

———. *Movie Crazy: Fans, Stars and the Cult of Celebrity*. New York: Palgrave Macmillan, 2002.

———. "Saving Privacy from History." *DePaul Law Review* 61 (2012): 973–1048.

———. "The *Sidis* Case and the Origins of Modern Privacy Law." *Columbia Journal of Law and the Arts* 36 (2012): 21–70.

Barnes, Kevin G., and John C. Nerone. *The Form of News: A History*. New York: Guilford Press, 2002.

Barnes, Robin D. *Outrageous Invasions: Celebrities' Private Lives, Media, and the Law*. New York: Oxford University Press, 2010.

Barron, James H. "Warren and Brandeis, The Right to Privacy: Demystifying a Landmark Citation." *Suffolk University Law Review* 13 (1979): 875–922.

Bartenstein Jr., Fred. "Recent Cases, Right of Privacy—Protection against the Publication of Newsworthy Information [Federal]." *Washington and Lee Law Review* 2 (1940–1941): 133–141.

Barth, Gunther. *City People: The Rise of Modern City Culture in Nineteenth-Century America.* New York: Oxford University Press, 1980.

Bartholomew, Mark. "Advertising and the Transformation of Trademark Law." *New Mexico Law Review* 38 (2008): 1–48.

———. "A Right Is Born: Celebrity, Property, and Postmodern Lawmaking." *Connecticut Law Review* 44 (2011): 301–368.

Battan, Jesse. "'The New Narcissism' in 20th Century America: The Shadow and Substance of Social Change." *Journal of Social History* 17 (1983): 199–220.

Baughman, James L. *The Republic of Mass Culture: Journalism, Filmmaking, and Broadcasting in America since 1941.* Baltimore: Johns Hopkins University Press, 1992.

Bell, Daniel. *The Cultural Contradictions of Capitalism.* New York: Basic Books, 1976.

Bellah, Robert N., Richard Madsen, William M. Sullivan, Ann Swidler, and Steven M. Tipton. *Habits of the Heart: Individualism and Commitment in American Life.* Berkeley: University of California Press, 1985.

Belli, Melvin. *Ready for the Plaintiff.* New York: Grosset & Dunlop, 1956.

Bender, Thomas. *Community and Social Change in America.* Baltimore: Johns Hopkins University Press, 1982.

Benedict, Ruth. *The Chrysanthemum and the Sword: Patterns of Japanese Culture.* New York: Houghton Mifflin, 1967.

Bent, Silas. *Ballyhoo: The Voice of the Press.* New York: Boni and Liveright, 1927.

Berelson, Bernard. "What Missing the Newspaper Means." In *Communications Research: 1948–1949*, edited by Paul Felix Lazarsfeld and Frank N. Stanton, 111–129. New York: Harper & Brothers, 1949.

Berger, M. Marvin. "Detecting Libel before It Appears." *Editor and Publisher*, May 29, 1937.

Berger, Meyer. "Surrender of Privacy." *Scribner's Magazine*, April 1939.

Bergstrom, Randolph. *Courting Danger: Injury and Law in New York City, 1870–1910.* Ithaca: Cornell University Press, 1992.

Bezanson, Randall P. "The Libel Suit in Retrospect: What Plaintiffs Want and What Plaintiffs Get." *California Law Review* 74 (1986): 789–808.

———. "The Libel Tort Today." *Washington and Lee Law Review* 45 (1988): 535–556.

———. "The Right to Privacy Revisited: Privacy, News, and Social Change, 1890–1990." *California Law Review* 80 (1992): 1133–1176.

Bezanson, Randall, Gilbert Cranberg, and John Soloski. *Libel Law and the Press.* New York: Free Press, 1987.

Bishop, Joseph B. "Newspaper Espionage." *The Forum*, August 1886.

Bledstein, Burton J. *The Culture of Professionalism: The Middle Class and the Development of Higher Education in America.* New York: W. W. Norton, 1976.

Bloustein, Edward. "Privacy as an Aspect of Human Dignity: An Answer to Dean Prosser." *New York University Law Review* 39 (1964): 962–1007.

———. "Privacy, Tort Law, and the Constitution: Is Warren and Brandeis' Tort Petty and Unconstitutional as Well?" *Texas Law Review* 46 (1968): 611–629.

Blumenthal, Albert. *Small-Town Stuff.* Chicago: University of Chicago Press, 1932.

Blumer, Herbert. *Movies and Conduct.* New York: Macmillan, 1933.

Booker, Frank E. "The Accusation of Communism as Slander Per Se." *Duke Bar Journal* 4 (Winter 1954): 1–15.

Boorstin, Daniel. *The Image: A Guide to Pseudo-Events in America.* New York: Vintage Books, 1961.

"The Boy Prodigy of Harvard." *Current Literature* 48 (1910): 291–293.

Boyd, Danah. "Facebook's Privacy Trainwreck." *Convergence: The International Journal of Research into New Media Technologies* 14 (2008): 13–20.

Boyer, Paul. *Purity in Print: Book Censorship in America from the Gilded Age to the Computer Age.* Madison: University of Wisconsin Press, 2002.

Boyer, Paul, Clifford Clark, Sandra Hawley, Joseph Kett, and Andrew Rieser. *The Enduring Vision: A History of the American People, Volume 2.* Boston: Wadsworth Cengage Learning, 2010.

Bratman, Benjamin C. "Brandeis and Warren's The Right to Privacy and the Birth of the Right to Privacy." *Tennessee Law Review* 69 (2002): 623–652.

Braudy, Leo. *The Frenzy of Renown: Fame and Its History.* New York: Vintage Books, 1997.

Breckenridge, Adam Carlyle. *The Right to Privacy.* Lincoln: University of Nebraska Press, 1970.

Breines, Wini. *Young, White, and Miserable: Growing Up Female in the Fifties.* Chicago: University of Chicago Press, 2001.

Brennan, James. "Never Give a Passenger a Break." *Saturday Evening Post*, February 28, 1948.

Brennen, Bonnie. *For the Record, An Oral History of Rochester, New York, Newsworkers.* New York: Fordham University Press, 2001.

Brick, Howard. *Age of Contradiction: American Thought and Culture in the 1960s.* Ithaca: Cornell University Press, 2000.

Briggs, Belinda. "A Monstrous Outrage." *Puck*, February 27, 1884.

Bronner, Simon J. *Consuming Visions: Accumulation and Display of Goods in America, 1880–1920.* New York: W. W. Norton, 1990.

Brown, Elspeth H. *The Corporate Eye: Photography and the Rationalization of American Commercial Culture, 1884–1929.* Baltimore: Johns Hopkins University Press, 2001.

Brown, Henry Billings. "The Liberty of the Press." *American Law Review* 34 (1900): 321–341.

Bruggemier, Gert, Aurelia Colombi Ciacchi, and Patrick O'Callaghan, eds. *Personality Rights in European Tort Law.* Cambridge: Cambridge University Press, 2010.

Burnham, John C. *Paths into American Culture: Psychology, Medicine, and Morals.* Philadelphia: Temple University Press, 1988.

Burress, Lee. *Battle of the Books: Literary Censorship in the Public Schools, 1950–1985*. Metuchen: Scarecrow Press, 1989.

Calhoun, Charles William. *The Gilded Age: Perspectives on the Origins of Modern America*. Lanham: Rowman & Littlefield, 2007.

Calvert, Clay. *Voyeur Nation: Media, Privacy, and Peering in Modern Culture*. Boulder: Westview Press, 2004.

"Camel Jockey." *Time*, January 18, 1937.

Cannon, Robert. "The Legislative History of Senator Exon's Communications Decency Act: Regulating Barbarians on the Information Superhighway." *Federal Communications Law Journal* 49 (1996): 51–94.

"Cape Cod Folks." *The Literary World*, July 30, 1881.

"Cape Cod Folks." *The Literary World*, September 10, 1881.

Carnegie, Dale. *How to Win Friends and Influence People*. New York: Pocket Books, 1981.

Cashman, Sean. *America in the Twenties and Thirties: The Olympian Age of Franklin Delano Roosevelt*. New York: New York University Press, 1989.

Chafe, William. *The Unfinished Journey: America Since World War II*. Oxford: Oxford University Press, 2003.

Chafee, Zechariah. *Government and Mass Communications, Volume 1*. Chicago: University of Chicago Press, 1947.

Chamallas, Martha, and Linda Kerber. "Women, Mothers, and the Law of Fright: A History." *Michigan Law Review* 88 (1990): 814–864.

Chamallas, Martha, and Jennifer B. Wriggins. *The Measure of Injury: Race, Gender, and Law*. New York: New York University Press, 2010.

Chamberlain, Ryan. *Pistols, Politics and the Press: Dueling in 19th Century American Journalism*. Jefferson: McFarland, 2009.

Chambers, Deborah. *Social Media and Personal Relationships: Online Intimacies and Networked Friendship*. Hampshire: Palgrave Macmillan, 2013.

Ciolli, Anthony. "Chilling Effects: The Communications Decency Act and the Online Marketplace of Ideas." *University of Miami Law Review* 63 (2008): 137–268.

Clark, Charles Edward, and Harry Shulman. *A Study of Law Administration in Connecticut: A Report of an Investigation of the Activities of Certain Trial Courts of the State*. New Haven: Yale University Press, 1937.

Clemons, L. S. "Right of Privacy in Relation to the Publication of Photographs." *Marquette Law Review* 14 (1930): 193–198.

"A Collect as You Go Tour of the Publisher's Chain." *Newsweek*, February 22, 1936.

"Comical Libel Suits." *The Independent*, November 24, 1881.

The Commission on Freedom of the Press. *A Free and Responsible Press: A General Report on Mass Communication, Newspapers, Radio, Motion Pictures, Magazines, and Books*. Chicago: University of Chicago Press, 1947.

Cooley, Charles Horton. *Human Nature and the Social Order*. New York: Charles Scribner's Sons, 1903.

Copeland, David. *The Media's Role in Defining the Nation: The Active Voice*. New York: Peter Lang, 2010.

"County Fair Picture." *Editor and Publisher*, May 30, 1964.

"The Craze for Publicity." *Century Illustrated Magazine*, February 1896.

Cross, Harold. "Current Libel Trends." *Nieman Reports*, January 5, 1951.

Cummings, J. Joseph. "Television and the Right of Privacy." *Marquette Law Review* 36 (1952): 157–166.

"Current Events." *Central Law Journal*, March 22, 1889.

Curtis, Michael Kent. *Free Speech: 'The People's Darling Privilege': Struggles for Freedom of Expression in American History*. Durham: Duke University Press, 2000.

Cushman, Philip. *Constructing the Self, Constructing America: A Cultural History of Psychotherapy*. Reading: Addison-Wesley, 1995.

Danielson, Caroline. "The Gender of Privacy and the Embodied Self: Examining the Origins of the Right to Privacy in U.S. Law." *Feminist Studies* 25 (1999): 311–344.

Davis, Jefferson James. "An Enforceable Right of Privacy: Enduring Legacy of the Georgia Supreme Court." *Journal of Southern Legal History* 3 (1994): 97–126.

Davis, Norris. "Invasion of Privacy, A Study in Contradictions." *Journalism Quarterly* 30 (Spring 1953): 179–188.

Dawley, Alan. *Struggles for Justice: Social Responsibility and the Liberal State*. Cambridge: Harvard University Press, 1993.

Dawson, Mitchell. "Law and the Right of Privacy." *American Mercury*, October 1948.

———. "Paul Pry and Privacy." *Atlantic Monthly*, October 1932.

Dayton, Cornelia. *Women before the Bar: Gender, Law and Society in Connecticut*. Chapel Hill: University of North Carolina Press, 1995.

DeCordova, Richard. *Picture Personalities: The Emergence of the Star System in America*. Urbana: University of Illinois Press, 1990.

DeFleur, Melvin. "How Massive Are the Mass Media? Implications for Communications Education and Research." *Syracuse Scholar* 10 (1990): 1–21.

D'Emilio, John, and Estelle B. Freedman. *Intimate Matters: A History of Sexuality in America*. New York: Harper & Row, 1988.

Demos, John. "Shame and Guilt in Early New England." In *The Emotions: Social, Cultural and Biological Dimensions*, edited by Ron Harré and W. Gerrod Parrott, 75. London: Sage, 1996.

Dennis, Richard. *Cities in Modernity: Representations and Productions of Metropolitan Space, 1840–1930*. Cambridge: Cambridge University Press, 2008.

Desjardins, Mary. "Systematizing Scandal: Confidential Magazine, Stardom, and the State of California." In *Headline Hollywood: A Century of Film Scandal*, edited by Adrienne L. McLean and David A. Cook, 206–231. New Brunswick: Rutgers University Press, 2001.

"Developments in the Law of Defamation." *Harvard Law Review* 69 (1956): 875–959.

Dewey, John. *The Public and Its Problems*. Denver: A. Swallow, 1927.

Dicken-Garcia, Hazel. *Journalistic Standards in Nineteenth Century America*. Madison: University of Wisconsin Press, 1989.

Dickler, Gerald. "Right of Privacy—A Proposed Redefinition." *United States Law Review* 70 (1936): 435–456.

DiSabatino, Michael A. "Civil Liability for Insulting or Abusive Language." *American Law Reports* 20 (1993): 773–812.

"Do Not Publish News of Libel Suits." *The Fourth Estate*, July 8, 1897.

Doan, Edward. "The Newspaper and the Right of Privacy." *Journal of the Bar Association of Kansas* 5 (1937): 201–261.

Doss, Erika Lee, ed. *Looking at Life Magazine*. Washington: Smithsonian Institution Press, 2001.

Drechsel, Robert E. "Negligent Infliction of Emotional Distress: New Tort Problem for Mass Media." *Pepperdine Law Review* 12 (1985): 889–918.

Dreiser, Theodore. *Sister Carrie*. New York: Bantam Books, 1958.

Dumenil, Lynn. *The Modern Temper: American Culture and Society in the 1920s*. New York: Hill & Wang, 1995.

Dyal, James A. "Images in the Lonely Crowd." *Vital Speeches of the Day* 31 (1965).

Ebert, John David. *Dead Celebrities, Living Icons: Tragedy and Fame in the Age of the Multimedia Superstar*. Santa Barbara: Praeger, 2010.

Eckert, Charles. "The Carole Lombard in the Macy's Window." In *Movies and Mass Culture*, edited by John Belton, 95–118. New Brunswick: Rutgers University Press, 1996.

Elder, Dana C. "A Rhetoric of Etiquette for the 'True Man' of the Gilded Age." *Rhetoric Review* 21 (2002): 150–169.

Emery, Edwin. *History of the American Newspaper Publishers' Association*. Westport: Greenwood Press, 1970.

———. *The Press and America: An Interpretive History of the Mass Media*. Englewood Cliffs: Prentice Hall, 1992.

Entin, Jonathan L. "Privacy, Emotional Distress, and the Limits of Libel Law Reform." *Mercer Law Review* 38 (1987): 835–858.

Ernst, Morris L., and Alexander Lindey. *Hold Your Tongue: Adventures in Libel and Slander*. New York: Abelard Press, 1932.

Ernst, Morris L., and Alexander Lindey. "What Price Reputation?" *American Bar Association Journal* 19 (1933): 103–107.

Ernst, Morris Leopold. *So Far, So Good*. New York: Harper & Brothers, 1948.

Ernst, Morris Leopold, and Alan U. Schwartz. *Privacy: The Right to Be Let Alone*. New York: Macmillan, 1962.

Ewen, Stuart. *Captains of Consciousness: Advertising and the Social Roots of the Consumer Culture*. New York: Basic Books, 2001.

"Expose Thyself." *Commonweal*, July 26, 1957.

"Fame and Notoriety." *The Nation*, October 17, 1889.

Farber, David. *The Age of Great Dreams: America in the 1960's*. New York: Hill and Wang, 1994.

Faulk, John Henry. *Fear on Trial; Alger Hiss and the Battle for History*. Austin: University of Texas Press, 1983.

Faulkner, William. "On Privacy: The American Dream: What Happened to It." *Harper's*, July 1955.

Felcher, Peter L., and Edward L. Rubin. "Privacy, Publicity, and the Portrayal of Real People in the Media." *Yale Law Journal* 88 (1978): 1577–1622.

Feldman, Stephen M. *Free Expression and Democracy in America: A History*. Chicago: University of Chicago Press, 2008.

Finkelman, Paul, ed. *Encyclopedia of American Civil Liberties, Volume 1*. New York: Routledge, 2006.

Fleischman, Frank. "A Boy Prodigy and the Fourth Dimension." *Harpers' Weekly*, January 15, 1910.

Forde, Kathy Roberts. "Libel, Freedom of the Press, and the *New Yorker*." *American Journalism* 23 (2006): 60–91.

———. *Literary Journalism on Trial: Masson v. New Yorker and the First Amendment*. Amherst: University of Massachusetts Press, 2008.

Forer, Lois. *A Chilling Effect: The Mounting Threat of Libel and Invasion of Privacy Actions to the First Amendment*. New York: Norton, 1987.

Fox, Stephen. *The Mirror Makers: A History of American Advertising and its Creators*. New York: William Morrow, 1984.

Fox-Genovese, Elizabeth. *Inside the Plantation Household: Black and White Women of the Old South*. Chapel Hill: University of North Carolina Press, 1988.

Friedman, Lawrence. "The Concept of Legal Culture: A Reply." In *Comparing Legal Cultures*, edited by David Nelken, 34. Aldershot: Dartmouth, 1997.

———. *The Republic of Choice: Law, Authority and Culture*. Cambridge: Harvard University Press, 1990.

Friedman, Lawrence M. *American Law in the Twentieth Century*. New Haven: Yale University Press, 2002.

———. *Guarding Life's Dark Secrets: Legal and Social Controls over Reputation, Propriety, and Privacy*. Stanford: Stanford University Press, 2007.

Friedman, Walter. *Birth of a Salesman*. Cambridge: Harvard University Press, 2004.

Fromm, Erich. *Escape from Freedom*. New York: Henry Holt, 1941.

Gaines, Jane M. *Contested Culture: The Image, the Voice, and the Law*. Chapel Hill: University of North Carolina Press, 1991.

Gajda, Amy. "Judging Journalism: The Turn Toward Privacy and Judicial Regulation of the Press." *California Law Review* 97 (2009): 1039–1106.

———. "What if Samuel D. Warren Hadn't Married a Senator's Daughter?: Uncovering the Press Coverage That Led to 'The Right to Privacy.'" *Michigan State Law Review* 2008 (2008): 35–60.

Garment, Leonard. "Annals of Law, The Hill Case." *New Yorker*, April 17, 1989.

———. *Crazy Rhythm: My Journey from Brooklyn, Jazz, and Wall Street to Nixon's White House, Watergate and Beyond*. New York: Times Books, 1997.

Gauvreau, Emile. *My Last Million Readers*. New York: E. P. Dutton, 1941.

"Gentleman Jockey Wins $2500 Award." *Editor and Publisher*, January 9, 1937.

Gergen, Kenneth. *The Saturated Self: Dilemmas of Identity in Contemporary Life*. New York: Basic Books, 1991.

Gershman, Jacob. "California Gives Teens a Do-Over." *Wall Street Journal*, September 25, 2013.

Glancy, Dorothy. "Privacy and the Other Miss M." *Northern Illinois University Law Review* 10 (1990): 401–440.

Glancy, Dorothy J. "The Invention of the Right to Privacy." *Arizona Law Review* 21 (1979): 1–40.

Gleason, Timothy. "The Libel Climate of the Late Nineteenth Century: A Survey of Libel Litigation, 1884–1899." *Journalism and Mass Communication Quarterly* 70 (December 1993): 893–906.

Godkin, E. L. "Libel and Its Legal Remedy." *Atlantic Monthly*, December 1880.

———. "The Right to Privacy." *The Nation*, December 25, 1890.

———. "The Rights of the Citizen: To His Own Reputation." *Scribner's Magazine*, July 1890.

Goffman, Erving. *The Presentation of Self in Daily Life*. New York: Doubleday, 1959.

Goldberg, David J. *Discontented America: The United States in the 1920s*. Baltimore: Johns Hopkins University Press, 1999.

Goldstein, Tom. *Killing the Messenger: 100 Years of Media Criticism*. New York: Columbia University Press, 2007.

Goodrich, Herbert F. "Emotional Disturbances as Legal Damage." *Michigan Law Review* 20 (1922): 497–513.

Gorman, Lynn, and David McLean. *Media and Society into the 21st Century: A Historical Introduction*. Chichester: Wiley-Blackwell, 2009.

Gormley, Ken. "One Hundred Years of Privacy." *Wisconsin Law Review* 1992 (1992): 1335–1442.

Graber, Mark A. *Transforming Free Speech: The Ambiguous Legacy of Civil Libertarianism*. Berkeley: University of California Press, 1991.

Graham, Kyle. "Why Torts Die." *Florida State University Law Review* 35 (2007): 359–432.

Grant, Roger. *Railroads and the American People*. Bloomington: Indiana University Press, 2012.

Green, Leon. "Fright Cases." *Illinois Law Review* 27 (1933): 760–780.

———. "Relational Interests." *Illinois Law Review* 29 (1934): 460–490.

———. "Right of Privacy." *Illinois Law Review* 27 (1934): 237–260.

Green, Martin Burgess. *The Mount Vernon Street Warrens: A Boston Story, 1860–1910*. New York: Charles Scribner's Sons, 1989.

Grodin, Joseph. "The Right of Publicity: A Doctrinal Innovation." *Yale Law Journal* 62 (1953): 1123–1130.

Guerard, Leon. *Personal Equation*. New York: W. W. Norton, 1948.

Gurstein, Rochelle. *The Repeal of Reticence: America's Cultural and Legal Struggles over Free Speech, Obscenity, Sexual Liberation, and Modern Art*. New York: Hill and Wang, 1998.

Hadley, Herbert Spencer. "The Right to Privacy." *Northwestern Law Review* 3 (1894): 1–21.

Haiken, Elizabeth. *Venus Envy: A History of Cosmetic Surgery*. Baltimore: Johns Hopkins University Press, 1999.

Halberstam, David. *The Fifties*. New York: Villard Books, 1993.

Hall, Kermit. *The Oxford Companion to the Supreme Court of the United States*. Oxford: Oxford University Press, 2005.

Hall, Kermit, and Melvin I. Urofsky. *New York Times v. Sullivan, Civil Rights, Libel Law, and the Free Press*. Lawrence: University Press of Kansas, 2011.

Halpern, Sheldon W. "The Right of Publicity: Commercial Exploitation of the Associative Value of Personality." *Vanderbilt Law Review* 39 (1986): 1199–1256.

Haltunnen, Karen. *Confidence Men and Painted Women: A Study of Middle-Class Culture in America, 1830–1870*. New Haven: Yale University Press, 1986.

Handley, Susannah. *Nylon: The Story of a Fashion Revolution*. Baltimore: Johns Hopkins University Press, 2000.

Harper, Fowler V., and Mary Coate McNeely. "A Re-Examination of the Basis of Liability for Emotional Distress." *Wisconsin Law Review* 1938 (1938): 426–464.

Hayes, Joseph. *The Desperate Hours*. New York: Random House, 1954.

"He Was Wrong." *Life*, September 25, 1895.

Henisch, Heinz Kurt. *The Photographic Experience: 1839–1914: Images and Attitudes*. University Park: Pennsylvania State University Press, 1994.

Hirsch, Arnold R., and Raymond A. Mohl, eds. *Urban Policy in Twentieth-Century America*. New Brunswick: Rutgers University Press, 1993.

Hirsch, Robert. *Seizing the Light: A History of Photography*. Boston: McGraw-Hill, 2000.

Hixson, Richard. *Privacy in a Public Society: Human Rights in Conflict*. New York: Oxford University Press, 1987.

Hochschild, Arlie Russell. *The Managed Heart: Commercialization of Human Feeling*. Berkeley and Los Angeles: University of California Press, 2003.

Hofstadter, Richard. *The Age of Reform*. New York: Knopf, 1955.

Holland, W. Bob. "The Passion for Publicity: Being an Account of the Ingenious Arts of the Press Agent." *Leslie's Monthly Magazine*, May–October 1904.

Horowitz, David. *Anxieties of Affluence: Critiques of American Consumer Culture*. Amherst: University of Massachusetts Press, 2004.

Houghton, Walter Raleigh. *American Etiquette and Rules of Politeness*. Chicago: Rand, McNally, 1889.

"House Party." *Time*, September 22, 1952.

Hoyt, Martha Seavey, Mary A. Stimpson, and Mary Elvira Elliot. *Representative Women of New England*. Boston: New England Historical Publishing, 1904.

Huff, Thomas. "Thinking Clearly about Privacy." *Washington Law Review* 55 (1979): 777, 794.

Hughes, Helen MacGill. "Human Interest Stories and Democracy." *Public Opinion Quarterly* 1 (1937): 73–83.

————. *News and the Human Interest Story: A Study of Popular Literature.* Chicago: University of Chicago Press, 1940.

Hulteng, John L. *The Messenger's Motives: Ethical Problems of the News Media.* Englewood Cliffs: Prentice Hall PTR, 1985.

"Ideal Homes." *The Unitarian,* August 1886.

Ingber, Stanley. "Defamation: A Conflict between Reason and Decency." *Virginia Law Review* 65 (1979): 785–858.

Jacobs, Glenn. *Charles Horton Cooley: Imagining Social Reality.* Amherst: University of Massachusetts Press, 2006.

James, William. *The Principles of Psychology, Volume 1.* New York: Henry Holt, 1890.

Jarecke, George W., and Nancy K. Plant. *Seeking Civility: Common Courtesy and the Common Law.* Boston: Northeastern University Press, 2006.

Johnson, Gerald W. "Freedom of the Newspaper Press." *Annals of the American Academy of Political and Social Science* (November 1938): 60–75.

Kacedan, Basil. "The Right of Privacy." *Boston University Law Review* 16 (1936): 353–395.

Kaestle, Carl F., and Janice A. Radway, eds. "A Framework for the History of Publishing and Reading in the United States, 1880–1940." In *A History of the Book in America,* edited by Carl F. Kaestle and Janice A. Radway, 10. Chapel Hill: University of North Carolina Press, 2009.

Kahn, Jonathan. "Privacy as a Legal Principle of Identity Maintenance." *Seton Hall Law Review* 33 (2010): 371–410.

Kalman, Laura. *Abe Fortas: A Biography.* New Haven: Yale University Press, 1992.

Kalven Jr., Harry. "The New York Times Case: A Note on 'The Central Meaning of the First Amendment.'" *Supreme Court Review* 1964 (1964): 191–222.

————. "Privacy in Tort Law—Were Warren and Brandeis Wrong?" *Law and Contemporary Problems* 31 (1966): 326–341.

————. "The Reasonable Man and the First Amendment: Hill, Butts, and Walker." *Supreme Court Review* (1967): 267–310.

————. "'Uninhibited, Robust, and Wide Open.' A Note on Free Speech and the Warren Court." *Michigan Law Review* 67 (December 1968): 289–302.

Karafiol, Emile. "The Right to Privacy and the Sidis Case." *Georgia Law Review* 12 (1978): 513–534.

Karsten, Peter. "Enabling the Poor to Have Their Day in Court: The Sanctioning of Contingency Fee Contracts, A History to 1940." *DePaul Law Review* 47 (1998): 231–260.

Kasson, John F. *Rudeness and Civility: Manners in Nineteenth-Century Urban America.* New York: Hill and Wang, 1990.

Kear, Lynn. *Evelyn Brent: The Life and Films of Hollywood's Lady Crook.* Jefferson: McFarland, 2009.

Kenyon, Andrew T., and Megan Richardson, eds. *New Dimensions in Privacy Law: International and Comparative Perspectives.* Cambridge: Cambridge University Press, 2006.

Kett, Joseph F. "Curing the Disease of Precocity." *American Journal of Sociology* 84 (1978): 183–211.

Kincaid, James. *Press Photography*. New York: American Photographic Publishing, 1936.

King, Andrew J. "Constructing Gender: Sexual Slander in Nineteenth Century America." *Law and History Review* 13 (1995): 63–110.

Klein, Herbert S. *A Population History of the United States*. Cambridge: Cambridge University Press, 2004.

Kyvig, David. *Daily Life in the United States, 1920–1940*. Westport: Greenwood Press, 2002.

LaCroix, Alison L. "To Gain the Whole World and Lose His Own Soul: Nineteenth-Century American Dueling as Public Law and Private Code." *Hofstra Law Review* 33 (2004–2005): 501–570.

Laird, Donald A. "Are You an Alibi Artist?" *Saturday Evening Post*, July 10, 1943.

Laird, Pamela Walker. *Advertising Progress: American Business and the Rise of Consumer Marketing*. Baltimore: Johns Hopkins University Press, 2001.

Lake, James. "Restraining False Light: Constitutional and Common Law Limits on a Troublesome Tort." *Federal Communications Law Journal* 61 (2008): 625–650.

Lane, Frederick S. *American Privacy: The 400-Year History of Our Most Contested Right*. Boston: Beacon Press, 2009.

Larremore, Wilbur. "The Law of Privacy." *Columbia Law Review* 12 (1912): 694–709.

Lasch, Christopher. *The Culture of Narcissism: American Life in an Age of Diminishing Expectations*. New York: W. W. Norton, 1979.

Laurent, Francis. *The Business of a Trial Court*. Madison: University of Wisconsin Press, 1959.

Laurent, H. *Personality: How to Build It*. New York: Funk & Wagnalls, 1916.

Leach, William. *Land of Desire: Merchants, Power, and the Rise of a New American Culture*. New York: Vintage, 1994.

Lears, T.J. Jackson. *Fables of Abundance: A Cultural History of Advertising in America*. New York: Basic Books, 1994.

———. "From Salvation to Self-Realization: Advertising and the Therapeutic Roots of the Consumer Culture, 1880–1930." In *The Culture of Consumption: Critical Essays in American History, 1880–1980*, edited by Richard Wightman Fox and T.J. Jackson Lears, 7. New York: Pantheon Books, 1983.

———. *No Place of Grace: Antimodernism and the Transformation of American Culture, 1880–1920*. Chicago: University of Chicago Press, 1981.

Leavitt, Bradford. "The Invasion of Privacy." *Pacific Unitarian*, May 1903.

Lee, Alfred McClung. *The Daily Newspaper in America*. London: Routledge/Thoemmes Press, 1947.

Leuchtenburg, William. *The Perils of Prosperity, 1914–1932*. Chicago: University of Chicago Press, 2010.

Levine, Lawrence. "American Culture and the Great Depression." In *The Unpredict-

able Past: Explorations in American Cultural History, 213–214. New York: Oxford University Press, 1993.

Levine, Lee, and Stephen Wermiel. *The Progeny: Justice William J. Brennan's Fight to Preserve the Legacy of New York Times v. Sullivan*. Chicago: American Bar Association, 2014.

Levy, Newman. "The Right to Be Let Alone." *American Mercury*, June 1935.

Lewis, Anthony. *Make No Law: The Sullivan Case and the First Amendment*. New York: Random House, 1991.

———. "The Right to Be Let Alone." *Journalism and the Debate over Privacy*. Mahwah: Lawrence Erlbaum Associates, 2003.

"Libel, Contempt." *Time*, June 9, 1934.

"Libel News." *The Fourth Estate*, April 7, 1898.

"Libel Suit against Author of A Bell for Adano." *Publishers' Weekly*, March 23, 1946.

Lifton, Robert Jay. *The Protean Self: Human Resilience in an Age of Fragmentation*. Chicago: University of Chicago Press, 1999.

"The Lingering Duello." *Century Illustrated Magazine*, May–October 1890.

"The Lounger." *The Critic and Good Literature*, March 1, 1884.

Lowenthal, Leo. "The Triumph of Mass Idols." In *Literature, Popular Culture, and Society*. Englewood Cliffs: Prentice Hall, 1961.

Lukas, Edwin J. "Letter to the Editor." *New York Law Journal*, August 16, 1940.

Lynd, Robert S., and Helen Merrell Lynd. *Middletown: A Study in Contemporary American Culture*. New York: Harcourt, Brace, 1929.

Lystra, Karen. *Searching the Heart: Women, Men, and Romantic Love in Nineteenth Century America*. New York: Oxford University Press, 1989.

MacDougall, Curtis D. *The Press and Its Problems*. Dubuque: W. C. Brown, 1964.

Mack, Erin, and Anita Allen. "How Privacy Got Its Gender." *Northern Illinois University Law Review* 10 (1991): 441–478.

MacNeil, Neil. *Without Fear or Favor*. New York: Harcourt, Brace, 1940.

Madow, Michael. "Private Ownership of Public Image: Popular Culture and Publicity Rights." *California Law Review* 81 (1993): 125–242.

Magruder, Calvert. "Mental and Emotional Disturbance in the Law of Torts." *Harvard Law Review* 49 (1936): 1033–1067.

Malone, Wex. "The Formative Era of Contributory Negligence." *Illinois Law Review* 41 (July–August 1946): 151–182.

Manley, Jared L. "Where Are They Now? April Fool!" *New Yorker*, August 14, 1937.

Marchand, Roland. *Advertising the American Dream: Making Way for Modernity, 1920–1940*. Berkeley and Los Angeles: University of California Press, 1985.

Marden, Orison Swett. *Masterful Personality*. New York: Thomas Y. Crowell, 1921.

Marien, Mary Warner. *Photography: A Cultural History, 2nd Edition*. London: Laurence King, 2006.

Marin, Peter. "The New Narcissism." *Harper's Magazine*, October 1975.

"Marjorie Kinnan Rawlings Wins Important Case in Florida Courts." *Publishers' Weekly*, June 29, 1946.

Martin, Everett Dean. *The Behavior of Crowds: A Psychological Study*. New York: Harper & Brothers, 1920.

Martin, Oliver. "Legal Aspects of Photography." *American Photography*, January 1945.

Mason, Alpheus Thomas. *Brandeis: A Free Man's Life*. New York: Viking Press, 1956.

Massaro, Toni M. "Shame, Culture, and American Criminal Law." *Michigan Law Review* 89 (1991): 1880–1944.

Mavity, Nancy Barr. *The Modern Newspaper*. New York: Henry Holt, 1930.

May, Lary. *Screening Out the Past: The Birth of Mass Culture and the Motion Picture Industry*. Chicago: University of Chicago Press, 1983.

McArthur, Benjamin. *Actors and American Culture, 1880–1920*. Philadelphia: Temple University Press, 1984.

McCormick, Charles H. *This Nest of Vipers: McCarthyism and Higher Education in the Mundel Affair, 1951–52*. Chicago: University of Illinois Press, 1989.

McLean, Sarah Pratt. *Cape Cod Folks*. Boston: A. Williams, 1881.

McLean, W. Archibald. "The Right of Privacy." *The Green Bag* 15 (1903): 494–497.

Mead, Terrance C. "Suing the Media for Emotional Distress: A Multi-Method Analysis of Tort Law Evolution." *Washburn Law Journal* 23 (1983): 24–63.

Mensel, Robert E. "'Kodakers Lying in Wait': Amateur Photography and the Right of Privacy in New York, 1885–1915." *American Quarterly* 43 (1991): 24–45.

Merrill, Samuel. *Newspaper Libel*. Boston: Ticknor, 1888.

Metzl, Jonathan. *Prozac on the Couch: Prescribing Gender in the Era of Wonder Drugs*. Durham: Duke University Press, 2003.

Miller, Nathan. *New World Coming: The 1920s and the Making of Modern America*. Cambridge: Da Capo Press, 2003.

Miller, Vernon. *Selected Essays on Torts*. Buffalo: Dennis, 1960.

Mills, C. Wright. *White Collar: The American Middle Classes*. Oxford: Oxford University Press, 1951.

Mintz, Jonathan B. "The Remains of Privacy's Disclosure Tort: An Exploration of the Private Domain." *Maryland Law Review* 55 (1996): 425–466.

"Miracle of the Bells Libel Suit Dismissed." *Publishers' Weekly*, February 11, 1950.

Montoya, Peter, and Tim Vandehey. *The Brand Called You: The Ultimate Brand-Building and Business Development Handbook to Transform Anyone into an Indispensable Personal Brand*. Personal Branding Press, 1999.

Moreland, Roy. "Right of Privacy Today." *Kentucky Law Journal* 19 (1931): 101–136.

Moskowitz, Eva S. *In Therapy We Trust: America's Obsession with Self-Fulfillment*. Baltimore: Johns Hopkins University Press, 2001.

Mueller, Gerhard. "Problems Posed by Publicity to Crime and Criminal Proceedings." *University of Pennsylvania Law Review* 110 (1961): 1–26.

Murnaghan, Francis. "From Figment to Fiction to Philosophy—the Requirement of Proof of Damages in Libel Actions." *Catholic University Law Review* 22 (1972): 1–38.

"My Experience as a Street-Car Conductor." *Lippincott's Monthly Magazine*, June 1886.

Neal, Robert Miller. *Newspaper Desk Work*. New York: D. Appleton, 1933.

Newell, Martin. *The Law of Libel and Slander in Civil and Criminal Cases*. Chicago: Callaghan, 1898.

Newman, Roger K., ed. *The Yale Biographical Dictionary of American Law*. New Haven: Yale University Press, 2009.

"Newspaper Brutality." *Christian Union*, December 5, 1889.

Nichols, Lewis. "Our Sacred Privacy Becomes a Memory." *New York Times Magazine*, October 11, 1931.

Nimmer, Melville B. "The Right of Publicity." *Law and Contemporary Problems* 19 (1954): 203–223.

———. "The Right to Speak from Times to Time: First Amendment Theory Applied to Libel and Misapplied to Privacy." *California Law Review* 56 (1968): 935–967.

Nizer, Louis. "The Right of Privacy: A Half Century's Developments." *Michigan Law Review* 39 (1940): 526–596.

Norman, Arnold Stanley. *The Magic Power of Putting Yourself Over with People*. Englewood Cliffs: Prentice Hall, 1962.

"Notes of Recent Decisions." *American Law Review* 36 (1902): 129–146.

"A 'Novel' Libel Suit." *The Literary World*, November 5, 1881.

O'Brien, Denis. "The Right of Privacy." *Columbia Law Review* 2 (1902): 437–448.

O'Shea, V. "Popular Misconceptions Concerning Precocity in Children." *Science* 34 (1911): 666–674.

Odgers, William Blake. *A Digest of the Law of Libel and Slander*. London: Stevens and Sons, 1896.

Ohmann, Richard. "Diverging Paths, Books and Magazines in the Transition to Corporate Capitalism." In *A History of the Book in America*, edited by Carl F. Kaestle and Janice A. Radway, 103. Chapel Hill: University of North Carolina Press, 2009.

———. *Selling Culture: Magazines, Markets, and Class at the Turn of the Century*. New York: Verso, 1996.

Oppenheimer, W. D. "Television and the Right of Privacy." *Journal of Broadcasting* 1 (1956): 194–201.

Orvell, Miles. *American Photography*. Oxford: Oxford University Press, 2003.

———. *The Real Thing: Imitation and Authenticity in American Culture, 1880–1940*. Chapel Hill: University of North Carolina Press, 1989.

Packard, Ashley. *Digital Media Law*. Malden: Wiley-Blackwell, 2013.

Packard, Vance. *The Naked Society*. New York: David McKay, 1964.

———. *The Status Seekers*. New York: David McKay, 1959.

Pallen, Conde Benoist. "Newspaperism." *Lippincott's Monthly Magazine*, November 1886.

Papacharissi, Zizi, ed. *A Networked Self: Identity, Community, and Culture on Social Network Sites*. New York: Routledge, 2011.

Park, Robert. "News as a Form of Knowledge: A Chapter in the Sociology of Knowledge." *American Journal of Sociology* 45 (1940): 669–686.

Park, Robert, and Ernest Burgess. *The City*. Chicago: University of Chicago Press, 1925.

Parker, David S. "Law, Honor, and Impunity in Spanish America: The Debate over Dueling." *Law and History Review* 19 (2001): 311–342.

"The Passion for Publicity." *The Outlook*, April, 25, 1896.

Pedrick, Willard. "Publicity and Privacy: Is It Any of Our Business." *University of Toronto Law Journal* 20 (1970): 391–411.

Peiss, Kathy. *Hope in a Jar: The Making of America's Beauty Culture*. Philadelphia: University of Pennsylvania Press, 1998.

Pells, Richard H. *The Liberal Mind in the Conservative Age: American Intellectuals in the 1940s and 1950s*. Middletown: Wesleyan University Press, 1985.

Pember, Don R. *Privacy and the Press: The Law, the Mass Media, and the First Amendment*. Seattle: University of Washington Press, 1972.

Pember, Don R., and Dwight L. Teeter Jr. "Privacy and the Press since *Time, Inc. v. Hill*." *Washington Law Review* 50 (1974): 57–91.

Pendergast, Mark. *Mirror, Mirror: A History of the Human Love Affair with Reflection*. New York: Basic Books, 2004.

Pfister, Joel. "Glamorizing the Psychological: The Politics of the Performances of Modern Psychological Identities." In *Inventing the Psychological: Toward a Cultural History of Emotional Life in America*, edited by Joel Pfister and Nancy Schnog, 167. New Haven: Yale University Press, 1997.

Pipel, Harriet F. "But Can You Do That." *Publishers' Weekly*, April 9, 1963.

Pilpel, Harriet F., and Theodora S. Zavin. *Rights and Writers: A Handbook of Literary and Entertainment Law*. New York: Dutton, 1960.

Poirer, Richard. *The Performing Self: Compositions and Decompositions in the Language of Everyday Life*. New Brunswick: Rutgers University Press, 1992.

Ponce De Leon, Charles. *Self-Exposure: Human Interest Journalism and the Emergence of Celebrity in America 1890–1940*. Chapel Hill: University of North Carolina Press, 2002.

Pope, Daniel. *The Making of Modern Advertising*. New York: Basic Books, 1983.

Post, Robert. "The Social Foundations of Defamation Law: Reputation and the Constitution." *California Law Review* 74 (1986): 691–742.

Postel, Charles. *The Populist Vision*. New York: Oxford University Press, 2007.

Potter, David. *People of Plenty*. Chicago: University of Chicago Press, 1954.

Pound, Roscoe. "Interests of Personality." *Harvard Law Review* 28 (1915): 343–365.

Powe Jr., Lucas A. *The Warren Court and American Politics*. Cambridge: Belknap Press, 2002.

"Precedent." *New Republic*, September 14, 1953.

"The Press: Freedom to Photograph." *Time*, August 9, 1954.

"The Press: Success in the Sewer." *Time*, July 11, 1955.

Probert, Walter. "Defamation, A Camouflage of Psychic Interests: The Beginning of a Behavioral Analysis." *Vanderbilt Law Review* 15 (1961): 1173–1202.

Prosser, William. "Intentional Infliction of Mental Suffering: A New Tort." *Michigan Law Review* 37 (1939): 874–892.

———. "Libel Per Quod." *Virginia Law Review* 46 (1960): 839–855.

———. "Privacy." *California Law Review* 48 (1960): 383–423.

Prosser, William L. *Handbook of the Law of Torts.* St. Paul: West, 1971.

———. "Insult and Outrage." *California Law Review* 44 (1956): 40–64.

Pruitt, Lisa R. "Her Own Good Name: Two Centuries of Talk about Chastity." *Maryland Law Review* 63 (2004): 401–539.

"Publishers' Corner." *Saturday Review of Literature*, July 15, 1950.

Quinn, Arthur Hobson. *The Literature of the American People: An Historical and Critical Survey.* New York: Appleton Century Crofts, 1951.

Rabban, David M. *Free Speech in Its Forgotten Years, 1870–1920.* Cambridge: Cambridge University Press, 1997.

Ragland, George. "The Right of Privacy." *Kentucky Law Journal* 17 (1928): 85–122.

Rascoe, Burton. "Libel's Lawyer." *Esquire*, August 1938.

Rawlings, Marjorie Kinnan. *Cross Creek.* New York: Charles Scribner's Sons, 1942.

Ray, R. Charles. "Torts—Libel—Slander—Defamation by Broadcast—Defamacast Actionable Per Se." *Houston Law Review* 1 (1963–1964): 58–60.

"Recent Cases, Libel and Slander—Liability for Publishing Photograph Which Created Optical Illusion Concerning Plaintiff." *Harvard Law Review* 49 (1936): 826–847.

"Recent Decisions, Torts—Right of Privacy—Biographical Sketch of Former Child Prodigy as a Matter of Public Concern." *Fordham Law Review* 10 (1941): 108–111.

"A Recent Instance." *Outlook*, October 4, 1902.

Reed, I. N. *The Ladies' Manual: A Guide to Women in Health and Sickness, from Youth to Advanced Age.* Chicago: I. N. Reed, 1883.

Rich, Burdett. "What Invasions of Privacy Are Unlawful?" *Law Student's Helper* 18 (1910): 238–240.

Richards, Neil, and Daniel Solove. "Prosser's Privacy Law: A Mixed Legacy." *California Law Review* 98 (2010): 1887–1924.

Richter, Amy. *Home on the Rails: Women, the Railroad, and the Rise of Public Domesticity.* Chapel Hill: University of North Carolina Press, 2005.

"Ridicule as Constituting a Cause of Action for Libel." *Western Reserve Law Journal* (1901): 196–200.

Rieff, Philip. *Triumph of the Therapeutic: Uses of Faith after Freud.* Chicago: University of Chicago Press, 1966.

Riesman, David. "Democracy and Defamation: Fair Game and Fair Comment." *Columbia Law Review* 42 (1942): 1085–1123.

Riesman, David, Nathan Glazer, and Reuel Denney. *The Lonely Crowd: A Study of the Changing American Character.* New York: Doubleday, 1950.

"Right of Privacy Undetermined." *Editor and Publisher*, April 25, 1936.

"The Right to a Good Name." *The Outlook*, December 26, 1908.

"The Right to Be Let Alone." *Atlantic Monthly*, March 1891.

"The Right to Privacy." *Youth's Companion*, December 10, 1891.

"The Right to Privacy." *Virginia Law Register* 12 (1906): 91–99.

"Right to Privacy in Nineteenth Century America." *Harvard Law Review* 94 (1981): 1892–1910.

Rodell, Fred. "For Charles E. Clark: A Brief and Belated but Fond Farewell." *Columbia Law Review* 65 (1965): 1323–1330.

Rosen, David, and Aaron Santesso. "Inviolate Personality and the Literary Roots of the Right to Privacy." *Law and Literature* 23 (2011): 1–25.

Rosenberg, Norman. *Protecting the Best Men: An Interpretive History of the Law of Libel*. Chapel Hill: University of North Carolina Press, 1990.

———. "Taking a Look at 'The Distorted Shape of an Ugly Tree': Efforts at Policy-Surgery on the Law of Libel During the Decade of the 1940s." *Northern Kentucky Law Review* 15 (1988): 11–56.

Rugg, Linda Haverty. *Picturing Ourselves: Photography and Autobiography*. Chicago: University of Chicago Press, 2007.

Sack, Robert D., and Richard Tofel. "First Steps down the Road Not Taken: Emerging Limitations on Libel Damages." *Dickinson Law Review* 90 (1985): 609–626.

Sandel, Michael J. *Democracy's Discontents: America in Search of a Public Philosophy*. Cambridge: Harvard University Press, 1996.

"Saving and Spending." *Harper's Bazaar*, June 1906.

Scheppele, Kim Lane. *Legal Secrets: Equality and Efficiency in the Common Law*. Chicago: University of Chicago Press, 1988.

Schickel, Richard. *Intimate Strangers: The Culture of Celebrity*. Garden City: Doubleday, 1985.

Schiller, Reuel E. "Free Speech and Expertise: Administrative Censorship and the Birth of the Modern First Amendment." *Virginia Law Review* 86 (2000): 1–102.

Schlanger, Margo. "Injured Women before Common Law Courts, 1860–1920." *Harvard Women's Law Journal* 21 (1998): 79–140.

Schlesinger, Arthur. *A History of American Life: The Rise of the City, 1878–1898*. New York: Macmillan, 1948.

———. *Learning How to Behave*. New York: Macmillan, 1946.

Schonberger, Victor Mayer. *Delete: The Virtue of Forgetting in the Digital Age*. Princeton: Princeton University Press, 2009.

Schramm, Wilbur, and William Rivers. *Responsibility in Mass Communications*. New York: Harper & Row, 1969.

Schwartz, Bernard. *The Unpublished Opinions of the Warren Court*. Oxford: Oxford University Press, 1985.

Schwartz, Gary. "Explaining and Justifying a Limited Tort of False Light Invasion of Privacy." *Case Western Reserve Law Review* 41 (1990): 885–920.

Schwartz, Hillel. *Never Satisfied: A Cultural History of Diets, Fantasies, and Fat*. New York: Free Press, 1986.

Schwartz, Paul M., and Karl-Nikolaus Peifer. "Prosser's Privacy and the German Right of Personality: Are Four Privacy Torts Better than One Unitary Concept?" *California Law Review* 98 (2010): 1925–1988.

Schwartz, Warren F., Keith Baxter, and David Ryan. "The Duel: Can These Gentlemen Be Acting Efficiently?" *Journal of Legal Studies* 13 (1984): 321–356.

Schweitzer, Marlis. *When Broadway Was the Runway: Theater, Fashion, and American Culture*. Philadelphia: University of Pennsylvania Press, 2011.

Schweitzer, Marlis, and Marina Moskowitz, eds. *Testimonial Advertising in the American Marketplace: Emulation, Identity, Community*. New York: Palgrave Macmillan, 2009.

Scobey, David. "Anatomy of the Promenade: The Politics of Bourgeois Sociability in Nineteenth-Century New York." *Social History* 17 (1992): 203–227.

Scott, Anne Firor. *The Southern Lady, From Pedestal to Politics, 1830–1930*. Chicago: University of Chicago Press, 1970.

Scott, Henry E. *Shocking True Story: The Rise and Fall of Confidential, America's Most Scandalous Scandal Magazine*. New York: Pantheon Books, 2010.

Seitz, Reynolds C. "Insults—Practical Jokes—Threats of Future Harm—How New as Torts?" *Kentucky Law Journal* 28 (1939–1940): 411–423.

Sennett, Richard. *The Fall of Public Man*. New York: Knopf, 1977.

Shamir, Milette. "Hawthorne's Romance and the Right to Privacy." *American Quarterly* 49 (1997): 746–779.

Shands, Nugent. "Libel-Optical Illusion-Prima Facie Actionable." *Mississippi Law Journal* 9 (1937): 250–251.

Shaw, Harry. "Pocket and Pictorial Journalism." *North American Law Review* 243 (1937): 297–309.

Shi, David. *The Simple Life: Plain Living and High Thinking in American Culture*. Athens: University of Georgia Press, 1985.

Shils, Edward. "Privacy: Its Constitution and Vicissitudes." *Law and Contemporary Problems* 31 (1966): 281–306.

Shorman, Rob. *Selling Style: Clothing and Social Change at the Turn of the Century*. Philadelphia: University of Pennsylvania Press, 2003.

Shugerman, Jed Handelsman. *The People's Courts: Pursuing Judicial Independence in America*. Cambridge: Harvard University Press, 2012.

Shuy, Roger. *The Language of Defamation Cases*. New York: Oxford University Press, 2010.

Sidis, Boris. *Philistine and Genius*. New York: Moffat, Yard, 1911.

Siebert, Frederick Seaton. *The Rights and Privileges of the Press*. New York: D. Appleton-Century, 1934.

Silverthorne, Elizabeth. *Marjorie Kinnan Rawlings: Sojourner at Cross Creek*. New York: Overlook Press, 1988.

Simmel, Georg. "The Metropolis and Mental Life." In *The Blackwell City Reader*, edited by Gary Bridge and Sophie Watson, 103–104. Oxford and Malden: Wiley-Blackwell, 2002.

Sivulka, Juliann. *Soap, Sex, and Cigarettes: A Cultural History of American Advertising.* Boston: Wadsworth, Cengage Learning, 2012.

Sklar, Robert. *Movie Made America: A Cultural History of American Movies.* New York: Random House, 1975.

"Slander Books." *Saturday Evening Post,* January 9, 1932.

Sloan, Bill. *I Watched a Wild Hog Eat My Baby: A Colorful History of Tabloids and Their Cultural Impact.* Amherst: Prometheus Books, 2001.

Smith, H. L. "The News Camera on Trial." *Forum and Century* 5 (1937): 267–270.

Smith, Janna Malamud. *Private Matters: In Defense of the Personal Life.* Reading: Addison-Wesley, 1997.

Smith, Michael E. "Judge Charles E. Clark and the Federal Rule of Civil Procedure." *Yale Law Journal* 85 (1976): 914–956.

Smolla, Rodney. "Emotional Distress and the First Amendment: An Analysis of Hustler v. Falwell." *Arizona State Law Journal* 20 (1988): 423–474.

———. *Suing the Press: Libel, the Media, and Power.* New York: Oxford University Press, 1986.

Smythe, J. E. "James Jones, Columbia Pictures, and the Historical Confrontations of From Here to Eternity." In *Why We Fought: America's Wars in Film and History,* edited by Peter C. Rollins and John E. O'Connor, 289. Lexington: University Press of Kentucky, 2008.

Snyder, Brad. "Protecting the Media from Excessive Damages: The Nineteenth Century Origins of Remittitur and Its Modern Application in Food Lion." *Vermont Law Review* 24 (1999–2000): 299–346.

Solove, Daniel J. *The Future of Reputation: Gossip, Rumor and Privacy on the Internet.* New Haven: Yale University Press, 2007.

Speed, John Gilmer. "The Right of Privacy." *North American Review* 158 (1896): 64.

Spring, Samuel. "Invasion of Privacy." *Publishers' Weekly,* February 2, 1952.

———. *Risks and Rights in Publishing, Television, Radio, Motion Pictures, Advertising, and the Theatre.* New York: W. W. Norton, 1956.

Starkie, Thomas. *A Treatise on the Law of Slander, Libel, Scandalum Magnatum and False Rumors.* London: W. Clarke and Sons, 1818.

"Statute Protecting Right of Privacy Constitutional." *Law Notes* 12 (1909): 184–185.

Stearns, Peter. "Stages of Consumerism: Recent Work on the Issues of Periodization." *Journal of Modern History* 69 (1997): 102–117.

Stearns, Peter N. *Battleground of Desire: The Struggle for Self-Control in Modern America.* New York: New York University Press, 1999.

Steigleman, Walter Allan. *The Newspaperman and the Law.* Dubuque: W. C. Brown, 1950.

Stevens, John D. *Sensationalism and the New York Press.* New York: Columbia University Press, 1991.

Stotesbury, Louis. "Famous Annie Oakley Libel Suits." *American Lawyer* 13 (1905).

Strossen, Nadine. "Freedom of Speech in the Warren Court." In *The Warren Court:*

A Retrospective, edited by Bernard Schwartz, 71–72. New York: Oxford University Press, 1996.

Summers, John H. "What Happened to Sex Scandals? Politics and Peccadilloes, Jefferson to Kennedy." *Journal of American History* (December 2000): 825–854.

Sumner, David E. *The Magazine Century: American Magazines since 1900*. New York: Peter Lang, 2010.

"Super-Sensitive Folks." *New York Sun,* reprinted in *Publishers' Weekly*, February 23, 1884.

Susman, Warren. "'Personality' and the Making of Twentieth-Century Culture." In *Culture as History: The Transformation of American Society in the Twentieth Century*, by Warren Susman, 275, 277. New York: Pantheon Books, 1984.

Swindler, William Findley. *Problems of Law in Newspapers*. New York: Macmillan Press, 1955.

Syndor, Charles. "The Southerner and the Laws." *Journal of Southern History* 6 (1940): 3–23.

Tagg, John. *The Burden of Representation: Essays on Photographies and Histories*. London: Macmillan, 1988.

"The Taste for Privacy and Publicity." *The Spectator*, June 9, 1888.

Tebbel, John. *A History of Book Publishing in the United States, Volume 4*. New York: R. R. Bowker, 1978.

Teel, Leonard. *The Public Press, 1900–1945: The History of American Journalism*. Westport: Praeger, 2006.

Thayer, Frank. "The Changing Libel Scene." *Wisconsin Law Review* 1943 (1943): 331–351.

Thomas, Brook. "The Construction of Privacy in and around The Bostonians." *American Literature* 64 (1992): 719–747.

Thomas, William G. *Lawyering for the Railroad: Business, Law, and Power in the New South*. Baton Rouge: Louisiana State University Press, 1999.

Thomley, Betty. "Miss and Makeup." *Colliers*, November 2, 1929.

Thorp, Margaret Farrand. *America at the Movies*. New Haven: Yale University Press, 1939.

Thurber, James. *The Years with Ross*. New York: Harper Collins, 1959.

"Torts: Right of Privacy: Matters of General or Public Interest." *Michigan Law Review* 39 (1941): 501–503.

"Torts: Right of Privacy of Former Child Prodigy." *California Law Review* 29 (1940): 56–96.

Toth, Emily. *Inside Peyton Place: The Life of Grace Metalious*. New York: Doubleday, 1981.

"Toward a Constitutional Theory of Individuality: The Privacy Opinions of Justice Douglas." *Yale Law Journal* 87 (July 1978): 1579–1600.

Trachtenberg, Alan. *The Incorporation of America: Culture and Society in the Gilded Age*. New York: Hill and Wang, 2007.

————. *Reading American Photographs: Images as History, Matthew Brady to Walker Evans*. New York: Hill and Wang, 1990.

"True Crime Inspires Tense Play: The Ordeal of a Family Trapped by Convicts Gives Broadway a New Thriller, 'The Desperate Hours.'" *Life*, February 28, 1955.

Turner, Frederick Jackson. *The Frontier in American History*. New York: Henry Holt, 1921.

Twenge, Jean M. *The Narcissism Epidemic: Living in the Age of Entitlement*. New York: Atria Books, 2010.

"$22,250 Settlement in Burton Suit." *Editor and Publisher*, January 23, 1937.

Twitchell, James B. *For Shame: The Loss of Common Decency in American Culture*. New York: St. Martin's Press, 1997.

"Untitled." *The Current: Politics, Literature, Science, and Art*, February 23, 1884.

"Untitled." *Puck*, May 4, 1887.

Vatter, Harold G., and John F. Walker. *History of the U.S. Economy since World War II*. Armonk: M. E. Sharpe, 1996.

Veblen, Thorstein. *The Theory of the Leisure Class; An Economic Study of Institutions*. 1899. New York: Macmillan, 1912.

Veeder, Van Vechten. "The History and Theory of the Law of Defamation." *Columbia Law Review* 4 (1904): 33–56.

Velie, Frances, and Caroline Menuez. "Twilight of a Genius." *Coronet*, February 1945.

"A Vote for the Press over Privacy." *Time*, January 20, 1967.

Wade, John. "Defamation and the Right of Privacy." *Vanderbilt Law Review* 15 (1962): 1093–1126.

————. "Tort Liability for Abusive & Insulting Language." *Vanderbilt Law Review* 4 (1950–1951): 63–115.

Wakefield, Dan. "From Eternity to Brooklyn." *The Nation*, November 16, 1957.

Walker, Stanley. *City Editor*. Baltimore: Johns Hopkins University Press, 1999.

Wallace, Amy. *The Prodigy: A Biography of William J. Sidis, America's Greatest Child Prodigy*. New York: E. P. Dutton, 1986.

Walsh, Justin E. *To Print the News and Raise Hell: A Biography of Wilbur F. Storey*. Chapel Hill: University of North Carolina Press, 1968.

Warner, Chas Dudley. "Newspapers and the Public." *Forum*, April 1890.

Warner, Harry P. *Radio and Television Rights*. Albany: Matthew Bender, 1948.

Warren, Samuel, and Louis Brandeis. "The Right to Privacy." *Harvard Law Review* 4 (1890): 193–220.

Waters, Mary C. *Ethnic Options: Choosing Identities in America*. Berkeley: University of California Press, 1990.

Watts, Amber. "Queen for a Day: Remaking Consumer Culture, One Woman at a Time." In *The Great American Makeover: Television, History, Nation*, edited by Dana A. Heller. New York: Palgrave Macmillan, 2006.

Watts, Trent A. *One Homogeneous People: Narratives of White Southern Identity, 1890–1920*. Knoxville: University of Tennessee Press, 2010.

Weinstein, Deborah. *The Pathological Family: Postwar America and the Rise of Family Therapy*. Ithaca: Cornell University Press, 2013.

Welke, Barbara. *Recasting American Liberty: Gender, Race, Law and the Railroad Revolution*. Cambridge: Cambridge University Press, 2001.

———. "Unreasonable Women: Gender and the Law of Accidental Injury, 1870–1920." *Law and Social Inquiry* 19 (1994): 369–406.

Wells, Harwell. "The End of the Affair? Anti-Dueling Law and Social Norms in Antebellum America." *Vanderbilt Law Review* 54 (2001): 1805–1848.

Welter, Barbara. "The Cult of True Womanhood, 1820–1860." *American Quarterly* 18 (1966): 151–174.

West, James. *Plainville, USA*. New York: Columbia University Press, 1945.

Westin, Alan F. *Privacy and Freedom*. New York: Atheneum, 1967.

White, G. Edward. "The First Amendment Comes of Age: The Emergence of Free Speech in Twentieth Century America." *Michigan Law Review* 95 (1996): 299–392.

———. *Tort Law in America*. New York: Oxford University Press, 2003.

Whitman, James Q. "Enforcing Civility and Respect: Three Societies." *Yale Law Journal* 109 (2000): 1279–1398.

———. "The Two Western Cultures of Privacy: Dignity Versus Liberty." *Yale Law Journal* 113 (2004): 1151–1222.

Whyte, William. *The Organization Man*. New York: Simon & Schuster, 1956.

Wightman, Richard, and T.J. Jackson Lears, eds. *The Culture of Consumption*. New York: Pantheon Books, 1983.

Winfield, Betty. *Journalism—1908: Birth of a Profession*. Columbia: University of Missouri Press, 2008.

Winship, Michael. "The Rise of a National Book Trade System in the United States." In *A History of the Book in America*, edited by Carl F. Kaestle and Janice A. Radway, 57, 60–61. Chapel Hill: University of North Carolina Press, 2009.

Wirth, Louis. "Urbanism as a Way of Life." *American Journal of Sociology* 44 (1938): 1–24.

Witt, John Fabian. *Patriots and Cosmopolitans: Hidden Histories of American Law*. Cambridge: Harvard University Press, 2007.

Wittenberg, Philip. *Dangerous Words: A Guide to the Law of Libel*. New York: Columbia University Press, 1947.

Wolfe, Tom. "The 'Me' Decade and the Third Great Awakening." *New York Magazine*, August 23, 1976.

Woodrow, Wilson. "The Fascination of Being Photographed and the Improvement on Photography." *Cosmopolitan* 35 (1903): 683.

Wyatt-Brown, Bertram. *Southern Honor: Ethics and Behavior in the Old South*. New York: Oxford University Press, 1982.

Yahoda, Ben. *About Town: The New Yorker and the World It Made*. New York: Scribner, 2000.

Yankwich, Leon. "The Protection of Newspaper Comment on Public Men and Public Matters." *Louisiana Law Review* 11 (1951): 327–346.

————. "The Right of Privacy: Its Development, Scope and Limitations." *Notre Dame Lawyer* 27 (1952): 499–528.

Yasser, Ray. "Warren Spahn's Legal Legacy: The Right to Be Free from False Praise." *Seton Hall Journal of Sports and Entertainment Law* 18 (2008): 49–84.

Young, William H. *The 1950s*. Westport: Greenwood Press, 2004.

Young, William H., and Nancy K. Young. *The 1930s*. Westport: Greenwood Press, 2002.

Younger, Irving. *The Irving Younger Collection: Wit & Wisdom from the Master of Trial Advocacy*. Chicago: American Bar Association Publishing, 2011.

Zaretsky, Eli. "Charisma or Rationalization? Domesticity and Psychoanalysis in the United States in the 1950s." *Critical Inquiry* 26 (2000): 328–354.

Zimmerman, Diane Leenheer. "False Light Privacy: The Light That Failed." *New York University Law Review* 64 (1989): 364–454.

————. "Requiem for a Heavyweight: A Farewell to Warren and Brandeis's Privacy Tort." *Cornell Law Review* 68 (1983): 291–367.

Zunz, Olivier. *Making America Corporate, 1870–1920*. Chicago: University of Chicago Press, 1990.

Index